PHILIP SLAYTON is in the Faculty of Law, University of Western Ontario.
MICHAEL TREBILCOCK is in the Faculty of Law, University of Toronto.

In this collection of twenty-five papers given at a conference sponsored by the Law and Economics program of the University of Toronto's Faculty of Law, the contributors tackle many of the varied problems being raised today about the conduct of the professions in society. The traditional self-regulating model has been questioned on many grounds and the number of self-employed professionals is declining. The enlargement of the area of state power and the emergence of ideas about fairer access to professional services also serve to bring the relations between society and professionals into debate. Sylvia Ostry, former federal deputy minister of consumer and corporate affairs, argues for more competition; Claude Castonguay speaks for the Quebec model of a supervisory public body. The book is divided into several parts: regulatory philosophies; self-regulation – who qualifies?; professional education; supply and access; paraprofessionals; employed professionals; and regulating continuing competence. There is an introduction by one of the editors and a concluding paper by Ivan Illich characterizing this as the age of disabling professions.

The work unites many aspects of a complex social phenomenon that has risen in Canada as in other countries. It will interest all concerned with the development of professions and their future evolution, whether professionals or paraprofessionals themselves or those upon whose interests the professions have an impact.

EDITED BY PHILIP SLAYTON
AND MICHAEL J. TREBILCOCK

p. 342

p. 12 - 113.

The Professions
and Public Policy

UNIVERSITY OF TORONTO PRESS

TORONTO BUFFALO LONDON

Canadian Cataloguing in Publication Data

Conference on the Professions and Public Policy,
University of Toronto; 1976.

The professions and public policy

Conference held October 15-16, 1976, and
sponsored by the Law and Economics Program of
the University of Toronto Faculty of Law.

ISBN 0-8020-5416-1

1. Professions – Canada – Congresses.
2. Professions – Law and legislation – Canada –
Congresses. I. Slayton, Philip II. Trebilcock,
Michael J. III. University of Toronto. Faculty
of Law. IV. Title.

HD8038.C2C65 1976   331.7'1'0971   C78-001129-5

Contents

PARAPROFESSIONALS

EMPLOYED PROFESSIONALS

REGULATING CONTINUING COMPETENCE

A CONCLUDING PERSPECTIVE

Preface

In today's post-industrial society the professions have emerged as one of the most important economic sectors. But while the phenomenon of professionalism has become increasingly pervasive, this development has not generally been reflected in a corresponding increase in the attention devoted to the professions in public policy debates. It is unlikely that we can afford this neglect much longer.

The essays in this volume are an attempt to define and focus the issues that fall to be considered in any re-evaluation of public policies towards the professions.

The essays trace their genesis, in every case except the introductory essay, to papers presented at a conference on the professions and public policy held in Toronto, 15 and 16 October 1976, and sponsored by the Law and Economics Program of the University of Toronto Faculty of Law. From the papers presented there the editors selected those that seemed to offer significant viewpoints on the most important issues of policy that emerged during the conference discussions. Authors of these papers were then invited by the editors to revise and refine their papers as essays for inclusion in this volume.

The editors wish to acknowledge several indispensable sources of assistance in bringing this book of essays foward to publication. First, two friends of ours, Murray Glow of A.R.A. Consultants Ltd, who played a central role in the conception of the conference, and Paul Stanley of the same firm, who oversaw much of the subsequent planning and administration of the conference, are owed a major debt of thanks. June Armstrong of the Conference Office at the Ontario Institute for Studies in Education displayed superlative competence in orchestrating the many detailed administrative arrangements. Verna Percival, secretary to the Law and Economics Program, has likewise carried similar burdens far beyond the call of duty. Rik Davidson, Prudence Tracy, and Larry

MacDonald of University of Toronto Press were also generous with their editorial assistance.

Last, but of course by no means least, we owe a special acknowledgment of thanks to the contributors of essays to this volume, who have so generously given of their time and energies both in preparing initial conference papers and in revising them subsequently as essays for this volume. Obviously, without their efforts this volume would not exist.

INTRODUCTION

MICHAEL J. TREBILCOCK

The professions and public policy:
the nature of the agenda

[The lawyer] *should always bear in mind that the profession is a branch of the*
administration of justice and not a mere money-getting trade.
(Law Society of Upper Canada, *Professional Conduct Handbook*)

All professions are conspiracies against the laity.
(George Bernard Shaw, Preface to *The Doctor's Dilemma*)

INTRODUCTION

Widely divergent perceptions of the social and economic role of the self-governing professions, perhaps reflected rather extremely in the prefatory quotations,
have always existed.[1] To some critics of the professions, they have been seen as
little more than anachronistic legacies of medieval guilds, with 'secret society,'
special privilege, overtones. To most members of the professions, they have been
seen as learned and noble callings, dedicated to ideals of public service before
personal gain.

Director, Law and Economics Program, Faculty of Law, University of Toronto. The
author wishes to acknowledge many helpful suggestions in preparing this essay from his
coeditor, Philip Slayton.
1 For historical perspectives on professionalism, see for example A.M. Carr-Saunders and
P.A. Wilson, *The Professions* (Frank Cass and Co., 1933); Jerold Auerbach, *Unequal
Justice: Lawyers and Social Change in Modern America* (Oxford University Press, 1976);
Burton Bledstein, *The Culture of Professionalism* (Norton, 1977); 92 Daedalus, *The
Professions* (Fall, 1963); W.J. Reader, *Professional Men: The Rise of the Professional
Classes in Nineteenth Century England* (Weidenfeld and Nicholson, 1966); C.L. Gilb,
Hidden Hierarchies: Professions and Government (Harper and Row, 1966); *Four Aspects
of Professionalism* (Canadian Consumer Research Council, 1977), esp. L. Bohnen, 'The
sociology of the professions in Canada'; M.S. Larson, *The Rise of Professionalism*
(University of California Press, 1977).

As Dr Ostry remarks in her paper in this book, in our present irreverent age, when few major institutions continue to be taken on faith, it was inevitable that the professions would be eventually exposed to searching public scrutiny.

In the recent past in Ontario, the McRuer Royal Commission on Civil Rights undertook a wide-ranging review of procedural and administrative issues pertaining to the decision-making processes of the self-governing professions.[2] At the same time, the Committee on the Healing Arts examined many aspects of the regulation of the health professions.[3] More recently a ministerial committee has been appointed by the attorney general of Ontario to examine aspects of the regulation of the professions of law, accounting, architecture, and engineering, in the province. In other provinces a similar pattern of inquiry has begun to emerge. In Quebec, the Castonguay/Nepveu Report on the professions and society[4] and the subsequent enactment of the comprehensive Quebec *Professional Code in 1973*[5] marked a significant new departure in direct government and public involvement in the regulation of the professions. In Alberta, two select committee reports on the professions were completed in April and December 1973,[6] and in Manitoba a governmental evaluation of public policy towards the professions has been in progress. At the federal level the Economic Council of Canada's *Interim Report on Competition Policy* in 1969 recommended more extensive use of competitive instruments in the regulation of the professions,[7] and the 1976 amendments to the *Combines Investigation Act*,[8] by extending the Act to the service sector, have moved some distance in that direction. Beyond Canada, a royal commission is undertaking a full-scale review of the English legal profession and an inquiry into the engineering profession has begun, while in Australia the New South Wales Law Reform Commission has recently embarked upon a similar inquiry. In the United States, official scrutiny of many professions, principally in an anti-trust context, has sharply increased.

2 See Ontario Royal Commission on the Inquiry into Civil Rights, *Report Number One*, Vol. III, section 4, 'Self-governing professions and occupations' (Ontario: Queen's Printer, 1968).
3 See Ontario Committee on the Healing Arts, *Report*, Vol. III, chap. 25, 'Regulation of the healing arts' (Ontario: Queen's Printer, 1970); see further, Ontario *Health Disciplines Act* S.O. 1974, c.47.
4 *Report of the Commission of Inquiry on Health and Social Welfare* (Quebec, 1970)
5 S.Q. 1973, c.43; see the essay in this volume by Castonguay.
6 *Report I*, April 1973, and *Report II*, December 1973, of the Special Committee of the Legislative Assembly of Alberta on Professions and Occupations.
7 Economic Council of Canada, *Interim Report on Competition Policy* (Queen's Printer, 1969)
8 S.C. 1974-75-76, c.76.

While acknowledging the irreverent nature of our age, certain factors can be more specifically identified which have cast the professions into sharper public relief.

First, and most importantly, it seems clear that the phenomenon of professionalism has become much more pervasive, despite some acute problems of definition, which we shall mention below. At the turn of the century, only about 4.6 per cent of the Canadian labour force were categorized as professional (broadly defined). In 1971 that percentage had risen to 12.7.[9] An ever-lengthening list of occupations has obtained, or is seeking, some form of self-governing status – in Ontario, at last count, twenty-two occupations had achieved some measure of self-government.[10] In Quebec, under the *Professional Code*, thirty-eight self-governing occupations are either accorded exclusive licensing powers or reserved professional titles.[11] As Jethro Lieberman points out in his essay in this book,[12] a major incongruity resides in the observed fact that demands for self-regulation, while often articulated in 'public interest' terms, almost always come from 'professions' themselves rather than from the public whose interests are said to be in jeopardy in the absence of such regulation.

Even within established professions, such as medicine and law, the ratio of professionals to population has sharply increased – in medicine in Ontario, from one doctor per 857 of population in 1951 to an estimated one doctor per 575 in 1977; in law from one lawyer per 1,357 in 1951 to an estimated one lawyer per 707 in 1977.[13] The public's contact with members of the professions is thus becoming increasingly frequent, often accelerated through subsidized service programs such as medicare and Legal Aid, and with this growing contact has come an increased public awareness of their social and economic importance.

Secondly, in an age of consumerism, clients and potential clients of the professions increasingly assert their interests in matters such as pricing, quality, and availability of often essential services.

9 Sylvia Ostry, *The Occupational Composition of the Canadian Labour Force*, 1967, Census (1961) Monographs (Canada: Bureau of Statistics) Table 2, p. 50; *Census of Canada 1971*, Vol. III, Part 2, 94-77, Bull. 32-3.
10 See McRuer, op. cit., note 2 above, at p. 1160.
11 Quebec Professional Code, S.Q. 1973, c.43 Schedule I.
12 See essay below by Lieberman; also *The Tyranny of the Experts* (Walker and Co., 1970).
13 *Census of Canada 1951*, Vol. IV, *Labour Force, Occupations and Industries*, Table 4, [Labour Force 14 years and over by occupation and sex, for Canada and the provinces, 1951]; *Census of Canada 1951*, Vol. I, *Population, General Characteristics*, Table 1; *Census of Canada 1971*, Vol. III, part 2, *Occupations by Sex for Canada and the Provinces*, Table 2; *Census for Canada 1971*, Vol. I, part 1, *Population Census Divisions and Subdivisions (Ontario)*, Table 6.

Thirdly, another feature of our age – society's emphasis on the importance of participatory democracy – has led inevitably to demands that affected interests somehow be able to contribute to, or participate in, the functions of government delegated by the state to the professions.

Fourthly, with the waning of the educational euphoria of the sixties which entertained the belief that higher education of any kind was in itself the key to success in life, young people have become increasingly pragmatic in choosing career paths and have turned in massive numbers to professional schools, as prospective guarantors of satisfying and remunerative careers. As queues lengthen for places in professional schools, and as the professions themselves become more densely populated, aspiring entrants have naturally become increasingly concerned over whether a place in the professions can be found for them.

Fifthly, despite the self-perception of the professions as other than mere money-getting trades, some elements of the public have come to believe, rightly or wrongly, that relatively high incomes in the professions, and relatively high rates of increase in those incomes over time, connote less than fully effective market and regulatory constraints on the economic behaviour of professionals. As Lees puts this perception, 'it is at least questionable whether professional people are quite the monks growing their own vegetables in selfless pursuit of the public good that their prnouncements and demeanour would often have us believe.'[14]

Finally, government as the bill-payer for the enormous and escalating outlays involved in professional education and in subsidy programs such as medicare and Legal Aid,[15] has an understandable concern with whether it can somehow make the tax dollar stretch further by shifts in public policy towards the professions.

All these factors, and probably others, have tended to coalesce in the last decade or so, and in large part explain an emerging public policy focus on the professions.

THE NATURE OF THE ISSUES

At least from an economic perspective, perhaps a useful analytical framework for identifying relevant policy issues in the regulation of the professions might envisage four separate and successive scenarios. First, one might hypothesize a perfectly efficient market for professional services and ask what assumptions

14 D.S. Lees, *Economic Consequences of The Professions* (UK Institute of Economic Affairs, 1966) at p. 17
15 Health expenditures in Ontario now comprise about one-third of the annual provincial budget.

would need to hold for a market to be so characterized (e.g. ease of entry, optimal information flows, no externalities etc). One might ask further, what distributive problems (e.g. access to services) such a market would leave unresolved. Secondly, one might hypothesize an unregulated market for a particular class of professional services and attempt to identify likely forms of market failure that would occur in the absence of regulation e.g. market concentration, cartelization, or collusion; suboptimal production and dissemination of information (e.g. regarding availability, quantity, quality, and pricing of services); perhaps mainly as symptoms of the foregoing, non-optimal forms of price determination, non-optimal quality/quantity/price calculi by consumers; the presence of significant, negative third-party effects. Again, in an unregulated market, as in a perfectly functioning market, the appropriateness of distributive outcomes would need to be evaluated. Thirdly, one might consider whether or not *present* regulatory arrangements effectively address these inferred forms of market failure, recognizing that all forms of regulation are to some extent imperfect, as are most unregulated markets, and that the imperfections of one must be carefully weighed against the imperfections of the other. Fourthly, one might seek alternative regulatory responses to market failures which exhibit fewer imperfections than both existing regulatory arrangements and an unregulated market.

Scenarios two (an unregulated market), three (present regulatory arrangements), and four (alternative regulatory strategies) might be tested in turn against their ability to provide acceptable responses to some obvious base-line questions within any set of professional functions. In allocative efficiency terms, three questions might be posed: 1/ How can policies best ensure appropriate matching of manpower skills to functions in terms of (*a*) formal entry tracks into a profession (avoiding problems of both under- and over-training relative to functions to be performed),[16] (*b*) the information available to consumers with

16 On the structure and objectives of professional education programs, see essays in this volume by Wright and Slayton; also Slayton, 'Professional education and the consumer interest,' in *Four Aspects of Professionalism*, op. cit., note 1 above; essays below by Mustard and Krever; E.C. Hughes et al., *Education for the Professions*, the Carnegie Commission on Higher Education (New York: McGraw-Hill, 1973). On paraprofessionals in the delivery of professional services, see essays below by Spitzer and Taman. The problem of formulating optimal quality thresholds shares important common features with problems of product safety regulation at large: see e.g. P.E. Sands, 'How effective is safety legislation?' (1968) 11 J. of Law and Ecs 165; W.Y. Oi, 'The economics of product safety,' (1973) 4 Bell J. of Ecs 3; N. Cornell, R. Noll, and B. Weingart, 'Safety regulation,' (US National Science Foundation, mimeo. 1976); M. Spence, 'Consumer misperceptions, product failure, and product liability,' (US National Science Foundation, mimeo. 1977); S. Peltzman, 'An evaluation of consumers protection legislation: the 1962 drug amendments,' (1973) 81 J. Pol. Ec. 1049; S. Peltzman, 'The effects of automobile safety regulation (1475) 83 J. Pol. Ec. 671.

which to make appropriate quality choices,[17] and (c) subsequent constraints against depreciation of professional competence over time?[18] 2/ How can the supply of an appropriate quantity of professional manpower to given functions best be ensured?[19] 3/ How can appropriate pricing behaviour and innovation on the part of professionals best be ensured?[20] In distributive terms we must ask how an appropriate distribution of professional services to client groups can best be ensured (i.e. questions of price and non-price barriers to access).[21] And finally we must ask, if regulatory arrangements are to be substituted for the market in any of these contexts, how policies can best ensure that appropriate regulatory norms are set and attained (i.e. institutional accountability).[22]

The essays which follow in this book, in 'decomposing' these questions into constituent parts, address more concretely the questions of formulating both appropriate performance objectives to be applied to professional markets and appropriate public policy responses for ensuring that those objectives are satisfied.

ALTERNATIVE REGULATORY PHILOSOPHIES

A number of generalized regulatory philosophies can be identified which offer alternative normative frameworks for public policy analysis of the professions. It is probably safe to say that single-minded reliance on any single philosophy is unlikely to produce widely acceptable outcomes. First, exclusive reliance on the concept of self-government in its most absolute sense will attract suspicions of monopoly, protectionism, and administered markets. It will be asserted that the regulation of the professions has become too important to be left only to professionals. As Lieberman puts this sentiment, 'at first blush, the claim to self-regulation is strange. We don't ask non-playing members of football teams to referee games involving their teams.'[23] Yet, on the other hand, extensive direct government regulation of the professions is likely to engender hostility both from the professions with a fierce and ancient pride in their autonomy and pro-

17 See contributions below by Olley, Younger, Benham and Benham; also Spence, op. cit., note 16 above; Cornell, Noll, and Weingast, op. cit., note 16 above.
18 See essays below by Prichard, Sheppard, and Thomas.
19 See in this volume Stager and Meltz, and Skolnik.
20 See R.G. Evans, 'Models, markets and medical care,' in Officer and Smith, eds, *Issues in Canadian Economics* (McGraw-Hill Ryerson, 1976); 'Modelling the objectives of the physician' (Symposium of Health Care Economists, Queen's University, 1974); and his essay below.
21 See Evans in this volume.
22 See Castonguay in this volume.
23 See Lieberman in this volume.

bably at least scepticism from many members of the public who have become less than sanguine about government's ability to engage in effective large-scale economic regulation. Moreover, given the concentrated resources, expertise, and stakes of the professions when matters of their own regulation are at issue – relative to other less-organized, more thinly spread interests – it may be at least questionable whether any public agency charged with oversight of the professions is likely to be able to avoid for very long a pro-professional bias of substantially less marked proportions than that sometimes attributed to agencies of professional self-government.[24] In both contexts the organized professions are likely to prove the dominant interest group in regulatory decision-making. It may well be the case that in some instances appropriately tempered forms of self-government hold comparative institutional advantages over direct government regulation. Unfortunately, present patterns of professional regulation do not yield any rational theory of the criteria that should inform the choice between direct government regulation and self-regulation (or indeed between any and no regulation). The definition of a profession has never been satisfactorily resolved. An obvious, politically based, definition, albeit of little normative value, would be to accept as professions whatever occupations have been successful in achieving self-regulating status. A more useful functional definition of what critical characteristics of an occupation should properly lead to it being viewed as a profession has always proved more elusive. With this unpromising backdrop, the question of which groups should qualify for self-government has become increasingly pressing as governments face growing demands by new occupational groups for the same self-governing professional status as has already been granted to older groups.[25]

But of course the debate between self-governing, and direct government, regulation of the professions is necessarily premised on the notion that some regulation of many 'professions' is called for. Some analysts fundamentally challenge this premise.[26] But in perhaps its most extreme form by Milton Friedman,[27] the argument is made that the exposure of professional service markets to the disci-

---

24 Cf. M.J. Trebilcock, 'Winners and losers in the modern regulatory system: must the consumer always lose?' (1975) 13 Osgoode Hall L.J. 619.
25 See contributions to this volume by Dussault and by Tuohy and Wolfson; also Tuohy and Wolfson, 'The political economy of professionalism,' in *Four Aspects of Professionalism*, op. cit., note 1 above; Bohnen, op. cit., note 1 above; G.F. Goert, 'Cybernetics, professionalization, and knowledge management' (1975) 35 Public Admin. Rev. 581. For problems posed by the concept of self-government in professions dominated by employed professionals, see essays below by Gunderson, Adams, Fraser, and Rose.
26 See in this volume Ostry and Benham and Benham.
27 *Capitalism and Freedom* (University of Chicago Press, 1962), chap. 9.

pline of unrestrained competitive market forces offers the best form of protection to consumers of those services. On this view, entry into the professions would be unrestricted as would e.g. price competition and advertising following entry. Indeed, in any important regulatory sense professions would cease to exist.

This view is, of course, of limited relevance in professional service markets where market forces have been seriously eroded by subsidy programs such as medicare under which services ostensibly carry a zero price. Moreover, even in unsubsidized markets this view, if unqualified, disregards the serious potential for information breakdowns between producer and consumer over such questions as whether a service is in fact needed at all, if so in what quantities and qualities, and depending on these factors at what price. The fact of the matter is that in some professional markets, particularly those embracing non-standardized services and relatively unsophisticated consumers, supply and demand are not independent variables. In important respects, suppliers determine the demand for their own services i.e. demand is not exogenous.[28] Where this is so, an unregulated market is likely to generate suboptimal outcomes.[29] To acknowledge this is not of course to be compelled to endorse present forms of professional regulation; nor to accept that regulation is justified for all so-called professions; nor, where regulation is justified, to accept that the same forms and intensity of regulation are appropriate irrespective of the strength of variables such as degrees of standardization of service, degrees of sophistication of clientele, magnitude of hazards involved, etc. Obviously factors such as these should determine whether there is a case for any regulation at all; if there is to be regulation, whether it should be designed to improve information flows only e.g. by professional certification programs, or whether it should be designed to control entry through exclusive licensing regimes.[30]

Whatever the appropriate role of competition policy in the professions,[31] it can probably be conceded to its proponents that exclusive licensing regimes have been used too pervasively and indiscriminately in the past in the regulation of

28 R.G. Evans, op. cit., note 20 above.
29 See essays in this volume by Olley and Younger.
30 Certification of professional competence does not involve excluding non-certified practitioners from the field; exclusive licensed regimes deny entry to unlicensed practitioners. For perspectives on these alternative strategies, see Friedman, op. cit., note 27 above; T.G. Moore, 'The purpose of licensing' (1961) 4 J. of Law and Ecs 93; L. and A. Benham, 'Regulating through the professions: a perspective on information control (1975) 18 J. of Law and Ecs 421; M. Lagacé, 'A review of Ontario's compulsory certificate programme in some selected trades' (Ontario Dept of Labour, 1971); also the essay below by Castonguay.
31 The jurisdictional problems in Canada in applying federal competition to the professions are formidable: see Kaiser in this volume.

the professions. The rigidities, and thus the inefficiencies, inherent in this form of market segmentation[32] and the dangers of protectionism entailed in any form of entry control, particularly one administered by existing suppliers, suggest greater caution in its use than has hitherto been the case.

A variant of the deregulation philosophy is that advanced by Ivan Illich.[33] Emphasizing less the economic monopolies exercised by the self-governing professions than their intellectual monopolies over bodies of knowledge and expertise, Illich asserts that the professions have needlessly 'professionalized' many functions in our society, creating unhealthy dependency relationships and reducing the autonomy and self-sufficiency of the individual citizen. For example, instead of designing subsidy programs to provide a doctor to everyone who 'needs' one – often determined by the medical profession's own definition of 'need' – Illich challenges us to redefine in fundamental ways our conception of needs and to reclaim this definitional function from professional 'needs-makers.' While clearly Illich is right that needs, or demands, for professional services are often not exogenous, operationalizing policies for ensuring that the demand for professional services is exogenously (i.e. independently) determined may often be impossible, given the very essence of many professional-client relationships and the inequality of information and expertise that necessarily inheres in them.

Beyond these various regulatory philosophies are approaches perhaps less sharply defined, such as 'corporatist' regulatory models premised on fuller representation of affected interests in the governing processes of the professions.[34] The rationale for such a model can be stated at two levels. First, given that professional self-government is merely a delegated form of government at large, presumably precepts of political accountability that are applied to government generally must have some realm of application to self-government by the professions. Secondly, if one believes that inputs in large part determine outputs in decision-making, then presumably fuller representation of affected interests in the government of the professions should generate decisional outputs which better weigh regulatory impacts on affected interests than in regimes where the professions control all the relevant inputs.

The appropriate roles and mixes of self-regulation, direct government regulation, deregulation, deprofessionalization, corporatist, and related regulatory

32 For an example of an exploration of these, in the context of the health professions, see E. Hodgson, 'Restrictions on unorthodox health treatment in California: a legal and economic analysis' (1977) UCLA L. Rev. 647; more generally, see W. Gellhorn, 'The abuse of occupational licensing' (1976) 44 University of Chicago L. Rev. 6.
33 See his essay below; also *The Limits to Medicine: Medical Nemesis* (McClelland and Stewart, 1976).
34 See in this volume Castonguay.

philosophies, both in relation to different professions, and in relation to differ-ent issues within a given profession, underlie most issues of public policy pertain-ing to the professions.

THE NATURE OF THE PUBLIC INTEREST
IN THE REGULATION OF THE PROFESSIONS

Whatever the merits of these various regulatory philosophies, some concept of the public interest in the regulation of the professions must inform public policy-making in this context. The public interest here, as elsewhere, is an elusive concept. Clearly a number of publics and subpublics are affected: 1/ a wide range of consumers and potential consumers of a profession's services, differing greatly in nature and scale of demands and degrees of sophistication; 2/ members of a profession, probably ranged along a wide spectrum of functions and exper-tise; 3/ paraprofessionals functioning in the area; 4/ related professions or poten-tial professions with overlapping stakes or ambitions in the area; 5/ aspiring entrants to these various professional groups; 6/ educational institutions and pro-fessional educators, usually functioning in a non-explicit market setting and arguably maximizing a complex of objectives not necessarily fully coterminous with market efficiency criteria;[35] 7/ various classes of third parties affected by externalities to professional-client relationships, e.g. third parties who rely on audited financial statements; 8/ taxpayers, who subsidize professional education programs and professional delivery systems; and 9/ the state, which, while re-flecting the foregoing interests, also embraces a much larger range of additional interests that are indirectly engaged once one moves from a partial equilibrium analysis of, e.g. one particular professional market, to a general equilibrium analysis of all the interacting forces in the economy as a whole (e.g. the determi-nants of the size and distribution of the state's investment in all forms of man-power training).

How these various interests should be weighted is in part a function of one's disciplinary perspective. Economics, traditionally, would focus on issues of allo-cative efficiency and attach less importance to the distributive impacts of alter-native policies. In a number of professions (e.g. medicine, law) major distributive issues obviously exist on the demand side, but less obviously also on the supply side.[36] If, for example, policies are under consideration which, for efficiency rea-sons, would shift around market shares among different professional and para-

35 See K. Arrow, 'Uncertainty and the welfare economics of medical care' (1963) 53 Am. Ec. Rev. 941 at 952.
36 See the essay below by Evans.

professional groups to produce more optimal manpower mixes, groups losing market shares will argue questions of distributive justice by pointing to uncompensated expropriations of prior statutory job (or property) 'rights.' This argument will be made with particular force when the existing scheme of entitlements has typically induced early capitalization of any monopoly rents initially generated by such a scheme so that investments by subsequent entrants are likely to show a relatively normal rate of return, whatever the underlying inefficiencies that may be obscured by this.[37] While distributive considerations such as these may be in conflict with efficiency criteria (and consumer welfare), the political process may be unable to avoid debates over professional regulation (as with other regulation) being cast primarily in distributive terms.

Traditional legal analysis in this context would perhaps focus predominantly on procedural concepts of justice and would concern itself with relatively limited issues of 'due process' in the decision-making activities (e.g. discipline proceedings) of the professions.[38] On the other hand much recent political analysis would emphasize the pluralistic nature of policy-making in this and similar contexts and would predict policy outcomes in terms of the political dynamics of interest group behaviour.[39] Pluralistic theories might yield policy prescriptions geared less to producing particular substantive outputs but more to altering the policy inputs (by improving access to the policy-making process). While policies designed to ensure that all affected interests are weighed in the policy-making process are hard to oppose, pluralist notions of policy-making tend to be less helpful in offering any theory for determining *how* those interests should be weighted once they are politically legitimated (other than in terms of the votes, or support, they represent to politicians). In the absence of a widely accepted, substantive theory of distributive justice, which appears a forlorn hope,[40] this problem will remain a critical one.

37 See G. Tullock, 'The transitional gains trap' (1975) 6 Bell J. of Ecs 671; essay below by Benham and Benham; for problems of calculating monopoly rents in the professions, see Riera et al., 'Human capital analysis: its application in the study of the consumer interest in the professions,' in *Four Aspects of Professionals*, op. cit., note 1 above.
38 See e.g. McRuer, op. cit., note 3 above.
39 See e.g. R. Dahl, *A Preface to Democratic Theory* (University of Chicago Press, 1956); M. Olson, *The Logic of Collective Action* (Harvard University Press, 1971); A. Downs, *An Economic Theory of Democracy* (Harper and Row, 1957); G.A. Schubert, *The Public Interest* (Free Press, 1960); C.E. Lindblom, *The Policy-Making Process* (Prentice-Hall, 1968); C.E. Lindblom, *The Intelligence of Democracy* (Free Press, 1965); *The Process of Public Decision-Making*, Ontario Economic Council, 1977.
40 Cf. John Rawls, *A Theory of Justice* (Harvard University Press, 1971); Robert Nozick, *Anarchy, State, and Utopia* (Basic Books, 1974).

No single talisman of the public interest is likely to attract an overwhelming social consensus. Inevitably, any set of public policies towards the professions will result in the divergent interests affected perceiving themselves, relative to other interests, as either 'winners' or 'losers.' Certainly it is not possible for any set of policies to make every interest a 'winner,' at least in distributive terms, much as it may sometimes be to the advantage of politicians and others to obfuscate this painful truth. One can confidently predict, therefore, that the issues discussed in the following essays will not be quickly resolved. Instead, we may anticipate continuing, and indeed heightened, controversies over the regulation of the professions as they continue to evolve into one of our most important economic sectors. If the essays in this book cannot end the controversies, perhaps they may at least assist in focusing the issues and informing the debate.

REGULATORY PHILOSOPHIES

SYLVIA OSTRY

Competition policy and
the self-regulating professions

Two hundred years ago Adam Smith proffered the following advice: 'people of the same trade seldom meet together, even for merriment and diversion, but the conversation ends in a conspiracy against the public, or in some contrivance to raise prices ... Though the law cannot hinder people of the same trade from sometimes assembling together, it ought to do nothing to facilitate such assemblies, much less to render them necessary.'[1] Smith was a profound cynic, but the essence of his message that power unchecked is power misused has proved itself over time. We are now beginning to appreciate the relevance of that message as it applies to the self-regulating professions.

The professions have, in some crucial respects, long enjoyed a public policy stance of benign neglect. While for some time there has been concern over individuals' access to professional services, it is only recently that the professions have themselves been put on the examining table and subjected to the kind of careful probing familiar to other important participants in the market process. Understandably, a critique of the professions is not something one enters into lightly. As one observer has put it, 'the professions operate in an atmosphere of sacerdotal reverence: the stillness of the courtroom, the antiquity of the solicitor's office, the embarrassed silence of the doctor's surgery. How unseemly to apply economic analysis to all that.'[2]

Chairman of the Economic Council of Canada; formerly deputy minister, Department of Consumer and Corporate Affairs, Canada. The author is indebted to Ron Hirshhorn for his invaluable assistance in preparing this article.

1 Adam Smith, *An Inquiry into the Nature and Causes of the Wealth of Nations* (London: Methuen and Co., 1904), 144
2 D.S. Lees, *Economic Consequences of the Professions* (London: Institute of Economic Affairs, 1966), 4

These, however, are irreverent times. Many have come to accept the wisdom of Shaw's dictum that 'all great truths begin as blasphemies'; and, 'unseemly' or not, the task of evaluating the role and structure of the professions and putting in place the needed safeguards has begun.

The professions were brought under Combines Law along with other service industries following the recent passage of Bill C-2.[3] As a result of this legislation Canada no longer has the dubious distinction of being one of the few developed countries to exclude the important and rapidly growing service sector from competition laws. What is significant about the amendments in the present context, however, is the opportunity they afford for a response to the special problems of the self-regulating professions. These problems have received some significant attention in recent years; most notable has been the work of the McRuer Comission and the Committee on Healing Arts in Ontario, the Castonguay Commission in Quebec, the select committee on the professions in Alberta, and the report of the Economic Council of Canada on competition policy.[4] In this paper I should like to describe some of the concerns that the Department of Consumer and Corporate Affairs has in this area, and to try to elaborate on some of the issues that emerge from the decision to extend competition policy to the self-regulating professions.

The argument for extending competition policy to the professions arises out of a recognition of the substantial benefits available when market forces are allowed to assert themselves. In other sectors of the economy we have found that performance is considerably improved in an environment that rewards superior productivity and penalizes waste and inefficiency. We have seen that effective competition encourages the development of new products and improved patterns of production, and generally helps promote the most efficient use of the economy's scarce resources. Also, we have, I believe, come to appreciate the considerable appeal of the simple system of natural justice wherein a free functioning market is the arbiter of who receives what. When economic rewards are affected by restrictions in the system or influenced by administrative decisions, differences in these rewards become less understandable, and often less acceptable. The influence of the market on individuals' perceptions of justice is extremely important and in itself provides a compelling argument on behalf of a competitive system.

3 *Combines Investigation Act*, R.S.C. 1970, c. C-23 as amended by S.C., 1974-75-76, C.76.
4 Ontario Royal Commission on the Inquiry into Civil Rights, *Report*, 1970 (McRuer Report); Ontario Committee on the Healing Arts, *Report*, 1970; Quebec Commission of Inquiry into Health and Welfare, *Report*, 1970; Alberta Select Committee of the Legislative Assembly on Professions and Occupations, *Report*, 1973; Economic Council of Canada, *Interim Report on Competition Policy*, 1969

For those who value the benefits of a market system there is much that is disturbing about the structure and role of the self-governing professions. The very notion of self-regulation is inimical to the concept of a competitive system where the market sets the terms of production and establishes the required discipline. And indeed, licensure laws often have an uncanny resemblance to cartel arrangements designed specifically to restrict competition among members of an industry; in this sense licensure can be seen as a way of enlisting the enforcement powers of the state to help in the very difficult task of organizing and policing an agreement to, for example, refrain from price-cutting.

The foregoing is not intended to call into question the motives of professional groups; what it does indicate is a concern about the effect of their behaviour and the costs that professional arrangements, however inspired, impose on society. The McRuer Commission noted that twenty-two self-governing professions and occupations in Ontario had been given 'statutory power to license, govern, and control those persons engaged in them.'[5] Under this and similar authority in other provinces, professional associations have been able to establish training and character requirements for prospective members, set fee schedules and determine the form of various charges, prohibit advertising and related competitive practices, and influence generally the form and manner in which professional services are supplied. It is not clear that all or even most of these restrictions have provided significant positive benefits to the public. What seems more apparent is their substantial effect in reducing competition, impeding innovation and change, and raising costs and prices for many professional services.

Some years ago the British Monopolies Commission looked at the general effect of certain restrictive practices in the professions. They summarized the concerns which arose from their examination of the evidence as follows: 'Collective arrangements which significantly limit the freedom of the parties in the conduct of their business may be expected ... to result in higher prices, less efficient use of resources, discouragement of new developments and a tendency towards rigidity in the structure and trading methods of those businesses. Such collective restrictions tend to reduce the pressures upon those observing them to increase their efficiency. They may also delay the introduction of new forms of service and the elimination of inefficient practitioners.'[6] This puts the problem well, though most observers would probably be inclined to express the latter point more forcefully. As Milton Friedman has pointed out, advances in knowledge and in methods of organization and production often come from the work of 'quacks' and 'crackpots' – those who are willing to try the new and the unortho-

5 Ontario Royal Commission on Inquiry into Civil Rights, Vol. 3, 1160
6 Monopolies Commission, *Part 1: The Report* (London: HMSO, 1970), 69

dox.[7] A freely functioning market tolerates this sort of diversity and encourages experimentation which is likely to improve upon producers' ability to meet consumer demands. But members of the self-regulating professions are strongly encouraged to conform to the prevailing orthodoxy, and if they want to remain in good standing they are often severely limited in the kind of experimentation they can undertake. Friedman conjectures that with a free market for medical care we would have perhaps seen the development of highly efficient medical corporations – what he terms 'department stores of medicine.' One can carry this sort of speculation in numerous directions, but the point is clear: the result of various professional restrictions has most certainly been to delay, if not prevent, the introduction of new forms of service and to lend support to the inefficient and uninnovative practitioner.

One of the most disturbing effects of market restrictions, as I mentioned, is that it leads to economic differentials which are difficult to justify. In the case of professional groups it has proven difficult to get a reliable quantitative reading of this effect; analysts have not been completely successful in disentangling the monopoly profits attributable to restrictions from the higher earnings that represent a legitimate compensation for greater education and training, greater ability, longer hours of work, increased responsibility, and other factors.[8] But this is not to say that evidence of excess or monopoly gains in the professions is lacking. The appearance of a long queue of willing entrants in itself suggests that returns to an occupation are more attractive than one would expect in a competitive market. And such queues of course have not been uncommon in the case of the most lucrative professions. This is especially the case if we count, as we should, those who meet the minimum standards and would join the queue had they not been deterred from standing in line by the higher effective standards actually used to ration entrants to the major professional schools.

Proponents of licensure laws argue that they are necessary to ensure a certain quality of professional service and to protect the consumer from fraud and incompetence. Certainly there may be a case for supporting the consumer in a market situation where he is likely to be severely disadvantaged by a lack of information and knowledge or where his decision is likely to have implications

---

7 Milton Friedman, *Capitalism and Freedom* (Chicago: University of Chicago Press, 1962), chap. 9
8 An interesting attempt to establish the quantitative impact of professional restrictions occurs in Milton Friedman and Simon Kuznets, *Income From Independent Professional Practice* (New York: NBER, 1954). See also, David Dodge, 'Occupational wage differentials, occupational licensing, and returns to investment in education: an exploratory analysis,' in *Canadian Higher Education in the Seventies*, edited by S. Ostry for the Economic Council of Canada (Ottawa: Information Canada, 1972).

for others in society which he would not be willing or able to consider. But how helpful are various licensure laws and restrictions to the consumer? And do the benefits that are available justify the substantial costs which accompany the imposition of professional controls? I suggest that if federal and provincial authorities had asked themselves these questions a long time ago the market for professional services would be very much different from what it is today.

Let us look first at the concept of licensing itself. One might well be suspicious of licensure at the outset because the pressure for licensing invariably comes not from the consumers it is to protect but from the trades and professions themselves. Licensing is a considerably less than ideal form of consumer protection. The fact that a professional met certain standards at the beginning of his career is clearly not much guide to his current competence. And while professional associations purport to investigate fraud and incompetence, the evidence on professional self-discipline – as well as the generally negative attitude to testimony against a professional colleague – would suggest that this activity is pursued with something less than undiluted zeal.

A recent study by the US Federal Trade Commission sheds some revealing light on the question of licensing.[9] The FTC made a comparison of the television repair industry in three separate areas: California, where there is a system of registration and a Bureau of Repair Services to investigate fraud, Louisiana, where there is a system of mandatory licensing by a board comprised of members of the industry, and the District of Columbia, where there are no controls of any type. The study found that the price of repairs in Louisiana, the state with licensing, was more than 20 per cent higher than in the other two areas. But no fewer instances of fraud were found in Louisiana than in the District of Columbia, the area without controls; and the highest quality of service was evident in California where the Bureau of Repair Services was at work. In other words, while licensing could well result in higher prices, it is far from a guarantee of product quality.

Similar results have emerged from studies of regulation in the Canadian trucking industry.[10] These studies attempted to compare intraprovincial trucking in provinces where the industry is firmly regulated – specifically British Columbia, Saskatchewan, and Manitoba – with that in Alberta where there is no regulation

9 Staff Report to the Federal Trade Commission, *Regulation of the Television Repair Industry in Louisiana and California – A Case Study*, November 1974
10 D. McLachlan, 'Canadian trucking regulations,' *Logistics and Transportation Review*, 8 No. 1 (1972), 59-81; J. Sloss, 'Regulation of motor freight transportation: a quantitative evaluation of policy,' *Bell Journal of Economics and Management Science*, 1, No. 2 (Autumn 1970), 327-66; J. Palmer, 'A further analysis of provincial trucking regulation,' *Bell Journal of Economics and Management Science*, 4, No. 2 (Autumn 1973), 655-64

and in some other provinces where there are lesser degrees of regulation; in Ontario, for example, there is no regulation of rates, while in Quebec, where there is also a regulatory authority, trucking rates have been de facto not regulated. No evidence was found in this work that carriers in the provinces which required licensing were as a rule safer than those in Alberta. Nor was there any indication that small shippers and small towns in the latter province were suffering from a lack of service. What these studies did find was a quite significant difference in costs and in trucking rates between regulated and unregulated provinces. In the most recent study, John Palmer estimated that de facto regulation leads to rates which are about two cents higher per ton-mile.[11]

These studies indicate to me that it is well to remain highly suspicious of the supposed benefits of licensure. Apparently I am not alone in this view. The McRuer Commission, the Castonguay Commission, and the Economic Council of Canada all saw the need to have the public viewpoint more firmly represented in licensing decisions and accordingly recommended that lay members be appointed to the governing bodies of professional associations. This would certainly be a positive move, and the actions some provinces have already taken in this direction are to be commended. Especially notable in this regard are the steps which have been taken in Quebec – via the enactment of a Professional Code and the establishment of a Professions Board – to ensure public representation in the administration of professional corporations, and generally to help prevent the abuse of power by professional bodies.[12] Developments of this sort should help to reduce the cynicism that often surrounds the activities of professional groups. And with lay representation the decisions of professional bodies should reflect a broader perspective and hopefully an improved understanding of what constitutes the public interest. In practical terms I would hope that the result would be a more careful consideration of such issues as the functions of paraprofessionals, and the length of professional training – both of which, of course, directly affect the price of professional services as well as the economic return to existing practitioners.[13]

11 Ibid.
12 See for example René Dussault and Louis Borgeat, 'La Réforme des Professions au Québec,' *Revue du Barreau*, 34, No. 3 (May 1974), 139-83.
13 An interesting discussion of the use of paraprofessionals is U.E. Reinhardt, 'Occupational licensure in the health care sector'; this constitutes appendix C of Dodge, 'Occupational wage differentials,' 167-73. With regard to professional training concern arises, for example, out of the finding by Andrew Roman that law training in Ontario is longer than anywhere else in the world; Roman also quotes an associate law dean as saying that a gold medal law student ten years before would today have difficulty acquiring a place at law school. Andrew Roman and Associates, *A Study of Legal Education in Ontario, 1970*, prepared for the Commission on Post-Secondary Education in Ontario (Toronto: Queen's Printer, 1970)

However, notwithstanding improvements of this type, licensing can be a very costly market restriction. This is the case both where licensing is by the industry and where control is exercised by a government agency or commission, as in trucking. This suggests, therefore, that we must also begin to make a much more critical look at licensure itself. We must recognize that licensing is likely to raise the price of professional services and that its influence on the quality of professional care could quite possibly be perverse. For example, by imposing sufficiently stringent entry requirements we could ensure that Ontario has the most highly qualified barbers anywhere. But the result would not necessarily be an improvement in the quality of male coiffure in the province. Faced with higher prices and a lack of low-cost alternatives some males would probably seek out the haircutting services of their wives; others would just go without a haircut for longer than usual. The effect of the licensing restriction, therefore, could conceivably be to make Ontario males a shabbier-looking lot than before.

Too often in the past we have failed to appreciate these sorts of implications. We did not try to tally the costs of regulation or to look beyond the traditional justifications for licensing. We should now realize that licensing exists in many cases where there are no major information problems or exceptional risks, and where the consumer is reasonably able to determine his own best interest. We should recognize that in some instances where licensing would seem warranted the costs may not justify it. And we should be aware that there are less restrictive alternatives to licensing, such as registration and certification, and that in many cases these may be more appropriate forms of intervention in the market.

Adopting a more critical stance towards demands for licensing and inserting a public presence on the governing bodies of professional associations are two approaches to the problems arising from self-regulation in the professions. A third response is to focus directly on the activities and rules of professional bodies and to try to ensure that these are in the public interest. This, of course, is the approach underlying the recent amendments to Canada's combines law.

Competitive forces have long been important in bringing the public interest to bear in the decisions of groups and individuals. So it is only logical, where there is reason to be concerned about the public interest as it relates to matters of price and efficiency, to begin to look to competition policy for a solution. The immediate question we are faced with, however, is whether or not competition policy can be made to apply to the activities of bodies which have received their authority under provincial statute. The simple answer to that very complex question is 'in some instances, yes.' In the *Canadian Breweries* case, Justice McRuer indicated specifically that, while commercial activities that are effectively regulated are generally not subject to the Combines Act, the law may apply to other activities of the same industries or firms: 'When a Provincial Legislature has conferred on a Commission or Board the power to regulate an industry and fix prices, and the power has been exercised, the Court must assume that the power is exercised in the public interest ... There may, however, be areas of competition in the market that are not affected by the exercise of the powers conferred on the provincial body in which restraints on competition may render the operations of the combine illegal.'[14]

In the Stage II proposals to amend competition law an attempt is being made to codify the jurisprudence in this area and to clarify the general relationships between regulated industries and the Combines Act.[15] The new proposals would make it clear that firms or groups are not completely immune from competition law merely because there are regulators in the vicinity. Under these proposals, conduct would be exempt from application of the law where it was regulated in the sense of being expressly authorized by a public agency not appointed by representatives of the regulatees. The public agency must be expressly empowered to regulate the activity and have expressly directed its attention to that activity. In addition, for competition law not to apply it must be shown, under the proposed provisions, that its application would seriously interfere with the attainment of the objectives of the regulatory legislation. It should be stressed that the question of the Act's application only becomes relevant when there is reason to suspect a violation of a criminal or civil provision of the law; the provisions in this area do not represent an attempt to challenge the authority of regulatory bodies to carry out their functions.

There is a related problem which we are also attempting to come to terms with in the Stage II revisions. It sometimes happens that a regulation aimed at achieving a perfectly legitimate objective for which a government agency is responsible lessens competition. While this cannot be avoided in some cases it may be unnecessary in others where both the objectives of the specialized agency and that of competition policy can be met. In Stage II it is therefore proposed that federal regulatory bodies be required to pursue their objectives in the manner that is least restrictive of competition.[16] This is an important proposal, and it should go some way towards reducing the conflict between competition policy and other legitimate government objectives.

At any rate, as regards the activities of the regulated professions, there are important matters to which competition policy would seem not to apply. I am thinking here particularly of the fee-setting arrangements emerging from provincial programs such as medicare and of the practice of setting entry requirements

14 *Regina* v. *Canadian Breweries Limited* [1960] O.R. 601, 629-30
15 Consumer and Corporate Affairs Canada, *Proposals for a New Competition Policy for Canada, Second Stage* (Ottawa: Minister of Supply and Services Canada, 1977), 26-30 and 140-1
16 Ibid., 28-30 and 141-2

to preserve professional standards. At the same time, however, there is an important range of activities carried out by professional bodies which is not covered by provincial law; here the revised Combines Act applies and has the prospect of becoming an effective instrument for asserting the public interest.

To keep things in perspective, let me emphasize that there is a good deal of uncertainty regarding the precise implications of Combines Law for the professions. The important Section 32 of the Bill, which pertains to agreements to lessen competition, only became applicable to the service sector on 1 July 1976. One still awaits a test of the legislation's strengths and weaknesses in this area.

With the recent revision, however, the Competition Bureau has begun seriously to examine a number of professional rules and activities. One of these is the restriction on the professional's right to disseminate information. This is perhaps the most prevalent practice among professional groups. It can also be a particularly pernicious one from the point of view of competition policy, as some recent studies in the United States illustrate. Lee Benham, for example, found that, owing to the lack of information and the resulting absence of price competition, prices for eyeglasses were 25 to 40 per cent higher in markets with greater professional control. He noted that these higher prices were 'in turn associated with a significant reduction in the proportion of individuals obtaining eyeglasses during a year.'[17] A study of advertising restrictions in the US drug industry came up with similar evidence of a significant loss to consumers.[18] One might reasonably expect that the burden of such losses weighs especially heavily on the shoulders of low-income consumers.

In defence of these restrictions it is argued that advertising is 'unprofessional,' that it could mislead the public and endanger necessary public trust and confidence in the professions. But the advertising of, for example, legal services need not resemble, say, the advertising of toothpaste. Advertising, far from being demeaning, can be a dignified and responsible method of informing the public about the type of services being offered and their price. In this regard one only has to look at the informative advertising sponsored by various interest groups and trade associations.

There are, to be sure, examples from the past of professional advertising of a somewhat startling character, as those opposed to increased information have

17 Lee and Alexandra Benham, 'Regulating through the professions: a perspective on information control,' *Journal of Law and Economics*, 18 (Oct. 1975), 421-47. See also Lee Benham, 'The effects of advertising on the price of eyeglasses,' *Journal of Law and Economics*, 15 (Oct. 1972), 337-52.
18 Letter by the Council on Wage and Price Stability to the FTC in the Prescription Drug Price Proceedings, 4 Aug. 1975; also, John Cady, *Restricted Advertising and Competition: The Case of Retail Drugs* (Washington: American Enterprise Institute, 1976)

not hesitated to indicate. However, these references to the past can be highly misleading. Professional practice and public attitudes and expectations are much different from what they were fifty or even twenty-five years ago. There is now as well important legislation to discourage rhetorical flights of fancy in advertising. This is not to deny that advertising can be misleading, and indeed degrading. This remains a possibility in the professions as elsewhere – notwithstanding existing legislative and other safeguards. However, the dangers in this regard do not provide a justification for the complete and firm control many professional groups have imposed over the flow of information.

The approach in Bill c-2 reflects this view and the general concern that, in many cases, restrictions on advertising are incompatible with their relative costs and benefits to the public. The focus in the legislation is on those restrictive arrangements which unduly lessen competition. Advertising arrangements that are not harmful to competition are specifically exempted (Section 32 [2]). There is also explicit recognition in the Act (Section 32 [6]) that protection of the public may require rules relating to professional 'standards of competence and integrity.' However, where such restrictive agreements cannot be justified as being 'reasonably necessary for the protection of the public,' and are likely to unduly lessen competition with respect to price or quality, they risk being in violation of Section 32 of the Act.

Another practice of concern is the attempt to control professional fees. Regulations governing fees are not as widespread as regulations on advertising. And where fee schedules do exist they are at times difficult to enforce.[19] It is not uncommon for a tariff schedule to be disregarded, for example, where the professional is selling his services to a large buyer with a substantial degree of bargaining power. But there are important areas where fees are effectively maintained – and at some considerable cost to society.

The issue was put quite well, I think, in a recent United States Supreme Court test of price-fixing in the legal profession. It was the important case of *Goldfarb* v. *Virginia*.[20] The prosecuting attorney, Solicitor General Robert Bork, asked why the antitrust laws should not apply to lawyers. 'The answer is said to be the ethical responsibilities of the bar,' he noted, but 'one searches in vain for the connection between professional ethics and price-fixing for professional services.'[21] One does indeed. The argument put forth, that fees must be set to preserve professional standards, is not at all convincing. Where it is desirable to

19 This point is made particularly in John Crispo, *Fee-Setting by Independent Practitioners* (Ottawa: Information Canada, 1972).
20 [1975] 95 S.C. 2004 (U.S. S.C.)
21 Quoted in Mark J. Green, 'The high cost of lawyers,' *New York Times Magazine*, 10 Aug. 1975

ensure a certain quality of professional service - and let me emphasize that in many cases it is not desirable to deprive the consumer of his choice in this way - where a certain level of quality is desirable, however, there are more effective and less costly approaches. The elimination of price competition has, as I have indicated, major implications for efficiency, for innovation and change, and for costs and prices in the industry. The attempt to impose a given fee structure, moreover, can lead to severe distortions with respect to allocation of time and talent within a profession. The restrictions on price-cutting along with most restrictions on advertising are undesirable of course from the point of view of consumers; one might expect that they are also fairly disagreeable to new entrants to the profession who, by being denied the opportunity to use these competitive devices, are put at a significant disadvantage.

In regard to pricing restrictions, it is again Section 32 of the Combines Act which is relevant. The question the courts will have to decide in each case is 'Does the practice of the association with respect to fees constitute an arrangement to unduly limit competition?' The general contention is that by publishing a fee schedule the professional body is only providing its members with a suggested list of charges. This may be the case, but the facts could indicate that the issuance of such a schedule amounts to much more than a suggestion. Where, for example, there is evidence of attempts having been made to enforce an agreed-upon schedule of fees, I would think it quite difficult to conclude that a price-fixing arrangement did not exist. Less direct evidence may point in the same direction. Where, for example, it is clear that most practitioners in an area raised their fees to a newly recommended level in the reasonable expectation that the tariff schedule would be substantially followed, the courts could very well find that the association has entered into an arrangement under the terms of Section 32 of the Act.

In this connection it is instructive to note the decision of the Ontario Supreme Court in the recent *Armco* case.[22] There was no direct evidence of a price-fixing agreement in this case, and indeed some of the published statements would tend to suggest quite otherwise. But there was evidence that after much discussion on the subject the industry had adopted an 'open pricing policy,' the key to which was publication of a price list by one of the firms and its prompt adoption by the remainder of the accused. The cumulative effect of the evidence indicated to Justice Lerner that there had been an arrangement to lessen competition unduly - a conclusion substantiated by the evidence of 'consistent and remarkable uniformity' in pricing.

It has been the custom of a number of professional associations to propose, discuss, authorize, and circulate fee schedules which have been widely adopted

22 *Regina* v. *Armco Canada Ltd* [1975] O.R. 521

by their respective memberships. There appears to be sufficient similarity between the situation in these cases and that in the *Armco* case to caution the wise
and wary against continuation of such practices. The prohibitions in the Combines Investigation Act are criminal law, and one cannot help speculating on the
ultimate consequences of prosecution of members of a group whose bylaws provide for suspension of a member who has been convicted of an indictable
offence.

In our efforts to come to terms with price-fixing and with other restrictive
practices in the professions we can benefit from the experience of other countries. The US record of achievement in this area is beginning to look especially
impressive. In the recent case of *Goldfarb* v. *Virginia* referred to earlier, the US
Supreme Court ruled for the first time that adherence to a fee schedule by professionals can amount to price-fixing in violation of federal antitrust laws. This
has paved the way for a number of actions: the Justice Department, for example,
has recently challenged the advertising bans of the American Medical Association
and the American Bar Association, as well as the pricing restrictions of the Institute of Public Accountants, the Society of Anaesthesiologists, and the American
Institute of Architects, among others. Professional groups in the United States
are getting the message, and many longstanding restrictions – such as those
incorporated in the American Bar Association's Code of Professional Responsibility – are being reviewed and amended.[23] The British government has also
become increasingly concerned about the practices of professionals. The Monopolies and Mergers Commission has just reported on the activities of various professional groups, and it is expected that the UK government will shortly respond
to the recommendations for a general liberalizing of advertising and other restrictions.[24]

I think that what we are seeing quite generally is a significant change in the
public attitude towards self-regulation. To a greater extent than ever before, people are making invidious comparisons and questioning whether it is necessary or
desirable to endow some groups with special powers. The decision in Canada's
case to extend competition policy to the self-regulating professions represents, I
believe, a positive and significant response to public concern on this issue.

At the same time, however, we should fully recognize the substantial barriers
against competition in the professions. In many cases it is not merely a problem

23 For a good discussion of developments and considerations related to the American Bar
Association's restrictions on advertising see William Smith, 'Making the availability of
legal services better known,' *American Bar Association Journal*, 62 (July 1976), 855-61.

24 The following are some of the reports issued by the Mergers and Monopolies Commission: *Accountancy Services, Veterinary Services, Stockbrokers' Services, Barristers'
Services, Advocates' Services.*

of anticompetitive rules – important as these are. The more general problem often is that the members of professional groups are led to think of each other not as competitors but as colleagues, or, to use Reuben Kessel's terminology fellow members of an 'in-group.'[25] One does not question the work of one's colleagues; never mind that such openness could lead to more effective decision-making by consumers and contribute to an improvement in professional standards. Clearly this perspective is not something that can be changed easily or quickly. It will require the co-operation of federal and provincial authorities and a commitment by both to strengthen the role of competitive forces in this important area of the economy.

25 R.A. Kessel, 'Price discrimination in medicine,' *Journal of Law and Economics*, 1 (Oct. 1958), 20-53

JAMES W. YOUNGER

Competition policy and
the self-regulating professions

My purpose in responding to Dr Ostry's paper is not to provide a systematic defence of the self-regulating professions, but to question the validity of the arguments employed for the purpose of justifying government regulation of the
professions under the Combines Investigation Act.[1] It is conceded that, under a
proper definition of a profession, not all occupations now afforded the status
of self-regulating professions in Ontario qualify as such. The argument for
exempting such occupations from the Combines Investigation Act must be pursued on different grounds.

Dr Ostry's argument may be summarized as follows: In the case of the production and distribution of goods competition improves efficiency in the allocation of resources and distributes economic rewards justly. Similar consideration
should apply to professional services. The argument in favour of self-regulating
professions is that the operation of market forces will not ensure a minimum
standard of quality in cases where the consumer is likely to suffer damage due to
inability to judge the quality of the services rendered (information breakdowns),
or where his decision is likely to have implications for others which he would
not be able or willing to consider (externalities). However, based on experience
in the television repair trade and the trucking industry Dr Ostry questions the
validity of this argument and asserts that the demand for self-government does
not emanate from consumers and that the costs of self-regulation may exceed
the benefits, neither of which is precisely measurable. Having reached this conclusion, the argument diffuses into a consideration of constitutional problems
and the application of the Combines Investigation Act to fee-setting and advertising restrictions.

Vice-president, Secretary, and General Counsel, The Steel Company of Canada, Ltd
1 R.S., C-23; amended by c. 10 (1st Supp.), c. 10 (2nd Supp.), 1974-75-76, c. 76

A preliminary reaction to this argument is that it proves more than the federal government is prepared to concede; if anything, it demonstrates that the Combines Investigation Act should apply to trade unions. However, the activities of unions are exempted from the Act by Section 4 (1) (a). It must therefore be concluded either that the government rejects the validity of the argument, that its competition policies are inconsistent and discriminatory, or that it is prepared to acknowledge that special considerations may apply to particular groups to justify their exemption from generally applicable competition policies. If the latter is the case, the arguments in favour of exempting professional organizations as outlined below would seem to be much stronger than those for exempting trade unions, on a logical if not on a political basis.

If Dr Ostry's argument proves too much, it also proves too little. Let us examine its premises a little more closely. Its basic position may be formulated syllogistically as follows: The allocation of resources by market forces is the most efficient means of allocation resources. The control of the allocation of professional services by professional bodies is not allocation of those services by the market. Therefore, professional self-regulation is not the most efficient means of allocating professional services. This argument is invalid because both the major and the minor premises are questionable.

The basic problem with the major premise is that, in common with many economic statements, it equates efficiency with price and assumes that the consumer is in a position where his primary interest is in price or where he is able to make an intelligent appraisal of quality in relation to price. While these are undoubtedly fair assumptions in most cases of sales of goods or simple forms of service, the case may well be different with professional services for the following reasons.

First, the market operates most effectively when the consumer is capable of making a fair assessment of quality in relation to price. In the case of most goods, most consumers can make this assessment based on their past experience or that of others on whose experience they can draw. This is not always the case, however. For example, the government regulates the manufacture and sale of drugs, and the Canadian Standards Association sets standards for a variety of products such as electric appliances because it is assumed that the consumer is unable to make a reasonable assessment of quality in the absence of such assistance. The same argument applies, a fortiori, to professional services. This argument, of course, begs the question of who should set the standards of quality, but it does indicate that the premise is not universally true.

Second, in most cases involving the sale of goods or non-professional services, the consumer is not confronted with an emergency that forces him into the market. Ordinarily he can defer his purchase until he has time to review his choice.

In the case of professional services not only is the consumer unable to judge the quality of the service but he is frequently forced by an emergency to make a choice on the spur of the moment, often with irreversible results. Under these circumstances he needs to be assured of some minimal professional competence.

Third, one of the fallacies inherent in much of the discussion of competition policy is that the market is one-dimensional and that the dimension is price. In fact, competition is multidimensional and relates to quality, service, variety, and so on, as well as price. A market can function quite effectively even if prices are relatively uniform. My own professional experience leads me to the conclusion that expertise and promptness are more important to most clients than price. This argument is supported by the initial conclusion of the Cohen Commission in the United States that, while some measure of competition in the accounting profession is beneficial, excessive price competition may detrimentally affect audit quality.[2]

Fourth, the market for professional services is different than the market for goods. In the case of goods, where the consumer can make an intelligent assessment of the relevant facts, it is desirable that the market offer a wide range of qualities and prices. However, if the consumer of professional services demands quality first, and if it is difficult for him to make a judgment as to quality, the market will function best if minimum standards of quality are assured. The only alternative is for the consumer to know the supplier. The average consumer knows from experience that he can trust certain institutions such as Eaton's, General Motors, or Canadian General Electric when he is purchasing goods and that he runs a risk in purchasing an unfamiliar brand or in dealing with an unfamiliar supplier. With respect to professional services, the average consumer has no such guidance, and, by the nature of the case, will find it difficult to acquire.

Fifth, in the case of most goods and non-professional services, there is little need for control of quality standards because consumers are making continuous demands on the market for similar goods and services and will suffer no serious or permanent damage as a result of a mistaken choice. The consumer who dislikes his haircut suffers little loss and no permanent damage, and can go to a new barber in a few weeks. The housewife who purchases a tough steak is in the same position. The market will tend, fairly quickly, to weed out the unsatisfactory supplier of such goods and services. However, the demand for professional services is discontinuous, and the risk of serious or permanent damage from incompetence is high. Since it is difficult for the market to deal with the problem of professional incompetence, some system for safeguarding quality seems desirable.

2 *Business Week*, 28 March 1977, p. 56

All of these considerations cast doubt on the validity of the major premise of Dr Ostry's argument as it applies to professional services.

Equally open to question is the validity of the minor premise, which asserts that control of the allocation of professional services by professional bodies is not allocation of these services by the market. The fallacy in this statement lies in the assumption that the self-regulating professions control the allocation of professional services. Such control must take the form of control either of the demand for, or supply of, such services. It seems quite clear that professional bodies have not interfered with the function of the market by prescribing consumer demand. On the contrary, the professions have encouraged consumers of their services to express their demand for both traditional and novel assistance and advice. In fact, practitioners in a number of professional fields have been diligent in anticipating the needs of their clients. While it is true that in the Middle Ages the courts tended to restrict the remedies of the subject to cases where an appropriate writ was available, the legal profession constantly strove to widen the scope of available remedies, as illustrated in the development of the action on the case. It is the ingenuity of lawyers that has gradually moved the law from the position of *ubi remedium, ibi jus* to *ubi jus, ibi remedium*. The expansion of the range and depth of services provided by the accounting profession in recent years is a clear example of how a profession has anticipated the needs and met the demands of its clients as conditions have changed. Nor can the professions be accused of restricting the right of clients to choose their own professional advisers except to the extent that some specialists have chosen to limit their own practices. No client is forced to choose a practitioner whom he does not trust or who lacks appropriate qualifications or expertise.

If the self-regulating professions have not interfered with the demand side of the market for their services, what of their effect on the supply side? The professions have been frequently accused of limiting the number of practitioners in order to enhance the income of existing members. Presumably even critics of the professions would agree that it is not objectionable to limit admission to the professions by setting certain minimum standards of character and competence. The experience in Great Britain, the United States, and Canada has tended, in the interests of the public, to move from an unrestricted right to practice to professional self-regulation. In the early nineteenth century there were virtually no restrictions on holding oneself out as a solicitor, a physician, or an accountant. Experience indicated the need for establishing appropriate standards of expertise,[3] and it can scarcely be denied that self-regulation has enhanced the expertise of practitioners to the benefit of their clients. If there is any cause for complaint

3 cf. Michael Birks, *Gentlemen of the Law* (London: Stevens and Sons Ltd, 1960), chap. 7.

it would seem to be that supervision of professional education and qualifications has not been sufficiently stringent and continuous.

In any event, aside from establishing tests for academic aptitude, the effect of professional self-regulation on admissions in most cases has been negligible. The law societies are probably the epitome of self-regulation, but the legal profession in Ontario has for many years been open to anyone who could meet the academic requirements and was of good character. In fact there has been a consistent tendency to admit to the bar more candidates than the profession can easily absorb. Similarly, there appear to be no undue restrictions on admission to accountancy or engineering.

The real constraint on admission to the professions is the capacity of educational facilities. Any limitation on these facilities in Ontario in recent years has been the responsibility of the provincial government, not of the professions. Complaints about limitations on admission to the legal profession centre on the universities, which are supported by the government, not on the Bar Admission Course, which is controlled by the professions. Similarly, admission to the professions of accountancy or engineering is limited only by the capacity of government-financed educational institutions. The medical profession represents a particularly striking case. Because medicare has converted medical services into an ostensibly free good, the demand exceeds the supply. The profession has not restricted admission to practice in any unreasonable way. However the government has decided to control the cost of such services by limiting the supply rather than discouraging the growth in demand. The limitation on the supply of physicians is the result of government policy, not of professional self-government.

Dr Ostry's minor premise therefore loses much of its validity. If it is an argument in favour of unrestricted admission into the professions, it flies in the face of historic experience. If it is an argument only in favour of fewer restrictions, the issue is not whether to draw the line, but where and by whom. On the question of who draws the line, the facts indicate that the government is responsible for more restrictive policies than the professions, and the premise is shown to be invalid.

Since it appears that there is considerable reason to question both the major and minor premises of Dr Ostry's basic argument, one must conclude that it has not been shown that professional self-regulation represents an inefficient means of allocating professional services. The implication that government control would be preferable to self-regulation is not borne out by the facts, which indicate that government intervention is likely to be more restrictive and arbitrary than self-regulation.

Yet it must be conceded that the argument as to the necessity of maintaining professional standards does not necessarily justify the existence of such standards in occupations which are not learned professions. The appropriate definition of a profession will be canvassed later in this paper. At this point, it is appropriate merely to disavow any intention to defend licensing legislation which restricts admission to occupations where consumers are able to make a reasonable appraisal of the quality of the services offered, where no serious or lasting damage will result to a consumer making an unwise choice, and where the market will discipline the unqualified supplier of services. There is a qualitative difference between the services rendered by a lawyer or a physician and those rendered by a hairdresser, a television repairman, or an automobile mechanic.

Dr Ostry's second argument is that the costs of self-regulation may exceed the benefits to society, although neither the costs nor the benefits are precisely measurable. This argument may be stated as follows: The costs of professional services to society are greater than the benefits. The costs of professional services are determined by the self-regulating professions. Therefore, the self-regulating professions represent a net cost to society.

Dr Ostry admits that the major premise of this argument is open to question because the costs and benefits are not precisely measurable, but she assumes its validity. There is no denying that the costs and benefits of professional self-regulation are not quantifiable, but the weight of evidence would seem to be against the truth of the proposition on the basis that the benefits of any other system would appear to be less and the costs greater. On the benefit side of the equation, it has been argued above that professional self-regulation in the learned professions is designed to benefit consumers and that it results in a more efficient allocation of such services than would a completely free market for such services. On the cost side of the equation the first argument is that the cost to consumers of professional services is no higher than it would be in the absence of self-regulation. The cost of such services is in the main determined by market forces. To enhance the price of such services it would be necessary that the professions be able either to limit the supply of services, to increase the demand for such services, or to control prices. It has been demonstrated above that any effective limitation on the supply of professional services, beyond certain minimal standards, is imposed by the government and not by the professions. It is obvious that professional bodies have no control over the demand for their services, and, at least in the case of law, accountancy, and medicine, growing demand is largely attributable to government action. This leaves open the question of the power of the professions to fix fees.

The extension of the Combines Investigation Act to the professions has in large part been motivated by the assumption that the unilateral power of the professions to fix fees is a significant interference with the allocation of resources by the market. The question is whether this assumption is factually well founded. Let us examine the situation in a few professions. Comprehensive fee tariffs exist in the medical profession. They represent minima, and physicians may charge more for their services. However, it must be recognized that because of medicare these tariffs are negotiated with the government, which has the ultimate right to dictate what fees will be allowed for purposes of medicare. No other profession has such an elaborate fee-setting mechanism.

In the accounting profession there are no tariffs of fees approved by the profession. Fees are negotiated between accountant and client on the basis of time and expertise. Chartered accountants are not permitted by their governing body to base their fees on the value to the client of the work done.

In the legal profession, tariffs relate principally to certain basic types of solicitor's practice. More complex matters and almost all barrister's practice is charged for on the basis of the time and skill expended and the value of the services to the client. Except for those members of the profession whose practice consists largely of real estate transactions and estates, the tariffs are of little significance. In any event, fee-cutting is common, the tariffs cannot be enforced, and the Law Society does not treat disregard of the tariffs as professional misconduct.

Even within the limited area to which tariffs of legal fees apply, there is a strong argument that their effect is not adverse to the interests of clients. The theoretical complaint is that they are related more to the value of the services to the client than to time expended by the solicitor. This complaint, of course, ignores the factor of the additional risk assumed by the solicitor. It is true that the result of adhering to the real estate tariff may mean that a client will pay more for legal services in the case of a transaction involving a larger purchase price where no serious legal problems are encountered than for a minor transaction that turns out to be very time-consuming. However, a change in the tariff would not result in any over-all reduction in fees but only in a redistribution of fees among clients. A solicitor has to obtain an adequate margin over his costs to stay in practice. If he charged strictly on a basis of time and skill, the tendency would be to shift a larger share of his fees to small estates and small real estate transactions. This result would be unjust for three reasons: first, the more important a transaction is, the more the services are worth to the client, and the more he ought to pay; secondly, the more money is involved in a transaction, the greater the risk to the solicitor, and the higher his fee should be; and thirdly, when a client becomes involved in a transaction, he is unable to appraise in advance what legal complications may arise, and there is something to be said for sharing this risk among all clients.

An examination of the facts relating to the power of the self-regulating professions to fix fees therefore indicates that it has no significant effect in insulating the professions from the discipline of market forces, because the areas covered by fee tariffs are either relatively narrow or subject to government regulation; that tariff fees in the aggregate are not excessive, and the only question relates to their distribution; and that there are sound arguments in support of the manner in which fees are distributed.

There is an additional argument to indicate that the costs to society of professional self-regulation are less than they would be in the absence of such regulation. The gist of this argument is that some control of admission to the professions is necessary to minimize the waste to society of talent and training that could not be fully utilized if the professions were overcrowded. Professional training is expensive to society both directly and indirectly. It is expensive to maintain the necessary educational facilities. This is a direct and measurable cost. To the extent that students take such training and are then unable to utilize it because of overcrowding in the profession, the cost of such training has been wasted. The indirect costs, however, are even greater. These are of two kinds. First, there is the waste of the lives of young people who spend years in training for a profession and then find that they either cannot find employment at all or cannot make an income commensurate with their ability and training. This is certainly the case in the legal profession. The profession should ensure that the supply of new layers is more closely related to demand. This might be done by requiring that no candidate may be admitted to the Bar Admission Course in Ontario unless he has first obtained an articling position and his principal has indicated in writing whether he is likely to have a position available in his firm by the end of the course, without necessarily committing himself to hiring the particular individual. Until recent years, it was essential that a student obtain an articling position before admission to Osgoode Hall Law School, and this system at least gave the student some indication of the state of the market. It is foolish to say, as some academics do, that time spent in training for an overcrowded profession is not wasted. It is a tragic waste of talent to graduate more professional people each year than the professions can readily absorb. There is, secondly, a longer-run cost to society. If what we need in the professions is quality, then we need to attract able young people. The effect of overcrowding the professions in the longer term will be that our ablest young people will turn elsewhere for their choice of occupation and that the quality of professional service will suffer.

These arguments indicate strongly that the costs to society of abolishing professional self-regulation would be greater than the present system and that the benefits would be less.

The minor premise of this aspect of Dr Ostry's argument is equally untenable. For the reasons adduced above, it is apparent that the influence of professional organizations on the cost of professional services is not significant. Since both premises are either doubtful or false, the conclusion that the self-regulating professions represent a net cost to society cannot be maintained.

The argument of this paper so far has been that Dr Ostry has failed to justify federal government intervention for the purpose of controlling the self-regulating professions on the basis of the arguments, first, that professional self-regulation is not the most efficient means of allocating professional services, and, secondly, that professional self-regulation represents a net cost to society. It may still be argued, however, that even if the professions do require regulation there should be greater government involvement in such regulation. This has already occurred in the case of the medical profession. Specifically, the argument might take the form of asserting that it is desirable that the Combines Investigation Act should apply to the professions in order to prevent such allegedly anti-competitive practices as setting fee schedules and limiting professional advertising.

To deal with this argument fully would require a separate paper since it involves serious constitutional questions as well as the value judgments inherent in any discussion of further government intervention in the private sector. The principal issues may be summarized as follows:

1 Self-regulation does not wholly preclude government intervention. The jurisdiction and authority of professional bodies are prescribed by the provincial government, and the governments that created them can intervene to prevent abuse of their powers.

2 Federal intervention in the affairs of the professions raises a peculiar problem. Jurisdiction over the professions has always been assumed to rest with the provinces. The provinces have exercised that jurisdiction and have given expression to a public policy designed to give professional bodies the power to regulate their members. Such self-regulatory powers have traditionally been exercised, inter alia, to preserve professional dignity by limiting advertising and, in some professions, to prescribe tariffs of fees. The federal government's right to regulate competition has been upheld as a criminal law jurisdiction and has traditionally been limited to areas where it is not in conflict with the exercise of provincial powers. It is highly undesirable for the federal government, under the guise of exercising its powers in respect of criminal law, to inject itself into an area of provincial jurisdiction where the provinces have expressed a differing concept of the public interest.

3 It has not been shown that federal intervention is necessary. This is surely a case for the application of Occam's razor.

39 Competition policy and the self-regulating professions

4 Self-regulation by the learned professions is supported by historical prece-
dent, and the onus is on the proponents of change to prove that it is necessary.
This Dr Ostry has failed to do.

5 More direct government control of the professions is undesirable because
government is more likely to make decisions based on short-run or ideological
considerations that may seriously damage both the professions and the consumers of these services.

6 Government ought not intervene directly in the affairs of the professions,
since it is not sufficiently close to and familiar with the training and discipline
of practitioners and the market for professional services.

7 The centralization of power in Canadian society and the politicization of
decision-making has already proceeded too far. Government intervention in the
affairs of the professions represents another step in this direction.

The preliminary reaction to Dr Ostry's paper is that if its arguments were to
be accepted it would demonstrate a peculiar inconsistency in government policy in that the Combines Investigation Act has been applied to the professions
and not to labour unions. The reason for this inconsistency must be ideological.
The government apparently sees the professions as a relatively high income,
visible, minority group. They are thus vulnerable to attack by a government
committed to an egalitarian policy of wealth distribution. In the opinion of this
writer, the federal government sees the Combines Investigation Act less as an
instrument for preserving the market system than an engine for controlling
prices, profits, and marketing policies, in short as a means of politicizing market
decisions. In the final analysis, the extension of the Act to cover professional services should be evaluated in terms of this ideological thrust.

The final question to be reviewed is one that is basic to the whole issue,
namely, what a profession is. Dr Ostry is correct in stating that 'licensing exists
in many cases where there are no major informational problems or exceptional
risks.' The arguments in this paper in favour of professional self-regulation are
applicable only to those occupations where practitioners are required to have
superior mental capacity and judgment and to undergo a long and arduous training; where the risk to the consumer from consulting an unqualified practitioner
is high; and where the consumer is not in a good position to make a choice.
These criteria are undoubtedly met by the professions of law, accountancy,
medicine, and dentistry. In the case of occupations such as engineering and
architecture, it is more difficult to support professional self-regulation because
most consumers of such services are sufficiently sophisticated that they can
make an adequate judgment as to the quality of the services being offered. Nor
are these criteria met where the provision of professional advice is incidental to

the sale of assets either as principal or agent. For this reason, the arguments in this paper are not applicable to occupations such as pharmacy, optometry, and real estate brokerage. There may be good reason in some of these cases for the existence of a body to supervise educational qualifications and discipline, but it is more difficult to argue for professional autonomy and exemption from the Combines Investigation Act than in the case of occupations that meet the above criteria. This paper should not be construed as attempting to justify the existence of twenty-two self-governing 'professions' in Ontario.

However, it is worth noting that the very existence of so many statutes providing for self-regulation and the rapid growth of provincial and municipal licensing of a variety of occupations indicates a different apprehension by provincial legislatures of the issues of public policy involved than does Dr Ostry's paper. Without arguing in favour of this trend, it should at least lead one to question the reasoning behind the extension of the Combines Investigation Act to services.

All of these considerations lead to the conclusion that the provision of professional services is an area where the operation of market forces alone will not ensure the public interest, where the costs of regulation do not exceed the benefits; that such regulation is best carried on by self-governing professional bodies; but that this status must be restrictively defined. It would therefore appear that the indiscriminate application of the Combines Investigation Act to professional services, while continuing to exempt the activities of trade unions, is inconsistent and inappropriate.

LEE BENHAM and ALEXANDRA BENHAM

Prospects for increasing competition in the professions

When the consequences of restrictions on competition in the professions are discussed, the emphasis has generally been on the gains to members of the professions involved, rather than on the full range of costs borne by members of the society at large. Economists are continually pointing out that barriers to entry into a given occupation mean higher earnings for the individuals within that occupation. A principal interest of economists who study the professions has been the extent to which professional practitioners capture windfall gains, that is, receive excessive earnings, as a consequence of barriers to entry and other professional restrictions. Implicit in these studies is the notion that these windfall gains constitute the major cost to society associated with such restrictions. Would that it were so.

The higher earnings received by many professionals because of such restrictions are often a small part, even an insignificant part, of the full costs associated with professional control.[1] Although other consequences of this control are

Department of Economics, Washington University at St Louis

1 Even in answer to the narrower question of what would happen to the earnings of professions if competition were permitted, conventional measures of excessive earnings are likely to be a poor indicator of the actual change resulting from more competition. The argument is as follows: A professional association can raise its members' earnings by restricting entry or reducing outside competition. Entry into that profession then becomes more attractive, and frequently queues of entrants develop. The profession can then raise its entry standards, often by requiring more years of education or higher test scores, to select the 'most desirable members of the queue.' Already established members of the profession benefit from these new restrictions, but 'high quality' new entrants may receive little if any more than from alternative careers open to persons with their qualifications. The competition for windfall gains thus tends over time to dissipate those gains. See Gordon Tullock, 'The transitional gains trap,' *Bell Journal*, Autumn 1975 (Vol. 9, No. 2), 671-8.

often enumerated, including higher prices to consumers, less specialization, reduced efficiency, and lower levels of innovation, many people apparently feel
that these other effects are quantitatively insignificant. We have investigated
some of these other effects of professional control in the market for eyeglasses.[2]
In this market the optometrists, the principal professional group, have sought to
emulate the conduct of other more firmly established professions. The results we
found illustrate some of the social costs incurred through such control.

Our study examined the prices paid for eyeglasses and the frequency of
obtaining eyeglasses across states in the United States as a function of the level
of professional control of the eyeglass market in those states. Some states have
much stricter professional controls than others. Using data on the prices for eyeglasses actually paid by consumers and the frequency with which individuals obtained eyeglasses during a given year we estimated the relationship between three
measures of professional control and a variety of consequences.

Prices paid by individuals were found to be about 25 to 40 per cent higher in
the states with greater professional control.[3] The elasticity of demand for eyeglasses was found to be approximately −1.0. This means that, as a consequence
of the higher prices, approximately 25 to 40 per cent fewer individuals in the
more restrictive states obtained eyeglasses during a given year. Furthermore, the
less-educated individuals in the sample appeared to be more adversely affected
by the restrictions: the impact on the prices they paid appeared to be greater.
These results are not the ones generally promised by the professions.[4] Indeed,
eye-care professionals have asserted that the actual utilization of eye care in the
United States is approximately half the optimal rate. The impact of professional
controls in this market is moving the public away from these espoused professional goals.

Other similar examples can certainly be found. Dr Ostry's essay refers to
studies of the costs associated with licensing in the trucking and television repair
markets. The number of studies now available is limited, but all the evidence we
have seen suggests substantial benefits from increased competition.

2 Lee Benham and Alexandra Benham, 'Regulating through the professions: a perspective
on information control,' *Journal of Law and Economics* (October 1975), 421-47. See
also Lee Benham, 'The effect of advertising on the price of eyeglasses,' *Journal of Law
and Economics* (October 1972), 337-52.
3 Some preliminary work by the American Optometric Association in response to this
study indicates that the higher prices paid in states with greater professional control are
not reflected in professionals' earnings there. This suggests that the higher prices paid by
consumers are in larger measure consumed by inefficient market organization.
4 It should further be noted that the results of our study do not measure the absolute
effects of professional control in the market we examined; they indicate only the differences between highly restrictive and somewhat less restrictive sets of professional controls.

If we agree that more competition is desirable, why not just implement it immediately? Even if the political will to take action currently exists, implementing competition is not as easy as it may appear. Competition is heartily disliked in most times and places by those persons and organizations directly involved. People will go to great efforts to protect themselves against the vicissitudes of competition. One common historical response to limit competition has been the formation of guilds. Guilds have a long history and appear to be much hardier and more viable than many other institutions. Many of us look back on a relatively short period in the nineteenth century which had comparatively little guild-like behavior as the natural state of affairs. A more realistic view of guild-like activities suggests that their influence will be around for a long time, although for a variety of reasons the magnitudes of the distortions introduced will vary. Professions are in many important respects the modern counterpart of the guilds.

This has implications for what we can expect to happen over time. It is unlikely that fundamental problems will be dealt with once and for all by changes in the law. Much of the impetus for changes, past and future, comes from professional providers, who are able to collude effectively against consumers and voters to restrain trade to their benefit. Even if reforms are introduced, the professions affected by such laws will exert continual pressure for changes in the law or reinterpretation of existing regulations.

In this connection, we must remember that public policy is shaped by what is perceived to be the problem. The professions' own views of the problems they face can significantly influence the set of issues that receive public emphasis and attract political attention. The professions will publicize certain problems while impeding dissemination of knowledge, and action, concerning other problems. As one example, consider the prompt and well-publicized attention given to performance failures committed by unlicensed practitioners. Contrast this with the attention given to a comparable failure by some respected (or at least licensed) member of the profession. Since the professions are in the position of strongly influencing the questions raised and the problems perceived, it should not surprise us if the answers are frequently congenial to their viewpoint.

Given these long-run and predictable pressures, it is important to find responses which will strengthen the defence mechanism of society at large against the efforts of professions, current and incipient. Some optimism on this issue arises from our belief that better informed voters and consumers will more effectively counter the moves of the professions. Our own experience in this area is consistent with this belief. Our view is that a key to increasing individual choice lies in the development of stable independent sources of information for the public. We should like to discuss several aspects of this information issue.

First of all, better data on the social costs of professional behaviour should be collected and made public on a continuing basis, as is currently done with, say, statistics on the consumer price index and the level of unemployment. These should include statistics on prices, utilization levels, rates of innovation, and costs associated with distortions of various sorts introduced by professional controls, such as limitations on the extent of specialization and prohibition of advertising. We are well aware of the difficulties associated with measuring such distortions. The task is not easy; there is likely to be substantial disagreement even among experts concerning what to measure and how to measure it. But the effort is warranted. The costs of such undertakings would be minuscule compared with the costs associated with current restraints in trade. Such regularly published indicators and estimates would provide at least one way of attracting general attention to the consequences of professional behaviour. These are not the only kinds of information which need improving. A fundamental argument made by many professional groups is that consumers are incapable of making reasonable choices with respect to practitioners, type of service, and so forth. But professionals very frequently make every effort to see that consumers remain uninformed as to the important alternatives available and as to the differential nature of the services offered by members of their profession. It is therefore certainly unfair to argue that failures in the operation of the market are due to the natural incompetence of consumers. Serious attention needs to be given to the problem of how to provide consumers with better information in this area.

Removing restrictions on the distribution of information by individual members of professions would be an important step. Current restrictions on advertising in many professions make it difficult for consumers to know the range of available providers, the prices at which services are being offered, or the new products and services introduced. Removing these restrictions would significantly increase consumer knowledge of available alternatives. It would also benefit those professionals who are more efficient, more innovative, or willing to furnish their services at lower prices, since they could then inform a large body of potential clients of the advantage of coming to them for professional services.

Beyond the information issue, there are of course other ways to increase competition in the professions. Certainly the public should be represented on the boards of the professional associations. (California has recently increased substantially the number of public members on professional boards of regulation.[5] In many cases the public members now constitute a majority.) One might

5 The California *Business and Professions Code*, amended by Senate Bills No. 2116 and 1839, approved by the governor and filed with the secretary of state, 22 Sept. 1976.

recommend, not entirely facetiously, that a prerequisite for board membership be lack of membership in the profession the board is to regulate. Board members could of course ask for expert advice but would essentially regulate the profession as consumers. Of course we have little ground for optimism about the survival capacity of such boards.

We heartily endorse Dr Ostry's proposal for critical reassessment of licensing. New licensing should be resisted. Old licensing should be removed wherever feasible. Our impression is that Canada handles the problem of lobbying by professional groups somewhat better than the United States, but we are still not sanguine about the benefits of registration and certification. From a profession's point of view, these are important steps toward developing the cohesion necessary to become licensed. Registration and certification often precede licensing.

It is commonplace to note that there is overemphasis on the extreme cases and underemphasis on the more general implications and costs of any policy. This is particularly the case for policies associated with professional behaviour. Our discussion has emphasized that a wide range of major outcomes needs to be considered when one is examining the impact of controls on and by the professions. These include the effects on over-all prices, distribution of services, levels of utilization, rates of innovation, the range of alternatives available to consumers, and the differential impact on various groups of individuals. As citizens become more sophisticated, they are less likely to accept very restrictive practices merely because of the character and high salience of a few adverse outcomes associated with less restrictive systems. The kinds of information flows we have discussed would be helpful in reducing the ability of professional groups to use events and statistics compatible with their own view of the world to shape public policy.

Some have characterized the professions in George Bernard Shaw's inimitable phrasing as 'a conspiracy against the laity.' Professions are much more than that, of course, but restraint in trade is a deeply imbedded part of the professional world view. A detailed understanding of the costs and benefits associated with these restraints is essential for sensible public policy regarding the professions. By developing the kinds of indices we have discussed and by removing restrictions that prevent professionals from providing more information to the public, Canada could set the standard for dealing with the professions.

GORDON E. KAISER

Federal competition law
and the professions:
problems of jurisdiction

As a result of the 1 January 1976 amendments,[1] the Combines Investigation Act[2] now applies to services, and accordingly the professions would appear to be within the jurisdiction of the Act. However, notwithstanding these amendments, the application of the Act to professional markets remains far from clear.

The major uncertainties flow from the fact that many services are already regulated to varying degrees by some level of government.

Provincial and municipal governments in particular are active in this regulation. In 1970 some 70 per cent of professional and technical occupations were subject to licensing by autonomous or semi-autonomous agencies, while 31 per cent of the craftsmen and production process occupations were subject to the same form of licensing.[3] Ontario licenses some thirty-three occupations,[4] while municipal governments in the province license some fifty-two trades and businesses pursuant to the Municipal Act[5] and ten other trades and businesses are subject to specific statutes.[6] To this list must be added a host of licensing restric-

Visiting research professor in law and economics, 1976-7, Faculty of Law, University of Toronto

1 S.C. 1974-75-76, Vol. II, Chap. 76
2 R.S.C. 1970, Chap. C-23
3 David A. Dodge. 'Occupational wage differentials, occupational licensing and returns to investment in education: explanatory analysis,' in Economic Council of Canada, *Canadian Higher Education in the '70s* (1972), 133
4 *The Apprenticeship and Tradesman's Qualification Act*, R.S.O. 1970, c. 24
5 *The Municipal Act*, R.S.O. 1970, c. 284
6 *Bread Sales Act*, R.S.O. 1970, c. 49, s. 3(1); *Dog Licensing and Livestock and Poultry Protection Act*, R.S.O. 1970, c. 133, s.6; *Ferries Act*, R.S.O. 1970, c. 165; *Game and Fish Act*, R.S.O. 1970, c. 186, s.39; *Milk Act*, R.S.O. 1970, c. 273, s.19(2), 5; *Pawnbrokers Act*, R.S.O. 1970, c. 341, s.2(1); *Public Halls Act*, R.S.O. 1970, c. 376; *Public Vehicles Act*, R.S.O. 1970, c. 392; *Theatres Act*, R.S.O. 1970, c. 459

tions pursuant to federal statutes. A recent report recommends that the authority of local governments to restrict entry into trades be extended by amending the Municipal Act to permit municipal councils to require the owner-operator of *any* business to hold a licence for the carrying on of business.[7]

This extensive government involvement in many service occupations, including the professions, may have the effect of insulating the professions in large part from the application of the Combines Investigation Act.

There are several reasons for concluding that the Combines Investigation Act may have limited application to the professions or to occupational licensing in general. First, the government or crown agencies may not be bound by the Act. Secondly, the Act may not apply to those activities which are effectively regulated by a provincial or municipal government. Thirdly, the defence of voluntary action, and fourthly, the defence of maintenance of reasonable standards of competence, raise difficult legal issues. Fifthly, the constitutionality of the Combines Investigation Act as it applies to purely local service markets is open to question.

CROWN IMMUNITY

The words 'person,' 'customer,' and 'company,' which are used throughout the Combines Investigation Act, will be presumed to exclude the crown. The common law rule that the crown is not bound by statute, except by express words or necessary implication,[8] is codified in both the federal and Ontario Interpretation Acts.[9] The Combines Investigation Act does not contain express words indicating that the crown, or its agents, is bound by it. Much of the Act is criminal law, and Section 2 of the Criminal Code[10] defines the word 'person' and simi-

---

7 *Municipal Licensing*: Report of the Advisory Committee of Municipal Clerks, 10 March 1976. This proposal would define business as 'the carrying on of a commercial or industrial undertaking of any kind or nature, or the providing of professional, personal or other services for the purpose of gain or profit.' Municipalities regard this licensing function as regulatory, not revenue-generating in effect, and the stated purpose is that 'municipal licensing should prevent circumstances arising in which public security is liable to be jeopardized, public morality disturbed, or public hygiene affected.'

8 P.W. Hogg, *Liability of Crown*, 1971, chap. 7; S.L. Goldenberg, 'Tort actions against the crown in Ontario,' *New Developments in the Law of Torts* (Law Society of Upper Canada, Special Lectures, 1973), 341; D.W. Mundell, 'Remedies against the crown,' *Remedies* (Law Society of Upper Canada, Special Lectures 1961), 149

9 R.S.C. 1970, Chap. I-23; R.S.O. 1970, Chap. 225

10 R.S.C. 1970, Chap. C-34

lar expressions as including Her Majesty and public bodies.[11] This consideration, however, would not apply to the reviewable practices under the Combines Investigation Act, which are not criminal offences, in contrast to provisions such as the conspiracy provisions.

If there are no specific words in the statute, and the presumption is that the crown is not bound, the major issue becomes: who is the crown? The question often is reduced to a determination of the degree of control the crown has over the subordinate body or person claiming the exemption. To take a current example, can a provincial liquor control board claim that it is exempt from the federal Anti-Inflation Act[12] because it is in fact the crown in the right of the province?

As provincial governments are usually involved in regulating the professions, it is necessary to consider whether the provincial crown enjoys the same exemption as the federal crown. It is generally agreed that the rule that the crown is not bound by statute, except by express words or necessary implication, exempts the crown in the right of the legislating government. The more difficult question is whether it operates to exempt the crown in the right of other governments as well. In *Gauthier* v. *The King*[13] the provincial crown was clearly bound because the Act in question expressly applied to His Majesty, but the court held that the federal crown was not bound by the Ontario statute. The words 'His Majesty' were interpreted as applying only to the crown in the right of Ontario. The same question was considered by the Privy Council in *Dominion Building Corporation* v. *The King*,[14] and there it was held that an Ontario statute was applicable to the federal crown, notwithstanding the absence of express words or necessary implication to that effect.

The law is equally unclear in the case of the contrary proposition: whether the federal Parliament can bind by statute the crown in the right of the province. In the *Go Train*[15] case, the Province of Ontario argued that the federal Railway Act[16] did not apply to Her Majesty in the right of the province by reason of Section 16 of the federal Interpretation Act. As indicated earlier, that section provides that no provision or enactment of any Act affects the rights of Her Majesty unless it is expressly so stated. The argument was dismissed by the Supreme Court of Canada on the grounds that the Interpretation Act did not apply, be-

11 *Canadian Broadcasting Corporation* v. *Attorney General (Ontario)* (1959), 16 D.L.R. (2d), 609
12 S.C. 1974-75-76, Vol. II, Chap. 75
13 (1918), 56 S.C.R., 176. The Supreme Court of Canada considered whether the federal Crown was bound by *The Ontario Arbitration Act*, R.S.O. [1914] c. 65.
14 [1933] A.C. 533
15 *The Queen* v. *The Board of Transport Commissioners,* [1968] S.C.R. 118
16 R.S.C. 1970, Chap. R-2

cause no rights of the provincial crown were affected. The Court held that apart from the agreement with Canadian National Railways, Her Majesty in the right of Ontario had no right to levy tolls for the carriage of passengers over the relevant part of the CNR lines, and therefore no rights were affected. A somewhat similar result was reached in the *Johnny Walker*[17] case.

This issue arose more recently in *Re Pacific Western Airlines.*[18] Relying on Section 16 of the federal Interpretation Act the Alberta government, which had purchased a controlling interest in Pacific Western Airlines, argued that it did not have to comply with the requirements of the Canadian Transport Commission as Sections 19 and 20 of the Air Carrier Regulations did not bind the provincial crown. The Federal Court of Appeal held that the provincial crown was bound by necessary implication; the crown was bound even within the meaning of Section 16 of the Interpretation Act, because otherwise the purpose of the Aeronautics Act[19] would be frustrated.

A doctrine similar to that of crown immunity has been developed in the United States. The 'state action' doctrine established by the 1943 decision of the US Supreme Court in *Parker* v. *Brown*[20] has served as the basis for exempting regulated industries from the American anti-trust laws. The importance of this concept is indicated by the fact that there are some eighteen decisions by the US Supreme Court on this issue to date.[21] In *Parker*, a private marketing program established by a group of raisin growers was adopted pursuant to a California statute authorizing the establishment of market and price controls. The court held that there is 'nothing in the language of the Sherman Act or in its history which suggests that its purpose was to restrain a state or its officers or agents from activities directed by its legislature.'[22]

17 *The Attorney General of British Columbia* v. *The Attorney General of Canada,* [1924] A.C. 222
18 [1976] 2 F.C. 52
19 R.S.C. 1970, Chap. A-3
20 317 U.S. 341 (1943)
21 *Keogh* v. *Chicago & N.W. Ry. Co.,* 260 U.S. 156 (1922); *United States Nav.* v. *Cunard SS Co.,* 284 U.S. 474 (1932); *United States* v. *Borden Co.,* 308 U.S. 188 (1939); *State of Ga.* v. *Pa. R. Co.,* 324 U.S. 439 (1945); *Far East Conference* v. *United States,* 342 U.S. 570 (1952); *United States* v. *Radio Corp. of America,* 358 U.S. 334 (1959); *Md. & Va. Milk Producers Ass'n.* v. *United States,* 362 U.S. 458 (1960); *Cal.* v. *FPC,* 369 U.S. 482 (1962); *Pan American World Airways, Inc.* v. *United States,* 371 U.S. (1963); *United States* v. *Philadelphi Nat. Bank,* 374 U.S. 321 (1963); *Meat Cutters* v. *Jewel Tea Co.,* 381 U.S. 676 (1965); *Carnation Co.* v. *Pac. Conference,* 383 U.S. 213 (1966); *Ricci* v. *Chicago Mercantile Exchange,* 409 U.S. 289 (1973); *Hughes Tool Co.* v. *Trans World Airlines,* 409 U.S. 363 (1973); *Otter Tail Power Co.* v. *United States,* 410 U.S. 366 (1973); and *Cantor* v. *Detroit Edison Co.,* 96 S.Ct. 3110.
22 Supra n. 20, at 350-1

REGULATED INDUSTRY EXEMPTION

The often-cited authority for the exemption of regulated industries from the Combines Investigation Act is the decision of McRuer J. of the Ontario Supreme Court in *Regina* v. *Canadian Breweries Ltd* where His Honour stated:

I conclude that when I apply the Act as an Act designed to protect the public interest in free competition, I am compelled to examine the legislation of the provinces to see how far they have exercised their respective jurisdiction to remove the sale of beer from the competitive field, and to see what areas of competition in the market are still open. Having made this examination, I must then decide whether the formation or operation of the merger lessened or has likely lessened competition to an unlawful degree in the areas where competition is permitted.[23]

If the industry is regulated, it would appear that the Combines Investigation Act has application only if the alleged anti-competitive behaviour prevents the working of the regulatory scheme. McRuer J. stated:

When a provincial legislature has conferred on a commission or board the power to regulate an industry and fix prices, and *that power has been exercised*, the Court must assume that the power is exercised in the public interest. In such cases, in order to succeed in a prosecution laid under the Act with respect to the operation of a combine, I think it must be shown that the combine has operated, or is likely to operate so as to hinder or prevent the provincial body from effectively exercising the powers given to it to protect the public interest ... There may, however, be areas of competition in the market that are not affected by the exercise of powers conferred upon the provincial body in which the restraints of competition may render the operations of the combine illegal.[24]

It is entirely possible that an industry is exempt from the Combines Investigation Act in Canada if the provincial statute merely authorizes regulation. McRuer J. in *Canadian Breweries* emphasized that the exemption turned on whether the power had been exercised by the provincial regulatory commission or board, but it may prove difficult to determine whether the power has been actually or effectively exercised. Deliberate non-action can constitute both actual and effective exercise of regulatory jurisdiction.

23 [1960] O.R. 601, 611
24 Ibid, pp. 629-30 (emphasis added)

The recent US Supreme Court decision in *Goldfarb* v. *Virginia State Bar*[25] makes it clear that anti-competitive activities, to be exempt from the Sherman Act,[26] must be compelled by direction of the state acting as the sovereign. In this case a minimum fee schedule published by a county bar association and enforced through the threat of disciplinary action by the Virginia State Bar was held to be subject to the Sherman Act. The Supreme Court of Virginia was authorized by statute to regulate the practice of law in the state by adopting a code of legal ethics and prescribing disciplinary procedures. The State Bar was legislatively authorized to assist the Court in investigating and reporting violations of the Court's ethical rules. The State Bar argued at the trial that it was specifically authorized to regulate professional conduct under authority of the highest court in Virginia. In dismissing the argument that the State Bar was exempt under the state-action *Parker* test, the Supreme Court held:

The threshold inquiry in determining if any competitive activity is a state action of the type the Sherman Act was not meant to proscribe is whether the activity is required by the state acting as sovereign. Here we need not enquire any further into the state action in question because it cannot be fairly said that the State of Virginia, through the Supreme Court rules, required the anti-competitive action by either respondent ... The fact that the State Bar is a state agency for some limited purpose does not create an anti-trust shield that allows it to foster anti-competitive practices for the benefit of its members.[27]

The latest decision by the US Supreme Court on the scope of the antitrust exemption for professions, *Bates* v. *State Bar of Arizona*,[28] immunized from the Sherman Act rules prohibiting price advertising by lawyers where those rules were adopted and enforced by state supreme courts. The Court held that the real party in interest was the state supreme court which adopted and enforced the rule, and accordingly the challenged rule was an act of state and shielded from antitrust attack. The Court did, however, hold that the Arizona rule preventing price advertising by attorneys was unconstitutional on the ground that it violated the attorney's right of commercial free speech under the First Amendment.

The *Canadian Breweries* test, arguably, is a different and wider exemption. It is enough if the state *authorizes* the activity and the regulatory agency exercises its regulatory jurisdiction; the exemption is not limited to regulatory acts *required* by the legislature.

25 421 U.S. 773 (1975), 95 S.Ct. 2004 (1975).
26 U.S.C.A. 15 ss 1407
27 Supra n. 25 at 790
28 97 S.Ct. 2691 (1977)

It may be argued that regulated industries would not be exempt under the reviewable practices provisions of the Combines Investigation Act. This argument would turn on the proposition that the *Canadian Breweries* exemption is confined to the specific wording of the relevant section of the Combines Investigation Act.[29] The authority for this argument is the judgment of Kerwin J. of the Supreme Court of Canada in *Re Farm Products Marketing Act*: 'It cannot be said that any scheme otherwise within the authority of the legislature is against the public interest where the legislature is seized of the power, and indeed the obligation, to take care of that interest in the province.'[30]

It might accordingly be argued that the regulated industry exemption operates only where the wording of the particular section of the Combines Investigation Act contains, as an element of the offence, the prescription that the defendant's act was 'likely to operate to the detriment' or against the interests of the public, and that the exemption is not as wide for those sections of the Act which express the element of the offence differently (for example, reviewable practices are prohibited where they 'substantially lessen competition').

This is not a very persuasive argument. The only reason why a practice becomes an offence or is prohibited under the Act is that the conduct is likely to be contrary to the interests of the public whether that conduct is an act substantially lessening competition, or operating to the detriment of the public, or limiting competition unduly.

It is important to note that the regulatory exemption in Canadian law does not turn upon the proposition that there is a conflict between the regulatory scheme and the Combines Investigation Act. Rather, as Kerwin J. noted, the proposition is that there is no conflict because conduct in accordance with the regulatory scheme must be deemed to be conduct in the public interest, and therefore there can be no offence under the Combines Investigation Act and no conflict. There may, however, be actual conflict in the cases of per se offences where a finding of 'unduly' limiting competition is not required. In a per se offence such as price maintenance, if the conduct as defined exists it is deemed to be contrary to law. In this situation there would be a case of real conflict, and it could not be presumed away. In cases of real conflict between validly enacted laws, the rule of paramountcy would apply. The federal legislature would prevail.

29 R.S.C. 1952, c. 314, s.32(1)
30 [1957] S.C.R. 198, 206

VOLUNTARY ACTION DEFENCE

One further difficulty in applying federal competition law to self-regulated professions is that it may be argued that no liability attaches because the regulatory regime does not require compliance on behalf of the professionals or the licensed occupation, but merely invites voluntary compliance. A classic example would be a suggested fee tariff.

This is a difficult issue. Courts will have to consider carefully whether the action was really voluntary, or voluntary only in form. In the *Goldfarb* case, the State Bar argued that the fee schedule was merely advisory. Its purpose, the defendants argued, was only to provide legitimate information to member lawyers in complying with Virginia professional regulations. The decision of the Court on this matter is instructive:

A purely advisory fee schedule issued to provide guidelines or an exchange of price information without a showing of an actual restraint of trade would present us with a different question ... The record here, however, reveals a situation quite different from what would occur under a purely advisory fee schedule. Here a fixed, rigid price floor arose from the respondent's activities: Every lawyer who responded to the petitioner's enquiries adhered to the fee schedule, and no lawyer asked for additional information in order to set an individualized fee.[31]

This defence was also rejected in a British Columbia case where the BC Professional Pharmacists' Society was charged with conspiracy pursuant to Section 32 of the Combines Investigation Act.[32] The Society had voted to impose a surcharge of one dollar per prescription as a charge to be made for prescription drugs of welfare recipients, and sent a newsletter to all pharmacists in the province urging them to adopt the practice of the surcharge. With respect to the argument that this communication was a recommendation only, the Court held:

While the motions were in form recommendations, the whole of the evidence, including the conduct following upon the passing of the motions, indicated that they were recommendations in form only, and in substance were agreements to associate with the scheme to impose the surcharge. The defence says that each pharmacy exercised its own judgment as to whether or not to impose the sur-

31 Supra n. 25 at 781
32 *R. v. British Columbia Professional Pharmicists Society and Pharmaceutical Association of the Province of British Columbia*, 1971, 64 C.P.R. 129

charge, and that this takes the case outside the realm of the Combines Investigation Act. It can be said of every case under the Act that the individuals exercised their own judgment in deciding whether or not to participate. Considering the whole of the evidence, it is apparent that the agreement was to impose a $1.00 price increase and strive to have this imposed at every pharmacy in the Province.[33]

Also relevant in this context are two recent Combines decisions, the *Armco* case, decided by the Ontario Court of Appeal, and *The Large Lamp* case, recently decided by the Supreme Court of Ontario.[34] Simply stated, even if the arrangement is voluntary in form, uniform price action may attract liability as an agreement or conspiracy unduly limiting competition contrary to Section 32 of the Act, under the 'conscious parallelism' theory of conspiracy. It has long been established that the agreement in a Section 32 prosecution does not have to be written.[35] The *Armco* and *Large Lamp* cases go further, and state that the agreement or conspiracy may be inferred from joint action or parallel conduct, a concept well-established in American anti-trust law since 1939.[36]

While an illegal agreement may be inferred from similar conduct by oligopolists, economists argue that similar conduct is only natural where there are few firms in industry selling a homogeneous product. Pennell J. in the *Large Lamp* case responded to this argument in the following terms:

But I am of the opinion that the theory of oligopolistic pricing is irrelevant to the determination of whether or not the accused have offended the proscription of them under the Conspiracy Section of the Act. As stated in the *Queen* v. *J. W. Mills & Sons Limited et al*, on page 317: 'The fact that under the theory of oligopolistic prices this would have been the same in the long run is irrelevant. No

---

33 Ibid, p. 145
34 *R.* v. *Armco* (1975) 6 O.R. (2d) 521, 21 C.C.C. (2d) 129, affd. 1975, 24 C.P.R. 2nd 145; *R.* v. *Canadian General Electric Company Limited et al.* 29 C.P.R. (2d) 1
35 *Weidman* v. *Shragge* (1912) 20 C.C.C. 117 at 134; 46 S.C.R. 1; *R.* v. *St. Lawrence Corp. Ltd* (1966) 3 C.C.C. 263, 5 D.L.R. (3d) 253 (Ont. C.A.)
36 In *Interstate Circuit* v. *U.S.*, 306 U.S. 208, 277 (1939) Stone J. stated: 'An unlawful conspiracy may be and often is formed without simultaneous action or agreement on the part of the conspirators ... Acceptance by competitors, without previous agreement, of an invitation to participate in a plan, the necessary consequency of which, if carried out, is restraint of interstate commerce, is sufficient to establish an unlawful conspiracy under The Sherman Act.' This 'conscious parallelism' rule was further developed in *U.S.* v. *Paramount Pictures Inc.*, 334 U.S. 131, at 142 and 161 (1948); *U.S.* v. *U.S. Gypsum Company*, 363 U.S. 363 at 393-4 and 401 (1948); *U.S.* v. *Line Material Co.* 333 U.S. 287 at 315 (1948); *F.T.C.* v. *Cement Institute* 333 U.S. 683 at 716 (1948).

persons are entitled to engage in anti-competitive trade practices or policies because this result may obtain in any event if all things are equal.'[37]

But Pennell J. went on to say: 'I do not say that proof of parallel business conduct conclusively established an agreement contrary to provisions of the Combines Investigation Act.[38] Thus, the courts must find something in addition to parallel conduct. In the *Large Lamp* case, the 'plus' which the Court found was evidence of a memo from the sales manager of one defendant to the district manager of the other defendant, indicating that a mistake had been made in a bid to one of its customers whereby a discount of 5 per cent was granted for cash payment instead of the normal 2 per cent discount. The memorandum went on to say that the profit which would ordinarily result from the sale would be donated to charity. In considering this evidence, Pennell J. stated:

It contradicts experience that a man occupying the position of a sales manager of CGE should inform his competitor of a breach of a CGE sales plan by a CGE agent, unless there was an arrangement between competitors ... To me this is a document which speaks volumes ... Genuine competitors do not make reports of their business transactions to their rivals as Mr Cox did. This was not the conduct of a competitor but of a sales manager who believed that the accused were united in an agreement, express or implied, to act together and pursue a common purpose.[39]

The relevant point here is that the fact that participation in the scheme is voluntary may be immaterial: if potential participants are likely to participate by the very nature of the scheme, and if such participation would limit competition unduly, then the participants may be liable under Section 32 of the Act.

STANDARDS OF COMPETENCE EXEMPTION

The fourth gateway is that provided in Section 32(6) of the Act as a defence to the conspiracy section:

In a prosecution under subsection 1, the Court shall not convict an accused if it finds that the conspiracy, combination, agreement or arrangement relates only *to a service and to standards of competence and integrity* that are reasonably

37 Supra n. 34, p. 31
38 Ibid, p. 31
39 Ibid, p. 31-2

necessary for the protection of the public (a) in the practice of a trade or profession relating to such service, or (b) in the collection and dissemination of information relating to such service.[40]

There are two observations to be made here. First, the term, 'standards of competence and integrity' is susceptible of a broad meaning. For the purposes of interpretation it should be noted that this exemption is narrower than the corresponding exemption which appeared as Section 92 in Bill C-256.[41] That section provided that professional associations would be exempt from the conspiracy prohibition, including price-fixing, provided that the conduct in question was expressly authorized or required by the federal Parliament, provincial legislature, or municipal bylaw, and was expressly required by law to be supervised or regulated by a board, commissioner, or other public party charged with protecting the public interest. Accordingly, professional fee tariffs and restrictions on advertising which may have been exempt under Bill C-256 may not be exempt under Bill C-2 as, arguably, they do not relate to standards of competence and integrity. Secondly, the section must be read as being an additional defence over and above the *Canadian Breweries - Farm Products Marketing* exemption.

Of these four defences which may arise in the application of the federal competition law to regulated or quasi-regulated services, it is clear that the first two are the most important. It is impossible to predict their real scope, but any major extension in the Act to services in general and to the professions in particular will probably require further legislative amendment. Such an amendment has in fact been recommended by the authors of the recently issued *Dynamic Change* report.[42] The authors state:

For broader considerations, we recommend that regulated industries should be *deemed* to be generally subject to the Combines legislation, and to be exempt from it *only* when (1) the restrictive conduct is specifically imposed by the legislation; and (2) the restrictive conduct is actively supervised by independent officials and not by representatives of the participants; (3) the restraint is *necessary* to the effective accomplishment of the legislative goal and is the least restrictive means available to achieve the legislative goal. Indeed, we recommend that all these three principles apply to all forms of monopoly control authorized by government.[43]

40 R.S.C. 1970 Chap. 22 as amended S.C. 1974-75, c. 76, s.14(7) (emphasis added)
41 Bill C-256, 1971
42 L.A. Skeoch and B.C. McDonald, *Dynamic Change and Accountability in a Canadian Market Economy* (Dept of Consumer and Corporate Affairs, 1976)
43 Ibid, p. 152

The inclusion of a provision in the Combines Investigation Act following the above wording would constitute a very important amendment to the law in that it effectively shifts the burden of proof. It is fair to say that the jurisprudence now is that regulated conduct is assumed or deemed to be exempt from the Act unless it is clear that the conduct is not constrained by the jurisdiction of a regulatory body. The amendment would shift the burden of proof and deem all conduct to be subject to the Combines Investigation Act unless those purporting to rely on the exemption satisfy the three tests defined in the proposed amendment. Of course, those activities which now are deemed by statutory provision to be exempt from the Combines Investigation Act, such as farm product marketing boards,[44] would presumably not be affected by an amendment such as that proposed.

In any event, until such an amendment is incorporated in the law, it would be difficult to state with any confidence that the federal law will apply extensively to self-regulating professions. To be effective, the amendment must do two things. It must specify crown liability to remove the crown immunity defence. And it must legislate out the *Canadian Breweries* defence. The *Dynamic Change* recommendations would serve these ends.

The *Dynamic Change* recommendations were followed by the federal government in legislation amending the *Combines Investigation Act* introduced in November, 1977. Section 4.5 of Bill C-13 provides that the *Combines Investigation Act* would not, for the most part, apply to regulated conduct, which is defined as conduct meeting the following conditions:

(*a*) the conduct has been expressly required or authorized by a *regulating* agency that is not appointed or elected by persons or representatives of the persons whose conduct is subject to be regulated by the agency; (*b*) the regulating agency mentioned in paragraph (*a*) is subject to supervision, in the case of a regulating agency that is an agricultural products marketing board, by a supervising agency that is not appointed or elected by the persons or by classes or representatives of persons whose conduct is subject to be regulated by such regulating agency; (*c*) the regulating agency is expressly empowered by or pursuant to an Act of Parliament, or of the Legislature of a province, to regulate that conduct in the manner in which it is being regulated, and has expressly directed its attention to the regulation of the conduct.

The proposed amendments focus on three important propositions; first, the activities of self-regulating bodies will not be exempt from the Act; second, the regulatory agency must be specifically empowered to regulate the conduct at

44 *Farm Products Marketing Act*, S. 1970-71-72, Chap. 65, s.33

issue; thirdly, the regulatory agency must expressly direct its attention to the regulation of the conduct.

In a previous draft of the legislation contained in Section 4.5 of Bill C-42, introduced in March 1977, a fourth principle was advanced; the activity would be exempt from the Act only where the Act would seriously interfere with the regulatory objectives. This requirement has been deleted from the latest proposals. Unlike Bill C-42, Bill C-13 exempts agricultural marketing boards to a substantial degree. Nonetheless, the nature of regulated conduct exempt from the Act is narrowly defined, and many activities currently thought to be exempt because of their regulated status would become subject to the legislation. The preconditions necessary for regulatory exemption follow closely the principles established in American antitrust cases.

The proposed amendments to the Act introduce another American innovation: Section 4.6 provides that the standards to be followed by regulatory commissions must give due weight to competition law principles. Specifically, the section requires that any Board empowered to fix rates, approve conditions of entry, regulate or approve mergers, or fix or approve the quantity or quality of products must exercise its powers to achieve its objectives in the manner which is least restrictive of competition.

If the regulatory board fails to meet these standards in arriving at its decision, that decision will be subject to review before the courts, but only where the review is initiated by the director of investigation and research. Under the American doctrine, such a decision is reviewable by the courts at the instance of any interested party.[45] This ground of appeal to the director is available, however, only in those cases where the director has intervened in the matter, pursuant to Section 27.1 of the Combines Investigation Act. Section 27.1 of the Act permits the director to intervene in public regulatory proceedings of federal boards or agencies. While the director's ground of appeal may be narrowly construed, it will serve to further decrease the scope of regulatory exemption under Canadian competition law.

THE CONSTITUTIONALITY OF THE ACT

The application of the Combines Investigation Act to the professions will also raise the question of constitutionality of the Act as it applies to services. Prior to

---

45 *The Competition Improvement Act of 1976.* Aside from the statutory requirement, the American courts have stated that in interpreting the regulatory statute, the agency should 'consider matters relating to both the broad purposes of the Act and the fundamental national economic policy expressed in the anti-trust laws.' *Gulf State Utility Co. v. Federal Power Commission* (1973) 411 U.S. 747 at 759; see also *U.S. v. First City National Bank of Houston* (1967) 386 U.S. 361.

1 January 1976, the Act was restricted to goods, and the inclusion of services within its ambit may raise some constitutional issues. Interestingly, in the *Goldfarb* case one of the issues raised before the Supreme Court of the United States was whether legal services had the necessary degree of interstate commerce to be subject to the Sherman Act. The Fourth Circuit Court held that the minimum fee schedule affected only local services, and hence did not satisfy the Sherman Act's interstate commerce requirement,[46] but a unanimous Supreme Court reversed the Fourth Circuit's judgment on this point. Speaking for the Court, Chief Justice Berger stated that 'the transactions which create the need for the particular legal services in question frequently are interstate transactions.'[47] Because out-of-state funds were often used to finance the purchase of homes in the State, and the loans were often guaranteed by federal agencies located outside of Virginia, the Court held that title examination was an 'integral part' of these transactions, and accordingly affected interstate commerce to a sufficient degree.

A recent article by Professors Hogg and Grover[48] concludes that the amended Combines Investigation Act is constitutional largely on the basis of the federal trade and commerce power. This reliance on the federal trade and commerce power is based largely on the American 'stream-of-commerce' approach to constitutional law, an approach which appears to have been approved by the Supreme Court of Canada in *Re Farm Products Marketing*[49] and some five decisions following that case.[50] The stream-of-commerce argument basically is that matters of a purely local nature can be subjected to a federal regulatory statute, if, when viewed in a larger light, they are part of a marketing process which is national in scope. To this must be added the consideration that the federal law can regulate local trading where it is necessary for federal regulatory integrity, or, put differently, federal jurisdiction is necessarily incident to effective regulation of national markets. While there is support for this argument, it is a concept which has developed largely in the context of commodity markets. The case for making local service activities subject to federal law is less persuasive. Services simply do not flow across provincial boundaries to the same degree as goods. Indeed, it may be argued that effective regulation of many service activities is best accomplished by the local government rather than the federal government.

46 *Goldfarb* v. *Virginia State Bar*, 497 F. 2d. 1, 15-19 (4th Ct. 1974)
47 421 U.S. 773, 783-4
48 Peter W. Hogg, Warren Grover, 'The constitutionality of the competition bill' (1976) 1 *Canadian Business Law Journal*, 197
49 Supra n. 29
50 *R.* v. *Klassen* (1959) 20 D.L.R. 2d, 406 (Man. C.A.); *Caloil Inc.* v. *Attorney General of Canada* (1971) S.C.R. 543; *Attorney General of Manitoba* v. *Manitoba Egg and Poultry Association* (1971) S.C.R. 689; *Burns Food Ltd.* v. *Attorney General of Manitoba* (1975) 1 S.C.R. 494; *MacDonald* v. *Vapour Canada Ltd.* (1976) 22 C.P.R. 1

CONCLUSION

Even if all of the jurisdictional problems that arise in the application of the Combines Investigation Act to professional services are assumed away, it is important to note that the competitive health of professional service markets may be much more substantially determined by policies of provincial governments affecting the supply of entrants to professional markets: entry 'bottlenecks' to such markets involving excessively high entry qualifications, manpower policy as reflected in the structure and capacity of educational institutions, excessively rigid entry tracks precluding optimal utilization of paraprofessional services, and so on. Supply-oriented issues such as these are likely to prove much more critical to effective competition in professional markets than such matters as fee schedules and bans on advertising which will probably be the principal targets of enforcement activity under the Combines Investigation Act.

CLAUDE CASTONGUAY

The future of self-regulation: a view from Quebec

INTRODUCTION

In 1966, the government of Quebec gave the Commission on Health and Social Welfare a mandate to study the professions in Quebec. This move was prompted by a perception of deficiencies in the legislation governing Quebec professions, rapid evolution of the professions, and many requests to modify the powers of existing professional corporations and to create new corporations. I was called upon to be chairman of the Commission from November 1966 to March 1970, and afterwards, as minister of social affairs, to implement the report published by the Commission in the summer of 1970.[1]

I went back to active practice as a consulting actuary at the time of the 1973 Quebec election. In the spring of 1974 the government of Quebec asked me to lead a task force on urbanization. Then, in October 1975, when the task force was beginning the last and arduous phase of writing its report,[2] the federal government asked me to join the Anti-Inflation Board.[3] The AIB is responsible for enforcing guidelines affecting the compensation of professionals. As provided in the Anti-Inflation Act, it must also play the role of a commission of inquiry and make appropriate proposals to contain inflation in the future.[4] Over the past ten

Actuary and president of the Laurentian Fund Inc.; formerly minister of social affairs, Province of Quebec

1 Government of Quebec, *Report of the Commission of Inquiry on Health and Social Welfare, The Professions and Society* (Vol. 7, Tome 1, Part 5) (Quebec: 1970)
2 Groupe de travail sur l'urbanisation, *L'urbanisation au Québec; rapport* (Quebec: 1976)
3 I resigned from the Board on 4 December 1976.
4 Anti-Inflation Act, S.C. 1974-75-76, c.75, s.12(1) (e)

years, events have therefore almost constantly involved me, in one way or another, in the evolving relationship between governments and the professions.

THE QUEBEC COMMISSION
ON HEALTH AND SOCIAL WELFARE

In its 1970 report the Commission observed that, in keeping with the concepts of a liberal society, professional corporations in Quebec had been granted very wide powers without any form of government control over how they used them. It noted that while professional corporations regulated public services, they were not linked in any way to the administrative structure of government.

The Commission noted that the legal provisions regulating various occupations varied widely. Some occupations were declared 'open,' others 'closed.' Among the closed professions, some, employing their monopoly of professional titles, were able to define the conditions for eligibility to practise: others were granted in addition the power to regulate the practice of the profession and hence to assume the control of such practice on behalf of society. The Commission emphasized the fact that differences in status, especially among the newer professions, did not proceed from a uniform definition of their 'raison d'être,' their relative significance to society, and the place they should occupy in it.

Finally, the Commission stressed that the laws governing professions had not been adapted to important developments such as the ever-increasing number of professionals in an employer-employee relationship, the growing emphasis on accessibility to professional services, and greater specialization constantly giving birth to new occupations or 'professions.'

In short, the Commission considered that the system of professional organizations reflected more the expression of the power of various groups in their struggle for professional status, with its inherent advantages, than social and professional needs. Here, in a few words, is how the Commission concluded its critical examination of the situation in Quebec:

Not only does professional law no longer express the needs of modern society but often it goes against the very ideological and technical concepts which prevail and which guide its evolution. As for professional organization, it presents the major and hardly acceptable inconvenience ... of no longer expressing the real state of professional disciplines and their reciprocal relations, without, however, meeting the specific needs of those basically concerned, the professionals themselves.[5]

5 Supra n.1, p. 23

The Commission considered that a sound policy for the organization and regulation of the professions is one that above all ensures the protection of the public interest. This policy should then try to reconcile the public interest with the indisputable advantages of a certain autonomy for the professions with respect to political and technocratic structures. Finally, the Commission believed it necessary to avoid abolishing what is valuable in existing institutions, while making sure that the professional organization constitutes a framework which allows for the adjustments required by our constantly changing society.

Nationalization of the professional organization, for example through government control boards, was rejected as inappropriate. The Commission clearly opted in favour of what it called 'moderated self-regulation of the professions.' It saw in this approach part of the solution to the problem of integrating professionals into society.

In order to apply this philosophy to professional legislation and organization, the Commission formulated a number of guiding principles. These principles were intended both to establish and to maintain the limits of professional legislation, and to clarify the role of professional organization as a framework providing public services.

The abolition of out-of-date conditions for practice
Where no justification could be found for certain conditions required in order to practice certain professions, the Commission recommended that they be abolished. For example, the report mentions professional privileges that bear no relationship to the protection of the public, and limitations on certain economic behaviour of professionals that have no direct or indirect effect on the quality of professional services.

The need to distinguish between the role of protecting the public
and that of defending the professional's economic interests
The Commission recommended that professional corporations no longer be given the role of defenders of the economic interests of their members, since this role conflicts with their main function. It proposed the development of professional unions parallel to professional corporations, and development of professional labour relations legislation.

Measures to integrate professional corporations into the public sector
To achieve such integration, the Commission proposed means such as the establishment and periodic revision of codes and regulations covering professional

practice, the study of problems brought about by scientific and social change, and the publication of periodic public reports.

The establishment of a unified system of professional legislation
To accomplish this aim, the Commission proposed the adoption of a professional code that would replace the existing heterogeneous set of professional laws. The proposed code would distinguish between three types of professional organizations: the professional corporation, enjoying monopoly of function or title and fairly extensive delegated powers; the professional association, an open body with neither delegated powers nor monopoly of title, but whose objectives are the promotion of the profession and the establishment of standards of excellence; and the professional union, a body to defend a group's socioeconomic interests. In view of the public service character of professional corporations, it was contemplated that the professional code and any future amendments would be proposed by the government and not by professional organizations as private bills.

The structure and operation of professional organizations made public
It was the opinion of the Commission that the delegation of legislative powers to professional corporations requires that the public as well as the government be represented on the boards of such corporations. The Commission also proposed various means to make corporation operations public – periodic public reports, public discussions of regulation proposals, lifting the veil of secrecy that surrounds corporations, and so on.

Integration of professional corporations into the public administration process
The Commission stressed the need to render systematic the relationships between the professional corporations and government.

IMPLEMENTATION OF THE QUEBEC REFORMS

In autumn 1971 the government announced its decision to go ahead with the reforms proposed by the Commission and tabled the *Professional Code* in the National Assembly, together with twenty-three related bills concerning a like number of already existing, or planned, professional corporations. The parties concerned were then extensively consulted.[6] Although the spirit and the funda-

6 As soon as they were tabled, the bills were referred to a parliamentary commission entrusted with studying them and hearing representatives from all concerned. For more than a year the commission sat at least once a week; it heard more than 150 submissions. In the autumn of 1972, after the hearings, the government tabled new versions of the bills. It was not until June 1973 that the National Assembly concluded its study. The bills were given assent on 6 July 1973 and came into effect on 1 Feb. 1974.

mental principles of the legislation were not amended as a result of this public consultation, it allowed the government to bring about very interesting improvements.

It is impossible in a relatively small space to describe in detail each and every provision of the legislation. I will restrict myself to those aspects of the reforms which are the most innovative and pertinent.

The status of professional corporations

The legislation strongly maintains the principle of self-regulation of the professions. However, two provisions qualify the application of this general principle: the appointment of public representatives to the boards of the corporations, and the creation of the Office des Professions, the main role of which is to ensure that the professional corporations perform their functions adequately.[7] Furthermore, the *Professional Code*[8] establishes criteria and conditions for the incorporation of new corporations and makes a distinction between professions with the exclusive right to practice and professions with reserved titles.

1 The creation of new professional corporations

Because of the large number of requests from groups eager to be recognized as professional corporations, the government set out in the *Professional Code* the criteria on which decisions will be based. These criteria, which must be interpreted in light of the fundamental objective of the legislation, protection of the public, are: (1) the knowledge required to engage in the activities of the persons who would be governed by the corporation which it is proposed to incorporate; (2) the degree of independence enjoyed by the persons who would be members of the corporation in engaging in the activities concerned, and the difficulty which persons not having the same training and qualifications would have in assessing those activities; (3) the personal nature of the relationships between such persons and those having recourse to their services, by reason of the special trust which the latter must place in them, particularly because such persons provide them with care or administer their property; (4) the gravity of the prejudice or damage which might be sustained by those who have recourse to the services of such persons because their competence or integrity was not supervised by the corporation; and (5) the confidential nature of the information which such persons are called upon to have in practising their profession.[9] Establishing these criteria cannot but reduce the possibility of arbitrary decisions and slow down

7 The Commission recommended in its report that this function be entrusted to the Department of Financial Institutions, Companies and Cooperatives. For a full discussion of the Office des professions, see René Dussault's contribution below.
8 S.Q. 1973, c.43
9 Ibid, s.25

the process of creating new professional corporations. It is interesting to note that the government felt the need to declare that it would be very parsimonious in creating new professional corporations; the criteria, in spite of their precision, are not free from subjective interpretations.

The government, by announcing its criteria and issuing its statement of intent, advised all concerned that it would exercise great caution before extending self-regulation to new occupational groups. The government showed its intention of checking the extension of controls over 'professional' activity, particularly when such controls are applied through self-regulation.

2 The distinction between exclusive professions and professions with reserved title

The *Professional Code* provides for two types of professional corporations. In the first type, the members of the corporation are granted the exclusivity of the practice of their professional activities as well as of the use of the related title. In the second case, only the use of the title is exclusive.[10]

The granting of the exclusive right to practise is governed by the following criteria:

The members of a corporation shall not be granted the exclusive right to practise a profession except by an act; that right must not be granted except in cases where the acts done by these persons are of such a nature and the freedom to act they have by reason of the nature of their ordinary working conditions are such that for the protection of the public they cannot be done by persons not having the training and qualifications required to be members of the corporation.[11]

It is clear that the determining factor in granting the exclusive right to practise a profession is not the level of training needed to practise but rather the setting in which the profession is usually practised. It was decided that the granting of a reserved title was sufficient to protect the public in the case of professionals who practise almost exclusively in a structured environment, subject to controls, recruiting procedures, standards, governmental accreditation, and so on. On the other hand, when for a given professional activity the relationship with the public is strictly personal and no other party witnesses the quality of the services

10 Of the 38 corporations acknowledged in the *Professional Code*, 17 were professions with reserved title, and 21 were professions with exclusive right to practise. The granting of a reserved title, while allowing anyone to practise the profession, informs the public that the holders of the title are qualified, must comply with a code of ethics, and are subject to periodic professional inspections.

11 Supra n.8, s.26

rendered, the government felt it important to grant the right to exclusive practice to the members of the corporation and entrust the latter with the responsibility of controlling the quality of services rendered.

In making a distinction between the exclusive profession and the profession with a reserved title, the government wanted to avoid the existence of an undue number of exclusive fields of practice. In this way, the risk of isolating the complementary sectors between which close co-operation is necessary and the possibility of conflicts between professionals are reduced, the scientific and technical progress of the professions is not unnecessarily impeded, and the distribution of adequate services to the public is not unjustifiably restricted.

In other words, as far as the status of professional corporations is concerned, the objective of the reform is to protect the future of self-regulation against the race for professional status. The excessive multiplication of professional corporations, especially those with a right to exclusive practice, under the pretense of protection of the public, with the real purpose being to gain the advantages associated with this status, would sooner or later bring about the demise of the self-regulation of the professions.

I cannot help but mention the fact that while generally proposals for the extension of controls originate within governments, and the persons to be subjected to these controls try to check and restrain them, it is often the other way around in the case of professionals.

The adaptation of the fields of professional practice

The legislative provisions governing exclusive professional corporations include a mechanism to adjust the definition of their fields by regulation. The objective of this mechanism is to reduce the rigidity of the delimitation of the fields of practice and to eliminate one of the major barriers to an improved distribution of professional services. Its basic purpose is to reconcile the need to close certain professions for the protection of the public with the imperatives of the evolution of professions. The reform puts the responsibility of bringing the necessary modifications to the fields of activity on the professional corporations themselves. In the final analysis, the objective is to lessen recourse to legislative intervention for the periodic adaptation of fields of practice.

The exposure of professional corporations to society

At the various levels of the administrative structure of each professional corporation, the *Professional Code* provides for the participation of people who are not members of the corporation and whose major responsibility is to represent the public interest. This representation is ensured at the level of the corporation's board of administration by two, three, or four members, according as the corporation has less than 500 members, between 500 and 1500 members, or more than 1500 members. These board members are appointed by the Office des professions after consultation. If the board of administration sets up an executive committee, it must include one lay member (there is an exception to this provision in the case of the bar). Lastly, the chairman of the disciplinary committee of each corporation is nominated by the lieutenant governor in council, after consultation with the bar, from among those lawyers who have been practising for at least ten years.

As regards the presence of lay members within the corporations, it is interesting to note that while the Commission had proposed the inclusion of government representatives, the *Professional Code* does not provide for them. It should also be emphasized that the lay members are named by the Office des professions and not by the government. These two aspects of the *Professional Code* are another demonstration of the desire to protect the professional corporations against the possibility of the government intervening too directly in the conduct of their affairs.

Among the various provisions aimed at making the professional corporations more open to the public, it is also worth mentioning that the Office des professions is required to publish annually the disciplinary decisions taken by the professional corporations.

The conflict between academic training and professional training

The necessity of reconciling the imperatives of academic training and those of professional training – the junction between theory and practice – has given rise to acute problems during the last few years. To solve these problems and enable the professional corporations as far as possible to grant permits to practise on the sole strength of recognized diplomas, the *Professional Code* provides that the lieutenant governor in council shall determine, through regulations, after consulting with the Office des professions, the Council of Universities, the educational institutions, and the corporations concerned, the terms and conditions for co-operation between the latter and the educational institutions in the development of study programs which lead to a recognized diploma for the purpose of the permit to practise, and in the preparation of examinations or other means for evaluating persons pursuing these studies.

This machinery differs appreciably from that proposed by the Commission. The latter recommended the adoption of the state diploma system. Under this system the government establishes by regulation, for the purpose of eligibility to practise, the minimum requirements with respect to duration of studies, program of studies, practical training, and so on. The diplomas granted by the universities, the colleges, and the other educational institutions that satisfy these requirements are recognized as state diplomas of equivalent value and give the right of admission to the professional corporations.

The mechanism provided for in the *Professional Code* gives greater protection to the autonomy of the professional corporations and of the educational institutions in entrusting them with an important responsibility, rather than submitting them to governmental regulation.

Admission to professional corporations

The *Professional Code* provided that as of 1 July 1976 no one who is not a Canadian citizen with a working knowledge of French can become a member of a professional corporation in Quebec. This requirement clearly shows that the study of French as a working language must in future be a fundamental concern of anyone considering making a professional career in Quebec.

This aspect of the legislation must be seen as another demonstration of the desire to integrate professionals into society. As the requirement for a knowledge of the French language is considered by the government to be essential, it should be noted that the professional corporations have no leeway in the matter, in contrast to other conditions with respect to the right to practise. In other words, where matters of a purely professional nature are involved, the principle of self-regulation applies; when the general objectives of society are being pursued, however, this principle takes second place.

The application of the professional legislation

Before the adoption of the *Professional Code*, the legislation incorporating professional corporations entrusted them with almost exclusive responsibility for regulating the practice of the professions. Within the framework of their regulatory, quasi-judicial, and administrative powers, the corporations enjoyed a very high degree of autonomy, the only real limit being the requirement to have some of their regulations approved by the lieutenant governor in council. The new organizational and management principles set out in the *Professional Code* have led to a change in the distribution of the powers governing professional activity as a whole in Quebec.

1 The functions and powers of professional corporations

While the professional corporation clearly remains responsible for exercising control over professional activity, the *Professional Code* now seeks to ensure through various mechanisms that the corporation fully assumes this responsibility.

Thus certain regulations involving matters of public interest must be adopted within the time limit determined by the Office des professions.[12] If regulations regarding any of these matters have not been adopted within the time limit, the Office can, on its own initiative, enact those regulations required for the protection of the public. Moreover, all regulations drawn up by the board of administration of a corporation, whether or not it be subject to the Office's power of substitution, must be published in the Quebec *Gazette* at least thirty days before being approved by the lieutenant governor in council.

The *Professional Code* requires each corporation to establish a professional inspection committee and a disciplinary committee. The role of the professional inspection committee, consisting of members of the corporation appointed by its board of administration, is to examine the level of professional competence of the members of the corporation, particularly by verifying the quality of the professional services they render. For this purpose, the files, books, and registers of each member of the corporation may be inspected. The corporation's board of administration, on the recommendation of the committee, may require a professional to take a refresher course and limit his right to practise his professional activities for the duration of this course.

2 L'Office des professions

The Office des professions, created by the new professional legislation, has several original features. It is interesting to note that its establishment was not provided for in the Commission's report.

It consists of five members appointed by the lieutenant governor in council.[13] Three of them, including the chairman and the vice-chairman, are chosen from a list of at least five names furnished by the Interprofessional Council. The Office is a monitoring and regulatory agency whose main function is to ensure that every professional corporation adequately fulfils its task of protecting the public. As well, the *Professional Code* and related legislation confer on the Office important administrative responsibilities with regard to the organization of new professions, the monitoring of professional corporations, and the submitting of

---

12 These regulations concern: (*a*) the code of ethics, (*b*) the arbitration procedure for disputed professional accounts, (*c*) the setting up of a compensation fund to be used to reimburse the sums used by a professional for purposes other than those for which they were entrusted to him, (*d*) the procedure of the professional inspection committee, (*e*) the rules for the preservation, use, and destruction of the files, books, and registers of a professional who ceases to practise, (*f*) the type of advertising the professional can use, and (*g*) the determination of the quorum for the general meetings of the members of the corporation.
13 They must be members of a professional corporation.

suggestions to those taking part in the application of legislation dealing with the professions.[14]

Conclusion

Despite the creation of the Office des Professions and certain new requirements imposed on professional corporations, the principle of self-regulation has been adhered to in the implementation of the Quebec reforms. For the future, it is clear that the context of the distribution of professional services will evolve over the years. It cannot be assumed that the mechanisms developed for the protection of the public by the *Professional Code* will always be satisfactory. Through the Office des Professions as a monitoring agency, the government, however, can keep well informed about the changes that need to be made in the Acts governing professions, while at the same time respecting the philosophy and principles of the reform.

DEFENCE OF THE
ECONOMIC INTERESTS OF PROFESSIONALS

I mentioned earlier that the Commission report recommended that a distinction be drawn between protection of the public and defence of the economic interests of professionals. This matter covers at least two major and distinct components: the negotiation of collective agreements within the framework of public plans, and the regulation of professional fees in private practice.

The negotiation of collective agreements
within the framework of public plans

In its first report on health insurance, submitted in 1967, the Commission recommended that the establishment of a schedule of fees or a method of remuneration and of working conditions for the purpose of health insurance be the subject of formal negotiations between the government and the professional unions representing the physicians. The Commission also insisted that professional corporations should no longer concern themselves with the defence of their members' economic interests and, consequently, should not participate in

14 On its own initiative, the Office may make recommendations to professional corporations or the lieutenant governor in council on: (*a*) the establishment of new corporations or the amalgamation or dissolution of existing ones, (*b*) the modification of the Acts governing professional corporations, (*c*) the introduction of measures designed to ensure that professionals receive the best possible training, and (*d*) means of getting corporations to take concerted action to find solutions to common problems.

the negotiations. In its report on the professions[15] the Commission reiterated these recommendations with respect to all professions.

The Commission noted in its first report that an appropriate legal framework for such negotiations was lacking. In fact, the *Labour Code* is designed solely for the salaried worker, while the Professional Unions Act, under which professional unions are incorporated, governs mainly the right of association and contains no provisions dealing with negotiations. The absence of a legal framework, according to the Commission, creates uncertainty with respect to the stages and the duration of the negotiations and the mechanisms to be used in case of difficulty or deadlock. In concluding its analysis, the Commission recommended that legislation be passed governing collective bargaining with non-salaried professional groups.

Since these recommendations were formulated, numerous agreements have been concluded between the government and various professional groups: in the context of health insurance with doctors, dentists, pharmacists, and optometrists, in the context of legal aid with lawyers and notaries. It is interesting to note that these agreements were negotiated with professional unions representing the professionals involved.[16] In these cases, the principle of the role distinction between professional corporations and professional unions was translated into reality.

I must however mention that in general the Quebec government has until now considered it preferable not to move towards the adoption of legislation designed to govern collective bargaining with non-salaried professionals. This situation in my opinion can easily have negative effects on the future of self-regulation of certain professions. In the absence of new negotiated agreements the members of a profession tend artificially to modify their practice in order to obtain the increase in their income that they cannot get through bargaining. Such behaviour only encourages government authorities to counteract this tendency by adopting controls over the exercise of the professions involved.

The regulation of fees in private practice
Before the adoption of the *Professional Code*, several professional corporations had the power to establish a schedule of fees which had to be submitted to the government for approval. In this fashion, minimum schedules of fees were set covering more or less exhaustively the range of professional acts and services likely to be performed. In addition, a number of corporations had adopted regu-

---

15 Supra n.1
16 Because of the very special problems encountered in determining the method of remuneration when the legal aid system was established, on that occasion the negotiation took place with the bar.

latory provisions forbidding their members from charging an amount lower than the fee scale stipulated. To do so would have been considered a breach of professional ethics.

In its report on the professions, the Commission insisted that professional corporations, to which society delegates the responsibility of ensuring the protection of the public, should not at the same time seek to protect the economic interests of their members. The Commission stated that professional corporations should not play a determining role in setting professional fees.

When the *Professional Code* was adopted, the responsibility of submitting fee schedules to the government was transferred from the professional corporations to the Office des professions.[17] This responsibility covers all professional corporation members who practise privately. Neither the Commission's report nor the *Professional Code* specifies whether the schedule must be made up of minimum or maximum fees. Nor is there any indication whether the schedule is mandatory or only indicative. For this reason, and also because the schedules adopted prior to the establishment of the *Professional Code* may possibly have been out of date because of inflation, the Office des professions initiated studies and consultations with the organizations concerned regarding the whole question of fees in private practice.

When it initiated these consultations, the Office underlined the new situation created by the adoption on 1 January 1976 of federal legislation which made the distribution of professional services subject to the Combines Investigation Act.[18] This Act now apparently prohibits a whole range of practices restricting competition in the field of services and appears to forbid collusive agreements between professionals in setting the amounts of their fees.

The coming into force on 1 July 1976 of this prohibition does not prevent provincial authorities from setting fee schedules for professional services rendered in private practice, and consequently does not affect the jurisdiction of the Office des professions in this field. The federal legislation does, however, create a new situation. In the absence of provincial regulation of professional fees, these will henceforth have to be set through the market within the framework of the Combines Investigation Act.

17 S.12(4) of the *Professional Code* states that the Office must 'suggest for approval to the lieutenant governor in council, after consultation with the corporation and bodies concerned, a tariff of professional fees for the services rendered by the members of the corporation, when the cost of these services is not fixed by collective agreement or determined by law.'

18 An Act to amend the Combines Investigation Act and the Bank Act and to repeal an Act to amend an Act to amend the Combines Investigation Act and the Criminal Code, S.C., 1974-75-76, c.76, s.30

Since the adoption of the *Professional Code*, my views on this question have become more precise because of changes that have taken place on the economic scene. The regulation of fees in private practice can only lead to a form of protectionism which has no place in the field of professional services. We must opt in favour of the laws of the marketplace. If this choice prevails, there will no longer be any question of minimum or maximum fee schedules or of any other form of fee regulation in private practice. On the other hand it will be essential that adequate information on fees charged by professionals be available to the public. This will require an important modification to the current situation, since there still exist restrictions on information of this sort.

OTHER CONTROL MECHANISMS

Although control over professional activity is clearly the responsibility of the professional corporations, they cannot assume all the tasks which such control requires, either because of incompatibility of the roles involved or for a variety of practical reasons. For example, within the framework of health insurance the evaluation of certain fee claims requires that a judgment be made upon the necessity or the appropriateness of professional services rendered by various categories of professionals whose services are covered. Since the professional corporations could not associate themselves with a control function so intimately related to the economic interests of their members, review committees were created in 1973 by the Health Insurance Act.[19] These committees, whose functions are to review claims for payment which appear unjustified to the Health Insurance Board, are composed of members of the profession concerned and a lay person appointed on the recommendation of the Office des professions.

TENTATIVE EVALUATION[20]

The acceptance of the reform
The Office des professions has been set up and its credibility well established. It has successfully accomplished the difficult task of creating four new corporations with the exclusive right to practise (chiropractors, denturologists, podiatrists, and hearing aid acousticians). It has proceeded, without criticism, to appoint lay members to corporation boards of administration. Dialogue and sustained relationships have been established between the Office and the corporations. As for the corporations, they have now modified their structure and their

19 S.Q. 1970, c.37
20 As of October 1976

operation in accordance with the provisions of the *Professional Code* and, where applicable, of the particular Act to which they are subject. Most of the means and mechanisms designed to integrate them more fully with the public administration have been established.

Stages under way

1 Creation of new corporations
Faced with numerous applications by groups requesting professional incorporation, the Office in 1974 launched a study on the evolution of professionalism in Quebec. This study was released in the autumn of 1976, and is described extensively elsewhere in this collection of essays.[21]

2 Delegation of professional acts
I have mentioned the fact that the *Professional Code* provides a mechanism to adjust the definition of fields of practice in order to reconcile the necessity for closing certain fields of activity with the imperatives of the evolution of the professions. In its third activity report the Office affirms its intention to see this mechanism effectively applied in the future.[22] In other words, we will soon be in a position to see more clearly whether professionals can assume this delicate task through their corporations, or whether the legislature will have to intervene.

THE FUTURE

Quality and accessibility of professional services are compatible with the principle of self-regulation of the professions. With regard to the extent and content of the application of this conclusion, it is still too early to come to a definitive conclusion. However, one can anticipate that the number of new occupations or 'professions' that will be formed into professional corporations, more particularly of the exclusive type, will be strictly limited.[23]

As a result of higher educational levels, increases in living standards, and greater consumer awareness, the pressures exerted on corporations to assume fully their responsibilities are likely to increase. The existence of other institutional options, notably in the field of health, in the framework established by

21 See Dussault's contribution to this volume.
22 Office des professions, *Third Annual Report of Activity, 1975-76* (Quebec: 1976). The current discussions bear on the delegating of professional acts from doctors to nurses, to medical technologists, and to technicians in respiratory therapy, and on delegation of acts from nurses to auxiliary nurses.
23 See Dussault's contribution to this volume.

employer-employee relationships, as well as in the issue of licenses to practise by governmental bodies, will inevitably add to these pressures.

As for those who aspire to the status of 'professionals,' their attitude is likely to change. The existence of far stricter criteria for incorporation, the withdrawal of the professional corporations from the role they have played in defending the economic interests of their members, the pressures being exerted on the corporations to assume fully their responsibilities, are all factors likely to dampen enthusiasm for professional status.

With regard to professional incomes, it is now clearly established that the level of incomes must be set through negotiations. Control mechanisms designed to eliminate abuses do not appear to have given the expected results, and unless there is an improvement in the situation the introduction of tighter controls can be anticipated sooner or later.[24]

24 See also, *Professional Fees in Private Practice*, Report of L'Office des professions, June 1977, in which it is recommended that the determination of professional fees in private practice in future be regulated primarily by market forces.

R.E. OLLEY

The future of self-regulation:
a consumer economist's viewpoint

INTRODUCTION

Professional self-regulation ranges from nearly complete to negligible. Those professionals who are members of tight corporate bodies, with extensive delegated power from government, enjoy a great deal of self-regulation. At the other extreme are those professionals, such as credit managers, management people, and so on, who have for all practical purposes no self-regulation. While most discussions, the present one included, deal with what may be called organized professionals, it constitutes a sometimes helpful counter-perspective to note that many professional people, such as economists and management consultants, function with virtually no self-regulatory capacity.

The ability of economic analysis per se to deal with the question of self-regulation is probably quite limited. Very little work has been done on the institutional framework within which economic life takes place. Virtually none is available on professional societies, which are a powerful and growing set of institutions. Indeed, in a recent article lamenting among other things the lack of work on why institutions grow and evolve, R.A. Gordon[1] fails to mention, among the many types of institutions noted, professional societies at all.

What economic analysis can do is offer some insights about what economic and other consequences one may expect under various institutional forms. These insights are valuable starting points, and are highly evocative of what may be

Department of Economics, University of Saskatchewan; chairman of the Board, Consumers' Association of Canada
1 'Rigor and relevance in a changing institutional setting,' *American Economic Review*, 66, No. 1, 1976, pp. 1-14

achieved.[2] But, in the absence of detailed empirical inquiry they cannot be regarded as definitive.

MARKET REGULATION

It is apparently most straightforward of all to postulate that the market should regulate the offering and pricing of professional services. The argument comes down to saying that the going price of professional services will call forth some number of practitioners. The price will change continuously so that the number of persons coming forward is socially optimal. People will enter or leave the profession until the returns to those remaining in it, non-monetary benefits taken into account, are just equal to the returns in other occupations, recognizing training differences.

At the same time, the public buys the grade of service it wishes under the delivery conditions it wishes, unemcumbered by regulations from professional societies or government. The law of the land protects against fraud, theft, deceit, and other misdemeanours, while the civil law provides recourse in the event of defective workmanship. The user of the service is presumed to have or to be able to obtain sufficient information on the quality of service being delivered by each professional and to match that to his requirements or budget.

With such a system, it is argued, there would be three main advantages. First, price would never be unduly enhanced. Second, service could be offered in the widest variety of qualities and under any or all delivery conditions that were efficient relative to the user's needs. Third, there would be maximum latitude for innovation, technological improvement, new procedures, and any other evolution that might be of value.

This is a persuasive way to look at the benefits from allowing no regulation. Unfortunately it does not come to terms with three key requirements for such a system to work well. These are supply adjustment for professionals, information, and the relation between product and price.

The first problem, the adjustment of supply to demand, might be said by the user to be a problem for the professionals. Some kind of premium would apply to earnings to take job uncertainty and other unknowns into account. This premium would be a matter for users to consider, since it would clearly affect price. In addition, the problems of matching supply and demand for various professionals in recent years indicates that mismatching of jobs and people cannot be

2 See, for example, Milton Friedman, *Capitalism and Freedom*, Chicago: University of Chicago Press, 1962, especially pp. 137-60, on which the following paragraphs are based in part.

treated as being merely a private problem. It spills over into political and social areas, and can create disorderly markets when the matching is not fairly close.[3]

The second, and more important, problem is information. It is easy enough to say that a wider choice of services will become available. However, most of the value of choice is dependent on the user's being aware of the variety and being able to interpret what each variation means. Without that knowledge, it is clear that the idea of variety is largely empty of practical significance.

But this leads also to a more profound question of information. There is always variety between individual professionals in terms of ability, quality of training, background of interests and preoccupations, currency of knowledge and information, and general competence. Professional services are complex products. To expect that the user could have even minimal capacity to assess these over a wide range of possible variation if there were no regulation, while doing the same thing for the thousands of other goods and services he uses, is simply unrealistic, not to say worse. The claim that consumers ask around before picking out a professional cannot be construed as more than seeking general reassurance, and then picking up second-order information, relative to the professional service itself, to determine which professional to use. The information assumption, namely very extensive pertinent knowledge about the professional, simply cannot be met.[4] Without it, the argument for regulation by the market alone is badly shaken.

The third problem is the relation between product or service and price. Economic models bearing on the efficacy of the market as a regulator of economic activity generally assume that price is separate from product. Price cannot affect the product. If it does, and product quality changes, a new product is said to have emerged with the same characteristic of invariant quality with respect to its price. Even for physical products, this important assumption is not tenable in most actual cases. Conditions of sale, service, warranties, aftersale service, and qualitative features of the product itself all can be, and are, changed when price is constrained. When the product is a service this is eminently more possible. To note one dimension where a professional service could be 'diluted' to meet a lower price or effectively bilk the client, one only has to recall that most professional services have a large 'invisible' content. This is the part of the service which rests on keeping up to date, checking out alternative possibilities, assessing possible symptoms, and following some possibly subtle considerations, which

3 See for example, R.G. Evans, 'Does Canada have too many doctors? – Why nobody loves an immigrant physician,' *Canadian Public Policy*, 2, No. 2, pp. 147-60.
4 It is sometimes suggested that information should be made available to the consumer to remedy this problem. The sheer volume, growth, and complexity of such information make this seem impossible.

may be important, much further than the customer thinks he needs. Any of these features of service and many others, could be modified without the user's ever knowing it. In effect, the product cannot be defined by the user at the time of purchase, or perhaps ever, unless he is as expert as the professional himself – a possibility so unlikely as to warrant no serious mention. Under these conditions the user cannot perform as he is required to do by the market model of regulation, and the applicability of that model is further shaken.

In short, the idea that the market can regulate any economic activity rests crucially on there being adequate information available to all concerned. From the perspective of the consumer who uses professional services this is not possible for many dimensions of the content and quality of the service. Lines of physical product with this feature would and do become candidates for the development of formalized standards of safety, then of performance.[5] Service lines where the product is highly malleable seem to beg for some mechanism to limit the range of information needed by the user to one that is manageable from his point of view.

MONOPOLISTIC SELF-REGULATION –
OR REGULATION BY PROFESSIONAL SOCIETIES

As an alternative to market regulation, an argument can be made in relatively formal economic terms that the supply of professional services should be organized as a monopoly. At the formal core of the model would rest economies of centrally managed supply, of regulated quality, and of technological development. Such an argument could be elaborated in the following terms, assuming in the theory that the monopoly position is not misused in some way.

Monopolistic management of the professional service (the industry) would assure an adequate supply of professionals at the lowest costs to the suppliers. The professional society would be able to anticipate the trends in demand, a complex enough process, better than individuals could. Expected requirements for professionals could be met by management of the licensing arrangements, the training programs, or both. This would avoid the case of waste from oversupply with attendant under- or unemployment. It would also avoid suboptimal supply because of shortages, with the consequent loss of possible satisfaction to consumers. Undersupply would not occur, assuming that returns to the individual were competitive with other activities, because potential entrants would

5 The whole work of the Canadian Standards Association, for example, is directed to meeting the need to provide lower limits to the range of product quality because the consumer or user cannot readily discern performance for himself.

know that a job could be expected, while oversupply would be met by refusing licenses. Where training is lengthy and complex, this kind of supply management would be valuable. Moreover, the appropriate place to control the flow would be at the beginning of training, to avoid the waste of being unable to find a use for expensive training.

Monopolistic control of training, carried out or heavily influenced by the professional society and executed directly or by some kind of suasion, would serve to meet the second condition of efficiency, namely the assurance of adequate quality in the service at a minimum cost to society. Where the user cannot ascertain the quality of the service for himself, controlled training conditions would assure him of at least some initial minimum quality of service being offered. The cost to society of that assurance would be least under effective monopoly, because of centralized assessment of training quality. At the same time, codes of ethics and other standards, laid down and enforced by the professional society, would assure acceptable minima to the ongoing quality of delivered service, again at minimum cost. Effectively, the professional society becomes the quality policeman in several dimensions, carrying ample power to discharge that task through licensing and delicensing rights.

Finally, monopoly control by the professional society would assure maximal technological improvement in the service. This would be most evident through the standards it demanded of training institutions. These standards would assure speedy application of new technology and transmission of new insights to professionals in training. Less evident, but no less possible, would be the society's imposed requirements under its codes and standards for conduct, in which would be embodied a requirement to use the best techniques, upon pain of censure or delicensing. This procedure would relieve the consumer or user of the services from the impossible task of trying to carry out such assessments for himself, and at relatively low cost to society in general or the user in particular.

Because the professional society would be monopolistically responsible for discharging all these tasks, society at large or any individual would have, in theory, a readily identifiable institution to turn to in the event of dissatisfaction. This would reduce the social and private costs of finding the right place to go to appeal some private or collective action within the profession. It would also minimize the costs of acting on the appeal.

The foregoing rationale of a professional monopoly for its own services can of course be elaborated in much more detail. As the argument is made, it meets the problem of narrowing the range of quality variations to something the consumer can manage. It also assures that the minimal quality drifts up over time as new knowledge is found to be valuable and applicable. Finally, it gets rid of disorderly market conditions from the mismatching of the supply of professionals with demand. For all these reasons, among others, the argument looks attractive and has apparently been persuasive to varying degrees over time.

This model, like the market model, contains critical unstated assumptions, principally in respect of behaviour. It also ignores the need for some kind of continuing process to trade off between the technically possible and economically appropriate.

Key to the socially acceptable working of the monopoly model is that it will not become an economically useful device for extracting excessive incomes and that it will be an effective device for discipline. As Mr Castonguay has noted in his essay, professional societies often in fact become devices to protect the economic interest of their members and to enhance incomes unduly. At the same time, the degree to which discipline can be exercised to ensure the highest reasonable minimum of service quality is widely argued to be limited. Professionals just do not like to testify against their fellows. The ordinary consumer of professional services often does not know if he has been short-changed and does not find any encouraging place to address complaints. The result is that the alleged discipline toward keeping service quality high is neither evident nor apparently strong. The likelihood is high of characteristic monopoly behaviour, namely taking too much income and showing limited interest in improving service quality or in adopting new techniques or knowledge.

In addition to this problem with what may be called internal adaptation, the monopolies will usually be slow to adapt to new social conditions which require either new forms and qualities of service, or new institutional arrangements for delivering the service. Mr Castonguay has pointed out that slow adaptation was perceived by the Quebec inquiries to be a central problem. Another example may be useful. In a report on the usefulness and workability of an agency to concern itself with child health, the following remarks appear: 'A number of new problems in child health are emerging with dimensions beyond the scope of a traditionally perceived medical health delivery system,' and 'A number of well-known problems are either becoming more serious or are being revealed to require more comprehensive responses than have been forthcoming in the past.'[6] These remarks were made in the context of finding a way to deal with various dimensions of child health where extensive co-operation with existing medical institutions will be absolutely necessary. Yet they are clearly symptomatic of a failure in adaptation by at least some existing institutions. This is how lack of adaptation by any kind of monopoly almost always appears to the consumer: his needs, perceptions, and priorities have changed, but the existing institutions have not responded.

6 Shirley Post, *Feasibility Study: Canadian Institute of Child Health*, a study for the Hospital for Sick Children Foundation, Toronto, 1976, unpaginated 'Summary'

The working characteristics of monopolistic self-regulation by the professions have led to demands for improvement in their performance and/or regulation, which may imply direct licensing by government.[7] Sometimes the suggestion goes as far as proposing complete deregulation to allow the market free play.[8] Neither extreme is very appealing, because each simple model, when applied, has its own set of serious problems as described. Yet, apart from the Quebec scheme, described by Mr Castonguay, alternative institutional arrangements are difficult to suggest, let alone find.

THE QUEBEC REFORMS

The Quebec *Code de professions* and its accompanying Office des Professions seem, from the observations of Castonguay, Dussault, and others, to have as their objectives to capture for the consumer the benefits of monopoly organization in professions where there are such, and to avoid the problems attendant on that model. The procedure appears to be a much elaborated version of the actions called for by the prairie provinces' Royal Commission on Consumer Problems and Inflation.

Three dimensions to the legislation and its application appear to be key. These are the separation of economic from the technical and organizational interests of professionals, the maintenance of a high degree of autonomy in the management of the licensed professions, and the creation of agencies and mechanisms to ensure that all possible benefits from new insight accrue to the public and that the professions respond to the public's needs. As Mr Castonguay correctly points out, it is much too early to evaluate the reforms, which always take some time to be shaken down in application. More important, and probably crucial to their success, is the matter of attitude, which Castonguay properly underlines. In the organization and delivery of professional services, attitudes or states of mind can profoundly influence the path taken by any set of reforms.[9]

The three main features of the Quebec reforms deserve further discussion with respect to their consumer implications.

First is the separation of economic from technical matters. Just how this will be accomplished is not clearly established. This is not surprising. If Part 1 of the

7 For example, *Report of the Royal Commission on Consumer Problems and Inflation*, Alberta, Manitoba, and Saskatchewan's Queen's Printer, Regina, 1968, p. 326
8 Cf. Friedman, *Capitalism and Freedom*
9 It is perhaps worth recalling, however, that Medicare in Saskatchewan, which was accompanied by tumultuous feelings, shook down fairly quickly into a competent medical care program, even in face of considerably more personnel changes than would normally accompany a professional reform.

Federal Combines Act is left unimpeded, fees of private practitioners will have to be set by market forces.

Just how completely the market will determine fees is not clear. In a number of unorganized professional fields, such as management consulting, fee structures all look pretty much alike without apparent collusion. Somehow 'the going fee' gets to be known and is used. This, of course, says nothing about the level of price, since one would expect prices to be highly comparable under competition. One dimension of market freedom shows up, however, in the widely varying fees charged by freelance operators, and in the possibility of job or special prices. This is perhaps all the market can do. Whether it can do even this much where the practice of the profession requires a (revocable) licence from the corporation is of course quite another matter. One cannot be sanguine that no mechanism will develop to make it clear what fee schedule is generally to be used and to make sure that the fee schedule is obeyed.[10]

The more serious problem of the interaction between price and quality of service, referred to above in connection with the market regulated model, is by no means resolved in the Quebec reforms. There can never be enough verification of services to prevent this interaction. It may be that provincial governments should allow fee schedules to be set, to function as maxima or minima, as the case requires. This would be most appropriately done by some provincial government agency proposing a fee schedule to the lieutenant governor in council. A mechanism of this kind would introduce a safeguard against excessively high prices but would ensure a careful scrutiny to make certain that fees were high enough to minimize interaction between them and the quality of service.

Certainly there is much to be said for reducing the preoccupation of some professional groups with mainly economic matters. However, it is very important not to pursue this objective to unrealistic extremes. The discharge of professional functions, whatever their technical or social attraction, also serves an economic function for most practitioners. That function is to meet some income objective. Complete separation of the economic and technical is unrealistic from the point of view of the practitioners, and probably of society as well.

Moreover, the economic influence on service has a valuable social function. Economic pressures from the buyer side of almost any market should lead to modifications in the products offered by suppliers. Up to the point where these variations in product mislead or harm the user, they should be encouraged. This implies that some mechanism has to be at work to reflect the evolving

10 Allowing advertising of professional services and prices would probably mitigate this problem and bring considerable benefits to the consumer. See Lee and Alexandra Benham's contribution to this volume and the references to Benham therein.

patterns of demand to the supplier. Price relationships are one powerful way of doing this, and no central agency like government can capture the range of adaptibility that the market, when working effectively, can produce effortlessly.

While this last argument causes some to advocate complete reliance on the market, it seems to lead more appropriately to having the professional organizations play some consultative role in the determination of the economic welfare of their members. This is again because of the relationship between price and product quality. Judgment on where to draw the line between acceptable and unacceptable price-stimulated variations in quality is much improved by considered professional participation in the decision. The conclusion, then, is that a reduction in economic preoccupations by professional societies is likely beneficial, but their complete removal from the societies' purview would be carrying the matter too far.

The second main feature of the Quebec reforms is the high degree of autonomy left to the professional societies in managing matters of a scientific, professional, or technical nature. This, of course, makes use of expert knowledge just where that knowledge can be most useful in administration. In that light, it is undoubtedly an appropriate emphasis. The only serious potential problem is the chance that professional preoccupation will increasingly neglect three dimensions of the dynamics of human development in perception and knowledge. Technical excellence could fail to respond to new varieties of technical potential, new organizational opportunities for service delivery, and, most importantly, new perceptions of what the user wants out of a professional service.

It is apparently to protect against this defect, as well as to ensure quality under any set of definitions that the third feature of the Quebec reforms was developed. This is the provision of mechanisms to bring what may be called the public interest directly to bear on the professional society. These mechanisms, coupled with tight definitions and a general reluctance to create new licensed professions, are apparently intended to assure quality and responsiveness where the professional self-regulated monopoly seems otherwise to be the best social device for delivering the service.

The new legislation takes as its over-all objective to ensure that the professional societies discharge the responsibilities which emerge out of the promised benefits from the society at their creation. This emphasis is very valuable, explicitly reminding those concerned that privilege implies responsibility, and that an accounting for the discharge of that responsibility may now, as a matter of law, be requested. Often overlooked in the evaluation of regulatory laws are the 'invisible' benefits that accrue from the fact that the regulated professionals must keep an eye on an informed potential reactor that cannot be ignored.

The criteria for setting up professional societies seem appropriate. As always, however, it is how these criteria are interpreted and applied that counts. The consumer can only wait, and hope that responsiveness to his needs will somehow be built into the application.

The regulations contain a set of considerations designed to ensure adaptation of professions to society's needs and changing conditions. First is the requirement that there be lay representation on the governing bodies. This appears to be more valuable than it really is. In my experience the internal dynamic of working committees or boards is such that all participants get caught up in the common rules of logic and schemes of perception. This is not always or even usually culpable co-option of the lay person, but rather a phenomenon more like acculturation to the milieu. Lay representatives who come from organized public interest groups, and who must report back to those groups, can usually maintain the difference of viewpoint requisite to an adequate discharge of their roles. Lay representatives without that requirement have no external environment which forcibly draws them back to the viewpoint they are supposed to bring. This feature of the Quebec legislation, which neglects to require that the public interest representatives come from organized public interest groups is in my view a serious defect in applying the principle of lay representation.

The second feature, aimed at adaptation, is a twin set of initiatives given to the Office des Professions which it is apparently enjoined to use. First, the office can initiate research, inquiry, or hearings into any matter bearing on the organization, performance, or conduct of a profession. It can publish the results and propose legislation on the basis of its findings. This is a potentially powerful device to assure continuing adaptability in the professional societies. The only potential problem would be if its investigations neglected to solicit with patience and vigour the viewpoints of the non-professional, that is, of the citizen user of the professional services. All too often inquiries into matters which profoundly affect the people end up as dialogues among professional experts and serve the citizen's perspectives negligibly or even negatively. Second, the office can, exclusively on its own initiative, propose to the professional associations or to the lieutenant governor in council changes in the status, scope, laws, training procedures, or nature of intersociety co-operation. Again, the only caveat would have to do with the degree to which the office made itself aware of lay user viewpoints. Otherwise, this, like the inquiry power, is a potentially highly useful device to enforce adaptation to changing conditions.

The third feature is the requirement that all professional societies recognized by the office have inspection and discipline committees, and that the latter's inquiries be published, along with their findings. Just what the inspection committees can do that goes beyond good administrative procedures is unclear. They cannot inspect the quality of services rendered to any significant degree. The discipline committees are likely to render more substantive benefits to the consumer. However they would look even better if they were required to carry out some kind of program to make themselves and their potential well known to the public. A profound problem remains untouched, namely that the consumer will only rarely be able to form an assessment of his grievance, and will even more rarely be able to make a case. Indeed, a reading of *Decisions Disciplinaires Concernant Les Corporations Professionnelles*[11] indicates that all the disciplinary actions treated involve the grossest forms of incompetence or dishonesty, usually with clear and dire consequences to the consumer. Grievances of a nature paralleling what one would routinely find being resolved under product warranties are nowhere to be seen. Some mechanism remains to be evolved to enable the consumer to identify cases where his problem is 'merely' shoddy service, and to enable him to bring these forward. This problem will continue to fester in consumers' minds.

CONCLUSION: THE PROTECTION OF CONSUMER RIGHTS

The consumer has a right, put as briefly as possible, to be able to have access to the widest reasonable choice of service types at a price which is the minimum consistent with the continued supply of those services. At the same time he has the right to adequate information, or reassurance, about those services, and to recourse in the event the service is defective relative to what it purported to be.

Ringing as this kind of summary of consumer rights may sound, it is fraught with problems, as the preceding discussion of the working of various organizational models has indicated and implied. These problems leave one with the strong sense that the consumer has the right only to a manageable set of professional service offerings which do not evolve and develop according to some rigid rules derived from a model but which derive from the open working of concerned participants in the service market. Protection does not come from the rigorous pursuit of some simplified model's prescriptions, but from honestly and openly managed institutions which respond to changing conditions.

Thus, the fundamental protective device for the consumers' rights is the interaction between his perceptions of his needs and the institutions which organize the serving of those needs. Impressive though it is, the market cannot be relied on exclusively to provide sensitive reactions to consumer needs. Some limits have to be placed on the market's range of reactions. Moreover, some key con-

11 Office Des Professions du Québec, Québec: Editeur officiel du Québec, 1976, Vol. 2, No. 2, décembre 1975

ditions for efficient working of the market are not met at all in the professional service industries. Hence the supplements to market institutions have to take these shortfalls into account.

Given these considerations, it seems unavoidable that professional societies will have an important role to play in protecting the consumer. When played at its best, this role will be to provide quality assurance, to bring newly proven knowledge into use, and to minimize the frequency and consequence of lapses in the human discharge of the service delivery system. It will also be a role which directs adaptations in technique, organization, and procedure to serve best the emerging needs for service and to do so in a way which maintains a basic adaptation of feasible quality standards to economically and socially workable definitions of the consumers' needs.

But monopolies, even in technical matters, have problems. It is easier to be comfortable, not to change, and to relax than to face the adjustments required by adaptation. Some kind of balance of power has to be struck to assure the consumer facing a monopoly that its responsibilities do not become underemphasized. The only likely agency to provide that countervailing force is the government. Thus the role of government has to be to create mechanisms which will assure the consumer that the professional societies, particularly those with licensing power, do indeed respond to existing and emerging consumer and social needs.

Government itself, of course, is capable of monumental misemphases and error in its own right. Thus one role of the professional society will have to be to protect the consumer as far as possible against that eventuality.

The system being tried in Quebec, where there is a basic statutory provision for regulation, coupled with an Office which has considerable functional independence, appears to be a laudable first step. It is experimenting to find a way to capture for the general public the benefits of monopoly self-regulation but to introduce the fundamental strength of the market, namely to keep the suppliers providing what the buyers want. Problems remain, as I have noted. The outcome depends fundamentally on attitude, in particular on whether a good-humoured desire to make the changes work can be maintained. Some mechanism which limits and supplements the free working of the market, and which limits and supplements the working of monopoly self-regulation, will have to be evolved to meet the consumers' needs not only as perceived by any model but especially by consumers themselves.

JETHRO K. LIEBERMAN

Some reflections on self-regulation

Because I am not versed in the Canadian experience of regulating professionals and because those who are have considered the matter at some length in this collection of papers, I plan to draw back and discuss the philosophy of self-regulation generally, with some reference to problems south of the border.

There are many possible definitions of professionals and professionalism. The definition matters, for according to a restricted meaning there are only two or three true professions, while according to expansive definitions anyone capable of soliciting a fee for services rendered (from astrologers to zen philosophers) is entitled to call himself a professional and invoke the time-honoured plea for guild-like control over his own affairs.[1] In other words, one of the clearest signs of professional status is the power, whether delegated by government or assumed in its absence, of private control over matters pertaining to a particular occupation. It is not the only indication, to be sure. Exclusivity of practice (primarily through licensing), lengthy training, and special relationships with clients are also marks of professional status. But in an age of pervasive regulation the ability to avoid both the market and the government is much prized.

Thus, for example, at a single session of the Wisconsin legislature in the early 1950s, the following occupational groups sought laws requiring that their 'practitioners' be licensed: caterers, canopy and awning installers, cider makers, coal dealers, dancing school instructors, egg breakers, frog dealers, labour organizers, meat cutters, music teachers, and beer coil cleaners. They were each unsuccessful. But scores of groups have succeeded in one state or another, so that over the

Legal affairs editor, *Business Week Magazine*; author of *The Tyranny of the Experts* (New York: Walker and Co., 1970)

1 An analysis of the definitions of professionals and professionalism and of the types of groups claiming professional status is made in Jethro K. Lieberman, *The Tyranny of the Experts* (New York: Walker and Co., 1970), chaps 1, 2, and 4.

years not merely lawyers and doctors and architects and accountants can claim to be professionals but also such diverse occupational types as photographers and dealers in scrap tobacco. What distinguishes them from the run-of-the-mill workers is that they are given some measure of control over the means by which their specialized labour is performed.[2]

At first blush, the claim to self-regulation is strange. We do not ask non-playing members of football teams to referee games involving their teams, nor do we assign businessmen to posts requiring them to investigate the commission of white-collar crimes within their companies. Why, then, do we with such seeming nonchalance let professionals assume similar power?

The answer stems from the recognition in the last century that caveat emptor was no longer a sufficiently prudent legal maxim for a host of activities in the emerging industrialized world. Despite the occasional plea of the free-market economist that laissez-faire is the better policy,[3] it is widely accepted today, for reasons that Professor Olley has adduced in his contribution, that the market is not an adequate regulator of harmful conduct. That is to say, the market allocates resources efficiently, but unaided by a legal system it will not take into account a host of injuries that are byproducts of the manufacture and distribution of goods and services. Factories pollute. Automobiles maim. Market-induced production of automobiles does not guarantee that they will be safe.

This possibility of injury is especially apparent in the case of professionals. In a complex, technological society we are all at the mercy of experts. The layman cannot protect himself against the misuse of the professional's expertise, and except within the narrow bounds of our own specialties we are all laymen facing a world of diverse and mammoth mysteries. To require that we take responsibility for judging all those whose services we require is utopian; no such responsibility can exist in the modern world.

Consequently professionals have come to withdraw at least a significant portion of their activities from the unregulated economic market. They oblige themselves to abide by a code of conduct whose hallmark is the forswearing of the temptation to take advantage of those entrusted to their care. The professional becomes a fiduciary. Service – in theory at least – takes precedence over self-interest.

Historically, this regulation has been carried out by the professionals themselves. For some, like law and medicine – the 'free' professions – self-regulation

2 For the Wisconsin experience, see Ruth Doyle, 'The fence-me-in-laws,' 205 *Harper's* 89 (1952). See also Lieberman, *Tyranny*, chap. 2.
3 Milton Friedman, *Capitalism and Freedom* (Chicago: University of Chicago Press, 1962), chap. 6

can be traced to the medieval guilds. But there is an anomaly here worth pausing to consider.

Medieval government was a pluralism of governing organizations. In England, there was not one legal system but many; in the seventeenth century, Coke counted as many as fifteen. The courts of common law were different political institutions from the chancery courts, and these in turn were to be distinguished from the courts of admiralty and from the ecclesiastical courts. Each was rooted in a different system of law, and where there was overlap the systems did not necessarily mesh. The courts would squabble among themselves over each other's right to hear a particular case, and there was no final authority to impose order.

Similarly, this 'chaos,' if you will, existed in the governing of the crafts. Central government did not yet exist in our sense; the sovereign power that resided in the monarch was not used to dictate precise codes for the conduct of professional duties. The sovereign delegated his power to the guilds, which, autonomously, fixed performance standards, fees, and entrance requirements. This was the only way by which government could realistically be conducted in those days; no central authority existed that could realistically carry out such prophylactic regulation.

Today there is. The state is now the central locus of authority for determining what is an injury to one person or to a group of people for which the law will provide redress. The medieval state had no particular concern about delegating what today we know as 'public' power, since all such power was the king's, and he could do with it as he liked. Today, however, the sovereign power is not someone's private possession; it is the power of the people themselves. Delegation of this power to private parties is a significant rupture in the legitimacy of the ensuing rules. Hence self-regulation by professionals on behalf of the public ought to be suspect. It is not at all coincidental that the motivation underlying the writing of ethical codes by the vast majority of professional guilds within the United States during the twentieth century has been the desire to exercise monopoly power on behalf of their members rather than on behalf of the public.

Self-regulation can have only two legitimate purposes. The first is to protect individual clients with whom the professional comes into contact. The second is to protect the public; that is, individuals with whom the professional does not have direct dealings. Thus, the first purpose is fulfilled by such rules as those requiring the professional to act as a client's trustee, to charge fairly, to keep confidences. To the latter purpose, protection of the public, are rules prohibiting the client and professional, for example, from conspiring together (thus lawyers should not help corporations violate fraud statutes).

The justification for self-regulation is that only professionals have the requisite knowledge to carry out these purposes. But the dangers of self-regulation may override this justification. Like its purposes, the dangers of self-regulation are twofold. The first is that self-regulation will not in fact work. The second is that it will work too well. Let me explain this seeming paradox.

If a group of people sharing a common tradition from which they profit is given the choice between doing a diligent job of prosecuting wayward members (an act that will tend to injure the group's public reputation) and hushing up the wrongdoing, there is little doubt that it will follow the latter course, keeping a low profile and acting only in the worst cases (defined, usually, as those cases that have inadvertently come to the attention of the public). This is precisely the course that disciplinary boards, even ostensibly public ones, have taken in the United States. The disciplining of lawyers for incompetence and often outright fraud, for example, is in a shockingly bad state of repair. A 1970 report of a special committee of the American Bar Association (called the Clark Committee, after its chairman, retired US Supreme Court Justice Tom C. Clark) said bluntly that the situation was 'scandalous.' In most states, the Clark Commission concluded, 'the prevailing attitude of lawyers toward disciplinary enforcement ranges from apathy to outright hostility. Disciplinary action is practically non-existent in many jurisdictions; practices and procedures are antiquated; many disciplinary agencies have little power to take effective steps against malefactors.'[4] Seven years after the scathing report was issued, little improvement has been seen.[5] The situation is no better in other professions. In medicine, the bizarre double suicide of two brother doctors in New York City in 1975 brought to public attention that a hospital had permitted them to use its facilities to carry on a practice knowing of their drug addiction and psychological difficulties. This was thought not to be an isolated case.[6]

The vast majority of lawyers actually suspended from practice or disbarred are subjected to such penalties only because they have been convicted of some crime in a public court. Sanctions for incompetent performance or conflict of

4 ABA Special Committee on Evaluation of Disciplinary Enforcement (Chicago: American Bar Association, 1970), p. 1
5 For follow-up studies on lawyers' discipline, see, for example, Eric H. Steele and Raymond T. Nimmer, 'Lawyers, clients and professional regulation,' 1976 *ABF Research Journal* 917; F. Raymond Marks and Darlene Cathcart, 'Discipline within the legal profession: is it self-regulation?' *ABF Research Contributions* (Chicago: American Bar Foundation, 1974).
6 See Linda Wolfe, 'The strange death of the twin gynecologists,' *New York Magazine*, 8 Sept. 1975, p. 43; Boyce Rensberger, 'Long Island doctor who lost license got backing,' *New York Times*, 15 April 1977, p. B2; Jane Brody, 'Addicted twin doctors endangered patients, assembly panel is told,' *New York Times*, 22 April 1977, p. B3.

interest are rare. (In England, incompetence does not even qualify as a breach of the standards of conduct mandated by the Law Society.)[7]

Yet incompetence and conflicts of interest are scarcely rare. Let me give just one example of the latter. In many of the eastern states, where lawyers are still essential to the conveyancing of real property, title insurance companies routinely give what they euphemistically call 'commissions' (and what I call kickbacks) to the lawyers for both the buyer and the lending institution. In New York State, until an Act of the legislature prohibited these kickbacks in 1974, the standard rate was 15 per cent. That meant that $45 of a $300 premium that the buyer was forced by the lending bank to pay to the title company was returned to the lawyer. Now under a fair reading of the canons of ethics as they applied in New York,[8] the buyer's lawyer was required either to assign this sum to his client or else to obtain his client's consent to keep it. Many lawyers did one or the other. But many lawyers did not. The New York State Insurance Department estimated that kickbacks retained by lawyers amounted to between $4 and $6 million annually.[9] Part of this sum, perhaps nearly half of it, was taken by bank lawyers who pocketed a kickback on the policy that the buyer paid for on behalf of the bank. This situation was notorious; every member of the official apparatus of the state bar knew what was happening, yet no attempt was ever made to investigate lawyers routinely pocketing such sums. And it is a telling point that the state legislature finally had to intervene rather than the state bar, which easily had it within its power to declare the acceptance of such kickbacks unethical under any circumstances.

The second problem of self-regulation – that it will work too well – follows directly from the first. In order to preserve the image of the profession, the codes of ethics will frequently inhibit conduct that the public, if it had a chance to vote, would probably approve. Thus lawyers are brought up on charges of defaming judges on occasions when the lawyers are speaking ex cathedra and not at all engaging in slander in the legal sense, and the general ethical rules against seeking publicity have worked in the United States to cover the doings of the legal profession in a great blanket of secrecy. Neither the bench nor the profession can tolerate the openness that the public needs. Ethics thus breeds conformity; unorthodox behavior is shunned.

---

7 See, for example, Murray Teigh Bloom, *The Trouble with Lawyers* (New York: Simon and Schuster, 1969).
8 New York State Bar Assn Code of Professional Responsibility, DR 5-107; New York State Bar Assn Committee on Professional Ethics, Opinion 320, 18 Dec. 1973
9 *Business Week*, 13 April 1974, p. 97

One of the most stunning examples of this phenomenon occurred in 1966 in Washington DC, where Monroe H. Freedman, then a law professor at George Washington University and now dean of Hofstra Law School in New York, happened to give a lecture one afternoon to the Criminal Law Institute, a private non-profit group that was undertaking to train lawyers for the job of representing indigent defendants at trial. Freedman's particular lecture was on the ethics of doing so, and in the course of the lecture he raised several intensely difficult questions, including the problem of condoning perjury by the defendant. Freedman suggested that there might be occasions when it would be proper and necessary to do so. There happened to be a reporter on the metropolitan staff of the *Washington Post* at the lecture, and the next day a headline appeared in the paper to the effect that Professor Freedman advocated perjury in the criminal courts. Within twenty-four hours Freedman was notified by the grievance committee of the District of Columbia bar association that he was being investigated for possible unethical conduct – not for doing but for speaking out. The proceeding dragged on for about four months and finally, after the national press had picked up the story, sputtered out. The only useful byproduct of this inane adventure was Professor Freedman's gaining a national reputation and his going on to write a series of penetrating articles and a book on the subject of legal ethics.[10]

Even more is at stake, however, than the use of codes of ethics to silence dissent. More frequently they are used to exact conformity of conduct claimed to be but not actually in the public interest. For example, suppose printers were assumed to constitute a professional group and were given the power of self-regulation, including the power to set down rules of conduct. What would we say if within that grant of power they claimed the authority to prohibit their members from setting type for any allegedly obscene or subversive book or periodical? Or suppose longshoremen were licensed and subject to discipline by their fellows: is it not plausible to imagine a politically-inspired boycott of foreign goods being unloaded in American ports (as in fact actually happened, under extenuating circumstances, some years ago)?[11]

The point is that the power of self-regulation always carries with it the power to *transcend the limits of the professionals' expertise.* This is especially true when professionals are allowed not only to police themselves but also to define

10 See Monroe H. Freedman, 'Professional responsibility of the criminal defense lawyer: the three hardest questions,' 64 *Mich. L. Rev.* 1469 (1966); Freedman, *Lawyers' Ethics in an Adversary System* (Indianapolis: Bobbs-Merrill, 1975).
11 For the story of a maritime union boycott of Egyptian ships in the New York port, see James W. Kuhn and Ivar Berg, 'The private right to frustrate public policy,' in *Values in a Business Society* (New York: Harcourt Brace, 1968), pp. 92ff.

themselves; that is, when they are allowed to regulate who may perform work related to the essential or core task of the profession. Thus in the United States lawyers are particularly vigorous in challenging the 'unauthorized practice of law.' Although private bar associations do not have the final word on the subject, the courts (composed entirely of lawyers) do, and it is not surprising to discover therefore that a host of activities that could be carried out far more cheaply by other types of practitioners are reserved exclusively to members of the bar.[12]

Lawyers in Arizona once put up a fierce battle to keep real estate brokers from invading their monopoly. The real estate salesmen were in the habit of helping customers fill in the blanks on printed contract forms. The state bar sued to enjoin them from doing so, and the state supreme court ruled that such transactions were legal in nature and that the right to conduct them was vested exclusively within the legal profession.[13] Not even an Act of the legislature could change this rule, the court said, since the regulation of the legal profession was inherently part of the judicial power, whose limits the state court professed the final word to essay. Incensed, the real estate people waged a fight to amend the state constitution to cool the presumption of both lawyers and court. Ultimately they succeeded in enshrining for themselves the constitutional right to fill in blanks in real estate forms.[14]

This power, to regulate how the profession is practised, is what Ivan Illich calls a 'radical monopoly'[15] and gives rise to what I have termed 'inconspicuous production,'[16] the desire to do little work (or work calling for relatively little skill) for high fees.

In the United States, the guild-like power of professionals through their quasi-public organizations is often exercised to control (or maintain) the fees of the practitioner. Thus lawyers until 1975 prescribed 'minimum fee schedules' as the 'ethical' way of doing business (until the Supreme Court struck these down as violating the antitrust laws).[17] I gather that in Quebec there is a fairly sharp division drawn between the power of the professional corporation to regulate con-

12 For discussions of unauthorized practice as an economic device, see James Willard Hurst, *The Growth of American Law: The Law Makers* (Boston: Little, Brown, 1950), pp. 319ff; Jethro K. Lieberman, 'How to avoid lawyers,' in Ralph Nader and Mark J. Green, *Verdicts on Lawyers* (New York: T.Y. Crowell, 1976), pp. 105ff; and the author's forthcoming book on lawyers' ethics (New York: W.W. Norton & Co., probable publication date, 1978).
13 *State Bar of Arizona* v. *Arizona Title & Trust Co.*, 90 Ariz. 76, 366 P.2d 1 (1961).
14 The story is told in Bloom, *The Trouble with Lawyers.*
15 Ivan Illich, *Tools for Conviviality* (New York: Perennial Library, 1970), pp. 54ff
16 See Lieberman, *Tyranny*, chap. 6.
17 *Goldfarb* v. *Virginia State Bar*, 421 U.S. 773 (1975)

duct and the power to regulate fees. Nevertheless, any professional corporation worth its salt can find ways to protect and enhance the radical monopoly at the expense of the public. The primary route to this end in the United States is through statutes and other regulations that restrict the methods of delivering and advertising the service. Thus the advertising of prescription prices for drugs and eyeglasses is banned in many states, and studies show that the prices paid to druggists and optometrists and opticians is markedly higher in states with the ban than in those without it.[18] Yet these regulations masquerade as a means of protecting the public health. (I should note that the Supreme Court during the past few years has finally come to its senses and realized that laws prohibiting advertising, at least those imposing a blanket prohibition, violate the First Amendment and so are void.[19])

There are other ways by which the professional corporation can affect the price of the service by regulating conduct. Let me mention only one, this time from England. During the past several years, local authorities have established so-called law centres which put lawyers on salary to represent the poor. These law centres do a fair bit of advertising, in the sense of announcing their existence and informing the public of the work they stand ready to do. In order for a solicitor to go to work at a law centre, it is necessary to obtain a 'waiver' from the Law Society, an institution which is somewhat analogous to the Canadian professional corporation. The reason for the waiver is to avoid the risk of being prosecuted for participating in a scheme through which legal services are advertised to the public. The Law Society began to condition the granting of waivers on a showing that there was a 'need' for the law centre in the particular locality. Translated, this meant that no waivers would be forthcoming if local solicitors would feel a competitive pinch (a rather silly proposition in any event, since few lawyers represent private clients who cannot afford to pay them). After considerable fuss, the Law Society backed down, and in consonance with British mores is now negotiating with other concerned parties on exactly what ground rules should apply in the granting of waivers.

All of these matters are serious problems in a regime of self-regulation. But Canada does not have such a pure regime. Government is apparently more intrusive in Canada (particularly in Quebec) than in the United States in the affairs of professionals. If the professional corporation fails to act, higher offices may compel it to act or even, seemingly, may supersede its judgment. Nevertheless,

18 See the Benhams' contribution to this volume.
19 *Bigelow* v. *Virginia*, 421 U.S. 809 (1975); *Virginia State Board of Pharmacy* v. *Virginia Citizens Consumer Council*, Inc. 44 L.W. 4686 (1976). *Bates* v. *State Bar of Arizona* 97 S.Ct. 2691 (1977)

the question of the composition of the professional corporation is still trouble-some, for it is this institution that will be making the majority of day-to-day decisions about the governance of the profession. Why should lay persons play so undistinguished a role, even in Canada? Why should lawyers be free of lay persons altogether? (In some American states, non-lawyers are at last being added to lawyers' disciplinary boards.)

I do not know what is so mysterious and complex about the governance of a profession that rules of ethics and the like can be drawn only by professionals. But in another sense this is a tortured question, I know, and one for which I have no sound answer. One remembers how professional practice was perverted under the Nazi regime, and the methods by which law and psychiatry are prac-tised in the Soviet Union today are chilling enough to give us pause at the sug-gestion that the power to regulate professional conduct be removed from the hands of professionals and vouchsafed to some governmental agency altogether. So it may be that the structure of regulation in Canada, at least that in Quebec, is the appropriate one. But it is one on which not all the evidence is yet in and the dangers of leaning too far in the corner of self-regulation must therefore con-tinue to be observed.

SELF-REGULATION: WHO QUALIFIES?

RENÉ DUSSAULT

The Office des Professions du Québec in the context of the development of professionalism

INTRODUCTION

Since the adoption of the *Professional Code*[1] in July 1973, the Quebec government has intervened more directly than before in the regulation of activities referred to as 'professional.' The supervising of professional corporations by means of the Office des Professions indicates that, in the field of professional services as in other sectors of economic and social activity, the legislator considers that producers cannot, alone and without external supervision, assume the defence of the interest of consumers and of the general public. However, the role of the Office is not restricted to overseeing corporations which have been recognized by the *Professional Code* and implementing regulations deriving from the legislation. The legislator has also assigned the Office the double mandate of suggesting the establishment of new professional corporations and of evaluating the usefulness of existing corporations, recommending their amalgamation or dissolution.

From its inception the Office des Professions has experienced heavy pressure urging the professionalization of occupations in Quebec. On the one hand as of April 1977 twenty-three groups of workers were asking for the recognition of the professional status of their activity and the granting of professional corporation status. On the other most of the corporations whose members have a reserved title have asked to become exclusive practice corporations, i.e., corporations whose members have a reserved field of practice and a reserved title. The Office, almost from the start, was thus confronted with a major problem of orientation. To what point should it promote the development of the profes-

Deputy minister of justice, Province of Quebec; formerly chairman of the Office des professions du Québec
1 Statutes of Quebec, 1973, C. 43.

sionalization of occupations in Quebec by encouraging the establishment of new professional corporations and by favouring the transformation of corporations with reserved title into exclusive practice corporations?

THE OFFICE DES PROFESSIONS DU QUÉBEC IN THE
CONTEXT OF THE DEVELOPMENT OF PROFESSIONALISM

In carrying out its mandate the Office has recourse to Section 25 of the *Professional Code*, which enumerates the factors to be taken into account when considering requests for professional incorporation. These factors, which are characteristic of professional activity, deal with the knowledge required for practising a profession, the practising professional's degree of independence, the difficulty of assessing the quality of a professional act, the personal nature of the relationship between the professional and his client, the gravity of the prejudice that a client may sustain, and the confidential nature of the information transmitted by the client to the professional. These factors remain open, however, to subjective interpretation. For instance, what conditions permit one to affirm that the gravity of the prejudice and the degree of independence are sufficient in a particular case and insufficient in another or that the nature of the relationship is sufficiently personal and the nature of information sufficiently confidential to justify recognition under the *Professional Code*? In reality, the *Code* by itself does not enable one to set the limits, to determine the threshold beyond which a given activity is sufficiently 'professional' to warrant regrouping in a corporation those persons engaged in that activity. Depending on whether one opts for a broad or narrow interpretation of Section 25, one can question the reasons for the incorporation of certain of the existing corporations or, conversely, favour a considerable increase in the number of professional corporations.

In the same manner, the eventual change of status of existing corporations with reserved title into exclusive practice corporations raises serious questions. Doubtless, the exclusive practice mechanism makes it possible to eliminate incompetent persons who could possibly cause serious prejudice to the public. But this same mechanism requires that the activity concerned be defined and its limits set with much precision. It erects barriers between the various specializations in a given sector and grants to the professionals concerned a total control of the market, which might entail an increase in the price of services.

Given this state of affairs, the Office considered it necessary, prior to taking a position on these questions, to study in greater depth the phenomenon of professional corporatism in relation to the public's need for protection and the demands of modern society. The Office conducted over a period of more than two years a thorough study of professions in Quebec and in the light of data obtained formulated a policy with regard to the development of professionalism in Quebec.[2]

In search of objective criteria
This study of professionalism in Quebec was conducted in three successive stages: first, the groups requesting professional incorporation were compared with corporations that already existed; second, research done on professions in North America was examined in order to define better the basic criteria set down in the *Code* concerning their establishment; and, third, certain activities of the professional corporations existing at the time of the adoption of the *Code* were analysed in an attempt to identify areas to stress in the effort to ensure the protection of the public. The first step showed that the groups seeking incorporation, as well as existing professional corporations, were not homogeneous. Consequently, the Office was not at this stage able to draft a coherent statement of characteristics common to existing professional corporations that could have served as a guideline for the establishment of new ones. The purpose of the second step was to identify attributes common to all socially or legally recognized professions and potentially offering a valid means of distinguishing them from other occupations. This step, which proved inconclusive also, at least revealed that no consensus exists at present on the identification and content of professional attributes, despite numerous efforts to this end over the last few decades.

Although it has not been possible to assign an unequivocal content to the basic factors set down in Section 25 of the *Professional Code*, the Office had cherished the hope that it could found its policy respecting the establishment of new corporations on the need to protect the public in the area of professional services. A close examination revealed, however, that the notion of 'protection of the public' is just as imprecise and subjective as the notion of 'profession' and that any consensus as to meaning is as unlikely in one case as in the other. Requests for incorporation received to date by the Office tend to confirm this point of view, because all are based on the necessity of protecting the public in a specific area of activity.

How can this need be evaluated in each and every case? How can the public which needs protection be identified? Does protection only refer to clients or individual consumers of professional services or does it also include the public or private company which uses these professional services or employs professionals? Does the concept 'public' apply to society at large? If it does, then what

2 *The Evolution of Professionalism in Quebec*, Office des professions du Québec, Quebec Official Publisher, September 1976

does the word 'protection' mean in this context, and what are the dangers against which society must be protected?

Given this state of affairs, the Office considered that it was in no position to draw up alone a formal definition of the expression 'protection of the public.' Such an undertaking seemed to it to be of a highly political nature, on a par with the definition of the expression 'public interest.' On the other hand, wishing to attenuate as much as possible the discretionary nature of its rulings on requests for professional recognition as defined by the *Professional Code*, the Office decided to rely on the third step of its study.

An approach based on the activities of professional corporations
The Office conducted a study among those professional corporations existing prior to the adoption of the *Professional Code* of four aspects of their activity traditionally recognized as important for the protection of the public. These aspects were as follows: discipline, continuing education, public information, and standards of practice. It was thought that such a study could show which characteristics of corporations did most to protect the public. These characteristics could then be used in guidelines to assess current and future requests for professional incorporation. This procedure, while in no way attempting to evaluate the quality of the work accomplished by the corporations, did seek to measure their level of activity in the four areas mentioned, and despite the relative character of these indicators generally proved to be a more fruitful endeavour than the preceding steps.

In general, the results obtained showed a low level of activity. Of the twenty-nine corporations studied, eleven had not taken action in any of the four areas chosen as indicators, and only two had taken initiatives in all four fields. When the results obtained are compared with such characteristics of professional corporations as legal status, year of incorporation, number of members, annual revenue, proportion of members in private practice, and clientele served, it becomes evident that the year of incorporation or, alternatively, the number of years a corporation has been in operation, was the characteristic most closely associated with the level of activity in protecting the public. One even discovers that the corporations are divided into two distinct groups corresponding to two significant periods in the history of the evolution of professional activity. First, corporations established more than fifty years ago are usually composed of members the majority of whom are in private practice. These corporations are exclusive practice corporations, have more revenue at their disposal, and are more actively engaged in protection of the public as measured by the four indicators: within this group of corporations, protection of the public appears to be favoured still further when the clientele served is for the most part made up of individuals. Second, corporations established more recently are usually composed of professionals who are not self-employed. These corporations are not exclusive practice corporations, have less revenue at their disposal, and do not carry on activities directed at protecting the public.

The mechanism of the professional corporation is thus less effective when extended to groups of persons who do not possess the characteristics of the older professions. In other words this mechanism has not been able over the years to adapt effectively to the evolution of social conditions and, more specifically, to the evolution of the manpower market. Before considering the extension of the professional corporation to new sectors of activity, it is therefore appropriate to review its origins and to study the factors which are at the root of its difficulties of adaptation, in view of the attraction that it continues to hold for the producers of services.

The activity of professional corporations viewed in an historical perspective
The professional corporations established in Quebec during the second half of the nineteenth century and at the beginning of the twentieth operated within an economic context founded on free enterprise. Producers of goods and services were often scattered among small-scale enterprises, and most professionals were in private practice, alone, autonomous, and isolated.

Generally speaking, the members of corporations established during this period worked over wide-ranging fields of general knowledge. Qualified manpower was scarce, the sum of knowledge was less than today's, and the compartmentalization of work was less pronounced. For each field of knowledge there existed a corresponding field of practice – medicine, dentistry, law, and so on – and each professional was able to offer services which covered the totality of his particular field. In this context, the establishment of professional corporations constituted a response to specific needs, as much for the professional as for the client: the need to identify the isolated professional with a homogeneous group, the need to standardize the services offered by independent professionals to clients who were not readily able to evaluate the quality of these services, and so on. Incorporation made it possible to stabilize, as it were, the distribution of professional services in a given sector while respecting at the same time the system of free enterprise. Mindful of defending the interests of their members, of advancing the cause of the profession, as well as of promoting the well-being of their clientele and of the public in general, these independent corporations constituted the only mechanism of control for the professions concerned. It appeared difficult to regulate otherwise the activities of independent producers practising individually and possessing monopolies over vast fields of knowledge. Thus it came about that the producers of services were delegated by the state the responsibility of safeguarding the interests of the consumers of these same services.

The rapid industrialization of Quebec society and the technological revolution brought about by the second world war considerably modified work conditions and manpower characteristics. Three phenomena in particular are worthy of note: the increasing proportion of salaried workers, the specialization of work activities resulting from the tremendous increase in the fields of knowledge, and state intervention in the production of essential services.

For a number of years now, the growing control of work activities by private and public enterprises has brought with it a gradual increase in the number of salaried employees in the qualified labour force. A great many members of professional corporations have become salaried workers. Because of this they are less isolated, less independent, often members of a union, and subject to formal and regular hierarchical control by their employers. The control exercised by professional corporations must be adjusted to these new conditions.

Moreover, professionals are less and less able today to claim to offer services which cover the entire range of a very wide field of knowledge. Their work is often fragmented and specialized. Manpower supervision is thus carried out more easily with these workers, called upon as they are increasingly to perform well-defined acts in specific circumstances according to proven methods. This narrowing of the fields of activity of skilled manpower facilitates the task of supervision in salaried areas and, in the opinion of the Office, modifies the role of professional corporations, given the steadily decreasing number of fields where an independent professional corporation constitutes the only control mechanism for professionals offering comprehensive services within a wide field of knowledge and practising their profession individually in private practice.

State intervention has become considerable in the area of professional services. The state is directly or indirectly the principal employer of professionals and the principal client of professionals in private practice. In addition, governments are able to pass legislation enabling them to regulate an occupation directly and can issue permits to those who engage in such activity. They can also pass various statutes of a more general nature which regulate the distribution of professional services in a more indirect manner. Consider, for example, the Quebec Act respecting Health Services and Social Services,[3] the Consumer Protection Act,[4] and the federal Combines Investigation Act.[5] Each of these Acts, consid-

3 Statutes of Quebec, 1971, C. 48
4 Statutes of Quebec, 1971, C. 7
5 Revised Statutes of Canada, 1970, C-23, amended by Statutes of Canada, 1974-5, C. 76. This amendment extended the application of this Act to the service sector.

ered separately, significantly reduces the expected contribution of professional corporatism to new sectors of activity. The simultaneous development of such restrictions over recent decades counsels great prudence with regard to the evaluation of the need for establishing new professional corporations.

THE POLICY OF THE OFFICE DES PROFESSIONS
WITH RESPECT TO THE DEVELOPMENT OF
PROFESSIONALISM IN QUEBEC

At the conclusion of its study, the Office des Professions arrived at the following policy with regard to the establishment of new professional corporations, the situation of existing corporations with reserved title, and the adaptation of professional corporatism to salaried areas.

Establishing new professional corporations
In the absence of data that could help clarify and render operational the general factors set down in Section 25 of the *Professional Code* concerning the establishment of a professional corporation, the Office intends to study one by one the requests received and, after discussions with the groups concerned, to evaluate in each case the appropriateness, in light of the criterion of protecting the public, of establishing a professional corporation or utilizing another type of regulation.

1 The conditions for granting professional self-regulation
In its evaluation the Office takes into account the fact that the conclusions of the study undertaken with respect to the corporations existing at the time of the adoption of the *Professional Code* indicate that those corporations which have the greater level of public protection activity have maintained, in various degrees, five distinct characteristics which can be grouped into two categories. The first category concerns the conditions of practice: (1) a high proportion of members in private practice, (2) a clientele composed mostly of individuals, and (3) a relatively vast field of knowledge. The second category concerns the conditions of operation of a corporation: (4) substantial financial resources and (5) a relatively high number of members.

The Office considers granting professional self-regulation only to groups that, in its opinion, possess these five characteristics. However, if there exists a serious risk of prejudice being caused to the public because of the professional acts of groups that, although in private practice and having a clientele of individuals, do not practise within a wide field of knowledge, the Office will direct such groups towards another form of regulation. In doing so it is not necessary for the Office to take into account the resources these groups have at their disposal. This type of regulation could take one or other of the following forms: regulation and periodic inspections carried out by a directly concerned government department or body; direct regulation by the Office des Professions; joint regulation by the Office and a government body, or by the Office and a professional corporation the competence of which appears adequate to the supervision of the activity in question.

The Office recognizes, however, that there might be exceptions to this general policy in cases where the members of a group seeking establishment as a professional corporation work within the field of activity of an existing corporation or in a related field of activity and possess training in large part equivalent to that of the members of that corporation. In circumstances such as these, the Office could consider it appropriate to encourage the integration of the members of these groups with the corporations in question.

2 The choice between reserved title and exclusive practice

The study conducted by the Office indicated that the exclusive right to practice of a profession increased the activity of a corporation in matters of protecting the public, provided that the corporation possessed the five characteristics mentioned earlier. Doubtless, these results could justify the Office's recommending in general the granting of exclusive rights to practice to groups which fulfil all the conditions for obtaining professional self-regulation. But the Office hesitates to adopt blindly such an attitude since the exclusive practice of a profession involves several major drawbacks. The granting of a field of practice to the members of a profession exclusively affords them total control of the market. The disadvantages for the public inherent in this situation are, as in the case of any monopoly, quite obvious.

Moreover, exclusive practice leads to increasing difficulties of application because within the field of knowledge occupied by one corporation new professions, with levels of training that often vary, are constantly developing. This situation leads to friction between the groups concerned, whether between professional corporations themselves or between incorporated and non-incorporated professions. Such difficulties can be unresolvable when it comes to specifying fields of practice. In this context the Office believes that the most realistic position consists in deciding for each group whether the advantages of a monopoly of practice, as far as the protection of the public is concerned, outweigh the foreseeable drawbacks. This evaluation obviously has to be specific to each group and its particular context of practice.

This policy, while recognizing that exclusive practice offers certain advantages in the matter of protection of the public, places its confidence above all in the future of the reserved title mechanism. The latter makes it possible to identify those persons who offer the best guarantees of competence in a given sector without involving such major drawbacks inherent in exclusive practice as the compartmentalization of specializations and the granting of total control of a market to a group of professionals. With these advantages in mind the Office studied the particular situation of existing professional corporations with reserved title.

The particular situation of
existing professional corporations with reserved title
Several of the seventeen professional corporations with reserved title which now exist under the *Professional Code* have requested transformation into exclusive practice corporations. Despite the difficulties involved in the utilization of the exclusive practice mechanism in sectors where professionals already benefit from it, these corporations with reserved title believe that it is impossible for them to exercise their role in protecting the public function efficiently because they are not able to control all persons practising the profession.

The Office does not share this point of view. It seems difficult to recommend such an extension of the exclusive practice mechanism, given all the consequences of granting such a monopoly. The Office is of the opinion rather that the reserved title mechanism can often constitute the most satisfactory means of controlling professional activities and that this will be even more the case in the future. The difficulties in carrying out their functions that dissatisfy the professional corporations with reserved title do not derive essentially from the fact that their members hold only the monopoly of a title. They result rather from the major changes which have occurred in the conditions of professional practice, notably, as mentioned earlier, the steady increase in the proportion of qualified manpower having salaried status, the compartmentalization of fields of knowledge, and the intervention of the state in the production of essential services.

In addition, the majority of corporations with reserved title do not command the resources necessary for the effective accomplishment of their tasks. In the opinion of the Office, the best way of correcting this situation would be to regroup the corporations with reserved title operating in the same field of activity or in related fields. Examples of possible regrouping can be drawn from the field of human relations – psychologists and vocational guidance counsellors – and from the field of accounting – certified general accountants and registered industrial accountants. Such regroupings would enable these corporations to obtain the human and financial resources required for the exercise of a protection of the public function and to work in a climate of harmony rather than in one of mistrust. It would also reduce the risks of confusion in the public mind as to the demarcation lines between their fields of practice.

Adapting professional incorporation to enterprises and institutions
To the Office it is clear that professional corporatism – a mechanism for self-regulation originally intended for independent producers – has at this time a challenge to meet in private enterprises as well as in public establishments or institutions. This problem concerns almost all of the corporations with reserved title as well as a great number of the exclusive practice corporations. Thus, the Office, desirous of implementing an Act – the *Professional Code* – which imposes the same obligations on all professional corporations, whatever the context of their members' work, will do everything in its power to facilitate the adaptation of professional corporatism to salaried areas. It will attempt to ensure the consolidation of the professional reform, the opening up of professional corporations to the public through the increased participation of directors named by the Office, and improvement of the quality of services offered by corporation members, by periodical review of their competence, by maintenance of a strict disciplinary procedure, and by exercise of appropriate control through the new legislation.

Moreover, the Office's interest in the implementation of the new professional legislation, particularly with regard to reserved professional titles and the application of disciplinary and professional inspection procedures in salaried areas, is taking concrete form in a number of studies currently being carried out. Upon their completion the Office intends, if appropriate, to recommend to the government legislative amendments enabling professional corporations to assume effectively their role in salaried employment contexts. In the fields more particularly related to private enterprise the Office intends to study the possibility of permitting the professional corporations in question to enforce standards to be respected by their members when such crucial questions as the quality of the products and services offered by the enterprise, the protection of the environment, and the safety of workers are involved. Of course, these interventions by professional corporations in salaried areas will have a better chance of succeeding if a certain collaboration on the part of employers and unions can be obtained. It is here that the greatest challenge to professionalism and the most important obstacle to its adaptation to' present working conditions is to be found. Without the collaboration of the employers and the unions, it will be more difficult to ensure the effectiveness of the disciplinary and professional inspection mechanisms provided for in these sectors.

If, following these efforts to adapt professional corporatism to salaried areas, clear progress in this respect is evident, the Office could reassess the necessity of obliging groups requesting professional self-regulation to observe the condition respecting private practice. In the absence of such progress, however, the Office would have to maintain this requirement, to question the self-regulation principle for certain existing corporations, whether those with exclusive practice or those with reserved title.

CAROLYN J. TUOHY and ALAN D. WOLFSON

Self-regulation: who qualifies?

In a society where self-development, self-expression, and self-actualization are taken as cultural goals, self-regulation has a faintly moralistic but nonetheless compelling ring. More pragmatically, in Canada and the United States, where federal anti-combines policies have sent many groups scurrying for protection under umbrellas of authority delegated to them by provincial and state governments, it is a hotly contested issue. Where is self-regulation appropriate?

In the first place, let us be clear about what it is that we are discussing. Self-regulatory bodies, such as the colleges of physicians and surgeons, the law societies, and the associations of professional engineers, are particular occupational groups organized for the purpose of establishing and maintaining certain standards of practice in their respective occupations and exercising regulatory power delegated by the state. Through their councils and committees, such groups admit to their memberships only those individuals who have attained these standards; they are charged with policing their individual members to ensure that such standards are maintained; and they may revoke, suspend, or otherwise alter the membership status of individuals who fail to do so. Such professional groups are granted the exclusive right to confer a particular title or designation, indicating that their members have been judged by their peers to have attained and maintained certain standards in their practices. This 'certification' may or may not be required by law in order to practice a particular skill or technique; where it is so required, it becomes a licence.

Self-regulatory status is a much-sought-after privilege, enhancing as it does both the political and the economic power of any occupational group. It is often achieved as the culmination of a political process of coalition and representation

Carolyn Tuohy is a member of the Department of Political Economy, University of Toronto; Alan Wolfson is a member of the Department of Health Administration, University of Toronto

before and within the institutions of public government. The question in this discussion, however, is not where or how self-regulation has been achieved but where it is appropriate. We are seeking principles upon which public policy toward the professions ought to be based.

The achievement of self-regulatory status may reflect the success of a political strategy before particular governments as much as or more than it reflects a functional necessity. We are unlikely, then, to uncover the normative principles of a sound public policy toward the professions by looking at the relationships between established professional groups and the state. A fresh look at these principles requires us at the outset to think in more abstract terms about where it is appropriate for the state to delegate some of its decision-making authority to professional groups. (For the purposes of this argument, we shall be making an important assumption: we shall assume the integrity of the institutions of the state. We shall assume, that is, that the state is not captured or open to capture by any particular set of interests. This assumption requires an abstraction from reality, of course, but it is an appropriate starting-point in a prescriptive piece such as this. One way to think about how the state *ought* to function is to think about how such an ideal state *would* function.)

Self-regulatory status is, as we have argued elsewhere,[1] one of the important dimensions of professionalism, and we cannot consider it apart from the question of what we mean by professionalism. It is important to be clear about our definition of professionalism because the term has become clouded in several ways. In the first place, it has come to connote devotion to the standards of competent craftsmanship and to the interests of a client above personal gain and has hence become 'a symbol of high-ranking among occupations.'[2] In the second place, academic studies of professionalism have tended to confuse rather than to clarify the definition of the term, since each academic discipline has taken a different focus. Sociologists have looked at professional careers and norms; economists have focused upon imperfect markets for professional services; and political scientists have been concerned with mechanisms and institutions of professional regulation.

To clear away this confusion of terminology we contend that professionalism is best defined in terms of the relationship between the providers and the consumers of a service. Professionalism does not refer, strictly speaking, to high levels of competence and altruism themselves. Rather it is a relationship established to ensure that specialized competence is brought to bear in making certain

1 Carolyn J. Tuohy and Alan D. Wolfson, 'The political economy of professionalism: a perspective,' in *Four Aspects of Professionalism*, Consumer Research Council, Department of Consumer and Corporate Affairs (Ottawa, 1976) pp. 41-86

2 E.H. Hughes, 'The professions and society,' *Canadian Journal of Economics and Political Science*, 6, No. 1 (February 1960)

decisions and to ensure that the client's interests are fully protected in the making of these decisions. It is, in other words, an agency relationship. The essence of the professional role lies in the exercise of decision-making authority, based upon specialized knowledge, on behalf of a client. The client delegates to a professional the authority to bring specialized knowledge to bear in making practical decisions on the client's behalf and in the client's interest. The professional, in short, acts as his client's agent.

The uniqueness of professional agency relationships lies in the fact that they exist at two levels: between the individual professional and his client, and between the professional group and the state. It is this latter relationship which forms the basis of self-regulation. The professional group, in effect, acts as the agent of the state in regulating its own members. The state delegates decision-making authority to the professional group, on condition that this authority be exercised in the public interest. The professional group is charged with acting as the state would act, given the relevant information and expertise.

Professionalism, then, is one way of controlling the application of specialized knowledge. It is not the only such mechanism. One might rely upon the market to protect the public interest in the application of specialized knowledge where that knowledge is embodied in a product whose quality can be judged by the consumer, and where consumer-producer relations have no significant effects on third parties – the market for watches is an example. Where specialized knowledge can be routinized and embodied in a set of specific rules, one can rely upon bureaucratic supervision as a mechanism of control – as in the case of safety inspectors. Professionalism, as we shall argue below, is a way of controlling another type of specialized knowledge. It is knowledge whose application requires the exercise of considerable discretion on the part of the decision-maker. Furthermore, it is knowledge which is embodied in a service whose quality cannot be judged by the consumer.

When are professional relationships appropriate? In particular, when is it appropriate for the state to establish an agency relationship with a professional group? The answer to this question is a matter of judgment in particular cases, and we do not intend to offer hard and fast criteria. What we will attempt to do in the following discussion is no more (and no less) than to suggest the questions which must be addressed in forming a judgment about the appropriateness of self-regulation.

AGENCY RELATIONSHIPS BETWEEN PRACTITIONERS AND CLIENTS

Agency relationships are established at the group/state level and at the practitioner/client level for analogous reasons. Let us consider first the establishment of agency relationships at the practitioner/client level.

It is rational for the individual consumer to seek a professional agent to protect his interest in making certain types of decisions – those requiring information that is costly to obtain and where mistakes are costly. Such decisions as those relating to the treatment of illnesses or the defence of legal rights require specialized knowledge and relate to what one sociologist has called 'vital practical affairs.'[3] In other words, professional relationships are appropriately established where the costs of access to information and the costs of error are high. By transferring decision-making authority to a professional agent in such circumstances the client reduces the likelihood that costly errors will be made, without having to acquire costly information himself.

The establishment of an agency relationship involves not only the transfer of decision-making authority; it also means that the professional agent assumes the responsibility for promoting only the client's interests. So long as the client himself is the decision-maker, he promotes his own interests naturally; no one has to assume this 'responsibility.' Once the decision-making function is removed from the client, in this case because of an information gap, the interests of the client will be promoted only in so far as the new decision-maker assumes this responsibility. The agency relationship is in fact established to ensure this transference of the client's interests to the new professional decision-maker.[4]

This, then, is what we mean by an individual agency relationship: a relationship in which an individual provider of services assumes the responsibility for acting on his client's behalf as his client would act, given the same expertise.

The client establishes an agency relationship to reduce his own costs of information and error; but he must also be aware that he may incur costs to the extent that this agency relationship functions imperfectly. His agent may misperceive the client's interests, or may act so as to promote his own private interests at the client's expense. How can the client be assured that his agent will fulfil his responsibilities? How is trust between client and agent established? These are fundamental questions, but they must be held in abeyance until we have given some consideration to agency relationships between groups and the state.

AGENCY RELATIONSHIPS
BETWEEN GROUPS AND THE STATE

When ought the state to establish an agency relationship with an occupational group for the purpose of regulating that occupation? In the first place, of course,

3 Morris Cogan, 'The problem of defining a profession,' *The Annals of The American Academy of Political and Social Science*, 297 (January 1955)
4 Tuohy and Wolfson, 'The political economy of professionalism,' p. 49

it must determine whether any form of regulation is necessary. Are there interests which are significantly affected by the transactions between practitioners and their clients or employers which are not protected within the practitioner-client or practitioner-employer relationship in the absence of state intervention? If so, the state must determine the appropriate mode of intervention for the protection of these interests, be they those of clients, practitioners, employers, or third parties. Regulation is not the only way of protecting such interests: the state also has at its disposal judicial instruments, such as the definition of civil liability, and fiscal instruments such as subsidies for training or service, which may be preferable to or supplementary to regulation. The choice of the appropriate mix of these policies is a complex matter of judgment, requiring an assessment of the nature of the unprotected interests and the organization of the industry in question, and it is a vast topic beyond the scope of this paper. What we wish to consider are the conditions under which it is appropriate for the state, having judged that some form of regulation is necessary, to delegate regulatory authority to an occupational group.

Self-regulation, as we have noted, implies an agency relationship between the professional group and the state and is appropriate under conditions analogous to those which influence an individual consumer in deciding to establish an agency relationship with an individual producer. The state, like the individual consumer, wishes to choose that option which maximizes the benefits subject to cost constraints. But, again like the individual consumer, the state may have no measure of the benefits of the service provided. Where this fundamental ignorance with regard to benefits prevails, the state's decision tends to turn upon estimates of cost – the costs of the information upon which decisions must be based, the costs of enforcing those decisions once taken, and the probable costs of error in making these decisions without sufficient knowledge. Where delegation of regulatory authority is seen as reducing any of these types of cost without an offsetting increase in the others, it is the preferred option.

Let us consider the costs of information. Where the distinctive competence of a group consists in the practical application of a specific body of knowledge, the regulation of that service activity requires, among other things, access to that body of knowledge. And the state may perceive the costs of that access to be high for a number of reasons. In particular, access is seen to be costly to the extent that the body of knowledge in question is *systematic*, involving the relationships among the parts of a system (be it a human body, a system of law, or a physical structure). The state may be persuaded that those who perform and who regulate the performance of acts which affect one part of this system must be aware of the system-wide implications of those acts, and hence that both practitioners and regulators must have a grasp of the entire large and complex body of knowledge. Mastery of such a knowledge base, however, is costly, requiring a long and expensive training.

The state may, of course, be prepared to pay the costs of hiring 'experts' from the group to be regulated. But the delegation of decision-making authority to a professional group may allow the state to reduce not only its information costs but also the costs of monitoring individual practices. Particularly where individual practitioners operate in many scattered private practices, these costs are likely to be high. The professional group, operating as an agent of the state, may be a more efficient mechanism of enforcement than the state itself. When members of the group experience a common extensive training process, required for the mastery of a specialized knowledge base, they are likely to develop strong allegiances to the group and its norms, and the group can call upon these allegiances in achieving compliance.

Finally, as at the individual level, delegation of decision-making authority is also appropriate where the costs of error are high. The more closely the service in question touches upon the 'vital practical affairs of man,' the more important it is that errors not be made in the regulation of that service. To regulate in ingorance of the specialized knowledge base of service may result in very costly errors; in such cases the state cannot risk acting without access to specialized expertise.

The information, error, and enforcement costs reduced by delegation, then, must be weighed in the state's judgment, but they constitute only one side of the balance. Like the individual client, the state must consider not only the costs *reduced* by delegating decision-making authority, but also the potential costs *incurred* through imperfections in the agency relationship. The profession may misperceive the interests which the state is seeking to protect, or it may unduly promote its own private interests in making decisions. For example, the profession may define its exclusive scope of practice more broadly than is warranted by its specialized knowledge base and inhibit a rational and cost-effective allocation of functions in its sphere. It may maintain the price of professional services at artificially high levels. It may police individual agency relationships so as to protect only the consumer interest in quality, while ignoring other dimensions of the consumer interest. And it may focus upon individual relationships to the neglect of the broader implications of its regulatory policy for the distribution of professional services.

An appreciation of the potential costs of delegation requires an understanding of the decision-making process within an agency relationship, and the biases of which it is susceptible. In this context, the interests, ideology, and industrial organization of the occupational group must be considered. We have speculated at greater length about these factors elsewhere;[5] let us simply note here that the state must identify the potential costs of delegating authority and must establish self-regulatory structures only where they can be designed to reduce these potential costs to the point where they are outweighed by the advantages of self-regulation. Indeed, in the design of these structures there is no sharp dichotomy between direct regulation by the state and self-regulation by the group. Nominees of the state may participate in the decision-making processes of the group, and vice versa. The state may review more or less closely the outcomes of these procedures. We can say, however, that a group-state agency relationship exists where regulatory authority is delegated to a body (i) constituted separately from the administrative apparatus of the state, (ii) composed primarily of representatives of the occupational group, and (iii) charged with the responsibility of acting as the state would act, given similar information and expertise. The specific constitution of such a body, and the degree of discretion it is allowed, are completely matters of judgment which involve the weighing of the costs of information, error, and enforcement against the risk of imperfect agents.

THE INTERDEPENDENCE OF AGENCY RELATIONSHIPS

Agency relationships at the group/state and the practitioner/client level are established for analogous reasons; they are also mutually reinforcing. The existence of agency relationships at one level makes it more likely that they will exist at the other; and the character of the relationships at each level shapes their character at the other.

Why does the existence of agency relationships at the practitioner/client level make it more likely that they will exist at the group/state level? In the first place, these relationships are likely to require some form of regulation, to ensure the protection of the consumer interest. In some sectors of the economy we rely upon the operation of the market to ensure that the consumer gets what he wants from the producer. But we cannot assume that the consumer of professional services is protected against unethical or incompetent 'agents' by his ability to seek another source of service if he is dissatisfied. The market is an effective mechanism for protecting consumer interests only in so far as it is competitive. And markets are competitive only in so far as, first, there is good information available to all about the nature of commodities and their prices (in particular, the consumer must be well enough informed to be able to judge the

5 We have analysed these problems in the functioning of agency relationships in more detail ibid, pp. 62-6, 68-71, 77-86.

value that particular goods or services hold for him) and, second, there are large numbers of producers and consumers, each of whom makes his decisions independently.

In professional markets, neither of these conditions exists. They cannot exist because of the very nature of the specialized knowledge in which professionalism is grounded. The consumer lacks the information with which he might evaluate professional services. The professional knowledge base may be so complex that the consumer is incapable of judging the skill with which the professional applies it. The consequences of the professional's decision may provide an ultimate test of his competence – a surgical operation may prove to have been necessary or unnecessary; a contract may or may not be legally enforceable; a structure may or may not withstand stress – but, as we have noted, the costs of error in these cases are so high that the consumer cannot afford to wait for such an ultimate test of competence.

The nature of professional knowledge affects not only the consumer's ability to evaluate service but also the relationships among the providers themselves. As we noted above, the mastery of a complex and specialized body of knowledge requires a long and intensive training process, during which the individual professional develops a strong allegiance to the professional group. Furthermore, a grasp of a very complex knowledge base may be beyond the ability of any one provider and may require the individual professional in practice to tap the expertise of his colleagues through a process of consultation, collaboration, and referral. The more specialized and complex the knowledge base of a professional group, then, the less likely it is that the decisions of individual providers will be taken independently of group influence.

The prevalence of individual agency relationships is therefore likely to mean that some form of regulation is necessary. It also increases the likelihood that self-regulation is the appropriate *form* of regulation. One reason for this is the fact that both the state and individual consumers must respond to analogous costs of information and error in deciding whether or not to establish agency relationships. But, even further, the existence of individual agency relationships themselves must affect the state's decision. The prevalence of individual agency relationships increases the costs of monitoring individual practices and of enforcing standards of practice. The exercise of discretionary decision-making authority by individual practitioners is by its very nature difficult to police. Moreover, to the extent that the individual locus of responsibility has permitted the development of numerous small-scale practices, the apparatus of surveillance needs to be relatively more complex, cumbersome, and costly.

Furthermore, the professional ideology associated with the performance of agency functions at the individual level is likely to make the professional group a more efficient vehicle for the enforcement of standards. On the one hand this professional ideology, inculcated during a lengthy training process, elevates the importance of group allegiance and reduces the costs of enforcement by the professional group. On the other hand it is an ideology which contains strong elements of suspicion and hostility toward bureaucratic mechanisms and particularly toward governmental bureaucracy. This hostility appears to derive at least in part from the nature of the professional's agency function, which involves the application of specialized knowledge to individual cases. In order to exercise discretion in individual cases, professionals hold that their judgment must be guided only by the laws of their respective discipline and the needs of their clients, and not by administrative rules or political exigencies. Recent technological, political, and economic changes are disrupting this professional ideological consensus; nonetheless, professional suspicion of bureaucratic and governmental mechanisms remains widespread.

In the face of such hostility, governmental agencies might have to increase continually the tightness of their surveillance of professional activity and the coerciveness of their measures of enforcement in order to wield their regulatory powers effectively. The enforcement of regulations may be much more cost-effective if the state recognizes the importance of 'professional autonomy' and delegates authority to the group itself. By pursuing the latter course, it may decrease the costs of achieving compliance by appealing to the positive values of self-discipline and peer review and by de-emphasizing state authority and coercion.[6]

The regulation of agency relationships at the individual level, then, is likely to require the establishment of a group/state agency relationship. Conversely, the establishment of an agency relationship at the group level is likely to encourage individuals to establish agency relationships. It is a signal to individuals that the state considers the field of practice important enough, the members of the group expert enough, and the risks of biases or flaws in the agency relationship low enough to warrant the delegation of authority. In the simplest terms, in the terms in which it is likely to be perceived by the citizens of our 'ideal' state, self-regulatory status is a symbol of the trustworthiness of a professional group, as judged by the state, and will shape the way in which consumers deal with individual practitioners.

Indeed, what is notable about trust in professional contexts is that its existence at one level reinforces its establishment at the other. Only when there is evidence at the group level that the profession takes seriously and honours its responsibilities to the state can the individual client rely upon the profession to

6 Ibid, pp. 60, 64-5

police its members and hence to enforce individual agency relationships. Conversely, the maintenance of trust at the group level is dependent upon a general acceptance of the trustworthiness of practitioners by their clients. When individual trust relationships break down, the ability of the profession as a whole to maintain a trust relationship with the state is seriously compromised. And to the extent that trust is diminished in the group/state agency relationship, the state will allow the group less discretion in the performance of its agency function: it will more tightly circumscribe the powers of the professional group and will more closely monitor its performance. In the extreme case, the breakdown of trust may lead to abandonment of the agency relationship altogether, and the assumption of regulatory powers directly by the state.

Our argument has placed considerable emphasis upon the interdependencies between agency relationships at different levels. Nonetheless, we do not consider the prevalence of individual agency relationships to be either a necessary or a sufficient condition for the establishment of a self-regulatory system. Even where little or no delegation of authority from individual consumers to practitioners occurs, regulation may be necessary to protect third-party interests; furthermore, the costs of information, enforcement, and error at the state level may argue for the delegation of regulatory authority by the state. The case of aerospace engineering may be relevant here. Conversely, where enforcement costs are relatively low and risks of bias in the group/state agency relationship relatively high (for example, in heavily concentrated service industries), the balance of cost considerations may weigh against the delegation of regulatory authority by the state, even in the face of widespread agency relationships at the individual level. The securities industry is a case in point. We would not consider occupations involved in agency relationships at only one level to be fully 'professional' – but that is a matter of definition and not of public policy. From the standpoint of public policy, the importance of considering individual agency relationships in the context of making decisions about the establishment of a group/state agency relationships lies in the probabilistic argument we have advanced: the existence of agency relationships at one level increases the likelihood that they will be established at the other. In deciding the appropriateness of a self-regulatory system, the state ought to consider not only the regulatory requirements of individual agency relationships but also the symbolic effect of the regulatory system upon those relationships.

CONCLUSION

The delegation of regulatory authority is one of a number of policy options available to the state for controlling the application of specialized knowledge. In making a judgment about the degree to which decision-making authority should be delegated and the scope of the delegated authority, the state must consider the following questions: Are there unprotected interests which are significantly affected by the transactions between individual practitioners and their clients or employers which require that these transactions be regulated in some way? And can the state reduce the net costs of information, error, and enforcement in the regulatory process by delegating regulatory authority to the professional group? We have argued that these conditions are most likely to obtain where agency relationships between individual practitioners and their clients prevail. Our argument has been cast at a high level of abstraction, but public policy needs to be informed by empirical data as well as by a theoretical perspective. In this context, we refer the reader to the paper by René Dussault in this volume. Although his analysis proceeds from an empirical base and ours from theoretical propositions, we feel that our approaches are mutually informative.

In its recent study, the Quebec Professions Board identified a number of programs which it considered to be indicators of public-interested activity on the part of professional bodies. It found that older professions, with a high proportion of their members in private practice and a broad base of specialized knowledge, were most likely, given the appropriate resources, to undertake such activities. These findings are quite consistent with what we have argued in this paper. They can be interpreted to mean that where group/state agency relationships have been established and have become stable over time, they are likely to function well. Each of the variables associated with public-interested activity in the Quebec study points to the existence of one of the conditions which we consider to warrant the establishment of agency relationships. Where private practice and individual clients are prevalent it is more likely that individual professionals assume responsibility for promoting their clients' interests – in other words, it is more likely that individual agency relationships exist. A broad scope of practice suggests that these relationships have been established to overcome information costs. Furthermore, age, to the extent that it increases the cohesiveness of group identity and ideology, is likely to increase enforcement costs to the state and to make the professional group a more efficient mechanism of enforcement.

Although the empirical findings of the Quebec study are consistent with our model of professional relationships, they cannot be the only guides to public policy. It is not the prevalence of private practice and individual clients and the breadth of the base of specialized knowledge per se which warrant the delegation of self-regulatory authority to professional groups, but rather the costs of information, error, and enforcement, and the likelihood of bias in professional relationships. Admittedly, these criteria are not easily applied as administrative guidelines in particular cases: their application requires the exercise of judgment on the part of policy-makers and is less politically defensible than the application of hard-and-fast rules. But in an area as complex as professional policy the exercise of judgment is unavoidable. Our model is an attempt to inform that judgment, to suggest the questions to be asked and the types of information to be gathered.

We wish to make two final comments regarding the future development of public policy toward the professions. The first is to note the importance of establishing bases of data regarding the costs of information, error, and enforcement as well as the costs of monopoly in various professional markets. Reliable indicators of these costs must be developed. The second is to emphasize the importance of addressing the question of professionalism in the context of large-scale enterprise. This is the question implicit in the Quebec Board's concern with the development of policy toward salaried personnel claiming professional status. The question is how to control the application of specialized knowledge by personnel who operate in quasi-professional and quasi-bureaucratic relationships. We are speaking of personnel whose individual responsibility to clients is remote, who are accountable to upper levels of a corporate hierarchy, but whose hierarchical superiors delegate considerable decision-making authority to them by virtue of their specialized expertise.

We need, then, to develop a new model, a new way of controlling specialized knowledge in large-scale enterprise, which is neither entirely professional nor entirely bureaucratic. It may be that we should be developing agency relationships at the level of the enterprise. We may have to resurrect and sharpen the concept of corporate responsibility, a task which will require an understanding of the structures of powers and incentives faced by specialized personnel in corporate enterprise.

In summary, the development of public policy toward the professions in the future will require an empirical understanding of the functioning of agency relationships at the individual and the state level, and a new approach to the control of specialized personnel in large-scale enterprise. Quebec has shown itself willing to devote resources to each of these endeavours. Other Canadian governments must join the effort.

PROFESSIONAL EDUCATION

D.T. WRIGHT

The objectives of professional education

It is impossible to consider the professions and public policy without at the same considering the role of education. Indeed, the very closeness of relationships between formal post-secondary educational certification and professional licensure seems to make the one scarcely separable from the other. My concerns arise from the rigidities and potential abuses in such relationships.

It is necessary, at the outset, to distinguish between certification and licensure. In our society we have tended to attach these words to societal institutions and ascribe to them functions based on these institutions. Thus certification becomes a function of education institutions and licensure one of professional organizations.

In his essay on occupational licensure Milton Friedman distinguishes three levels of control.[1] The first is registration, an enumeration. The second, certification, is explained as follows: an 'agency may certify that an individual has certain skills but may not prevent, in any way, the practice of any occupation using these skills by people who do not have such a certificate.' Licensing is defined as 'an arrangement under which one must obtain a license from a recognized authority in order to engage in the occupation.'

Not too long ago most professions examined candidates directly, independent of educational experience and institutions. Individuals could qualify through various forms of apprenticeship to licensed practitioners. Although university programs were developed in many professional areas, it was possible in most professions until recently to become licensed without having to participate in formal

Deputy secretary for social development, Province of Ontario; formerly chairman of the Commission on Post-Secondary Education, Ontario

1 'Occupational licensure,' in *Capitalism and Freedom* (Chicago: University of Chicago Press, 1962) 144-5

education beyond the school level. Candidates for professional licensure in engineering and architecture still have the right to sit examinations set by the professional associations. Few do. In law, the training/apprenticeship system in Ontario was closely controlled by the Law Society, and university degrees in law were not fully acknowledged until 1957. While study in a university faculty has been an essential requirement in medicine and in dentistry, these professions have maintained their own independent licensing examinations. For professional licensure in chartered accountancy, a field for which the development of directly related university degree programs has lagged, a degree, *any* degree, became a prerequisite to the writing of professional examinations only in 1971.

The tendency to depend primarily or entirely on educational certification as a basis for professional licensure has increased the costs in time and money of becoming qualified to practise. There has been a trend as well to lengthening of courses of study. This tendency reflects the difficulty of measuring outcomes or outputs and the practice of accepting inputs as a proxy – so that the cost of a program, or the number of months or years of study, become measures of utility. More, by definition, is better. This practice is of course strongly inflationary. And it causes both direct and opportunity costs to be increased still further.

The developments just outlined appear to many people, of course, to be synonymous with 'higher standards' and therefore desirable. Nor can one deny the value of linking the details of professional practice to scientifically-based principles. But the real benefits and costs must be carefully identified. What really matters is competency, and we must achieve it efficiently. Where the process denies competency or protects incompetency or is unnecessarily expensive, the whole society loses. The 'control' function of licensure and the inhibition or denial of competition have attracted many criticisms. Perhaps the most incisive of these is that of Milton Friedman, who attacks licensure on the twin grounds of economic inefficiency and infringement of freedom in *Capitalism and Freedom*.[2] Friedman argues that present systems infringe on the freedom both of those who wish to purchase or consume services and of those who would wish to provide them. He states that licensure, by limiting entry to a profession, establishes a monopoly position in which producer interests inevitably prevail over the interests of consumers. Further, heavy economic and social costs are incurred when individuals who want to practise are prevented, and when the public is deprived of such, presumably less costly, services. Such arguments may appear to us to be unreasonably radical (radically conservative that is). But it is of compelling interest to us in Canada to note that in the United States today a powerful and apparently general trend in the direction of deregulation is evident.

2 Ibid

If, as appears most likely, this produces improvements in efficiency and productivity, lower prices, and the like, then the impact on Canada, where trends still appear to be strongly in favour of further regulation and additional government intervention generally in the economy, is bound to be powerful.

In the 1960s there appeared to be a consensus that equal opportunity could be obtained through education and that education provided the kind of social escalator that benefited talent and endeavour. Broadening of access to post-secondary education became one of the most important social goals for Canada. And however we may interpret the results, it must be acknowledged that a considerable democratization of access to education stands as a major social achievement of the past twenty years.

In the process, the role of a general or liberal education has been transformed. The rhetoric of convocation addresses has always held that the primary benefit of a university education (particularly in the liberal studies) lay in the opportunity it provided for learning. But until the late 1960s a BA actually guaranteed, at the very least, a job as a teacher. In the last few years, however, the rhetoric has become the reality: a BA is now more a mark of learning than a ticket to a job. Some of my university friends see considerable merit in this development: it is tending to sort out those who wish to learn from those who were just seeking a piece of paper. While all of this may induce dismay, especially amongst recent graduates, in fact it must be acknowledged as the inevitable consequence of recent social and educational policy.

The fact that the resulting mass access to higher education has deprived those who graduate of the near-certain benefits of elite status once associated with university graduation should not be a matter for surprise. The benefit of a status that has become common is bound to be less than when it was more rare.

While the education system generally has become more accessible, the same is not generally true of the professional faculties. Numbers gaining entry to the professions have not increased nearly as rapidly as total university enrolment or graduations. Pressure for entry has become exceedingly strong, even in those areas such as law and engineering where there have been the largest increases in the number of places available. With alternative routes of access to professional licensure now more or less closed the dangers of rigidity are of course greater. As well as the fundamental issues identified by Friedman, a particularly important social issue that has also arisen is that of determining who wins entry to professional faculties in the universities.

Michael Young intended *The Rise of the Meritocracy* (Thames and Hudson, 1968) to be a satire. But it has come to pass that the narrow definition of merit reflected in competitive entry to programs leading to professional licensure has become a principal determinant of status in our society. We must ask whether this will be appropriate or sufficient for the conditions with which our society must cope in the future. Canada has come to its present strength largely through the opportunities provided in a flexible individualistic society with a good deal of the pioneer/frontier spirit that characterized the United States. Will Canada continue to be able to cope, let alone thrive, with an increasingly bureaucratized, even sclerotic, structure?

What is most alarming is the critical lack of adaptability evident in these rather vital components of our social system. The proponents of what some call sociobiology suggest that we could learn much by examining the behaviour of other organisms. And in most biological systems the organisms unable to adapt to continuously changing conditions are those most likely to perish. Of course the reason for the invention of the guild was the desire for protection, and today's practices, in which 'closed' systems prevail in many parts of the labour market reflect the same, understandable, human need. The danger arises of course because such forms of protection are of little value if they in turn weaken the larger society.

To overcome this rigidity and inertia it is necessary to have educational and professional systems reflect the character of the particular society of which they are parts, and necessary especially to redesign those systems in the image of the contemporary social environment. In this respect we are still perhaps more fortunate than those societies with longer histories. We are less fettered by the inertia of tradition. And we should use that accident of history to our advantage. We should look to those motivations of our pioneers that led them to bring new approaches to new problems. The steel plough had to be invented before the North American prairies fell to agriculture. What is to be sought, then, is to develop systems suited to the needs of our society rather than to continue adapting procedures inherited from other times and other ways of life.

What general features might such systems have? First and foremost, professions would probably be clustered in broader groupings than is now the case. The case for clustering rather than ranking is that democratization of professional groups is as essential to the success of a new model as was the democratization of educational access to our economy in the sixties. One might expect a greater range of services offered by a broader range of paraprofessionals. The right of the individual citizen to choose either to work or to engage in education at any time of life without incurring penalties for non-conformity would be safeguarded. Thus, education would be a throughway rather than a terminus. Multientry/multiexit professional education groupings would allow individuals to leave formal education for work and to re-enter without penalty. Individuals without high levels of formal schooling who had learned on the job would be able to challenge the systems for entry by licensure through competency testing.

The systems, then, would be adapted to increase our capacity to handle social needs by encouraging the development of the highest competency without unduly increasing the cost of providing professional care. In short, what is to be sought from such social innovation is the optimum competency/cost/efficiency outcome for our own, particular, Canadian society.

PHILIP SLAYTON

Professional education and the consumer interest: a framework for inquiry

This essay has a modest purpose. It suggests that traditional professional education has a narrow basis. It outlines some adverse consequences of viewing the purpose of professional education in simple terms. I sketch the skeleton of an alternative approach that might avoid some of the disadvantages of the present system. Finally, the beginning of a research agenda is proposed, an agenda intended to facilitate sound evaluation of existing professional education programs and detailed development of alternatives.

What is the scope of a discussion about professional education? Indeed, what occupations can rightfully be described as 'professions?' The definitional question has tantalized many commentators. Elaborate lists of professional 'attributes' have been compiled.[1] Fierce battles have been fought over whether or not any given occupation is entitled to be called a profession.

I will avoid this particular controversy. In the main, the debate seems to reflect a political process – the attempt of organized occupational groups to win statutory powers of self-regulation.[2] Discussions of 'professionalization,' or ela-

Faculty of Law, University of Western Ontario. This essay is based on a paper of the same title published in 1977 by the Consumer Research Council, Government of Canada. The author is grateful for the criticism and advice of Michael Trebilcock, Faculty of Law, and Carolyn Tuohy, Department of Political Economy, University of Toronto.

1 See, for example, Wilbert E. Moore, *The Professions: Roles and Rules* (New York: Russell Sage, 1970), chapter 1; Government of the United Kingdom, Committee on Legal Education, *Report* (London: HMSO, 1971), 35; Edgar H. Schein and Diane W. Kommers, *Professional Education* (New York: McGraw-Hill, 1972), 8-9; Office des Profession du Québec, *L'évolution du professionnalisme au Québec* (Québec: Office des Professions, 1976).

2 See Howard M. Vollmer and Donald L. Mills, eds, *Professionalization* (Englewood Cliffs, NJ: Prentice Hall, 1966), and Jethro K. Lieberman, *The Tyranny of the Experts* (New York: Walker, 1970).

borate semantic exercises, interesting as they may be, are outside my self-imposed jurisdiction.

I am concerned here with occupations that exhibit three characteristics. First, they have powers of self-regulation granted by statute. Second, they provide a service to the community that is in widespread demand and is generally regarded as in some way essential. Third, a prerequisite to entering the occupation is a lengthy education, largely theoretical but often with a practical component as well. For my purposes these three occupational attributes are particularly important. The granting of powers by statute suggests a commensurate responsibility to exercise those powers for the benefit of the community. The providing of an essential service makes the occupation that does so of interest and concern to every citizen. And the educational requirement for entry is the subject of my essay: how well attuned is it to the particular responsibilities of the occupation in question?

Many so-called professions are excluded by these criteria. Chiropractors and hearing-aid acousticians,[3] for example, likely do not meet either the service or educational requirements. Research chemists or professors of classics are generally not members of statutorily recognized professions and may not provide services widely acknowledged as essential. And so on. The occupations that appear most interesting in light of the criteria are those that are often considered the 'traditional' professions – preeminently law and medicine, and to a lesser extent occupations such as architecture, engineering, dentistry, accountancy, and the rest.

The traditional professions are often described as the 'learned professions.' I have noted already that the occupations I am discussing, as they are presently organized, require much education. Generally the first formal step towards becoming a professional is pursuing theoretical studies at a post-secondary institution.[4] These studies may be preceded by or include some form of general liberal education, because many professions believe, and reflect the belief in their entrance requirements, that a 'good' professional must be a humanitarian and perhaps a humanist, as well as a 'scientist,' and thus must have a liberal, as well as a professional, education. Theoretical training transforming the recipient into a man of learning is normally followed by a period of practical training or apprenticeship. The reason is that most people trained for a profession subsequently engage in its practice, and it is generally thought that to practise medicine, law, or whatever, a purely theoretical training is insufficient.

---

3 In Quebec, they are 'professionals' by virtue of s.1(c) and Schedule I, s.1(a) of the *Professional Code*, S.Q. 1973, c.43.

4 In some countries at some times no formal training at all was required for some professions. In the United States, for example, it was not until the end of the nineteenth century that physicians and lawyers normally received a theoretical education.

The contemporary structure of professional education is affected by widely-accepted notions about the working environment the professional will enter once trained. Most members of the traditional professions still regard typical professional practice as solo practice or practice in a small partnership, and expect to be paid on a fee-for-service basis by a number of individual clients.[5] They still believe – notwithstanding a liberal pre-professional education – that the professional can think and act autonomously, without relating to or working with professionals of a different sort. These notions prevail even though, as Schein and Kommers point out, 'the employment settings of most professionals have shifted dramatically away from the single-practitioner model toward corporate employment.'[6] They prevail though, as Schein and Kommers note also, the needs of society appear to be changing rapidly, and rapidly changing needs require an interdisciplinary problem-solving approach.[7]

I suggest that this approach to professional education leads to an inflexible model unable to respond to changing circumstances and important pressures – what might be called the 'static paradigm.'[8] An extensive preliminary – generally liberal – education is required. A theoretical professional education, normally a university education, follows. Finally, the practical knowledge and techniques necessary for interpreting and applying theory so that a profession can be practised are acquired through an apprenticeship of some kind. Despite some

5 That doctors still think this way is strikingly illustrated in articles by Peter Banks MD ('Stick it on the mantlepiece') and M.A. Baltzan MD ('The cake is bottom-heavy') in (1975) 112 *Canadian Medical Association Journal* 656-8. Banks and Baltzan are replying to Sidney S. Lee MD and Lawrence M. Butler, 'Paying the doctor: the three-layered cake revisited' (1975) 112 *C.M.A. Journal* 642.

6 Supra n.1 at 15

7 Many others have noted the developments described by Schein and Kommers. See, for example, Sir Alexander Carr-Saunders, 'Metropolitan conditions and traditional professional relationships,' in Robert Moore Fisher, ed, *The Metropolis in Modern Life* (New York: Doubleday, 1955).

8 Here I am indebted to Thomas Kuhn. In his brilliant book *The Structure of Scientific Revolutions*, 2d edn (Chicago: University of Chicago Press, 1970), Kuhn has advanced the nature of scientific education as one explanation of the priority of paradigms in science. He writes: 'Scientists ... never learn concepts, laws, and theories in the abstract and by themselves. Instead, these intellectual tools are from the start encountered in a historically and pedagogically prior unit that displays them with and through their applications' (46). The consequence of the priority of paradigms is that normal science is a 'mopping-up' operation: 'Closely examined, whether historically or in the contemporary laboratory, that enterprise [normal science] seems an attempt to force nature into the preformed and relatively inflexible box that the paradigm supplies' (24). Kuhn is concerned with what might be termed the internal paradigm, corresponding roughly to scientific curricula. But clearly the internal paradigm is in part a function of what one might describe as the external paradigm – the pattern of scientific education.

attempts at liberal education, the process tends to be autonomous; that is, reference is to a finite and indentifiable body of knowledge and collection of techniques peculiar to the profession in question. And all is designed, in the main, to offer success in self-employment.

What are the consequences of this paradigm of professional education for the nature, quality, and quantity of professional services provided the consumer?

The inflexible view that a profession is learned – that its practice requires liberal education followed by extensive training in a body of theoretical knowledge – may result in ignorance of, and lack of interest in, practical low-grade professional activity;[9] indeed, professionals may consider the provision of such services as beneath them (although the view that a profession is an occupation, requiring something akin to an apprenticeship, may in some measure mitigate these effects). The notion that a professional is typically self-employed will likely strongly encourage a professional to offer services that provide a good financial return and will stimulate an entrepreneurial frame of mind. (One should note that there is nothing inherently undesirable about being entrepreneurial, and that the market for professional services is in some degree regulated by government, which may limit the entrepreneurial instincts of professionals.) Finally, the presumption of intellectual autonomy may well produce professionals who are unable or unwilling to engage in certain kinds of work (requiring interdisciplinary skills or sympathies) and whose vision may be limited in many respects.

What is the 'consumer interest' in professional services? The notion of consumer interest, although difficult as a broad concept, has some clarity here. The general problem that consumers are also producers, a state allegedly producing psychological 'aberrations,'[10] is of little relevance to professional services. First, relatively few people are engaged in providing these services. Second, the economic machinery to which most consumers are probably committed is not obviously the machinery providing professional services. Some professions exhibit some 'free enterprise' characteristics – for example, solo practice and fee-for-service – but in general the structure of the professions and the mechanism for delivery is sui generis. The consumer clearly stands apart from those who provide the service he seeks.

---

9 A recent empirical study of Chicago lawyers has shown a substantial correlation between prestige within the legal profession and the degree of intellectual challenge presented by the subject matter of the specialty. The study also shows that legal specialities that deal with personal suffering lose social standing as a result. See Edward O. Laumann and John P. Heinz, 'Specialization and prestige in the legal profession: the structure of deference,' [1977] *American Bar Association Research Journal* 155.

10 See Michael J. Trebilcock, 'Winners and losers in the modern regulatory system: must the consumer always lose?' (1975) 13 *Osgoode Hall Law Journal* 619, at 622ff

Furthermore, although there is not one single consumer interest in professional services, the various interests that exist share many characteristics. There are incontestable, particular, and shared needs for certain professional services (notably certain kinds of medical care) which provide a basic content to the notion of a consumer interest in professional services.

Accordingly I think it permissible to advance a description of a prima facie consumer interest in professional services. The consumer interest's first and most important component is access.[11] Access has many aspects. There must be enough of the professionals in question. They must be geographically well distributed. They must offer a wide range of skills. Cost must not be prohibitive. There must not be psychological barriers inhibiting the consumer from approaching the professional (this may imply, for example, that professionals be drawn from all sections of the community, and that services be delivered in ways that put the consumer at ease).[12]

The second component, coming into play when access is achieved, is quality. Access is more important because poor services are likely better than none. Good services, however, are best of all. Quality in this context is a simple concept and is measured by consequences.[13] Quality health care is care that when possible maintains or restores good health. Quality legal services are services that when possible avoid or solve legal problems for the client. Clearly there are situations when the concept of quality is difficult of application. What, for example, is quality health care of a terminally ill patient in great pain? What is quality legal service for a person accused of a crime who admits the offence? But difficult cases do not mean that there is not a simple core concept of quality.

Access and quality do not stand separate and apart, each from the other; they are related in a complex and important way. The optimal nature of this relationship may be the greatest public policy question facing the professions. What is the tradeoff between quality and price? How much quality should the system sacrifice to improve access?

Does professional education of the kind I have described promote accessible services of the appropriate quality?

11 On the complexity of the notion of access, see Robert Evans's contribution to this volume.
12 See 'Pickering Commission Report' (1973) 109 *Canadian Medical Association Journal* 1160. Of those surveyed, 46.4 per cent felt the single most important quality of a doctor was good human relations.
13 Of course the notion of measuring by consequences raises many difficulties. Does one examine the consequences for individual consumers, or in aggregate? In the former case there are problems such as time lags; in the latter there are difficulties in objectifying and aggregating essentially subjective judgments.

Consider access. For adequate access there must be enough of the professionals in question to service the community in a reasonable manner. Views will, of course, differ on what is reasonable service; how many people it takes to provide it; and who can best provide what service. But for any particular kind of service general agreement could likely be reached on a minimum or threshold number (for example, how many general medical practitioners per hundred thousand people are necessary to maintain properly a community's health).[14]

The present system of professional education does not directly address itself to this most fundamental aspect of access. That is because the static paradigm is inward-looking, directed to the attributes and environment of the professional himself, and not outward-looking, contemplating the need to be filled or the demands to be met.

Although the static paradigm does not address itself to the quantitative aspect of access, it is not neutral in effect. Curiously, the presumptions seem to pull in opposite directions. The emphasis on self-employment puts the professional in the marketplace (a strange and controlled kind of marketplace, but a marketplace nonetheless).[15] Accordingly, supply may in some measure respond to demand. But the extraordinary preparation required for a profession that is considered a learned occupation works to stifle supply at the source.

Geographic distribution is another part of access. Most agree that it would be desirable for some professionals to establish themselves, not in the cities of Canada, but in rural or remote communities. Professional education appears to have little relationship to this problem. Geographic distribution is more obviously a question, for example, of licensing (do not license for practice in places where there is an oversupply relative to elsewhere) or tax policy (provide tax relief for those who pursue their occupation in outlying areas). Yet in some ways the nature of professional education is relevant. Intellectual autonomy of a profession, promoted by some aspects of professional education, may discourage an appreciation of factors encouraging location in less populated parts of Canada; a highly specialized and research-oriented doctor, for example, will want to be near teaching hospitals, laboratory facilities, and a large population experiencing

---

14 *The Report of the Committee on the Healing Arts* (Toronto: Queen's Printer, 1970) stated that 'in the present state of our social and economic knowledge, the criteria for 'adequacy' of a public service must be arbitrary; there are no precise means of measuring the optimum quantity of the service which 'ought' to be available' (Vol. 2, p. 54). It is true that there are no precise means, but to say that criteria for adequacy are accordingly arbitrary is to be excessive.

15 The Committee on the Healing Arts considered, with respect to medical services, that 'orthodox economic market analysis is irrelevant because, through public policy, we have deliberately created a situation in which both supply and demand are administered' (ibid).

sufficient problems requiring his particular expertise.[16] Orientation towards self-employment may encourage professionals, when establishing themselves, to exclude contemplation of social service in favour of market considerations. The relationship between factors such as these and the distribution component of access is subtle and speculative. But one can fairly say that the static paradigm of professional education does not address this question.

The range of professional skills required by the consumer is enormous, ranging from the simplest to the extraordinarily complex. Some doctors remove splinters; others treat cancer. Some lawyers arrange uncontested divorces; others solve tax problems for giant corporations. Some architects plan kitchens; others design cathedrals. Yet the static paradigm of professional education does little to recognize the diversity of need. That professions are 'learned' is taken to mean, for the most part, that all professionals must attain at least a minimum but demanding level of learning. That they are intellectually autonomous permits ignorance of the full complexity of near infinite needs. That they are self-employed permits well-financed needs to be met first, or in some cases exclusively.

Yet another aspect of access is the cost of professional services (bearing in mind again the importance of the access/quality tradeoff). On this question comment is particularly difficult. Medicare, legal aid, and other similar plans that are or may come into existence no doubt promote access through subsidy policies, although there are 'professions' that as yet remain largely or completely untouched (it is said, for example, that only the rich and the poor can afford lawyers, while the middle class needs them most). In the long run such schemes may not eradicate the access problem, but merely change its shape. The exchequer is not a bottomless pit; if professional services remain extremely expensive, subsidy programs may not increase the general level of access, although access for the economically-deprived might improve.[17]

The many years spent by a professional in acquiring education (i.e. investing in human capital)[18] encourage, and may even justify, substantial fees for services. The consequences of the attitude that a professional occupation is a learned

---

16 See Laumann and Heinz, supra n.9.
17 The Committee on the Healing Arts ignored this point when it commented: 'Supply is determined largely by considerations of quality of standards and quantity of resources which the Province is prepared to devote to medical education; demand is determined largely by public programs of health insurance which provide consumers with access to physicians' services without being subject to market restraints. In other words, medical services are not rationed by price' (Supra n.14, 54-5).
18 See Gary S. Becker, *Human capital; a theoretical and empircal analysis, with special reference to education*, 2d ed (New York: Columbia University Press, 1975).

occupation (putting aside for the moment any justification that this presumption might have) affects access adversely by raising the cost of professional services. This aspect of the access problem is further aggravated by emphasis on self-employment. Professional services are in great demand. To the extent that fees can be set in the marketplace (in the face of increasing government intervention), they will be considerable.

Finally, with respect to access there is the matter of 'psychological' barriers. This factor may be elusive, but it seems real nonetheless. For instance consider the well-known reluctance of persons to seek legal advice.[19] It is difficult to attribute this phenomenon to any particular cause, but one can observe, again, that the static paradigm of professional education apparently does not address itself to the problem. By encouraging development of monolithic professions, presenting one face to the world, this model makes approach to most professions by the average consumer a forbidding process. Traditional curricula place little emphasis on development of interpersonal skills that will promote understanding once contact has been made. Admission policies may keep out members of minority groups that could best deal with the problems of those groups. And so on.

It seems that consumer interest in access is not well served by the prevailing system of professional education. The presumption that a professional occupation is a learned occupation adversely affects the supply of professionals, the range of skills available, and the cost of professional services. The marked tendency to intellectual autonomy does not promote an equitable geographic distribution of professional services, or the establishment of a satisfactory range of skills. Emphasis on self-employment discourages equitable distribution and provision of a wide range of skills, and tends to elevate costs. A learned, intellectually autonomous occupation practised by the self-employed does not promote optimal access to the service provided. An educational system that accepts and encourages these characteristics is not in the interests of the consumer of professional services.

It is in some measure otherwise with respect to the consumer interest in the absolute quality of professional skills. In this part of the discussion I am disregarding access to skills and the access/quality tradeoff problem. I refer only to the quality of professional service obtained by those who can get it.

Professional expertise is above all a function of professional education (the other important factor is experience). The emphasis on learning in the traditional model certainly promotes quality of service. But there are countervailing tendencies promoted by the static paradigm. Tendencies to intellectual autonomy may prevent professionals from perceiving some aspects of the problem

19 Cf. the Pickering Commission Report, supra n.12.

with which they are dealing. Emphasis on self-employment, and particularly fee-for-service regimes, may impair quality service by encouraging professionals to reduce time spent dealing with any particular case, and by serving to emphasize a curative rather than a preventive approach. But because of the primordial significance of learning for quality, and the emphasis on learning in the static paradigm, on balance that paradigm serves well the second component of the consumer interest in professional services.

Hence we have a dilemma. One part of the consumer interest is, in good measure, satisfied by the static paradigm. Another, by and large, is not satisfied. The modern challenge to professional education is to develop a dynamic model which will permit a move to greater access, while appropriate quality is protected. This objective perhaps can be accomplished by refinement of the access/quality tradeoff. The concept of quality or level of service relevant to need must be further developed. It should be developed by changes in the professional structure, with corresponding and facilitating changes in the structure and content of professional education.

To protect quality, the general, learned character of the professions must be maintained. There must be no widespread derogation of learning and its emphasis in the paradigm. But to promote access the approach to learning must be modified so that the supply of professionals increases; emphasis on intellectual autonomy and self-employment must be adapted so as to encourage a more equitable geographic distribution of professionals; in general, efforts must be made to promote the offering of a wider range of skills; presumptions that professionals are learned and self-employed must change to the extent that those presumptions result in elevated fees; and attitudes and practices that create psychological barriers for the consumer must be abandoned.

If the emphasis on learning is modified (not abandoned), then the supply of professionals will increase, the offering of a wider range of skills will be promoted, and professional fees may (in some measure) be brought under better control. That is because, if one has regard for the concept of appropriate learning, guaranteeing a relevant level of service for the need in question, it becomes evident that at present many professionals are overeducated. The consequences of overeducation are extraordinary, educational preparation putting professional careers beyond the grasp of many, the availability of a uniform and narrow range of skills, and a high cost of professional services.

What is desirable is a structure of professional education based on a concept of appropriate learning. This structure would be part of and reflect a new professional structure providing multiple levels of service, with specialists at the apex of the service pyramid and so-called paraprofessionals at the base. At the apex, substantial institutional specialization might be desirable, with particular professional schools (on a provincial or even national basis) offering advanced training not widely available. At the base one might find diploma programs in community colleges, night schools, and similar institutions, for paraprofessionals of many kinds.[20] Multiple entry and exit points would provide mobility. With such a system, educational hurdles for many who aspire to be providers of 'professional' services would be substantially reduced, and the supply of professionals would likely increase significantly. One anticipates a commensurate tendency for costs to decline, since not only would the supply be greater but the human capital invested by many of the new professionals would also be less than in the past. Finally, a wider range of service levels would be available.

Professional education's content in programs of all lengths and kinds would be modified as part of these developments. What is required is interdisciplinary and service-oriented curricula. So, for example, 'lawyers' of every stripe, from the corporation tax counsel to a legal paraprofessional doing simple property conveyance work, should be encouraged to explore the function of law and lawyers in society and should be taught to appreciate the impact of lawyering on the whole community.[21] So too, to give another illustration, primary care in medicine must be emphasized at least as much as the frontiers of research. Needs of this sort have been recognized in Canada. For example, a 1970 report on engineering education in Ontario stated that 'the role of an engineer requires him to face situations in which he takes account of psychological, sociological, aesthetic and political factors as well as scientific and technological matters ... The modern engineer requires more than traditional skills, and for success in the future he must have a basic knowledge and understanding of the applied humanities.'[22] Kenneth Lynn has put the problem well: 'our professionals need to liberate themselves ... from monopolistic notions of who should do what job and narrow-minded conceptions of their obligations to the community at large.'[23]

Curricula revision must, of course, reflect the new character of professions restructured to provide multiple levels of service. One curriculum will be impossible in a non-monolithic profession; as a more sophisticated view of professional

---

20 For an interesting review of the literature dealing with these possibilities in the legal profession, see Eric Mills Holmes, 'Education for competent lawyering – case method in a functional context' (1976) *Columbia Law Review* 535, at 536-8.

21 Perhaps lawyers should be taught what Alfred Conrad has called 'macrojustice.' See his article, 'Macrojustice: a systematic approach to conflict resolution' (1971) 5 *Georgia Law Review* 415.

22 Committee of Presidents of Universities of Ontario, *Ring of Iron: A Study of Engineering Education in Ontario* (1970), 39

23 Kenneth S. Lynn, 'Introduction' (to the issue 'The Professions') (1963) 92 *Daedalus* 649, at 653

'learning' develops, a variety of curricula will develop within any one professional genus. The extent to which training will be interdisciplinary and service-oriented will depend on who is being trained for what. Paraprofessionals providing services of limited scope might not need to be philosophers and humanists, but they may need a considerable awareness of their optimal role in the community so as better to serve the community. For the research scientist the equation may be reversed: better to be a philosopher than an activist. Always there will be a subtle interplay between the professional role and the length and content of professional education.

As the professional structure is modified, so emphasis on self-employment will have less and less validity, a change that presumably will find expression in various ways within professional education programs. Already within some professions many are salaried, engineering being perhaps the most striking example; within almost all professions there is a tendency in this direction.

An outline of the new system emerges. The existing model of the professions should be modified to permit multiple levels of education; the professions should be restructured so that only the level of skill appropriate to the problem is brought to bear; individual professionals should be educated only to the point necessary for them to provide the service that is their responsibility within the structure. Multiple curricula must be developed for multiple levels of education. Curricula will differ not only in rigour and comprehensiveness but also in the extent to which they are interdisciplinary and service-oriented. It is reasonable to expect that if well-thought-out changes of this sort are introduced, the availability of professional services – in terms of quantity, geographic availability, cost, and even attitude – will increase substantially, with no relevant sacrifice of quality. In short, the legitimate consumer interest in professional services will be satisfied.

My argument has been theoretical. I have attempted to identify attributes of the contemporary system of professional education that tend to interfere with provision by the system of appropriate services to those who need them. I have suggested directions of educational development which might help meet the consumer interest in a more effective fashion. How can these lines of inquiry be developed? What is the 'research agenda?'

In the first place, a model of professional education objectives must be developed. Such a model would likely be based on a sound appreciation of the demand for professional services,[24] on a desire to match supply (in terms of pro-

---

24 Here much empirical work is required. An instructive United States study is Barbara A. Curran, *The Legal Needs of the Public: The Final Report of a National Survey* (Chicago: American Bar Foundation, 1978).

fessional qualifications) closely to demand, avoiding the overtrained/under-trained phenomenon, problems of numbers, geographic distribution, and the like, and on an understanding of the relationship between professional education and both the services available and their delivery mechanism. The model would, in addition, inevitably reflect a number of public policy decisions dealing with political and other priorities. Then, existing educational programs should be evaluated in light of the developed model, with special attention being paid to general tendencies for divergence from the model and the reasons for these divergences. At this point it might prove necessary to examine in detail who controls professional education, what their particular interests are, how these interests are pursued, and the inter-relationships between the relevant controlling institutions. It should then prove possible to describe desirable institutional reforms and plan for their implementation.

J.F. MUSTARD

Health professional education

INTRODUCTION

The education of health professionals has gone through a number of developments over the centuries. During the latter part of the last century and the first part of this century the issues around standards in medical education and the relationship of schools of medicine to universities were the focus of attention. More recently the emphasis has focused on changes in education programs and admissions policies in relation to social pressures and needs. A major force affecting the future is the potential increased involvement of government in health care and the control of the number of health professionals through regulation of education programs.

Over the centuries the education of individuals for careers as health professionals has taken place in a variety of settings and involved a variety of groups. Although medicine has had a long association with some universities in western countries, it is only within the last seventy years that most of the institutions for educating physicians have become part of, or affiliated with, universities. The Karolinska Institute, which is Sweden's largest and perhaps most famous medical school, has been an independent medical institution with no affiliation with any university since its foundation in 1810. In England the twelve London medical schools are based in hospitals, some of which had their origins in the twelfth century. It was only after the first world war that any significant attachments to the University of London were developed, and in some cases the links are still tenuous. In the United States prior to 1910 a number of proprietary schools were established and operated for profit by their faculties. Most of these institutions had very low standards. Even the universities with medical schools had their pro-

Dean, Faculty of Health Sciences, McMaster University

blems because the faculties were mainly composed of practising physicians whose allegiance was to their professional societies and hospitals rather than to their universities and education programs. Charles Eliot, when he became president of Harvard in 1869, expressed his feelings as follows: 'It seems almost incredible that the grossly inadequate training above described should be the recognized preparation for aspirants to a profession that was once called learned, and which pre-eminently demands a mind well-stored and a judgement well trained – a profession in which ignorance is criminality, and skill a benefaction – a profession which penetrates the most sacred retreats of human love, joy and sorrow, and deals daily with the issues of life and death.'[1] He did try to correct some of the defects in Harvard's medical school.

Flexner's Report for the Council of Medical Education of the American Medical Association aroused the public to recognize that the level of medical education in North America was far below acceptable standards.[2] Forty-six of the 131 schools of medicine in existence in 1910 were closed or absorbed by stronger institutions, and most that remained established a university affiliation. The primary result of the Flexner Report has been the establishment of high quality medical schools with university affiliations that have emphasized the scientific basis for rational diagnosis and therapy. From this report was also introduced the concept of accreditation of all medical schools by a peer group to minimize the self-interest effects of professional and other groups. There is little doubt the accreditation process has improved the standards of medical schools. Flexner later stated what he thought the philosophy of education for doctors should be: 'A medical school cannot expect to produce fully trained doctors, it can at most hope to equip students with a limited amount of knowledge, to train them in the method and spirit of scientific medicine, and to launch them with a momentum that will make them active learners, observers, readers, thinkers, and experimenters for years to come.'[3] The Royal Commission on Medical Education in the United Kingdom further emphasized this point in 1968.[4] Its report observes that modern medical practice is based on rapidly changing scientific and technical knowledge, and thus there is a need for practitioners who can keep abreast of the tide. The authors conclude that this is only possible if the physicians are educated to think scientifically and to study and learn for themselves.

1 C.W. Eliot, *Annual Report of the President of Harvard College, 1869-70, 1870-1*
2 A. Flexner, *Medical Education in the United States and Canada* (Carnegie Foundation for the Advancement of Teaching. Bulletin No. 4, 1910)
3 A. Flexner, *Medical Education* (New York: Macmillan, 1925)
4 Royal Commission on Medical Education (1965-8) *Report* CMND 3569 (London: HMSO)

This brief outline of some of the events and problems associated with the education of physicians over the last hundred years illustrates some of the difficulties in the education of health professionals. There is a need for ensuring that the graduates are capable of continuous self-directed learning, are able to solve problems, and are able to function within the complex social organizations in which health problems occur and are treated.

Health professional education programs and health care institutions are subject to continuous change in response to the pressures of social and scientific events, professional interactions, and government policies. One of the significant developments during this century has been the increase in new health professional groups to cope with the various opportunities, needs and demands of our society's health system. Of the fifty-six health disciplines identified in Canada in 1973, twenty-one were classified as new, with the first graduates appearing in 1970 or later.[5] These groups range from the traditional learned professions (e.g. university programs in dentistry, medicine, nursing, and pharmacy) to the technical groups in health care such as laboratory technologists. This development has been largely due to the application of modern science to health care, leading to very complex and expensive arrangements for the care of sick persons in acute care hospitals. Some believe this has distorted our arrangements for providing care, so that we no longer effectively cope with health problems at the community level. This leads to undesirable social and economic costs.

In addition, there is the more complex issue of each individual's own responsibility for his or her health. Clearly the more responsibility the individual assumes for his or her own health, the less the demand on the health professionals. Thus, in any consideration of education programs for health professionals some thought should be given to how much of the information made available to students in the health sciences should be made available to other students. For example, within a university should the bulk of the resources in the schools of medicine, dentistry, nursing, pharmacy, and public health be devoted to education of students in the professional programs or should a proportion of the resources be used to educate other university students about health and human biology? How much education in health and human biology should students in the social sciences receive (many of whom may become involved in public policy as it relates to health)?

The subject of health professional education and public policy involves consideration of the following points in respect to medicine and nursing: education

5 J.R. Robertson, *Report on Health Manpower Output of Canadian Educational Institutions* (Ottawa: AUCC 1973)

programs, admission to health professional programs with limited enrolment, team work, health care and education, and the impact of government policy and funding on professional education.

EDUCATION PROGRAMS

Many schools have educational objectives for their undergraduate programs which include such items as the following:
– Since knowledge in the health sciences will continue to change, the student must be prepared for the scientific approach to health problems and for continuing self-education.
– Since health professional education influences attitudes and expectations it is important that the program be broadly based and give the student a true perspective of all parts of the health system and its health care problems.
– Since much of health care has to be given by different groups of health professionals, students from different professional programs should have joint practical learning experiences so that they are better prepared for future teamwork.
  The impact of the pressures generated by new knowledge and society's demands and expectations create some interesting problems for institutions trying to develop a curriculum to meet the above and other objectives.

THEORETICAL AND PRACTICAL EDUCATION

In the preparation of health professionals it is necessary that they master a body of knowledge and, in addition, acquire the necessary skills to be effective practitioners. For many years these two aspects of the education of health professionals were separated. However, with the great growth in our knowledge in the human biological sciences and the demands for extending the students' clinical experience to include a broader community base, major changes have been made in the undergraduate education programs. Questions have been raised about the basic biomedical sciences. Should only the material relevant to human health problems be taught? In trying to cope with this question most institutions have attempted to integrate the basic biomedical sciences with their clinical programs. This has not been without some problems for faculty and students. In order to allow the students to see the relevance of some of the basic knowledge to clinical problems, students are now introduced to clinical problems very early in the curriculum. Thus the boundary between the theoretical and practical has become blurred.

CLINICAL TEACHING

The value of clinical teaching within teaching hospitals dealing with relatively rare diseases or extremely complex technical procedures has been challenged.[6] The response to this challenge is still uncertain. There has been a definite move in most universities to ensure that the students' clinical experience is more broadly based to include not only the health problems seen in the traditional teaching hospital but also the community health problems. Attempts are being made to broaden the base for clinical education so that students become aware of the environment in which the individual lives and the influence that social, economic, and lifestyle factors have on an individual's health, and the care that can be provided when an individual becomes ill. Despite these changes, there are still major deficiencies in the education programs, such as lack of experience for the students in handling the health and social problems of the older person[7] and the effects on health of environmental factors related to certain occupations. In attempting to develop education programs in these areas, academic institutions come into a direct interaction with government policies in a publicly funded health system. For example, if there is no well-established program for providing co-ordinated and integrated health care in the community, how do you provide clinical experience for students in a setting that does not exist? Changes in clinical education are sometimes slow since, in health care, the speed of transition is affected by previous capital investments, entrenched professional positions, established social hierarchies, statutory mazes, certification procedures, and economic limitations.

BEHAVIOURAL AND SOCIAL SCIENCES

There has been an attempt to introduce into the education of health professionals more awareness of the relation of behavioural and social sciences to health problems. The physical and biological sciences emphasis is still present in the curriculum but no longer dominates it to the exclusion of the behavioural and social sciences. However, the integration of these two sectors is difficult. At the clinical level of training, integration is often hampered by the public policy that fragments community health, social services, acute care hospitals, chronic care institutions, and psychiatric institutions.

6 R.V. Christie, *Medical Education and The State* (Washington DC: US Government Printing Office, 1976)
7 L. Auerbach and A. Gerber, *Study on Population and Technology - Perceptions 2* (Ottawa: Science Council of Canada, 1976)

RESEARCH

The shifts in values and emphasis have caused concern as to whether university programs in the health sciences are able to prepare a portion of the students for careers in research in the health field. In the opinion of some, the new emphasis away from research has led to a downgrading of the value of science in health education programs. Research in the health field requires not only people concerned with the basic biomedical sciences but also individuals who can work in the fields of applied and developmental health research and in the field of research directed towards making effective use of knowledge. Failure to interest some health professional trainees in research careers, particularly in the clinical care areas of health research, or in research directed toward acquiring understanding to ensure maximum application of useful knowledge, will make it difficult to provide for more effective, efficient health care and to introduce measures which may modify environmental and lifestyle factors that contribute to ill health. Government policy for the support of research and career positions is another factor of importance that influences student interests in research careers. The present policies of our governments are having a negative influence. If the scientific basis of health sciences education is to be maintained, there is a need to interest more health sciences students in research careers.

ADMISSIONS

Since physicians in our society are among the privileged in terms of careers and economic reward, medicine is at present an attractive professional program for many students. However, because government policy restricts the number of physicians trained in Ontario, the number of applicants that can be accepted into medical school each year is only a small proportion of the qualified applicants. Since the education costs of physicians are largely funded by government, and since the lifetime earnings of a physician are substantially greater than those of other members of society whose taxes support education, what should the policies be for admission to a restricted program?

In a publicly funded education system, who should be admitted to these programs and who should be excluded? Furthermore, in a publicly funded system, who should determine the policies which govern admittance to these education programs?

At the present time admission to these programs is largely under the control of the faculties within the universities. In general, the criteria they set are based upon the applicants' previous academic performances and educational backgrounds. With a large number of qualified applicants, is it fair to differentiate solely on the basis of academic grades? When the academic grades of universities are not completely comparable, what element of luck and discrimination enters into the selection process?

Another method of selection involves the use of a combination of factors such as academic performance and assessment of the students' personal qualities. This process, usually including an interview, may involve only faculty, or it may be more broadly based, involving a team composed of members of the faculty, of the community, and possibly of the student body. Limited as interview processes are, one with a broadly based representation will probably have a different pattern of selection than one with its membership drawn from the faculty. Another approach which could be used in a publicly funded system, although it would probably be unacceptable to our culture, is to have the students who wish to enter professional schools such as medicine nominated by their community, providing they have the necessary academic standards to meet the admission requirements of the professional program.

I think there will be strong pressure in a publicly funded system for increased public participation in the selection of students for restricted health professional programs such as medicine and nursing. An alternative may be to admit all applicants meeting a minimum standard and, at the end of each following year, fail those who do not meet higher standards. This is the policy in some European schools. Any restricted education program funded by government runs the risk of local public pressure restricting the student enrolment to the immediate area surrounding the school. This has some potential adverse effects if we are trying to develop a strong national identity with movement of our citizens to different parts of our country.

Another issue in admissions policy is the previous educational background of the applicants. With the development of the scientific basis of medicine there has been an almost universal trend to requiring students wishing to enter medicine and nursing to have a solid grounding in the physical and biological sciences with relatively less experience in the social sciences and humanities. This has raised the question whether selecting students from a fairly restricted background in physical and biological sciences does not lead to health professionals with a less-than-desirable breadth in their academic backgrounds. In some schools attempts have been made to broaden the base so that individuals are eligible for admission to the programs regardless of their university background. Able, mature students from a non-biological science background, in the experience of all schools with such admissions policies, are, in their ability to cope with problems in human biology, indistinguishable from students coming from the traditional physical and biological sciences background after a period of six months to one year.

The impact of our change in attitude towards careers for females has led to society and schools of medicine reducing whatever discrimination previously existed against female applicants. The reverse is probably true to some extent for nursing programs in universities. The full impact of the changes in medical and nursing school admission policies for professional careers for males and females in the health sciences and the possible changes in education programs is not known.

Finally, some attempts are being made to allow mature students who are in health careers but have no university education to be admitted to medicine and university health sciences graduate programs. This is necessary if we are to allow for some vertical and lateral mobility of students from the different education and training programs in the health sciences.

TEAMWORK

Nursing educators have long understood the need for a co-ordinated approach in the provision of care, but the physician has primarily worked as an independent individual with full responsibility for making decisions about the diagnosis and care of an individual patient. Over the years the increased complexities of diagnosis and care have usually required that more than one professional be involved. The concept of teamwork is difficult to introduce into professional training programs when our traditional concept of physicians is as solo practitioners with complete responsibility for the care of an individual. New physicians have to learn to work with each other as well as with other health professionals.

A variety of attempts have been made to introduce the concept of teamwork into the education programs of health professionals. In some schools the students are brought together in groups set up randomly every two or three months. Within these small groups students are expected to learn how to study in collaboration with their colleagues and develop the necessary personal skills for group interaction. Part of the group process is that they criticize each other in terms of group and personal behaviour. There is no doubt that the addition of a format such as this to an undergraduate program puts stress on the students. Whether they learn to work with others in such a format is difficult to tell.

Broadening this approach so that students learn to work with other health professionals is far more difficult. This, of course, cannot be achieved unless there are actual settings in which health professionals work together as a team. Thus the development of programs which provide for interprofessional experiences in terms of teamwork and the provision of care is extraordinarily difficult and is dependent upon the policies which influence the health care system and the attitudes of professional groups.

This point emphasizes one of the major difficulties in the clinical training of health professional students. The education program is enormously dependent upon the patterns of practice that exist in the society in which the institution is based. It is important that one recognize the limitations on innovation of clinical education programs if the environment in which students must receive their clinical experience is set in a traditional mode. If students are to appreciate new arrangements in health care, it is essential for the education programs to be involved in the arrangements for the provision of health care. Demonstration models of health care can be set up so that students can learn about the provision of care under new arrangements as well as those that are traditional in society. This is particularly important in trying to develop new attitudes and approaches for health professionals in the future. Not only does it affect concepts of group arrangements in which the students may learn the team approach for provision of health care, but it also has a major impact on their perception of the values given to the different professional roles in the health care system. We do not have effective means in our society for a proper partnership among educational institutions, government, and health-care institutions for developing new arrangements for health care.

In nursing it is very difficult to arrange for nurses in hospitals and other institutions to have a joint responsibility to the service institution and to the university faculty. The nurses' primary loyalty is to their service institutions. In clinical education it appears important that the clinical teacher has a dual responsibility to education and service. In clinical departments in medicine where this has been done, innovation is possible in clinical education, and the standards of clinical education are generally high. Other programs, such as nursing, need similar arrangements. Unfortunately it is government funding policies which largely determine the arrangements that exist, and these are not easy to change because of the different ministries and service institutions involved.

HEALTH CARE AND EDUCATION

During the last decade there has been considerable pressure from citizens, social scientists, governments, and some health professionals for changes in the present health care system.[8] These include: improved accessibility and availability of health services, a more effective and efficient health care system, and extension into neglected areas such as care of the aged and chronically ill, alcoholism, drug addiction, occupational health, and mental health.

---

8 *Report of Health Planning Task Force* (Ontario, 1974); *New Directions in Education for Changing Health Care Systems (CERI)* (Paris: OECD, 1975); Ontario Economic Council, *Issues and Alternatives, 1976 – Health* (Toronto)

This pressure has led to objectives being set in many provinces toward the development and expansion of comprehensive community-based primary health care.[9] Although some observers anticipate that improved primary health care will reduce health costs, this is unlikely for several reasons.[10] Money will have to be invested to establish an improved primary care system. A good system of primary care, however, may decrease overutilization of hospital resources and inappropriate use of highly specialized resources. Health is a field in which new discoveries and techniques create a demand for continual additions to the repertoire of services offered. It is also important to remember that demand rises to match available resources when the usual market controls are absent. The health care system is not subject to usual market controls. What can happen with the development of an effective primary care system is a more effective use of resources with gains in access to, and quality of, health care and improved citizen satisfaction.

This movement towards primary health care calls for changes in the traditional partnership between education and health services. Schools for physicians, nurses, and other health professionals have in the past conducted the bulk of their teaching within the confines of one or more specialized hospitals. Long-standing traditions of institutional and faculty autonomy, historical unions with specific hospitals, and academic priorities which centre on complex or rare illnesses work against an easy transition. Furthermore, the funding for parts of a professional school's program are often hospital-based and even when they are not, geographic and financial factors make it very difficult for the institutions to gain access to primary care settings. Changes in the system, however, must not erode the positive qualities now present in our arrangements for providing effective acute care and basic research.

With public funding of health care and education it is difficult for all of these developments to occur without close co-operation between provincial authorities and the education institutions.

Brotherston has emphasized that a policy of pursuing an expensive education program for preparing scientifically trained doctors and nurses for primary care should carry with it a policy to create the surroundings and arrangements for practice most conducive to the work and morale of the professionals created by the education process.[11] There is evidence that some of our problems stem from

9 *Report of Health Planning Task Force* (Ontario, 1974); J. Hastings, 'Report of the Community Health Centre Project,' *Canad. M.A.J.* CUII (1972) 361; Ontario Council of Health, 'The nurse practitioner in primary care' (Toronto, 1975)
10 Ontario Economic Council, *Issues and Alternatives, 1976 – Health*
11 J. Brotherston, *Evolution of Medical Practice in Medical History and Medical Care*, edited by G. McLachlan and T. McKeown (London: Oxford University Press, 1971)

a dislocation between education and the attitudes created by it, and the practice arrangements for doctors and nurses in the community. This leads to the last point – the relationship between government policies and professional education.

GOVERNMENT POLICY AND FUNDING AND HEALTH PROFESSIONAL EDUCATION

The increased involvement of the government in providing the funds for health care and for education of health professionals has created some interesting pressures in the system which have major long-term implications for health manpower and the nature of education programs.

If the government perceives that the number of physicians in society determines health care costs and believes that health care costs must be controlled, then it becomes necessary to control the number of physicians in the health care system. However, some believe that the percentage of our gross national product devoted to health care is related to available resources and public expectations and is only indirectly influenced by the number of physicians. Despite the uncertainty of the factors determining health costs, it is apparent that there will be increasing attempts to control health manpower. This implies that the career choices of health professionals will be ordered and directed. If this is desirable, how should it be done in a democratic society?

Some analysts believe that the manpower problem can be solved by controlling the output of the health professional education programs. To do this a central body will have to determine the scope and composition of the health professional education programs. This leads to the question of who determines how many dentists, dermatologists, family physicians, obstetricians, nurses, and so on are required in society. Until recently the factors determining manpower have been the number of places society made available for the education of health professionals, the career opportunities available to graduates, immigration, and the rewards of the different careers.

The pressures in the present system are leading to the decisions having to be made by the people who provide the funds, i.e. by the government. These decisions will tend to be arrived at through a dialogue involving the government, educational institutions, and professional groups. The impact of control on the numbers and types of health professionals graduating has implications for the flexibility and scope of the education programs and will ultimately change the basic characteristics of professional education and professional roles in society.

This problem is evident in the postgraduate training of physicians. In Ontario such training is largely funded by the Ministry of Health. The student numbers are set by the Ministry of Health, in consultation with the Ministry of Colleges and Universities, and the over-all mix of specialists to non-specialists is also set by the Health Ministry. The trainees have formed a bargaining unit in an attempt to improve their working conditions and level of remuneration. This has led to negotiations between teaching hospitals and the Association of Interns and Residents, with, of course, government involvement since government is the source of funds. How long will it be before these negotiations will be centralized because the government funds the programs and establishes the numbers of trainees? How long before the negotiations will include the conditions of the postgraduate education programs and the procedures and standards for evaluation? I suspect these developments will occur sooner than most of us are prepared to admit, with some interesting effects on the education programs. If the numbers entering the postgraduate programs are closely matched to the manpower needs, how will the certifying bodies, such as the Royal College of Physicians and Surgeons, conduct examinations in which, as now, there is a significant failure rate? If we have to ensure that most people entering the program have jobs at the end of their training period, what happens to the philosophy of 'the best person for the job?'

There will probably develop a policy which will determine, against provincial manpower guidelines, the numbers and types of faculty in the health sciences. I suspect the control of manpower and costs will also lead to further unionization of the professions in health, including physicians. Such developments are not necessarily bad, but unless they are carefully thought out they will have profound effects on our attitudes and expectations and on our flexibility in health sciences education programs. All of these changes could lead to rigidly standardized education programs.

Another area of interaction between government and health sciences education programs is in innovations in health care. In keeping with the general recognition of the need to upgrade our primary health care services, including enhancing the status of the health professionals in this field,[12] most of the schools of medicine and nursing in this country have strengthened their programs to prepare nurses and physicians for careers in primary care. A number of larger university schools of nursing have mounted certificate or diploma programs with the goal of preparing nurses for the primary care sector. In some of these the results have been assessed in research studies. In situations in which nurses and physicians jointly provide primary care as co-practitioners in a team arrangement, the studies show a high level of patient acceptance, personal satisfaction on the part of the practitioners, and increased ambulatory care with a reduction

12 Hastings, 'Report'

in institutional care.[13] Despite the fact that there is an established education program with interim funding from the Ministry of Colleges and Universities in an area of importance for new developments, there is still no clear policy from the Ministry of Health that would make it possible for graduates of these programs to have careers as nurse-practitioners. The Ontario Council of Health recommended an action plan in 1975. However, this innovation in health professional education is out of phase with government policy. Career opportunities are lost for the graduates, and necessary changes in health care delivery do not occur. This means the education programs will be stopped or changed with all the attendant difficulties if it is deemed desirable to start the programs again.

CONCLUSION

The involvement of government in the education of health professionals will increase. In order to maintain some stability, rational planning, and flexibility, I think we will have to give consideration to the following developments: 1 / There will need to be established permanent means of co-ordinating and integrating government policies and actions in health care and the education of health professionals. 2 / There will be pressure for provincial health care policies to foster conjoint education/health care actions at the district level, and the institutions (academic and health care) at this level will have to develop mechanisms to implement such actions. 3 / The control of health manpower will require close co-ordination between government and health sciences education institutions in terms of student numbers and faculty positions. 4 / Provincial health policies will have to be developed and clearly stated.

The ramifications of these developments are considerable. I do not think these policies should be developed within the narrow confines of the experts in the health sciences faculties and the civil service. There will be a need to establish a public body with the power to review government action and make public recommendations to which the government must respond within a stipulated time; otherwise the development and implementation of policy in health and health sciences education will be controlled by a small group with limited public accountability. In a democratic state it is important that public policy in a publicly funded sector be given close public scrutiny. Strengthening the power of the Ontario Council of Health to be similar to that of the Ontario Council of

13 W.O. Spitzer et al., 'Burlington randomized trial of the nurse practitioner,' *New Eng. J. Med.* (1974) 290, 251; K. Scherer et al., *First Survey of Nurse Practitioners and Associated Physicians: Methodological Manual and Final Report* (Hamilton: McMaster University, 1976)

University Affairs could create such a public body in health. If we do not give attention to this issue now, the result could be a standardized, rigid, almost totalitarian system of health professional education and health care, which I think is undesirable for our society.

HORACE KREVER

Professional education

Although I have had the stimulating opportunity of studying the professional education of those who practise their professions in the health field in Ontario, and although I believe that, for the most part, the problems of professional education are essentially the same in all the senior professions wherever they are practised, I have decided to confine myself to the issue of education in and for the legal profession. My vantage point is that of one whose experience includes that of a student, a practitioner with the responsibility of overseeing the practical training of a good number of articled students-at-law who had successfully completed their professional courses at several Canadian universities, a law professor with more than ten years' experience at two Ontario universities, a member and chairman of the legal education committee of the self-governing body regulating the profession and having the *legal* responsibility for *all* legal education, and, more recently, as a 'consumer' who daily sees the performance of the finished product of our system. I mention this experience only because there are few, if any, other students of legal education with the advantage of having served in as many capacities in our highly pluralized educational system, and this fact may explain what to many may appear to be the idiosyncratic point of view expressed in this paper. Indeed, a problem necessary to emphasize is the absence of any integration of, or even any recognition of, the need to think of the various periods of legal education as parts of a continuum or a single process rather than as a sequence of discrete interests each having its own raison d'être and, in its behaviour, unconcerned with the role or performance of the other interests or parts. The explanation for this state of affairs is, in large measure, historical, but is, nevertheless, not one which we can continue to regard as a justification. I

Justice of the Supreme Court of Ontario; formerly a member of the Committee on the Healing Arts, Ontario, and a member of the Faculty of Law, University of Toronto

shall return to the subject of the separateness of the various educational empires again because it is, to my mind, the most urgent problem facing professional education for lawyers today.

As in the case of all other 'true' professions, professional legal education is characterized by the inherent and perpetual problem of combining judiciously the sound theoretical base of the intellectual body of knowledge that is the hallmark of what I have called the true professions with a training in the practical application of the principles found in that intellectual body of knowledge, before the new practitioners are certified as competent to a public incapable of judging competence without assistance. No jurisdiction I know of is satisfied with its solution to this control problem. In recent years, at least in Ontario, the relationship between professional legal education and certification of the professional has grown so close that, for all practical purposes, it has become impossible to study law, either as part of the humanities or as part of the social sciences, in an Ontario university without enrolling in a faculty of law whose principal, if not exclusive, commitment is to the education of persons who intend to become members of the legal profession. In the light of the history of higher education, the proposition that law is capable of being studied as an intellectual discipline otherwise than in institutions devoted to the instruction of students with professional goals is no longer controversial.

In the evaluation of legal education in Ontario, however, the very success of the university in the struggle over the right to teach the intellectual concepts of the law as an integral part of the preparation of practising lawyers has made impossible the emergence of any authority with responsibility, in fact as opposed to law, for the smooth co-operation or even co-ordination of the various stages of pre-certification professional education in law.

A brief historical reference is now necessary. The most significant year in the evolution of legal education in Ontario was 1949. Then, as now, the legal authority for certifying persons as competent to practise law was the Law Society of Upper Canada, a creature of statute consisting of benchers, practising lawyers almost exclusively, elected by members of the profession. It is safe to say that until 1949 the dominant element of legal education was apprenticeship. The only professional law school in the province – Osgoode Hall Law School – was owned and operated by the Law Society and was unaffiliated with any university. University education was not a prerequisite to admission to the Law School; one could be admitted to the professional study of law with only high school matriculation, provided one had the necessary apprenticeship experience. Lest any unintended inference be drawn from what I have said, I digress to point out that not a few of an earlier generation of Ontario lawyers, who made a strong and positive contribution to their profession and the larger society, were 'matriculant students.' But modern needs of a post-war society required the end of a system under which the necessary education of those of its members who were to be entrusted with such responsible advice and counsel could be left to chance and self-help. Moreover, the Law School was not one in which attendance was full-time. Concurrent lectures and office training were employed. There were, in fact, only a handful of full-time law teachers, among whom the influence of Harvard Law School was strong. Speaking today, I am sure it will cause no controversy to say that the benchers of 1949, in whose care the Law School rested, were out of touch not only with education but also with the profession. In their decision that year to 'improve' legal education by placing stronger emphasis on office training at the expense of academic study, they set off a chain of events that has not yet ended. To condense years of bitter struggle and giant steps forward, I content myself with summarizing events inadequately by saying that the eventual result was the acceptance of the universities as the proper bodies to be responsible for the academic part of the preparation of lawyers, and the retention by the Law Society, as a consequence of its obligation to certify competence, of the responsibility for practical instruction. This responsibility is discharged by the system of articles of clerkship and the teaching portion of the Bar Admission Course.

It is beyond dispute that today's benchers are men and women who are incalculably more aware than their predecessors of the needs of the larger society of which they are also members and of the views of their much larger profession. Sensitive to the intellectual and emotional struggle of the universities for their rightful role in legal education, they are, however, practically devoid of the ability to exercise much of their legal authority over academic legal education and instead leave that authority where functionally it belongs – in the hands of the universities. It is my belief that, since winning the right to teach law as part of the student's preparation to practise law, the university law schools, as the first acknowledgment of that right becomes more and more remote in time, and forgetting, overlooking, or dismissing as unimportant their original argument that they could better educate lawyers for the practice of law in modern society than the licensing or regulatory body, and secure now in the heart of the university, which generally disdains 'trade schools,' that the university law schools are becoming less concerned about the needs of their students as future lawyers and totally uninterested, or at least uninvolved, in the process of legal education after the point at which the LL B degree is granted.

On the so-called practical side of the process on the other hand the difficulties are no less acute. Concerned about the gravity of the responsibility of ensuring that those it certifies as competent to advise clients, directly and without supervision, are indeed competent, the benchers of the Law Society, whose demonstrable qualities of excellence as lawyers do not include expertise in educational theory or practice, attempt to ensure the acquisition of practical skills by twelve months under articles and six months in the teaching portion of the Bar Admission Course. The unevenness of the articling experience has been acknowledged publicly; that qualifying to practise law does not, as the articling system assumes, necessarily qualify the practitioner to properly instruct or train students-at-law needs no proof. The articling experience is entirely unsupervised by the Society and is widely conceded to be longer than necessary for proper instruction. The teaching portion of the Bar Admission Course – the six-month period of intensive classroom instruction by practising lawyers, intended to compensate for the unequal nature of the articling experience – operates, even though now decentralized by the establishment of courses at Ottawa and London, under the handicap of large numbers of students, a curriculum which is essentially the same as that with which it began in 1957, course content which duplicates university law school courses, and no expertise or effective mechanism for reviewing curriculum policy except for the full-time director and his dedicated staff who are so fully occupied with the day-to-day functioning of the course as to have no time to devote to policy development.

Change in professional education does not come easily. Conservative by nature, professional persons are never quickly persuaded of the need for change. Strong vested interests abound. It is difficult to demonstrate to successful practitioners that the way in which they were prepared for practice is not the way future members of the profession should be prepared. When, in 1973, after a long and careful examination of legal education was made, the report of the Special Committee on Legal Education of the Law Society of Upper Canada was presented, the recommendation that the requirement of service under articles as a condition of qualifying for practice should be abolished, was rejected out of respect for the perceived hostile reaction of members of the profession. The recital of the shortcomings and deficiencies of the articling system in the Report went unchallenged, but to this day no change has been made in the system. More recently, discussion has centred on a proposal to abolish the six-month teaching portion of the Bar Admission Course and merely distribute its teaching materials, acknowledged to be of high quality, to students-at-law during their period of articles, giving them access to 'tutors' strategically available throughout the province for consultation and assistance that their principals are unable to provide. In my view, this proposal, if adopted, would be a retrograde step. At no time has it been suggested that the university law schools should consider modifying their programs to take into account any changes that might be made in the post-university, pre-certification training. Nor has there been created an effective authority charged with the responsibility of ensuring co-ordination and co-operation among the separate parts of the complicated system of pre-certification education. I reject as artificial the traditional concept of the conflict between the academic and practical in legal education and am persuaded that it is too often raised as a justification for avoiding responsibility. It is my opinion that the institutions with the greatest potential for the acquisition of expertise in educational matters involved in professional preparation for certification are the universities. In many respects the state of legal education is that of medical education in the pre-Flexner era.

Accreditation of law schools, as contrasted with medical schools, is unknown in Canada, and the law schools, in the light of their hard-won autonomy in the face of the regulatory body will with good reason not permit any threat to academic freedom, even if only in the form of inquiry into their methods and objectives. Pre-certification education, acknowledged by all who have examined it to be unnecessarily lengthy, to involve needless repetition, and to cause frustration in students at an age at which many, if not most, have acquired marital and family responsibilities, requires a unifying force. In my opinion the chief criterion for the institution to be entrusted with the task should be competence or potential competence for the task. Only one institution in our society satisfies that criterion.

Historically, the assumption underlying our system of professional certification of competence to practise was that once a candidate proved himself or herself to be initially competent to be licensed to practise, he or she was competent for life. Recent re-examination of professional certification has everywhere shown that assumption to be without validity. It is true that the risk to which the public is exposed by less than fully competent practitioners is much more serious in the case of the science-based professions than in the case of the legal profession. Nevertheless, the principle that in an era of rapid social change, of changing values and of increased legislative and judicial activity never previously contemplated, the lawyer who does not keep up to date in doctrines and procedures puts his or her clients at risk cannot be the subject of serious controversy. Nor are the mechanisms of third-party liability insurance and disciplinary procedures satisfactory safeguards against practitioners with diminished competence. Automatic recertification upon payment of annual fees requires rethinking. Satisfactory solutions, however, have not yet been found. Continuing educational programs are carried on with commendable regularity and quality. But as in the case of other professions, the problem does not lie with those legal practitioners who regularly attend the programs; it lies with the majority who never attend. In passing, it may not be out of place to point out, again by way of contrast with other senior professions, that, in law, university faculties, as institutions, play no significant role in the continuing education of practising lawyers.

The difficulties involved in continuing education in law, it must be admitted, are greater than in other professions, such as medicine and dentistry. Although specialization is an existing reality in legal practice, particularly in metropolitan parts of the province, official recognition of the specialist has not yet occurred. Self-accreditation as a specialist is for obvious reasons, given the opportunity it affords for misrepresentation to an uninformed public, prohibited as unprofessional conduct. The absence of specialty recognition compounds the difficulty of compulsory continuing education as a condition of periodic recertification. It is surely only in those fields of law which one practises that it is necessary to ensure continuing competence. To examine a practitioner who confines himself or herself to the practice of estate planning, for example, in a way that requires the candidate to have the general proficiency of one being initially certified as competent to be admitted to practice would be futile as well as unfair.

To resort to a system, as some jurisdictions are contemplating, which demands that every practitioner demonstrate attendance, for a given number of hours annually, at continuing education programs does little to ensure involvement in a learning experience. The development of satisfactory methods of evaluation in the area of law that is relevant for a particular practitioner is a challenge of formidable proportions. Despite all of these very real difficulties, however, there can be little doubt that the future of professional regulation will mean as much concern for continuing competence as regulation of the practice of law has shown for initial competence, without in any way decreasing the importance of finding solutions to the growing problems of pre-certification education.

Law has much to learn from the experience of other professions, particularly medicine. Without minimizing the magnitude of the educational problems of the medical profession, I suggest that the model of medical education is well worth using as a guide, at least to the extent of the reliance upon the universities for both undergraduate and continuing education and the sense of responsibility with which the universities have accepted that role.

SUPPLY AND ACCESS

DAVID STAGER and NOAH MELTZ

Manpower planning in the professions

INTRODUCTION

Manpower planning has been the subject of discussion and heated debate for more than a decade. Proponents have claimed that planning will enhance economic growth, particularly when it relates to professional and skilled manpower.[1] Opponents have claimed that such planning distorts the market and will lead to excess supply or excess demand and in either case is costly in terms of economic resources.[2]

Our objective in this paper is to outline the general issues in manpower planning, briefly look at what is being done today in Canada, and then offer some suggestions concerning directions manpower planning might take. This paper is not intended to be a comprehensive review of the subject, since other studies have gone into far more depth.[3] Instead, we want to raise what we consider to be the major questions concerning how and what manpower planning is done.

David Stager is a member of the Institute for Policy Analysis, University of Toronto; Noah Meltz is director of the Centre for Industrial Relations, University of Toronto

1 See H.S. Parnes, 'Manpower analysis in educational planning,' in H.S. Parnes, ed., *Planning Education for Economic and Social Development* (Paris: Organization for Economic Cooperation and Development, 1964) 73-80
2 See W. Lee Hansen, 'Labor force and occupational projections,' Industrial Relations Research Association, Proceedings of the 18th Annual Winter Meetings, New York, December 1965, 10-20 and comments 20-30; Howard R. Bowen, 'The manpower vs free-choice principle,' in Larry F. Moore, ed., *Manpower Planning for Canadians: An Anthology* (Vancouver: Institute of Industrial Relations, University of British Columbia, 1975) 233-41.
3 See John W. Holland and Michael L. Skolnik, *Public Policy and Manpower Development* (Toronto: Ontario Institute for Studies in Education, 1975); and Sar A. Levitan, Garth L. Mangum, and Ray Marshall, *Human Resources and Labor Markets*, 2d edn (New York: Harper and Row, 1976) chaps 6 and 13.

There appears to be no generally accepted definition of 'manpower planning.' Perhaps it would be more accurate to say that there are both broad and narrow interpretations of this term. Both of these approaches tend to be concerned only with policies affecting the supply side of the labour markets, leaving the demand side to policies focusing on the level and conditions of employment or on welfare services.[4] The wider view of manpower planning encompasses issues such as quality of training, in-service training and continuing education, competence testing, and the organizational characteristics of specific labour markets. The narrower view of manpower planning is concerned primarily with numbers; that is, with the number of persons available – or potentially available – to specific labour markets. In this paper we deal almost exclusively with the latter interpretation of manpower planning.

One should also draw the distinction between private and public manpower planning. Many employers, including some of the larger ones, pay little attention to explicit manpower planning, and particularly to continuous long-term planning. For those firms or organizations which do have an administrative division responsible for manpower, the emphasis tends to be on staffing needs in the near-term and on job descriptions, pay schedules, and on-the-job training. Public manpower planning necessarily takes a longer, broader view of labour supply.

OBJECTIVES OF MANPOWER PLANNING

The basic objective in public manpower planning is to avoid or to minimize a shortage or surplus of specific types of labour at a given wage rate. This is usually the prevailing wage rate, although the objective may be to increase supply in order to lower the relative price in a specific labour market. This basic objective may be related to other public policy areas. Manpower planning is obviously a component of general economic planning: target growth rates and specific output goals require that the appropriate stock of manpower is available to meet these higher-order objectives.[5] It is also necessary to co-ordinate manpower planning with other public concerns – immigration, regional development, science policy – to assure compatibility and consistency of such policies. Even if none of the preceding problems were present, a public manpower policy would be neces-

---

4 See Noah M. Meltz, 'Implications of manpower and immigration policy,' in Lawrence Officer and Lawrence Smith, eds, *Issues in Canadian Economics* (Toronto: McGraw-Hill Ryerson, 1974) 245-57.

5 See Sylvia Ostry and Mahmood Zaidi, *Labour Economics in Canada*, 2d edn (Toronto: Macmillan, 1972) 158-81.

sary to take account of what economists would call 'positive externalities,' namely the social benefits associated with particular occupations. By definition, these benefits are not taken into account in individuals' decision-making; hence there would be underinvestment in some areas of manpower development if these decisions were left to the private market.

Although we are taking as the objective of manpower planning that specific labour markets should be in equilibrium (quantity supplied equals quantity demanded at the prevailing wage), some persons would describe situations as 'shortages' or 'surpluses' even when the markets were in equilibrium. As income differentials narrow – for example between professors and plumbers – some professors might suggest that there is a shortage of plumbers simply because their relative incomes have changed. Similarly one hears of the 'shortage' of cleaning ladies as it becomes increasingly difficult to find domestic help at what was considered to be the traditional and proper relative wage.

Another view of labour shortages or surpluses is based on rates of return to investment in education and training. It has been suggested that even though labour markets might be in equilibrium, a substantial and persistent difference in the rates of return to different occupations reveals imperfections in the operation of such labour markets which require correction through public manpower and other policies.[6] Current rate-of-return estimates show physicians and dentists well ahead of lawyers and engineers,[7] while the reverse was true in the early 1930s.[8]

Yet a third alternative view of the shortage/surplus question is that recurring short-run shortages and surpluses, however defined, are inevitable in any dynamic economy.[9] There will be a 'temporary shortage' in the very short run if demand increases quickly – particularly for occupations with longer training periods – but this should require no policy action. However, if demand is steadily increasing relative to supply, then we will face a 'chronic shortage' due to the supply lag, and public intervention will be required if a steady increase in the relative wage for that occupation is to be avoided. The danger in this situation is evident in the university teacher case: the demand for academics increased steadily through the 1960s, university salaries and subsidies for PHD students

6 M.J. Bowman, 'Educational shortage and excess,' *Canadian Journal of Economics and Political Science*, Nov. 1963, 446-62
7 Commission on Post-Secondary Education in Ontario, *Cost and Benefit Study* (Toronto: Queen's Printer, 1972) 93-103
8 J.R. Walsh, 'Capital concept applied to man,' *Quarterly Journal of Economics*, Feb. 1935, 255-85
9 K.J. Arrow and W.M. Capron, 'Dynamic shortages and price rises: the engineer-scientist case,' *Quarterly Journal of Economics*, 73 (1959), 292-308

were increased substantially, and then demand slackened while PH D output continued at roughly the same rate.[10]

ALTERNATIVE TECHNIQUES
IN MANPOWER FORECASTING

While these latter two views of labour market imbalances have substantial merit, we are concerned here only with the 'equilibrium at a given wage' approach because this is the most commonly assumed objective in manpower planning. This approach requires a forecast of the demand for specific kinds of labour services and a forecast of supply. Various forecasting methods used on the demand side can be grouped in three categories: employer surveys, ratios and trends, and econometric models.

The employer-survey method consists simply of a questionnaire seeking individual employers' estimates of the number of persons they will need in various occupational categories at a specified time in the near future – usually twelve to thirty-six months hence.[11] Responses are aggregated to determine the global manpower needs. The ratio or trend method has several variants. For some occupations, such as teachers, dentists, or physicians, the prevailing or desired ratio of practitioners to population is applied to the forecast population, and the required manpower in the specific occupation is calculated directly. Alternatively, the ratio may be expressed as the percentage of the total labour force represented by members of the given occupation. This percentage could be held constant or varied in accordance with value judgments about the appropriate level of service that should be provided to the population. A variation of this method is a simple extrapolation of trends in the composition, or occupational mix, of the labour force.

The use of econometric models is a somewhat more sophisticated method: the manpower needs are estimated by specifying the detailed labour requirements for producing the forecast output of final goods and services. Such models can range from the very simple statement of a labour/output ratio to a complex computerized model allowing for variations in technology resulting from changes in relative factor prices and improved productivity.

Forecasts of labour supply are derived from basically one technique. This begins with the number of persons currently in the labour force in a specific

10 M. von Zur-Muehlen, 'The PH D dilemma in Canada: a case study,' in Sylvia Ostry, ed., *Canadian Higher Education in the Seventies* (Ottawa: Economic Council of Canada, 1972) 75-131
11 See Canada Department of Labour, *Employment Outlook for Professional Personnel in Scientific and Technical Fields 1962-1964*, Professional Manpower Report No. 13 (Ottawa: Queen's Printer, December 1962).

occupation; this number is then adjusted by estimating the increases and decreases that will occur over the time period in question. Estimates of graduates from specific educational programs (such as law, medicine, engineering, etc.) will depend on estimates of the population (particularly in the appropriate age group) and the percentage of this population enrolling in and completing the program. This number will be further adjusted according to the expected labour force participation rate for graduates of a specific program and the percentage of these who will enter the given occupation. One must also take account of previous graduates who will enter or re-enter the labour force after some absence, and the number of persons who will be added through immigration and transfers from other occupations where this is possible. There will also be attribution due to death, retirement, transfer to other occupations, withdrawal from the labour force, and emigration. In short, several important and difficult assumptions must be made in estimating labour supply; when relative salaries, educational financing, and social values are changing rapidly, such estimates can vary widely depending on one's choice of assumptions.

An alternative approach to this matching of supply and demand estimates is to estimate the rate of return to investment in education or training for various occupations. The rationale in making rate-of-return comparisons, as noted previously, is that occupations for which there is a persistently high private rate of return relative to other occupations are deemed to be experiencing a chronic shortage of manpower. This conclusion, however, must be tempered by an examination of the operation of specific labour markets to determine whether adjustments should more appropriately be made on the demand side,[12] and whether substantial differences in private non-monetary benefits can account for some of the rate-of-return variation.[13]

SOME PROBLEMS WITH THE FORECASTING METHODS

Some of the problems inherent in the rationale and techniques for manpower planning are self-evident. The assumption of what constitutes an equilibrium wage rate or the belief that public policy should aim for a specific wage rate are too important to be left to the manpower planners – or to members of specific professions or occupations. In fact, most manpower forecasts have simply tended to ignore wage rates. Second, the time horizon in manpower forecasting is necessarily long; that is, the more expensive the training required, the greater the need

12 For example, by improving the productivity of professional manpower providing services directly to the public.
13 See for example, D.A. Dodge and D.A.A. Stager, 'Returns to graduate study in science, engineering and business,' *Canadian Journal of Economics*, May 1972, 182-98.

for avoiding misallocation of resources, yet expensive programs tend to be long programs and hence to require long horizons or 'lead times' in their planning. But longer time horizons open the possibility for greater social and economic change, and hence wider margins of error in planning.

A third general problem area encompasses all the assumptions and data requirements entailed in the various techniques that have been described. These include assumptions about the rate and nature of economic expansion in particular regions of the economy, about relative prices and the elasticity of substitution among productive factors, and about personal tastes, social values, and political decisions. Fortunately – at least from the point of view of planning – the basic variables tend to change slowly; the serious difficulty is in forecasting or identifying a change in the direction of the basic forces. A recent example is found in university enrolments: planners had forecast a slowing down in the growth of enrolments in the early 1970s, but no one anticipated the absolute decline experienced in some provinces.

The fourth problem concerns the link between manpower planning and educational planning. Obviously a major determinant of manpower supply is the number of graduates from educational and training programs; hence manpower planning is frequently associated with educational planning. This linkage, however, is not an easy one. Questions concerning the destination of graduates have been raised in the context of manpower supply forecasting: What percentage of the graduates will immediately enter the labour force? Into which geographic areas and occupations will they go? The more fundamental question is one of determining the appropriate level and kind of skills or knowledge required to enter a specific occupation. The variation in educational preparation for any given occupation is evident in the data drawn from the decennial census. For example, of the 15,075 males who were employed in 1970 as electrical engineers, about 58 per cent had a university degree, 11 per cent had completed some university, 19 per cent had completed Grades 12 or 13 or some non-university further education, 9 per cent had attended high school to the end of Grades 9, 10, or 11, and 2 per cent had less than Grade 9 schooling.

What is deemed to be an appropriate educational preparation for an occupation is clearly changing over time. One of the most succinct pieces of evidence of this is in a paper by David Sewell.[14] When he examined the education of workers in 232 non-managerial occupations in 1961, he found that 28 per cent of this group were in occupations where the average educational level was more than one-half a school year below the level which employers for those occupa-

---

14 David Sewell, 'Educational planning models and the relationship between education and occupation,' in Ostry, ed., *Canadian Higher Education*, 45-74

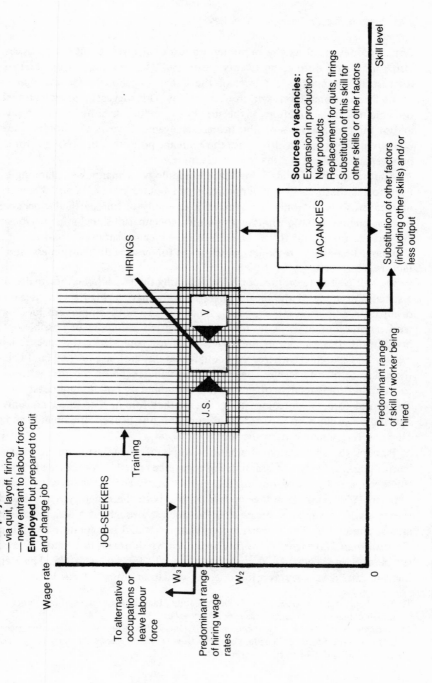

FIGURE 1 Simplified flow diagram of an individual labour market

tions had described as the minimum educational level for new employees. He also found that during the twenty years 1941 to 1961, about one-half of the increase in the educational level of the Canadian labour force was due to increased educational levels within occupations. This suggests that educational 'requirements' are a function of the supply of graduates, rather than the reverse, and/or that the measures of educational achievement (years of schooling) are not consistent over time. In either case the evidence poses serious problems for a link between educational and manpower planning.

Another problem underlying the methodology of manpower planning is the need to take into account the operation of labour markets. As noted earlier, the market involves not only the demand and supply of one particular occupation but also the interrelationships among various occupations, including persons who are outside the labour force. The adjustment mechanism in the market can have a number of possible responses which make forecasting difficult unless all of the factors are known.

We will elaborate on this point by indicating the possible factors involved and a specific example of the recent operation of a market. Figure 1 focuses on one occupation but shows the possible reactions of both employers looking for workers and workers looking for jobs.[15] Each has a number of possible options in addition to a change in the wage rate. They could leave the specific labour market and search elsewhere, they could drop out entirely, or they could change their skill or quality levels. The final result will depend on the alternatives open to each and their relative attractiveness (in monetary and non-monetary terms). To plan or forecast outcomes perfectly, we therefore have to know not only the demand and supply in a particular occupation but in fact all demands and supplies and their relative attractiveness.

Perhaps the most recent dramatic example of the adjustment mechanism of labour markets is that of graduate (or registered) nurses. For Canada as a whole, this occupation showed one of the highest levels and rates of vacancies from 1968 to 1975, ranking in the top five during six of these eight years.[16] The most recent data, however, indicate that vacancies throughout Canada have been almost eliminated. The Department of Manpower and Immigration's publication *Occupational Shortages, Total by Region* shows shortages in Canada of seventy-six persons in August 1976 compared with 722 for August 1975. The Department defines a vacancy as a job opening which an employer has been trying to

15 This diagram is reproduced from Noah M. Meltz, 'Identifying sources of imbalance in individual labour markets,' *Relations Industrielles*, 31 (1976), 224-46.
16 Department of Manpower and Immigration, *Canada Manpower Review*, second quarter, 1974, 19; and Statistics Canada, *Quarterly Report on Job Vacancies*, various issues from second quarter 1974 to first quarter 1976

fill continuously for at least thirty days and a shortage as the net number of vacancies on hand. The figure of 722 in Code 3131130, Nurse, General Duty, was the largest number of long-term vacancies of any seven-digit occupation on the list in August 1975. The decline in shortages did not occur in Ontario or British Columbia, since by 1975 there were few vacancies. The decline took place in the Atlantic, Quebec, and Prairie Regions.[17] Our suspicion in the absence of more concrete data and analysis is that a major factor contributing to this decline in vacancies was the large increase in salaries which took place for nurses, first in British Columbia in 1974, then in Ontario, and in other provinces subsequently. The Ontario increase was almost 50 per cent, bringing beginning general duty nurses to a present (1976) starting salary of $13,380 after completion of the two-year community college training program.[18]

The labour market mechanism likely operated as follows. The increase in salaries increased the supply of nurses in several ways. First, the turnover of nurses probably declined as the more attractive salaries induced nurses to remain employed rather than leaving at as rapid a rate as had been the case. In 1966 it was estimated that the annual turnover rate averaged 60 per cent.[19] Second, nurses who had been outside the labour force or in other occupations were likely attracted back into the profession. Third, persons (primarily women) considering career choices would now find this occupation relatively more attractive than before, since the rate of return had risen substantially, and would attempt to enrol in the training programs. Since these developments occurred at a time when the demand for teachers was declining, and when training, at least in Ontario, moved from the three-year hospital program to two years in community colleges, the trend to increased applications and enrolments would be accelerated. At the same time the increased salaries would probably have the effect of reducing somewhat the demand for graduate nurses unless governments were prepared to absorb all of the extra salary costs.

Unless manpower planners had been able to anticipate the substantial increase in salaries for nurses, their forecasts would have overestimated demand and underestimated supply.

17 The vacancies by region for general duty nurses were as follows:

	Atlantic	Quebec	Ontario	Prairie	Pacific	Total
August 1976	6	46	3	10	11	76
August 1975	240	189	20	224	49	722

18 Background information for this section was provided by Evelyn Wong, Ontario Nurses' Association, and Carl Posluns, Ontario Hospital Association. We would like to thank them for their assistance. The interpretation of the data is ours.

19 A.G. Atkinson, K.J. Barnes, and Ellen Richardson, *Canada's Highly Qualified Manpower Resources* (Ottawa: Department of Manpower and Immigration, 1970) 163

Richard Freeman's recent article on the market for new lawyers also indicates the effects of the operation of the market.[20] He found that 'the decision to enroll in law school is significantly affected by economic conditions in the profession,'[21] with the salaries of young lawyers being inversely related to numbers of graduates. The result is that 'the market undergoes highly dampened cobweb-type fluctuations with a peak-trough period of three to four years.'[22] He suggests that: 'the market for lawyers will likely be depressed in the mid-seventies when the large classes of the late sixties/early seventies graduate.'[23]

EXPERIENCE WITH MANPOWER PLANNING

Although manpower planning has been widely discussed during the past decade, in fact very little manpower planning goes on in Canada. Aside from ad hoc efforts to look at supply and demand in particular sectors, such as the Royal Commission on Health Services, there has been little ongoing manpower planning. The Department of Manpower and Immigration has prepared several forecasts of likely demand,[24] but it has not yet included a reconciliation of supply estimates with demand.[25] The Department's most recent project is the use of the CANDIDE econometric forecasting model to project manpower requirements. The project is termed COFOR (Canadian Occupational Forecasting Program). The data released so far deal with non-professional occupations. The Department also prepares short-term outlooks under the Forward Occupational Imbalances Listing (FOIL).[26]

Other groups have attempted to include the supply side to a greater extent. Cecily Watson and Joseph Butorac projected manpower stocks in Ontario and then modified 'the figure in the light of various supply and demand factors.'[27]

20 Richard Freeman, 'Legal "cobwebs": a recursive model of the market for new lawyers,' *Review of Economics and Statistics*, 57 (May 1975), 171-9; cf. P. Pashigian, 'The market for lawyers,' *Journal of Law and Economics*, 20 (April 1977), 53-86.
21 Ibid, 179
22 Ibid
23 Ibid
24 See B. Ahamad, *A Projection of Manpower Requirements by Occupation in 1975* (Ottawa: Department of Manpower and Immigration, 1969); Noah M. Meltz and G. Peter Penz, *Canada's Manpower Requirements in 1970* (Ottawa: Queen's Printer, 1968).
25 For a discussion of the Department's plans, see 'Canadian Occupational Forecasting Program,' *Canada Manpower Review*, fourth quarter, 1973 (Ottawa: Department of Manpower and Immigration, 1973) 15-17.
26 See *FOIL, Forward Occupational Imbalance Listing*, 2, No. 1, April 1976 (Ottawa: Department of Manpower and Immigration, 1976)
27 Cecily Watson and Joseph Butorac, *Qualified Manpower in Ontario 1961-1986* (Toronto: Ontario Institute for Studies in Education, 1968)

Edward Harvey and K.S.R. Murthy in their recent study have made explicit projections of supply and demand for graduates of engineering, chemistry, business, and commerce.[28] Their projections used the CANDIDE model on the demand side.

There are a number of reasons for the relatively few examples of manpower planning even in the most basic form of supply and demand projections. The first set of reasons is conceptual, namely the difficulties discussed earlier of selecting the most appropriate format or of attempting to take into consideration the possible interactions in the market. The second difficulty is empirical.[29] Aside from the decennial population census we do not adequately know the current employment situation or unemployment situation for detailed occupations. In reviewing the data on historical trends and projections of the number of lawyers in Ontario, Meltz found confusion among the data bases specially relating to the actual number of lawyers.[30] In addition, there were some questions about the reliability of the supply estimates and differences in the demand estimates. When data are finally released from Statistics Canada's *Occupational Employment Survey*, the first gap will be remedied. The lack of unemployment data may be ended if unemployment insurance data can be related to the more global estimates for occupation groups from the Labour Force Survey. Current vacancy data are, of course, now available through the Job Vacancy Survey. Other data needs which have yet to be met are comprehensive wage and salary figures and information on flows of people into and out of occupations.[31]

Even where projections have been prepared, there is no reason to expect that a unique set of figures will be produced. As with other exercises in 'futures,' forecasts can differ depending on the underlying assumptions they make and the models used. For example, a recent paper by Betty M. Vetter compared the widely different projections of supply and demand for science and engineering doctorates in the United States prepared by the Bureau of Labor Statistics and the National Science Foundation.[32] She says: 'in the physical sciences, NSF anti-

28 Edward Harvey and K.S.R. Murthy, *Supply of and Demand for New Graduates in Engineering, Chemistry, Business and Commerce* (Toronto: Technical Services Council, 1975)

29 For a recent discussion of labour market information, see Economic Council of Canada, *People and Jobs: A Study of the Canadian Labour Market* (Ottawa: Information Canada, 1976) chaps 5 and 10.

30 Noah M. Meltz, *A Review of Historical Trends and Projections of the Number of Lawyers and Judges in the Ontario Labour Force*, prepared for the Committee of Ontario Law Deans (Toronto: Institute for Policy Analysis, University of Toronto, 1974)

31 For a complete discussion of these points, see Economic Council of Canada, *People and Jobs*.

32 Betty M. Vetter, 'Higher education in the changing employment market,' a paper prepared for the American Council on Education, Fifty-Eighth Annual Meeting, Washington DC, 9 Oct. 1975

cipates that 10.5% of the doctoral workforce will not be able to find science/ engineering positions in 1985, while the BLS projection shows an over-supply of 44%.'[33] If it is so difficult to get some agreement on likely manpower trends, is it possible to consider the more comprehensive notion of manpower planning?

SHOULD THERE BE ANY MANPOWER PLANNING AT ALL?

At the beginning we noted that some persons question the value of attempting any manpower planning. Having set out the major conceptual and empirical difficulties in attempting manpower planning, we offer the following observations.

1 There is a role for projections of manpower requirements and supplies as long as the assumptions underlying the projections are made explicit and projections are frequently revised.

2 Manpower projections should be related to analysis of current and recent past developments in the operation of the labour markets for specific occupations; this is particularly important in the professions, which in most cases require a long lead time for changing domestic supply institutions.

3 Additional data are needed to undertake current labour market analysis more effectively. These data needs have been discussed in depth in the Economic Council of Canada's recent study *People and Jobs.*

4 A more comprehensive approach to manpower planning must go beyond simply changing enrolment in educational institutions. The broader examination of labour markets we suggested would require consideration of alternatives such as demand-side adjustments, changes in wage and salary rates, changes in immigration policy, etc.[34]

5 Private manpower planning should be encouraged to include labour market operation and projections along with purely personnel matters. Ultimately, firms and government agencies themselves can have an important input into the manpower planning process.

6 As a final point, we suggest that the alternatives should not be thought of as either comprehensive manpower planning or pure laissez-faire. As noted earlier, when there are long lead times the market will tend to produce booms and busts in what economists refer to as a cobweb effect. We suggest a mix of projections and current market analysis, along with the use of a range of policy variables beyond simply altering supply by changing the outputs of the education or immigration systems.

This bring us virtually to the point from which we began, namely the matter of objectives in manpower planning. The quantity and quality of such planning as occurs in our economy will depend on who provides what answers to the question of objectives.

33 Ibid, 3   34 See Meltz, 'Implications of manpower and immigration policy.'

MICHAEL L. SKOLNIK

Beyond manpower forecasting: some reflections on its meaning for the professions

A major problem which confronts any attempt to produce prescriptive statements on manpower planning for the professions is that there is no generally accepted notion of what manpower planning is; and in fact there are probably few areas of public policy where there is less consensus on such fundamentals as terminology, objectives, location of responsibility for decision-making, and policy tools available. As a colleague and I observed in the opening sentence of a book entitled, *Public Policy and Manpower Development*,[1] 'the plain semantic fact with which an effort to define and delimit manpower policy must cope is that the simple word "manpower" has no established meaning in any of the social sciences or in popular discourse.' When the word 'manpower' is coupled with the term 'planning,' the potential for ambiguity is increased, particularly as a consequence of the widespread tendency to employ such terms as manpower policy, manpower programs, and manpower forecasting interchangeably with manpower planning. Given this ambiguity, it is advisable first to clarify how the term 'manpower planning' will be used in this paper, before commenting on manpower planning for the professions. The brief remarks in the following section are included not for the sake of semantic virtue but because the most efficient way to define manpower planning is to indicate how it differs from related terms with which it is often confused.

MANPOWER PLANNING VS MANPOWER POLICY

The widespread use of the term 'manpower' is a relatively recent phenomenon, dating back not more than about three decades. The primary reason for using

Director of administration, Ontario Institute for Studies in Education; formerly director of research, Ministry of Labour, Province of Ontario
1 John W. Holland and Michael L. Skolnik, *Public Policy and Manpower Development* (Toronto: Ontario Institute for Studies in Education, 1975) 2

the word 'manpower' instead of 'labour' or 'worker' is to connote workers with special qualifications (e.g. highly qualified manpower or skilled manpower), or those who are presumed to be almost unemployable because they lack such qualifications. Highly qualified manpower is an object of manpower policy, a term with generally positive connotations. The positive connotations of manpower policy have to do, first, with the considerable public subsidy that enables these people to acquire their qualifications and the consequent concern that they be employed in a position appropriate to their credentials, and/or, second, with the belief that their employment is urgently needed for expansion of an important industry or because of the perceived necessity of the service they provide.

Manpower policy has been defined as 'the implicit or explicit commitment to a pattern of behaviour intended to increase the rate of returns accruing to society from the resource that is the population in its present state.'[2] As such, manpower policy is concerned with the most economical development and the most productive and personally satisfying use of society's actual and potential manpower resources. The domain of manpower policy consists potentially of all legal, institutional, and attitudinal factors which determine how manpower is developed and used. Particularly important are those factors which influence significantly the availability, quality, skill-mix, geographical distribution, and efficiency of manpower, as well as the process by which people and jobs are matched.

In less abstract terms, the principal objectives of manpower policy involve avoiding surpluses and shortages of manpower, achieving the best matching of a worker's skills and qualifications with the tasks and responsibilities to be performed, increasing productivity, and improving the quality of work life. Manpower policy implies a commitment to design and/or manipulate legal, institutional, and technological systems in such a way as to further the above objectives.

While national or provincial manpower *policy* implies a commitment to these objectives, that does not necessarily require substantial direct government involvement in specific decisions about how manpower will be developed and used. In contrast, national or provincial manpower *planning* connotes a direct involvement by government in influencing or modifying particular decisions of households and business establishments. For example, a manpower policy may include general guidelines regarding public subsidization of training and criteria for entry into various occupations. On the other hand manpower planning may connote precise procedures for the state to use in determining how many individuals should be trained and licensed in a particular field.

2 Ibid, 22

As noted earlier, manpower policy has generally positive connotations. Few people would object to their society having a manpower policy. Indeed, most people would regard a manpower policy as a staple of modern statecraft, and probably would not have strong emotive responses to the concept of a manpower policy.[3] In contrast, the concept of state manpower planning can be expected to evoke strong responses, and many would object to instituting provincial or national manpower planning. It is obvious that economist Kenneth Boulding had manpower planning in mind when he made the following widely quoted statement: 'I find the whole manpower concept repulsive, disgusting, dangerous, fascistic, communistic, incompatible with the ideals of a liberal democracy, and unsuitable company for the minds of the young.'[4] The literature to which Boulding was reacting would suggest that whatever else manpower planning includes, it at least means that the state (with or without consultation of worker and business organizations) determines the numbers of people who will be allowed to train and/or work in various occupations. Implementation may be via some fairly indirect mechanism such as manipulation of training fee, price, and wage structures or more directly through a quota system. After all, manpower planning at the enterprise level includes determining the number of people in various skill categories that the enterprise will hire and employ. It is thus easy to see why national manpower planning has come to have a similar connotation. It is this connotation of the state control over training and entry that makes manpower planning attractive in some quarters and repugnant in others.

THE RATIONALE FOR
MANPOWER PLANNING BY THE STATE

In the liberal democracies, government intervention in the economic lives of individuals and business is deemed warranted where such intervention is thought to prevent or correct socially undesirable results and where the benefits of the intervention exceed the costs. The rationale for state intervention in the development and utilization of manpower is that the outcome of the interactions among decentralized decisions of countless households and employers of manpower, even within the framework of a broad manpower policy, does not generate satisfactory results in terms of productive or equitable use of society's resources, and that such intervention will produce substantial benefits in terms of both equity

3 There may be objections to the contents of a particular manpower policy or to the way that policy is applied, but that is another matter.
4 Kenneth E. Boulding, 'An economist's view of the manpower concept,' in National Manpower Council, *Proceedings of a Conference on the Utilization of Scientific and Professional Manpower* (New York: Columbia University Press, 1954) 11

and efficiency. At present, opinion is divided on this proposition. The numerous items of evidence advanced in support of the need for manpower planning by the state include cases of graduates from lengthy and expensive educational programs being unable to find employment, working in jobs that people without such training appear to do very well, or being snapped up by employers from other countries; large industrial developments *almost* being held up by lack of qualified manpower; and excessively high earnings by certain groups of workers, which is regarded as inequitable by itself, but also contributes to inflation as other workers try to emulate them. More sophisticated writings show how the models of successive over- and underproduction of hogs or apple trees long known to agricultural economists can apply to over- and undersupply of highly trained manpower.[5] There is even some limited empirical evidence demonstrating the applicability of such models to 'products' of certain educational programs.[6]

It is possible to set out a lengthy list of the conditions which are necessary in order for the interaction of the unco-ordinated decisions of individual households and employers to generate a reasonably efficient matching of the demand for and the supply of manpower by occupation. There are about a dozen such conditions, of which the principal ones[7] are:
- sufficient wage flexibility for changes in wage rates to signal changes in demand or supply;
- expected economic returns must have a prominent (not necessarily exclusive) role in career choice;
- absence of undue social-psychological constraints on career choice;
- absence of substantial financial barriers to career preparation;
- flexibility of career preparation structures to adapt to changing occupational demands;
- absence of excessive 'bandwagon' phenomena in career selection;
- absence of extreme rigidity in employment structures;
- absence of frequent irregular shifts in demand for different types of skills.
The science of labour market analysis has not reached the point where what is meant by reasonable, excessive, extreme, etc. in this list of conditions can be stated precisely, or where one can say how seriously the efficiency of the de-

5 These are generally referred to as 'cobweb' models, because the line segments which connect successive points of intersection on a supply and demand chart form a cobweb-like image. For an introduction to such models see Richard G. Lipsey and Peter O. Steiner, *Economics* (New York: Harper and Row, 1966) 138-41.
6 Richard Freeman, 'Legal cobwebs: the changing market for lawyers,' *Review of Economics and Statistics*, May 1975
7 For a complete list, see John W. Holland et al., *Manpower Forecasting and Educational Policy* (Toronto: Queen's Printer, 1972) 31-66.

centralized system is impaired by various degrees of absence or presence of these conditions. There is reason to doubt the operation of some of these conditions at least at certain times for certain occupational groups. For example, it appears that the greatest increases in salaries of nurses have occurred during a recent period of labour market balance or excess supply rather than during earlier periods of shortage. The energy crisis appears to have resulted in an irregular and dramatic shift in the demand for some engineering and construction skills, of a kind unlikely to occur at any time for doctors, dentists, or lawyers. With ideal or even satisfactory supply-demand matching via the decentralized approach with limited direct state planning dependent upon so many specifications, it is likely that at least some improvements can be realized by market interventions working at the edges of the system. Some of the above conditions are more amenable to change through public policy than others. For example, the social-psychological factors which influence career choice may be among the least amenable to change, compared to, say, the financial barriers to career preparation. Some types of intervention increase the need for additional interventions, while others reduce that need. In general, interventions which attack institutional barriers reduce the need for further intervention. A policy which emphasizes the reduction of such barriers (e.g. making career preparation systems more flexible) may not warrant being referred to as manpower planning. Of course many of the so-called institutional barriers exist for very good reasons, or at least there may be serious consequences of removing them. For example, Michael Piore has shown that under seniority systems a great deal of informal on-the-job training of younger workers by older workers takes place which the latter may be afraid to give in the absence of such systems.[8] Clearly there is a need for much more knowledge about the short- and long-run effects of various intervention strategies and how they interact. Without that, and knowledge of the extent to which the various conditions listed above exist, one simply cannot say whether the most efficient policy consists of attacking inhibiting institutional and legal structures, or interfering more directly to control supplies of and/or demands for manpower, i.e. manpower planning.

Still, the extent of our ignorance on such matters can be reduced. One of the cornerstones of the case for manpower planning is the assumption of rigidly fixed manpower requirements. The essence of this assumption is that production systems require a specific number of persons in each of particular occupational groups for a given level of output or service. The argument implies that it is not possible to substitute workers with one skill for workers with another skill. If

8 Michael J. Piore, 'On-the-job training and adjustment to technological change,' *Journal of Human Resources*, Fall 1968, 436-8

more than the required number of workers in an occupation are present, the excess will be unemployed. If there are fewer than the required number, production will decline, and workers in other occupations will be unemployed (until the lowest common multiple is reached). If manpower requirements are as rigid as this model assumes, then it is extremely important to make precise manpower requirement projections and to take appropriate action to ensure that the actual supplies meet those projections.

While this type of assumption may fit the blending of materials in chemical and metallurgical processes, there is increasing doubt as to its applicability to human beings.[9] Where it does apply most is where human beings are used as machines (e.g. keypunch operators) or where legal or contractual arrangements so dictate. The latter state appears to hold frequently among certain professions and increasingly in large bureaucratized organizations. Whether such restrictions on how many persons in a particular occupational category are permitted to perform specific tasks, on balance, serve the public interest is difficult to say. However, the following manpower planning implication is of great concern: where there are such rigidities influencing the numbers of people of various occupational categories required, it will be extremely costly to have the wrong numbers of qualified people – and it will be very unlikely that qualified people will be supplied in the correct numbers *without* direct manpower planning by the state (and maybe even with such planning). In short, a market system requires substantial flexibility to operate efficiently, and the more rigidities built into it, the more there is a need for state manpower planning. Occupational groups pressing for various kinds of restrictions to protect their work sphere are, at the same time, helping to create the rigidities which make more direct government intervention necessary. For such groups then to appeal to the government 'to let the market alone' is to ignore the fact that the measures which they advocate would work to cripple the market.

THE ROLE AND LIMITATIONS
OF MANPOWER FORECASTING

It is inherent in the notion of manpower planning that the active role played by government in influencing manpower supplies and demands would be guided by manpower forecasts. The close connection between manpower planning and manpower forecasting is evidenced by the fact that frequently articles with titles

---

9 For a summary of empirical studies on this question, see George Psacharopoulos, 'Substitution assumptions versus empirical evidence in manpower planning,' *De Economist*, Nov.-Dec. 1973, 609-25.

which refer to manpower planning are devoted entirely to making or analysing manpower forecasts. Such a blurring of the distinction between the two concepts is understandable, because it is generally conceded that effective manpower planning is impossible without reliable manpower forecasts. Insofar as this concession is valid, it does not augur well for the possibilities of effective national or provincial manpower planning. The cumulative experience of manpower forecasting is not encouraging. There is some disagreement among experts as to whether the principal limitations are conceptual, methodological, informational, or institutional.

The concept of manpower requirements is quite fuzzy. What does it mean to say that Ontario will 'require' x thousand lawyers in 1985? What will happen if there are 5 per cent fewer than x lawyers in 1985? The methodology of manpower forecasting, in spite of, or more likely because of, its simplicity, is sound for combining various contributory factors into a consistent set of forecasts. The main methodological problem is that of dealing with the uncertainty implied in the term 'future.' It is easier to look back a thousand years than forward a day.

Information for most manpower forecasts is terribly inadequate. To some extent, information deficiencies can be remedied at a price – but a huge price. However, solving the information problem involves much more than money. The kind of information needed and the format in which it is needed depend upon how the forecast is going to be used. Yet most manpower forecasts are not used, and rarely is there a clear idea of the intended use when they are undertaken – notwithstanding the frequently made claim that the main purpose is 'to give a better feel for the future.' An even greater problem is that the people supplying the information usually are not party to the use of the forecasts. As such they feel little responsibility and have no commitment to the quality or rigour of the information. They may not even understand what is being asked of them. This makes for poor information. There are exceptions, where the suppliers of the information do have a commitment to the end use, and in these cases the results are often very good. Mostly these cases involve forecasting *within* an organization.

Persons who supply information for use in making manpower forecasts cannot be expected to have a commitment to the use or purpose of the forecasts when that commitment is lacking in those who initiate the forecasts. The absence of any sense of purpose or institutional context for using the results is said by some experts to be the over-riding obstacle to further development of the art of manpower forecasting.[10] This lack of a sense of purpose is sometimes

10 This is the conclusion of a recent evaluation of the state of manpower forecasting in the United States. See S.C. Kelley et al., *Manpower Forecasting in the United States: An Evaluation of the State of the Art* (Columbus: Center for Human Resource Research, Ohio State University, 1975).

said to be a consequence of the unreliability of the forecasting technique. To that extent, there is a 'catch-22' situation: the information base for forecasts cannot be improved unless there is a commitment to using them; and such commitment cannot be obtained until there is more confidence in the forecasts.

If there is a way out of this dilemma it must be through making a strong commitment to the use of manpower forecasting and then hoping that on the strength of that commitment reliable forecasts can be developed at a reasonable cost. Even then there is no guarantee that sufficiently reliable forecasts can be produced. However, an even more important consideration in deciding whether to make such a commitment to manpower forecasting is the influence which the manpower forecasting paradigm has upon the way in which human resource development and utilization is perceived. The manpower forecasting paradigm reflects a somewhat cynical attitude which inhibits imaginative and flexible approaches to development and utilization of human resources. Four distinct aspects of this negative influence of the manpower forecasting paradigm are identified below.

De-individualization of career guidance
One of the most common justifications given for investing resources in making forecasts of manpower requirements is to develop such forecasts for use in career guidance. However, at best such forecasts can reflect only the present and near future occupational outlook. Even then it is impossible for one student to take into account how peers will react to the same forecasts, and therefore how to use the forecasts. For the student who wishes to maximize his opportunities, the rational response may even be to select the field that is forecast to have the worst opportunities – on the assumption that no one else will go into that field. Thus, the guidance counsellor may have to become an expert not only in manpower forecasting, but also in game theory.

A more fundamental question is whether it is reasonable for individuals to make decisions that will determine, not just their careers, but in large part their life styles on the basis of manpower forecasts which at best can indicate opportunities for the next *few* years? Surely the most important factors in an individual's career selection should be his or her interests, aptitudes, and abilities. It would be unfortunate if such factors were relegated to second place, behind some transient manpower forecasts. It may be out of fashion to think of a profession as a 'calling,' but it is not hard to imagine deceptively authoritative manpower forecast figures achieving domination over considerations of personality, self-image, and aptitude in career guidance discussions. In the long run an individual's desires for a satisfying and remunerative career are likely to be served better by following his or her abilities and interests than by following the latest manpower forecasts.

'Peg-in-a-hole' mentality

The manpower forecasting model is based on a 'peg-in-a-hole' philosophy of people and jobs. The job (hole) is taken as given, and the objective is to fit the person (peg) to the job. Adoption of such a philosophy conflicts with notions of personal dignity and individuality. The traits that distinguish one individual from another make it difficult for each individual to fit the job as it was designed. This mentality also inhibits seeing (or looking for) potentialities for personal growth and development. If a person fits the job, then personal growth threatens to bring problems of mis-fit.

Earlier it was suggested that many of the rigidities in employment structures are institutional – legal or contractual regulations, administrative policy, and convention – rather than the result of technology. Acceptance of the peg-in-a-hole mentality of manpower forecasting desensitizes people to the fact that these institutional rigidities *can* be changed. In fact, the peg-in-a-hole mentality conditions people to accept additional institutional rigidities.

The manpower assembly line

In the manpower forecasting model, human resource development is viewed as assembly line production. As with factory products like television sets, the idea is first to forecast the demand for various models or different occupational groups, and then to issue orders for the correct numbers to be produced by the factory. The assembly line view of human resources development results in an overemphasis on lengthy and expensive pre-employment training. Frequently graduates of such programs find difficulty obtaining jobs commensurate with their training, or discover after a short time on the job that they do not like the type of work for which they were trained. On the other hand there is a tendency toward neglect of the needs of employed workers for in-service training and retraining, and of employers' needs to have the skills of their workforce upgraded and updated. To some extent these neglects are being met by an increasing emphasis on continuing education. However, the assembly line mentality may influence continuing education as well as pre-employment training. When this happens, continuing education is viewed simply as 'retooling,' or upgrading very specific workplace skills, without assisting and encouraging individuals to re-think their career aspirations and search for new directions of personal and vocational development.

Preoccupation with numbers

The practice of manpower forecasting focuses almost entirely upon numbers, principally the numbers of persons entering, engaged in, or completing various types of training and the numbers employed, seeking employment, or sought by employers. To the extent that manpower planning discussions emphasize the forecasting side, and accordingly give prominence to the peg-in-a-hole mentality and the assembly line view of human resource development, they will likely ignore a variety of important qualitative issues regarding manpower development and utilization. Some of these issues have especially important implications for manpower in the professions. Three qualitative issues concerning manpower in the professions are discussed in the next section.

QUALITATIVE ISSUES CONCERNING MANPOWER
DEVELOPMENT AND UTILIZATION IN
THE PROFESSIONS

Strengthening the linkage between
prospective entrants and employers/clients
Historically one of the strong points of much professional training has been the close linkage that trainees have had with practising professionals as well as with clients and/or employers. Not only has this contributed much to the quality and relevance of training, but it has also provided trainees an opportunity for much better informed and realistic career choices than are possible for youths engaged in programs which have no such linkage. It is not known how many students drop out of professional training programs in the early stages because their exposure to the actual work situation makes them realize that they would not be happy in that type of work. Others may settle upon a particular area of specialization early in their training because of the work related experience. These are opportunities not available to students in fields that have little direct connection between the classroom and the workplace.

Another advantage of the close linkage between trainees and employers has been the maintenance of a reasonable balance between supply and demand without substantial direct government intervention. Where employers have had a major responsibility for the training of professionals they have sought to ensure the training of sufficient numbers to meet their own needs but have not been willing to train much larger numbers and cause a substantial oversupply. Of course where the majority of professionals are self-employed and the training volume is determined largely by peer professionals, undersupply is quite possible.

Given the advantages of a strong linkage between training and employment of professionals, it is ironic that this linkage is being weakened, and professional training in Canada is tending more in the direction of formal programs in universities and colleges at a time when with regard to other occupations there is growing criticism of Canada's over-reliance on institutional as opposed to on-the-job training compared with other countries,[11] and increased interest in establishing co-operative work-study programs.[12] Also, it seems more than coincidence that a serious concern about oversupply of nurses in Ontario should arise shortly after the traditional linkage between the trainees and the principal employers has been weakened and a system of educational institutions interposed more prominently between them. Recent constraints on health care expenditures may have contributed somewhat to this situation, but one hypothesis worth considering is that the traditional linkage between hospitals and trainees worked to prevent serious oversupply. When that linkage was weakened, without the introduction of other control mechanisms, there was no in-built check on oversupply. The author is not qualified to assess whether other benefits of the restructuring of nursing education in Ontario outweigh the potential costs referred to above. The main point to be noted here is that in a decentralized system the weakening of the linkage between decision-makers, in this case prospective nurses and their employers, likely necessitates some counterbalancing mechanism for preventing oversupply. The most likely counterbalancing mechanism is some form of central control by government over numbers trained.

In emphasizing the advantages of the traditional modes of professional training, one should not fall prey to undue nostalgia for a system which resulted sometimes in exploitation of trainees and in manipulation of supply to maintain exorbitant earnings. To the extent that exploitation occurs, it can be dealt with by protective legislation, as exists for work conditions and occupational health and safety. As for the frequently alleged 'excess' earnings of some professionals, it is important to distinguish between professions where self-employment predominates and those in which most are employees. It is primarily in some of the former that there is concern about excess earnings. In these cases employers are not a predominant force, so that the possible benefits of the linkage between prospective employers and prospective trainees does not apply. In such fields a good case might be made for greater state involvement in influencing supply.

Rationalizing relationships among different professionals
Professionals, like craft unionists, managers, bureaucrats, and others who have the opportunity to do so, tend to guard their vocational jurisdictions. There is

11 This is one of the main themes of Economic Council of Canada's Eighth Annual Review, *Design for Decision Making: An Application to Human Resources Policies* (Ottawa: Information Canada, 1971) 104-9.
12 As evidenced by the recent statement by the federal minister of manpower and immigration regarding federal government encouragement of co-operative education. See Hon. Bud Cullen, *Employment Strategy* (Ottawa: Office of the Minister of Manpower and Immigration, 21 Oct. 1976) 11-12.

now much concern about whether some of these divisions of responsibility are conducive to the most efficient use of professional manpower and the highest quality of service. It is alleged frequently, for example, that the allocation of responsibility between engineers and engineering technologists could be greatly improved by employing more engineers and fewer technologists, or vice-versa.[13] As specialization increases, these questions are likely to take on more significance.

Clearly, there is a need for research into alternative ways of allocating responsibilities among different professional groups. Yet even if there were a wealth of pertinent research findings on this subject, there would remain the problem of how decisions about change would be made and implemented. Except where one group is almost totally subordinate to another, there is no arena for the different professions to interact in making hard decisions together about the allocation of work responsibilities. It is thus left to the government to listen to all groups and then impose decisions. However, in a society not committed to state manpower planning it is unlikely that the government will have the technical capability or the perceived authority to bring about efficient rationalization, except in those quite visible situations where it is apparent to everyone that occupational roles are out of kilter. Even then, government is likely to gather the momentum and support for making such changes only infrequently. It is difficult to say just what are the potential gains in efficiency and quality of service that might result from a continuous effort to rationalize divisions of responsibility among various professions, but it is not hard to imagine that the bulk of those potential gains will not be realized under present circumstances. Perhaps the establishment of a council of professions with a mandate to examine such problems could make a contribution.[14]

Professionals in large organizations
The habit of thinking of professionals as self-employed lingers on even when increasing proportions of professionals are being employed in large organizations. A current concern about work in such environments today has to do with productivity and quality of work life.[15] Thus far, concerns of productivity and

13 For a discussion of such allegations see M.L. Skolnik, 'An empirical analysis of substitution between engineers and technicians in Canada,' *Relations Industrielles*, April 1970, 285-8.
14 In this connection the reader is referred to the role of the Office des Professions du Québec concerning the setting of limits between various professional specializations. See René Dussault's contribution to this volume.
15 For a useful introduction to the growing literature on the relationship between productivity and quality of worklife see Raymond Katzell and Daniel Yankelovich et al., *Work, Productivity and Job Satisfaction: An Evaluation of Policy-Related Research* (New York: The Psychological Corporation, 1975)

working conditions have emphasized assembly-line tasks and so-called menial jobs. Yet many professional activities have become highly routinized and repetitive, and in other ways (e.g. unionization) the traditional distinctions between professional and non-professional have become blurred. Society may justifiably give priority attention to conditions in low-paid, tedious, socially necessary jobs. However, productivity is everyone's concern, and if there are substantial gains to be made from identifying ways to increase the productivity of professional work they should be sought out. If the resources that have gone into manpower forecasting could instead be used for the study of professional jobs, how they are performed and how they interact with other related jobs, there would likely be greater returns on the investment.

CONCLUSION

The term manpower planning does not have a well-established definition. Most frequently it connotes a considerable role to be played by the state in determining the number of persons that will be permitted to train for and engage in particular types of work. The rationale for such centralized direction by the state derives from several assumptions about education, technology, and economic organization. One of the principal assumptions is that as the economy evolves it will need or demand a different inventory of occupational skills at each stage of its evolution. A second assumption is that these needs can be predicted in some detail reasonably far into the future. Further, it is assumed that the evolution of technology and economic organization is immutable, and accordingly that people and educational institutions must adjust to this evolutionary process. Finally, it is assumed that the adjustments necessary in order to achieve a reasonably efficient matching of manpower supply and demand will not occur simply through the interactions of decentralized decisions among countless individuals, employers, and educational institutions.

There is little empirical basis for accepting most of these assumptions.[16] For example, the cumulative experience of manpower forecasting has failed to establish that manpower needs can be predicted accurately. Occupational research has shown that considerable flexibility in the mix of skilled manpower is possible and that similar organizations can operate with quite different occupational compositions. These findings suggest that occupational needs are not determined

16 Howard R. Bowen refers to such assumptions as 'misconceptions' in 'The manpower vs the free-choice principle,' in Larry F. Moore, ed, *Manpower Planning for Canadians: An Anthology* (University of British Columbia: Institute of Industrial Relations, 1975) 233-41. The author has borrowed from Professor Bowen's provocative discussion of the limitations of the manpower approach to educational planning.

primarily by technology or immutable forces, but by law, administrative procedure, contractual arrangement, and established convention.

While the assumptions underlying the above manpower planning paradigm do not accurately reflect real world conditions, the consequences of accepting that paradigm are more serious than merely inaccurate forecasts and ineffective application of a theoretical model of planning. One's paradigms influence one's perceptions and give focus to one's curiosity. Acceptance of the manpower planning-cum-forecasting paradigm conditions one to regard existing occupational barriers as inevitable and inhibits the search for more flexible approaches to human resource development and utilization. Yet, more flexible approaches to human resource development and utilization are needed in order to increase productivity, improve the quality of service, widen the range of opportunities, and make work more personally satisfying. In particular there is a need to enhance the direct linkages and communication among the various parties whose decisions cumulatively determine the way human resources are developed and work is performed. Through such communication there can be *mutual* adjustments between an increasingly better educated population and an increasingly more complex economic structure. Influencing education and professional activity in such a way as to encourage rather than restrain creativity and innovation is a difficult task, and one which requires planning. It is unfortunate that manpower planning has come to signify a mechanistic approach to fitting people into predestined slots when the greatest challenges for manpower planning lie in developing approaches that will facilitate realization of the creative potential of dedicated and talented people.

ROBERT G. EVANS

Universal access: the Trojan horse

CONCEPTS OF ACCESS, UNIVERSAL OR OTHERWISE

Access to professional services, in a general sense, is very hard to be against. The concept of a professional service implies a special relationship with the public interest, which is sometimes expressed in the idea of there being a need for professional services, rather than a demand. Society at large seems to be much more concerned about my ability to acquire the services of a competent professional, most particularly in the health care fields, than about my ability to acquire the services of a Rolls-Royce, or even of a hot dog. At least, universal access to Rolls-Royces or hot dogs is not a public issue.

There are of course a number of possible justifications for this special sense of public interest in professional services, and the resulting extensive structure of public or private regulation which surrounds their providers in most modern societies. The concept of need, while usually ill-defined, reflects a sense that deprivation of such services at a critical time can seriously impair an individual's ability to participate in society. Medical or legal services particularly may be 'needed,' not in order for consumers, in the economists's jargon, to achieve maximum welfare with their given incomes, but in order for them to continue in existence as consumers. In a perfect world, such services would never be needed; we would not get ill or fight with each other. 'Needed' services are not wanted of themselves; rather they are required to avert some unfortunate consequence. Hence the general agreement that access to professional services is A Good Thing and to be encouraged.

As a positive concept, however, the meaning of access is rather fuzzy. It is far easier to conceptualize its negation, lack of access, in terms of the various types

Department of Economics, University of British Columbia

and strengths of barriers which may exist to acquiring services. This approach is also more natural for an economist, because we can treat such barriers as prices or costs of acquiring services. Such prices may of course be both monetary and non-monetary. We are then able to identify several different types of barriers or service prices, which will explain why improving access can mean very different things to different people. It is particularly important to recognize that the redistribution of economic costs and benefits among different people which results from any measure to 'improve access' in a particular dimension may be dramatically different from that of some other measure aimed at the same or another type of access barrier.

POINT-OF-SERVICE CHARGES

The monetary form of 'access barrier,' the direct price or point-of-service charge, is the most obvious impediment to 'universal access.' When professional services are supplied in a private marketplace, those who would have access to such services must give up economic resources to acquire them. It is important, however, to distinguish the point-of-service charge from the general issue of the cost of professional services. Services are never 'free' under *any* institutional arrangement. The only issues are the extent to which access to such services by a particular user shall be made contingent upon payment of all or a part of their cost by that user, and of course the level of that cost. In this dimension one can lower access barriers by transferring part or all of the cost of services for a particular user to revenue sources (private insurance premiums or taxes) which are not directly related to use. Either public or private insurance, or private (charitable) or public subsidy have this effect. Alternatively one can attempt to reduce the cost of professional services directly by encouraging or requiring reorganization of the process of supply.

In general the insurance or subsidy approach can have greater access-enhancing effects. Point-of-service charges can be driven to zero, as they have been for medical services by medicare. On the other hand such access is bought at the cost of removing all or most of the existing market constraints on supplier pricing behaviour and on utilization. Medicare experience suggests that both total and unit costs of services increase as a result. Efforts to improve the efficiency of production of professional services and thereby lower their price, by contrast, serve both to improve access and to lower over-all costs.

There is an important difference between the subsidy and the efficiency approach to access improvement when looked at from the point of view of the supplier of professional services. A subsidy or insurance approach by which a third party pays all or part of the cost of services on behalf of the recipient generally tends to increase total expenditure on professional services. This may result either because utilization of services rises at current prices when access barriers are removed, or because professionals find that they are able to raise prices without losing clientele under the subsidy arrangements. These two effects may be difficult to disentangle after the fact, particularly if price/quantity data are rather weak in the pre-subsidy/insurance system.[1] Their combined effect, however, is to increase the receipts of professionals through both rising average incomes and expanding numbers. By contrast, a strategy of promoting efficiency lowers cost barriers to access by lowering the unit costs of professional services. This may be associated either with lower professional incomes or with fewer professionals each working more efficiently (e.g. by making more use of aides), but in either case it represents a threat to the earning levels of existing professionals. Hence the general professional support for access-improvement through some form of insurance or subsidy rather than more general system reorganization.[2]

NON-MONETARY BARRIERS TO ACCESS

Access barriers are much broader, however, than simply point-of-service charges. They include geographic barriers, in the sense of excessively high time, money, and inconvenience costs of travel to a professional. When residents of under- or unserviced regions complain of inadequate access they often mean that such travel is much more expensive and time-consuming for them than for residents in more fortunate areas. In a generalized sense the price of professional services for them is much higher. As a result they may go without professional services which are not 'inaccessible' in some absolute sense, but merely too costly to be worthwhile.

1 A partial, though statistically unsophisticated, attempt to disentangle such effects for public hospital and medical insurance in Canada is reported in Robert G. Evans 'Beyond the medical marketplace: expenditure, utilization, and pricing of insured health care in Canada,' in S. Andreopoulos, ed., *National Health Insurance: Can We Learn From Canada?* (New York: John Wiley, 1975). A point which emerges strongly, however, is that price/quantity reactions to health insurance do not appear adequately described by the simple-minded mechanism of lowered out-of-pocket cost implying expanded consumer demand. The professional is not a passive 'supplier.'

2 Of course, professionals have always displayed mixed feelings about any form of public intervention. Presumably they have weighed short-run income gains against longer-run (and wholly justified) fears of 'outside interference' or public accountability (depending on one's point of view). When public pressure for cost control develops in a personal service industry, it can be expressed in only two ways – cutting provider incomes and/or forcing providers out of the industry. This elementary piece of arithmetic is often neglected by advocates of schemes for cost-reduction in health care – once a system is built up it is quite traumatic to scale down.

Barriers may also be due to conflicts between the convenience of providers and users of services. If professionals refuse to provide, or restrict, services outside normal business hours, access will differ between those members of the population for whom time off work or away from home is costly (lost pay or babysitting charges) and those with more flexible schedules. Social class barriers are asserted to exist because of the tendency for professionals to be heavily recruited from upper socioeconomic groups; they may not share the same cultural values or even language as their clients/patients. This 'social distance' may create difficulties of communication and costs in terms of social discomfort for some members of the population. Finally there are sheer information barriers which obviously correlate with all the others – if one does not recognize when services are needed, or know how to locate a competent professional, or how to talk to one, or how much the service should or will cost, then access to such services is restricted regardless of their actual price or location.

Such non-price barriers to access show up in a particularly important way in the case of professional services for which monetary barriers have been lowered or removed. Geographic barriers are obvious; people in regions with few physicians use fewer services *per capita* than people in well-supplied regions even though point-of-service charges are zero for both.[3] Since medical services are tax-financed, an equity problem is obvious. Dental insurance, private or public, shows up non-price barriers related to social class, cultural values, or information, as utilization remains closely correlated with socioeconomic class even within insured populations.[4] The use of hospital emergency wards or outpatient clinics rather than private physicians appears to be associated with socioeconomic class and also related to physicians' office-hour choices.[5] Health professionals

3 Cross-provincial data (Canada, Department of National Health and Welfare, Health Economics and Statistics Division *Earnings of Physicians in Canada 1962-1972* Ottawa [n.d.]) show an almost exact correlation between expenditures per capita on physician services and number of physicians per capita. There is also a tendency for fees to be higher in high-spending provinces, but this does not explain the relation. In Ontario, A.J. Culyer has shown a correlation of 0.76 between physician availability across regions and use of physician services (measured by expenditure per capita on a constant (1974) fee schedule) (*Measuring Health: lessons for Ontario* [Toronto: University of Toronto Press for the Ontario Economic Council, 1978] 170). Other within-province studies consistently show the same pattern.

4 D.W. Lewis and B.I. Brown *Dental Manpower/Population Ratio Estimates for Canada under Four Situations* Health Manpower Report #1-73 (Ottawa: Department of National Health and Welfare, March 1973)

5 A most thorough recent survey of access issues in health care, with emphasis on non-price barriers, is L. Aday and R. Andersen, *Access to Medical Care* (Ann Arbor, Michigan: Health Administration Press, 1975). Pages 18-20 in particular deal with use of clinics and emergency units.

have been much more studied; but doubtless utilization of the services of lawyers, accountants, and architects is even more highly correlated with income,
and would continue to be so for non-monetary reasons even if price barriers to
access went to zero.

ACCESS TO WHAT? PROBLEMS OF UNIVERSALITY

The existence of significant non-monetary costs associated with access to professional services, costs which are very different for different groups in the population, points up at least two serious difficulties with the concept of 'universal'
access. If universal is taken to imply equal access for everyone, with barriers reduced either to zero or to some 'fair' level, whatever that may mean, then universal access is probably impossible to achieve. To attempt to achieve it would
require revolutionary changes in professional organization. A centralized administration would be necessary to ensure that professional personnel were adequately distributed geographically. Recruitment practices would have to be
changed so that professionals were generally representative of the population.
Extensive information and outreach networks would be needed to ensure that
everyone was equally aware of the availability and capability of services. Truly
universal access on equal terms would be a formidable undertaking.

Even if it could be achieved, however, such universality would raise serious
equity problems. Obviously provision of professional services to some groups in
the population is much more expensive than to others – the residents of small
and/or remote communities are an immediate example. If universal access means
equal access for all in all dimensions, such residents will be imposing significant
costs on residents in urban or metropolitan areas. For most goods and services
supplied through the private market, we expect that there will be price differentials between central and remote communities, generally favouring the former;
and that people choose to live in high-cost communities either because of corre-
spondingly high wages or because of other advantages of the environment. Is it
equitable to impose some of the costs of this choice on city dwellers?

On the other hand it is also inequitable to tax people to pay for services
which non-price barriers prevent them from receiving. This problem applies in an
attenuated form to all professional services, as the educational system subsidizes
professionals heavily. Different non-monetary barriers to access both to professional education and to the resulting professional services imply that the benefits
of these subsidies are not equally available to all. But the equity problem becomes much more severe when attempts are made to reduce the direct monetary
barriers to services. Medicare, for example, greatly increases the cross-subsidy
from those who face high non-price barriers to those who face low barriers, since

it passes all direct dollar costs through the tax system. Hence partial attempts to deal with the access problem can make equity problems much more severe.

It thus appears that truly universal access to professional services is probably illusory because the various barriers to access are so complex, and in any case universality raises difficult issues of equity. Partial concepts of universal access which focus only on point-of-service charges, such as the medicare approach, not only are very far from universal access but also create even more difficult equity problems by their failure to deal with non-price barriers. This suggests that we look behind the concept of universal access as a social objective in itself, and ask what higher level objectives it might be intended to promote.[6]

UNIVERSAL ACCESS AS PROMOTION OF UTILIZATION

The most obvious justification of universal access to professional services is the expansion of their utilization. This objective has been most explicit in the case of medicare. Financial barriers were perceived as inhibiting people from receiving 'needed' care; removal of these barriers was intended to expand the use of services. In economic terms, professional services may be 'merit goods' such that society as a whole has an interest in ensuring that individuals receive them in 'needed' amounts. These needed amounts are such that individuals left to their own resources in private markets will not purchase as much of these services as society collectively judges that they should. Thus society must step in to encourage increased utilization, either by lowering the costs of utilization faced by the individual or by increasing the value which the individual places on such services. In extreme cases, of course, the costs of needed services may be well beyond the individual's own resources.

The difficulty with promoting utilization is that it implies an external standard or judgment about what utilization ought to be. The normal convention in economics is to assume that individuals are the most competent judges of their own needs and the socially best level of utilization is that which consumers choose, taking account of the resource costs of their choices. The concept of a professional service, however, is rooted in the relative ignorance of the user of such services. The utilization of professional services is the outcome of an interaction between the preferences of the user and the advice given or restraint im-

6 An attempt to develop a set of such higher-level social objectives, and to relate them to health insurance, is Robert G. Evans and Malcolm F. Williamson, *Extending Canadian Health Insurance: options for pharmacare and denticare* (Toronto: University of Toronto Press for the Ontario Economic Council, 1978). In that study, specific quantitative estimates are developed within a framework similar to that sketched out in this paper.

posed by the professional, with the professional often being the most important factor. This advice is in turn influenced by perceptions both of the user's interests and of the professional's own interests, economic or otherwise. A social interest in promoting utilization implies that society collectively has a standard of appropriate utilization levels separate from the actual utilization which emerges from the relations of professional and user.

Concern with universal access, or with lowering current access barriers, implies that this socially optimal level of use is above current levels. In health care parlance there is an 'iceberg of unmet need' out there in society, and something ought to be done about it. But such an external standard, if it is to represent a justifiable social objective, must not merely be formulated as 'more.' In the first place, professional services are not a homogenous entity, nor are the services of a given professional. For some types of services we are concerned about *overuse*, even at current market prices. We would not wish, through pharmacare, to encourage more use of prescription drugs. Some patients may fail to receive 'needed' drugs because of financial barriers, but many others are currently over-utilizing.[7] Excessive use of hospital services is a serious problem in Canada, and one which predates hospital insurance even if awareness of it does not. Excessive surgical intervention in North America has been a long-smouldering concern.[8] Promotion of dental services utilization is clearly a legitimate social objective, particularly for children, in order to reduce the prevalence of dental decay and subsequent tooth loss. But initial experience with 'universal access' in Quebec and Nova Scotia which does no more than remove price barriers suggests that what is promoted is further preventive servicing of dubious utility on children who were already under care before public dental insurance.[9] The utilization expansion which actually occurs is overuse.

7 An extensive survey of the medical literature on excess utilization, together with a radical interpretation, is given by I. Illich *The Limits to Medicine* (Toronto: McClelland and Stewart, 1976). Less strident, but similar, is the message of A. Chaiton et al., 'Patterns of medical drug use – a community focus,' *Canadian Medical Association Journal* 114 (10 Jan. 1976). Other similar commentary is widespread.

8 Most recently expressed in the Study of Surgical Specialists in the United States (SOSSUS) carried out under the auspices of the American College of Surgery, again Illich reports a number of the studies in the medical literature in *The Limits to Medicine*.

9 This emerges from interpretation of data on public children's dental insurance in the 1974 and 1975 issues of *Statistiques Annuelles*, Régie de l'Assurance-Maladie du Québec (Québec, 1975, 1976). Utilization rates are extremely low except in central Montreal, and the pattern of services provided clearly indicates a service population which has been under continuing care. Nova Scotia has cut back on reimbursement of preventive services in its plan because of high rates of provision and dubious efficacy (*Canadian Dental Association Journal*, June 1976, 'Newsbeat').

Examples of perceived overuse of professional services may also arise in the legal field. Proponents of no-fault automobile insurance argue that much of the litigation surrounding accidents may serve no useful social purpose, and similar comments have been made about the legal work required in land conveyancing in jurisdictions which do not have the Torrens system of title registration. In these activities what is needed is not more legal services, but less. Judicare is not an obvious solution.

In general, then, we cannot defend universal access in terms of a social interest in across-the-board increases in utilization of professional services. For some types of professionals, or more specifically for some types of services of some professionals, there may well be an 'unmet need' which society in general has an interest in helping to meet – restorative dentistry for children seems a generally accepted example. But in other areas overuse may be as much or more of a problem, and universal access which is interpreted as merely the reduction or elimination of all price barriers is likely to exacerbate this problem.

This formulation of the utilization problem has implicitly defined the standard of 'appropriate' utilization in terms of the objectives of the professional. Pharmaceuticals are overutilized, for example, if reduced drug use would have no harmful effects and possibly beneficial ones on the health of the user. But there is an additional economic problem of overutilization embodied in the notion of universal access, even if professionals could be relied upon to ensure that overservicing in a technical sense never occurred. If all barriers to access are removed, then both users and professionals are being signalled that resources to be used in the production of professional services are effectively free – which they most certainly are not. To society as a whole, all goods and services are costly in the sense of using up resources which have alternative uses. If professional services are supplied and used up to the point of zero marginal or additional benefit – all that can be done for the patient has been done – then resources which have positive value in other uses have been used to provide professional services which have (almost) zero value. The use of dentist time to provide preventive services with positive but very small benefits, much lower than the costs of provision, is an obvious example. Any professional with an average imagination can always think of some additional services which might be helpful. So universal access promotes overutilization in an economic sense. It appears that the justification of access on the grounds of promoting utilization requires not only the development of social standards of appropriate utilization of professional services complex enough to identify specific areas of over- and underuse, but also the adjustment of these standards to reflect the social cost of such services. If this cannot be done, universal access begins to look more like a program of market development for the professional services industry.

UNIVERSAL ACCESS AS WEALTH REDISTRIBUTION

Apart from its impact upon utilization patterns of professional services, universal access as noted above can have significant economic redistributive effects on any given base pattern of utilization. As a public objective, this has sometimes been expressed in the health field as 'spreading the burden' of care. Obviously any public program which lowers either price or non-price barriers to care by transferring part of the costs to some collective group, either an insured population or taxpayers, transfers wealth to high users of services at the expense of low- or non-users. Two such forms of transfer need to be distinguished, however, the insurance effect and the pure wealth transfer effect.

Professional services for which demand or need is dependent upon some uncertain contingency, such as becoming ill or being sued, represent an unpredictable expense and a net reduction in the user's welfare. One would prefer that the uncertain event had not occurred and the services had been unnecessary. In advance of the uncertain event occurring or not occurring, a group of people facing equal risks of loss from the uncertain event may pool their risks, contributing a premium equal to their expected loss (size of loss multiplied by probability of occurrence) plus some administrative charge, and agreeing that anyone actually incurring the loss will be reimbursed. By insurance, each group member exchanges a large but uncertain loss for a smaller, certain one (the premium). But *before* the event, no transfer of wealth from one insured participant to another occurs. After the fact, of course, a transfer occurs from those who do not need services to those who do. As long as the premium charged each participant reflects his or her expected loss, however (plus a share of administrative cost), a pure insurance plan is neutral with respect to the wealth distribution among participants.

Public 'insurance' programs, however, especially for professional services, do not have this neutrality feature. Costs of the program are met from taxes, although for cosmetic reasons some programs include a 'premium' which is effectively compulsory. The key point is that taxes or premiums are in no way related to expected use. Universal access through a public program of insurance, public delivery, subsidy, or whatever, thus transfers wealth from those whose expected use of services is low to those with high expectation of use. Medical insurance, for example, transfers resources from young adults to the elderly, and on a large scale. There exist, of course, young adults who turn out in any year to require medical services, and elderly persons who do not. But the probability of use, and the expected amount of use, is on average higher for an elderly person. Insofar as costs of participating in the program do not reflect this, the program transfers wealth as well as reducing risk.

It is not necessary, in principle, that a public insurance-type program have this wealth-transfer feature. There are a variety of reasons, such as economies of scale, adverse selection, or reactions by providers, why the private marketplace might be unable to provide a socially optimal level of insurance coverage.[10] A government might intervene with a (fairly complex) public insurance program which was distributionally neutral, solely to remedy such a market failure in the private 'market for risk-bearing' or insurance industry. A public program of this sort would have little connection with universal access; and in any case actual public programs to promote access always seem to embody significant distributional features.

The question to be answered for any particular type of professional service, then, is what is the pattern of use currently and how will universal or even improved access affect it? If any member of the population has roughly the same expectation of using a given service as any other, then universal access through elimination of price barriers has no redistributive effect. (Of course the choice of taxes to raise the required public sector revenue may affect wealth distribution). If the service is one which tends to be used more by groups generally considered deserving of public subsidy, then the transfer effects may be considered 'good.' As noted above, public medical insurance subsidizes the elderly. Pharmaceutical insurance or subsidies do the same. Since the elderly are generally perceived as less well off than average – particularly the elderly and ill – such a transfer seems to accord with general social preferences.

On the other hand consumption of dental services is very closely and positively related to socioeconomic class. Universal access in the form of denticare, lowering price barriers but not non-price ones, would thus represent a transfer program from the average taxpayer, primarily to middle- and upper-income groups. The distribution across income classes of the utilization of other professionals' services is not well researched. In fact there is some doubt about the relation between medical service use and income class, in that needs for services may well be higher among the 'more deserving' elderly and poor; but utilization for a given need level may rise with socioeconomic class.[11] As a generalization, however, it is probably the case that use of professional services outside the health

10 See Evans and Williamson, *Extending Canadian Health Insurance*, chap 1.
11 A study of the distribution of medical expenditures by income class in Ontario has just been completed by P. Manga, 'A benefit incidence analysis of the public medical and hospital insurance programs in Ontario' (unpublished PH D dissertation, Department of Economics, University of Toronto), and a preliminary version was presented to the Meetings of the Canadian Economics Association, Laval, June 1976. Especially important may be a tendency for upper-income people to use specialists rather than general practitioners for a given service.

care area is more sensitive (positively) to income level and hence that measures to lower access barriers will as in the Denticare case favour upper income groups.

This conclusion could be changed, of course, if reduction in access barriers actually increased utilization to a point where everyone had approximately equal expectation of use. This would, as noted above, require dramatic changes in professional organization to lower non-price barriers as well as price barriers. But if it could be successful, where would the professional services come from? In dentistry, for example, there is nowhere near enough manpower to supply the whole Canadian population with services at levels considered optimal by dentists and received by relatively affluent populations under continuing care. Price barriers might be removed, but non-price barriers would have to remain as rationing of some form would go on. This may not be true of all professions – pharmacy may well have significant surplus capacity in the form of pharmacists working only part-time as dispensers. But as noted above it is not clear that more use of pharmaceuticals is an appropriate social objective. It is very doubtful that enough lawyers or accountants exist to serve all members of society at the same level as the wealthier members are served. And even if the total professional service capacity of the economy could be expanded to provide such levels, it is not clear that Canadians collectively would wish to expand the share of their resources devoted to the professions in this way. Total expenditures on truly universal, optimal dental care, for example, could rival those of medicare.[12] The possibilities for law and accountancy are hard to guess. But if such expansion does not take place, then universal access may be a long way short of universal.

UNIVERSAL ACCESS AND THE EFFICIENCY
OF PROVISION OF PROFESSIONAL SERVICES

Thus the problems inherent in access-promotion through the insurance/subsidy mechanism lead us back to issues of cost, efficiency, and the organization of professional service suppliers. Truly universal access requires reduction of price and non-price barriers. If non-price barriers are not removed, or at least significantly lowered, then for some professional services at least access will remain very unequal and removal of price barriers will merely make the general wealth distribution problem worse. But if universal access can be achieved, costs may rise enormously both from the difficulty of lowering the access barriers themselves, and from the increased use of services which may result. (If of course increased service use does not result, then the justification of universal access must be its

12 Quantitative estimates for Ontario under a variety of assumptions are worked out in Evans and Williamson, *Extending Canadian Health Insurance*, chap. 4.

redistributive effect alone, and as noted for some professional services this would be redistribution from poor to rich). The possibility of achieving any needed expansion of output, and particularly of achieving it at levels of costs acceptable to the public sector, thus highlights an issue which should be a primary objective of public policy, the efficiency of the process of production of professional services. Universal access, as a public objective, cannot be separated from the need to influence the supply side of the professional marketplace. And this need goes beyond the problems of ensuring geographic availability of services and reducing informational and social barriers; it includes intervention to influence the process of production itself and to promote improved efficiency and lower costs.

The professional relationship between supplier and user of services makes the problem of defining and achieving efficiency in the usual sense significantly more complex than for 'normal' goods and services. In the conventional market model we rely upon the profit-seeking behaviour of suppliers to lead to efficient, least-cost production, the competition among suppliers to establish prices which reflect these most efficient costs, and the choices of consumers to determine which goods and services are worth this cost (and how much of each). None of these mechanisms applies in the case of professional services. The service becomes professionalized precisely because the individual consumer cannot know his own needs. The professional becomes the agent of the consumer in determining what, and how much, to consume. This creates an inherent conflict of interest between the professional as economic principal, provider and seller of services, and as agent for the buyer and user. Hence the oft-noted ability of suppliers to create part, at least, of the demand for their own services.

To mitigate some of the more obvious problems in such a conflict of interest, the professional relationship is generally sheltered to some degree from market forces by barriers to entry (licensure) and exemption from laws against collusion by suppliers. This in turn means that competitive market forces cannot generally be relied upon to ensure that prices of professional services reflect their costs. Hence the difficulty of defining a 'fair' price for services. The cost of professional services is in large part the income of the professional, so that when professionals set a fair price, they are in fact setting fair incomes for themselves. Such judgments are not entirely disinterested; and many commentators have noted that, at least for professions which have unsatisfied would-be entrants at current income levels, incomes must be above levels which a free market would set.

And finally, since one of the primary 'factors of production' in the supply of professional services is the time of the professional, the professional entrepreneur is in an economic sense the buyer of his or her own labour services. This creates a further conflict of interest between the professional-as-entrepreneur, interested in minimizing production costs, and the professional-as-worker, interested in maintaining the demand for skilled time. Cost-minimization through delegation of services to auxiliary workers, for example, given a fixed total volume of services produced, may lower unit costs of production but at the same time lower the utilization of professional time itself. Profits of the professional enterprise may rise, but the take-home pay of the professional falls. Hence the professional enterprise may not choose least-cost ways of producing output, but instead may be biased toward overuse of high-cost professional time.

Thus the problem of promoting efficiency in the production of professional services encompasses not only the problem of achieving minimum 'unit costs' of production but also that of ensuring that these costs are in fact reflected in prices, and that the mix of services provided is appropriate or needed. On this last point the problem of efficiency shades into the problem of utilization promotion. Overservicing is both an efficiency problem in that it uses up expensive resources and a utilization problem in that it may be directly harmful to the user. (This latter problem, however, is more of an issue in health care than in other professional services.) The peculiar institutional structure of the professions weakens the normal economic forces which lead toward efficiency in each of these three dimensions.

In each dimension, as well, the net income of the professional plays a critical role as a strategic variable. The continuation of pharmacists in the role of counters of pills and pourers of medicines, the resistance of dentists to dental auxiliaries who can drill and fill teeth, the glacial progress of the physician-assistant / nurse-practitioner / intermediate-level health professional with the proven capability of taking over a significant share of general practice, all can be traced to the threat that auxiliaries impose to the earnings levels of the current stock of professionals. Experimentation has demonstrated over and over again in each of the health disciplines that a significant or very large proportion of 'professional' activity can be delegated, with no loss of quality, to less highly trained auxiliaries. Efficient provision of professional services would require a much higher auxiliary-to-professional ratio, and many fewer professionals. Unit costs of services could be reduced, and only the universities would suffer. But in the short run, efficient use of auxiliaries would create a surplus of professional services, and of professionals, and resulting losses of income. Hence it does not occur.[13]

13 Again the literature in this field is vast and scattered. A recent collection of articles is J. Rafferty, ed., *Health Manpower and Productivity* (Lexington, Mass.: D.C. Heath, 1974), esp. J. Hadley, 'Research on health manpower productivity: a general overview.' Evans and Williamson, *Extending Canadian Health Insurance*, chap. 6, attempts to explore some alternative theoretical explanations for the reluctance of health practitioners to hire auxiliaries. A recent and extensive theoretical and empirical study is that of A.-P. Contandriopoulos and J.-M. Lance, *Une Modèle de la Prevision du Main-d'Œuvre Medicale*, a report supported by the Canadian Department of National Health and Welfare (NHG-605-21-48) McGill University, Montreal, 1976.

The role of professional incomes in the problem of relating service prices to costs is obvious; any divergence between the price of professional services and their cost goes directly into professional incomes. Similarly, economic incentives to overservicing are created when the cost to the professional of providing additional services to a user, i.e. the marginal costs, are lower than the income received therefrom. The professional must balance profitability against ethics, and when the service probably does no harm, may do some good, and in any case is paid for by the government, ethics become harder to maintain.

Relating these various forces to universal access, it appears that lowering barriers to access in general makes efficiency problems worse. Insofar as access is interpreted as access to the existing system of professional services provision, a reduction particularly of price barriers to access removes some of the professional constraints to overservicing (since the patient/client is no longer hurt financially). The market linkage between service prices and costs is removed, since users no longer pay prices, and service prices come to be set administratively through negotiation. Physicians in Canada negotiate fee schedules, but the real debate is over incomes. It is possible that administrative mechanisms may turn out to be more successful than a highly imperfect market in limiting the 'economic rents' or above-market returns of professionals. Most importantly, however, lowering barriers to access to the existing system of provision appears to make it more difficult to improve the efficiency of that system. Since the costs of overusing professionals to produce professional services appear in some professional areas at least to be relatively large (in the neighbourhood of 30 per cent of unit costs for dentistry and pharmacy[14]) the losses from forgone productivity increases are quantitatively serious.

Universal access, at least in the price dimension, tends to freeze in place existing patterns of service provision insofar as it removes economic barriers to service use. Users then have no incentive to respond to differentials in service prices. A producer of professional services who decides to lower costs of production by increasing efficiency cannot expand the market by passing price reductions on to users. And as pointed out above, increased efficiency on a given workload base means more idle time for the professional and lower total income. Moreover, partial improvements in access dilute the political constituency for change. Removal of financial barriers appears as a direct benefit to the population of users; the associated costs are buried in the general tax system. The members of society subjected to high non-price barriers will be geographically remote or otherwise disadvantaged, and in any case their concern will be for better access to the system, not for any form of change. Public programs to extend access to the exist-

14 Evans and Williamson, *Extending Canadian Health Insurance*, chaps 3 and 5

ing system of service provision tend to validate that system and create yet further vested interests supporting it. Although truly universal access to professional services appears to be revolutionary in implication, simply removing price barriers to access is highly reactionary in enshrining current modes of provision. How serious a disadvantage that is depends on how significant are the potential productivity gains given up.

ACCESS BY MANY ROADS – THE ABSENCE OF A UNIVERSAL FORMULA

Summarizing the foregoing, truly universal access to professional services appears almost certainly impossible and is probably not an appropriate social objective in any case. Rather, there exist a variety of different types of barriers, monetary and non-monetary, which inhibit potential users of services and impose various costs on the actual users. Some of these costs are related to the provision of professional services itself, others are not. Corresponding to these different types of barriers are a variety of different forms of social policy to improve access. But no one form of policy is likely to be suitable for all types of professional services, since the underlying social purposes to be achieved through improved access vary from one type of service to another.

The most obvious form of access promotion, reduction of price barriers to zero, has very different results for different types of professional services. Its impact on the distribution of wealth and the level of under- or overservicing of patients in the medicare case is still under debate. But it seems fairly clear that, if extended to dental services, such a partial access-improvement program would have a negative influence in transferring wealth from low-income non-users to high-income users. The distributional impact of pharmacare on the other hand would probably be positive on balance in that it transfers wealth to high users of drugs who tend to be the elderly and chronically ill. With respect to utilization-promotion, however, a simple reduction in money prices of access would tend to encourage more drug use, which appears at present to be a harmful effect. Denticare would also encourage more utilization, which, given the prevalence of dental disease, would be a desirable effect. Unfortunately, in the case of dental care non-price barriers seem to be sufficiently high that these utilization effects are relatively weak.

In general, access policies focusing on price barriers alone are likely to be undesirable for professional services whose use is closely and positively related to income, since if non-price barriers are high the program has bad distributional effects and if they are low the resulting expansion of desired utilization will probably outrun system capacity and create rationing barriers. Other contraindications are professional services where overservicing by professionals or overuse by consumers is perceived to be a significant problem, currently or potentially, since reduction of price barriers is an across-the-board stimulus to utilization regardless of the benefits to the user. Nor in this case can one take refuge in the judgment of either user or provider with respect to benefits. If the user were a competent judge the service would not be professionalized, and a professional who is a wholly unbiased and fully informed agent of the consumer would be a saint.

Alternatively, one could attempt to improve access by improving the competitiveness of the professional services market. Such a policy, if successful, could lower service prices significantly in some professional fields at least by stimulating the adoption of currently available cost-reducing technology. It would thus go part way toward reducing price barriers to access. Moreover, a more competitive professional services market could help to lower non-price barriers as well by placing more pressure on professionals to move to where users are and to make themselves more accessible through choice of working hours or efforts at communication. The medicare model, by contrast, discourages improvements in efficiency and may even increase geographic non-price barriers if, for example, public reimbursement enables more professionals to earn adequate livings in urban areas.

The difficulties with the approach through increased competition among professional providers, apart from the difficulties of breaking down habits of many years of collusive behaviour sanctioned both by legislation and by professional value systems, arise from the problem of defining the professional 'product.' Aggressive competition may open the way for both overservicing and quality dilution – presumably the social justification for professionalization in the first place. Thus the usefulness of such a public strategy depends on the possibility of defining a professional product in such a way that its quality can be externally monitored and its volume well defined. An obvious example is the product of pharmacy, the dispensed prescription. As the Saskatchewan drug insurance system shows, one can separate the drug component cost of a prescription from the dispensing cost and reimburse only the former. Then if pharmacists are required to set the dispensing charge independently, and permitted to advertise, drug users will be able to price-shop among pharmacists in an informed manner, and one would expect the usual market forces to encourage more efficient dispensing. It may be that this principle, of subdividing professional services to isolate those about which a consumer may make informed choices, could be extended to a number of aspects of legal work, particularly the 'average,' or 'uncomplicated' transactions surrounding drawing up a will or selling a house. The recent US Supreme Court decision in *Goldfarb* vs *Virginia Bar* seems to point in this direction, as does the extension of Canadian anti-combines legislation to cover services.[15] Unfortunately there appear to be serious loopholes in the new Canadian legislation which will lead to its having little or no impact on the collusive structure of some at least of the important professional markets.[16]

A third alternative method for improving access is direct public provision. Particularly when non-price barriers are high, and promotion of utilization is considered desirable, this may be a preferred alternative. In the provision of children's dental care, for example, there appears a general consensus among those who have studied alternative delivery systems that a public dental service based in the school system can (and does) achieve levels of utilization much higher than those of a private practice system even without point-of-service charges. Both geographic and inertial barriers are significantly lowered. Moreover, such systems seem to have the potential for dramatically reducing service costs, since they can be built around dental auxiliaries. Most actual or projected programs have auxiliary-to-dentist ratios in the range of thirty to one, compared with two or three to one in private practice.[17] There are obviously other areas of professional services where direct public provision is a superior alternative – programs for control of infectious disease through immunization or case-finding, for example. Again, high utilization rates are socially desirable, and non-price barriers to use are very important. Trying to base a program of mass immunization or vD control on a private practice system is both expensive and ineffective. But one would not move from these examples to advocate public service delivery for *all* professional services; a public legal or accounting service, for example, would have overtones of 1984.

15 See for example, the contribution by Kaiser to this volume.
16 The difficulty becomes clear if we consider how a vigorous 'competitive' strategy could possibly pay off for a practitioner in a field such as dentistry. Cutting prices might increase the demand for the services of that practice, but most practitioners are already quite busy, and it would be hard to generate enough revenue from new business to make up for lost revenue on the previous workload as a result of price cuts. The only way to benefit from such a policy would be for the practitioner to increase output dramatically by expanding auxiliary use and to take a significant share of business away from his colleagues by offering and advertising lower prices. But his colleagues collectively retain the power under the new legislation to prevent him from doing this; use of auxiliaries can be regulated under provincial Dentistry Acts, and Section 32(6) of the Combines Investigation Act permits collective action to regulate 'quality' in any case. An individual practitioner unable to expand his output can hardly gain from competitive pricing behaviour! Freedom to advertise and to set his own prices becomes an empty provision.
17 The relative uniformity of these conclusions, despite significant variations in methodology and approach, shows up in the provincial studies of children's dental care conducted in Saskatchewan, British Columbia, and Quebec, and analysed in some detail in Evans and Williamson, *Extending Canadian Health Insurance*, chap. 5.

It appears, therefore, that there are a number of different methods of improving access to different types of professional services, some of which do more harm than good, and none of which are likely to reach complete 'universality' in the broadest sense. Policies should be tailored to the individual professions, and sometimes to specific components of the services of a particular profession. Moreover, access is as much a characteristic of the process of provision of professional services as of the demand for them by users – in economic terms one must be prepared to influence the supply side as well as the demand side. A narrow-minded preoccupation with point-of-service charges alone, or a mechanical extension of medicare to denticare, pharmacare, judicare, or whatever, may have beneficial effects in some cases, but is likely to prove both a regressive wealth transfer and a windfall gain in market development and earning opportunities for the professional sector. What the general public would gain in benefits to counterbalance these costs is not at all clear.

PARAPROFESSIONALS

WALTER O. SPITZER

Evidence that justifies the introduction of new health professionals

INTRODUCTION

The rational introduction of innovations in clinical and other health services calls for the application of scientific experimental methods where possible. Whenever new types of health practitioners deal directly with patients, the importance of comprehensive and rigorous evaluation of the situations created cannot be over-stressed.

An essential component of an appraisal of the new health professionals is an evaluation of the educational programs in which these workers are trained. Most of the programs developed to prepare physician extenders during the last five to ten years have had one of two major contrasting orientations. In one group of programs, the successful graduate has been exposed to a procedural orientation and trained primarily to acquire specific skills to execute certain tasks under pre-determined conditions. The second approach characterizes the new health worker as a true professional, a practitioner who exercises clinical judgment. The program developed by Silver and Ford in Colorado is the best example of this orientation to the physician extender and has been widely emulated or adapted in the United States and Canada.[1] In Canada, the second approach has been the one generally adopted; this has developed into a practice in which physicians and

Faculty of Medicine, McGill University; director of the Centre for Advanced Studies in Primary Care, Montreal General Hospital
1 H.K. Silver, L.C. Ford and S.C. Stearly, 'Program to increase health care for children: the pediatric nurse practitioner program' (1967) 39 *Pediatrics* 756

nurses have become copractitioners in rendering care.[2]

The model for evaluation of the impact of the new health professional presented here is based on studies of the nurse practitioner which have been completed or are under way in the province of Ontario. In Canada, given the current or impending surplus of nurses in many areas, there has been no justification to develop a completely new category of health worker.[3] The demonstrated acceptance of the nurse as a primary care practitioner in the United States and Canada, and the strong foundation of education and experience of health sciences which a nurse contributes even prior to the acquisition of new skills, have commended her as the most suitable professional to adopt the redelineated roles now proposed and implemented.[4] Those working in the field in Canada recognize that the circumstances and availability of nurses elsewhere may determine that other approaches to augmentation of primary care resources need to be considered. However, it is proposed that the decision should be made on the basis of rigorous evaluation and evidence, rather than on opinion or vested interests.

In Canada, our most urgent health care problems are those that concern first-contact care. Accordingly, priorities in the development and redeployment of new health professionals allied to the physician have been restricted largely to the realm of primary care. This does not deny the fact that for at least two decades paramedical professionals have been effectively expanding their roles in specialty practice and in the hospital setting. Neither does it oppose any further evolution of the roles of other allied health professionals and particularly of the nurse. However, for the foreseeable future, current emphasis and apparent re-

2 W.O. Spitzer and D.J. Kergin, 'Nurse practitioners in primary care. I. The McMaster University educational program' (1973) 108 *Canadian Medical Association Journal* 991

3 J.R. Smiley, *Mobility, service, and attitudes of active and inactive nurses* (Toronto: Ontario Ministry of Health, 1968); H.R. Imai, *Report of a preliminary survey to explore the nursing employment situation in Canada in terms of the number of 1971 graduates of Canadian schools of nursing registered/licensed for the first time in 1971 who were able or unable to obtain permanent employment in nursing as of September 30, 1971* (Ottawa: Canadian Nurses' Association, 1972)

4 Health and Welfare Canada, National conference on assistance to the physician, Ottawa, 6-8 April 1971; College of Family Physicians of Canada, *Proceedings of a workshop on the role of allied professionals in the delivery of primary health care* (Toronto, 1971); W.O. Spitzer and D.J. Kergin, 'The nurse practitioner: calling the spade a spade' (1971) 38 *Ontario Medical Review* 165; T.J. Boudreau, *Report of the committee on nurse practitioners* (Ottawa: Health and Welfare Canada, 1972) 41-52

quirements have directed our attention toward the ambulatory sector, to primary care in particular. Our evaluation focus will be on the nurse practitioner in primary care, but the principles employed are applicable to other health professionals; they are also easily adapted for use in settings different from those in which we have conducted our experiments.

To further understanding, we give a definition of the type of new health professional under assessment: A nurse practitioner is one who works as a member of a team, usually on a one-to-one basis with a physician. Although such an individual may function physically separate from the doctor (e.g. in different examination rooms or in a satellite dispensary which may be located several miles from a main community health care centre), the nurse practitioner is in frequent, indeed daily, close interaction with the physician in the management of patients. Characteristically, a substantial number of patients are exposed to both the physician and the nurse in a large proportion of individual episodes of care.[5] It cannot be stressed sufficiently, however, that the nursing copractitioner, within the scope of responsibility and authority delineated, engages in clinical judgment and makes decisions based on clinical and general assessments of patients.

Introduction of the nurse practitioner as a decision-making copractitioner is a substantive departure from the conventional mode of clinical management of patients in primary care. The ultimate effects of this innovation can parallel or transcend the significance of new procedures, new drugs, and other therapeutic measures. Therefore, a strategy just as rigorous as that of the evaluation of new pharmaceuticals, therapeutic agents, or surgical procedures has been adopted in Ontario. The discussion which follows will identify significant parallels in the strategy suggested for evaluation; it is the strategy which has been successfully implemented for several decades in the evaluation of pharmaceuticals.

The strategy has the following seven tactics: surveys of need for health services and of potential sources of new health professionals; safety and efficacy of the new health professionals; assessment of quality of care; efficiency, from the perspective of the provider and from that of society; acceptance and satisfaction on the part of both providers and consumers; assessment of transfer of function; and long-term surveillance. We shall now consider each of these in turn.

5 Spitzer and Kergin, 'The nurse practitioner'

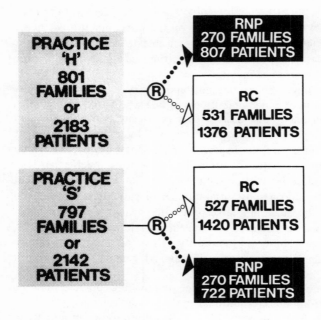

FIGURE 1 General design of the Burlington randomized trial of the nurse practitioner. The symbol R shows the randomization of the original practices to form the RC group of patients who were assigned to receive conventional medical care and the RNP patients who were assigned to nurse practitioners. The two RC groups were thereafter considered as a unit, as were the two RNP groups. SOURCE: G.P. Sweeney and W.I. Hay, 'The Burlington experience: a study of nurse practitioners in family practice' (1973) 19 *Canadian Family Physicians* 101

SURVEYS OF NEED FOR HEALTH SERVICES AND OF POTENTIAL SOURCES OF NEW HEALTH PROFESSIONALS

Good surveys are an irreplaceable prelude to the introduction of new health professionals or to any other major changes. First, it is important to establish or verify the actual perceived need for such new health professionals. In Ontario, manpower studies on the ratios and distributions of all categories of physicians in the province from 1961 to 1971 showed an acceptable population-to-physician ratio and even an adequate population-to-family physician ratio (1723:1). However, there was evidence of maldistribution which badly affected large segments of the population, especially in the remote northern areas. In the late 1960s and early 1970s at least three independent studies gave evidence of an unquestionable surplus of nurses in many parts of Canada and in most areas of Ontario.[6]

Other Ontario studies show that the public are generally satisfied with the health care services they receive and hold the scientific ability of doctors in high regard, but that they have serious concerns about the availability of family physicians and general practitioners in first-contact care. This finding was most clearly shown in a study commissioned by the Ontario Medical Association in which 64 per cent of the general population reported dissatisfaction about non-clinical aspects of first-contact care. Only half the people were confident of getting a doctor in an emergency situation. One-fifth were not confident that, having telephoned their doctor, they would be able to reach him the same day. Other surveys in Ontario have shown consistent findings.[7]

The preliminary indicators enumerated above, some of which were available to program developers and investigators in 1970 and early 1971, suggested the appropriateness of attempting new ways of augmenting primary care service. They justified giving priority for such plans to underserviced areas. Educational programs were then designed and launched that would increase the clinical skills of nurses so that they could function as nurse practitioners where they were needed.

SAFETY AND EFFICACY

The most important questions about a new approach to patient care are the same as might be asked for any other form of treatment: is it safe? is it efficient? Accordingly, for the evaluation of the nurse practitioner in primary care we

6 Smiley, supra n. 3; Imai, supra n. 3; F.A. Pickering, *Report of the special study regarding the medical profession in Ontario* (Ontario Medical Association, 1973) 15-23; W.S. Hacon, 'Health manpower in Canada' (1973) 64 *Canadian Journal of Public Health* 9
7 D.L. Sackett, W.O. Spitzer, M. Gent, and R.S. Roberts, 'The Burlington randomized trial of the nurse practitioner: health outcomes of patients' (1974) 80 *Annals of Internal Medicine* 137

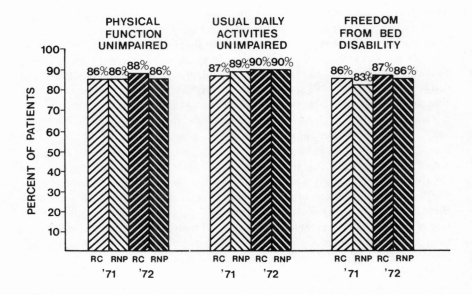

FIGURE 2 Physical status of patients in surveys during baseline (1971) and comparison (1972) periods (Burlington trial). These results are based on 521 subjects in the RC group and 296 in the RNP group who were assessed in both 1971 and 1972. SOURCE: W.O. Spitzer, D.L. Sackett, J.C. Sibley, R.S. Roberts, M. Tech, M. Gent, D.J. Kergin, B.C. Hackett, A. Olynich, 'The Burlington randomized trial of the nurse practitioner' (1974) 290 *New England Journal of Medicine* 251

planned the type of randomized clinical trial used to investigate new therapy, with patient outcomes as the principal measure of effectiveness. This resulted in the Burlington Randomized Trial of the Nurse Practitioner.[8]

As shown in Figure 1, about eight hundred eligible families in each of two

8 W.O. Spitzer, D.L. Sackett, J.C. Sibley, R.S. Roberts, M. Tech, M. Gent, D.J. Kergin, B.C. Hackett, and A. Olynich, 'The Burlington randomized trial of the nurse practitioner' (1974) 290 *New England Journal of Medicine* 251; Sackett et al., 'The Burlington randomized trial'

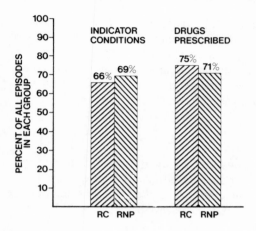

FIGURE 3 Percentage of episodes of care rated adequate (Burlington trial).
The denominators for these percentages were a total of 392 episodes for indicator
conditions (225 in the RC group and 167 in the RNP group) and 510 episodes for
drugs (284 in the RC group and 226 in the RNP group). SOURCE: W.O. Spitzer,
D.L. Sackett, J.C. Sibley, R.S. Roberts, M. Tech, M. Gent, D.J. Kergin, B.C.
Hackett, A. Olynich, 'The Burlington randomized trial of the nurse practitioner'
(1974) 290 *New England Journal of Medicine* 251

practices in the city of Burlington were randomized so that each doctor continued with conventional care for two-thirds of them, or about 530 families
each. Each nurse practitioner became responsible for 270 families. A family was
eligible for the trial if one of its members had been treated in one of the practices
in the prior eighteen-month period or if they identified one of the physicians in
the trial practices as their family physician; 1,598 families (4,325 individuals)
satisfied these eligibility criteria.

Figure 2 shows the physical aspects of health status of the patients at the beginning and at the end of the trial. At the outset, in 1971, the two groups were
similar in physical function, in the ability to carry out the usual daily activities,
and in freedom from bed disability. The comparable status of the patient at the

end of the trial period in 1972 is also shown. The results for all three measurements remained essentially the same in both groups. Similarly, the results of emotional function and social function measured at the end of the trial year were almost identical in both groups. During the one-year experimental period, the difference in death rates between the conventional and nurse practitioner groups was not statistically or clinically significant.

QUALITY OF CARE

In addition to assessment of safety and efficacy by assessing health outcomes, it is also important to determine whether the introduction of the new health professional affects the quality of care rendered. In the series of studies on the nurse practitioner in Ontario, we evaluated the quality of care as part of the Burlington trial. The manner in which commonly used drugs were recommended was appraised and the management of certain indicator conditions was assessed. An indicator condition is a distinct clinical entity such as a symptom, disease, state, or injury which occurs frequently in the type of practice under surveillance and in which the outcome can be affected favourably or adversely by the choice of treatment. The adequacy of management for ten indicated conditions and thirteen drugs was rated according to explicit criteria which had been established by a professional peer group of family physicians, not university-affiliated, practising in the same region. The identity of the selected conditions and drugs was not known to the copractitioners. Figure 3 shows the results that can be obtained from this kind of evaluation using indicator conditions applied to a single-blind fashion. Among indicator conditions, 392 episodes were assessed, and 66 per cent were rated adequate in the conventional group (RC), while 69 per cent were rated that way in the nurse practitioner group (RNP). For drugs, 510 prescriptions were assessed; 75 per cent were rated adequate for the conventional group and 71 per cent for the nurse practitioner group.[9]

Figure 4 compares the manner in which consulting specialists rated referrals blindly from the nurse practitioner group, the conventional group, and a community control group (CC). The scores are expressed as a percentage of maximum

9 J.C. Sibley, K.V. Rudnick, J.D. Bell, R.D. Bethune, W.O. Spitzer, K. Wright, 'Quality of care appraisal in primary health care: a quantitative method' (1975) 83 *Annals of Internal Medicine* 46; Spitzer et al., 'The Burlington randomized trial'

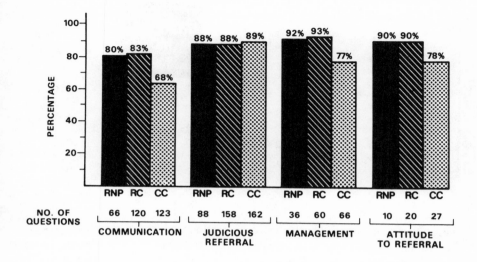

FIGURE 4 Evaluation of referrals from practitioners as assessed by consulting specialists (Burlington trial). The symbol CC represents community control group. The number of questions are those in each category of inquiry about patient referrals. SOURCE: J.C. Sibley, K.V. Rudnick, J.D. Bell, R.D. Bethune, W.O. Spitzer, K. Wright, 'Quality of care appraisal in primary health care: a quantitative method' (1975) 83 *Annals of Internal Medicine* 46

attainable favourable judgments on questions that were grouped as: those concerning communication among professionals, the clinical judgment in the process, the type of management given to the patients before and after the referral, and the attitude of the physicians or nurses about the referral. The performances of the RNP and the RC groups were similar, and both were appreciably better than for the CC group, except on matters of judgment.[10]

10 Sibley et al., 'Quality of care appraisal'

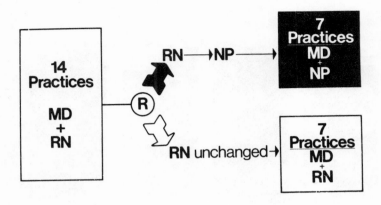

FIGURE 5 Design of the Southern Ontario randomized trial of the nurse practitioner. R represents randomization process. SOURCE: W.O. Spitzer, D.J. Kergin, M.A. Yoshida, W.A.M. Russell, B.C. Hackett, C.H. Goldsmith, 'Nurse practitioners in primary care. III. The Southern Ontario randomized trial' (1973) 108 *Canadian Medical Association Journal* 1005

EFFICIENCY

From the perspective of the provider
The equal outcomes for physical function, social function, emotional function and mortality and the comparability of quality of care provided suggest equality of effectiveness. It is therefore appropriate to proceed to examine the efficiency of the nurse practitioner. Efficiency can be studied from the standpoint of the providers of care (to date, private medical practitioners), or it can be examined from the standpoint of society.

Many determinations of the efficiency of nurse practitioners were done in a project which was known as the Southern Ontario Randomized Trial of the Nurse Practitioner.[11] In contrast to the Burlington trial, where patients had been

11 W.O. Spitzer, D.J. Kergin, M.A. Yoshida, W.A.M. Russell, B.C. Hackett, and C.H. Goldsmith, 'Nurse practitioners in primary care. III. The Southern Ontario randomized trial' (1973) 108 *Canadian Medical Association Journal* 1005

randomized, nurses and practices were allocated to two groups. Five months before the trial began, the office nurses of fourteen eligible practices had applied for the new training to qualify as nurse practitioners. Seven nurses were randomly assigned to receive nurse practitioner training, and their corresponding practices became the experimental group. The remaining nurses and practices became the control group, as shown in Figure 5.

The contrasting methods compared during the twelve months of the trial were as follows. In the conventional practices (the control group), office nurses would provide professional and non-professional assistance to the doctor of each practice in their customary way. Ongoing management of patients would continue to be planned exclusively by the physician, based on his clinical judgment. In the nurse practitioner practices (experimental group), the nurse would act as copractitioner according to ground rules described earlier. One practice from each group dropped out in the earlier part of the trial, leaving six in each group for most of the comparisons done.

The Southern Ontario trial focused on the effects of the new kind of practice on doctors and nurses. Among the research issues explored, the key financial question was the following: Is the modified deployment of physicians and nurses profitable to a family medicine practice? In this study the experimental period coincided with fiscal year 1971. Actual financial performance was assessed based on accounting and tax records for 1970 and 1972. During the following year, records were available in four control practices and all six experimental practices.

Table 1 shows the changes in average gross and net incomes. There was a small drop in both categories of doctors' income in experimental practices, and a substantial increase in both categories for the controls. As shown in Table 2, there were also changes in the nurses' net incomes between the baseline period and the follow-up period. Part of the effect on net incomes of physicians might be attributable to the increases in nurses' incomes.[12]

The analysis of revenues and costs during two years of experience in the study practices of the Burlington trial shows that each family physician had a reduction in income of $11,950 per year after the nurse practitioners assumed their new roles.

12 W.O. Spitzer, W.A.M. Russell, and B.C. Hackett, 'Financial consequences of employing a nurse practitioner' (1973) 40 *Ontario Medical Review* 96; W.O. Spitzer, B.C. Hackett, and W.A.M. Russell, 'Financial consequences of employing a nurse practitioner. II: Changes in income of physicians and nurses' (1973) 41 *Ontario Medical Review* 269

TABLE 1
Changes in actual gross and net income per physician of experimental and
control practices (Southern Ontario trial; determined from practice accounting records)

	Average income ($)		
	1970	1972	Change (%)
6 Experimental MD gross	68,764	67,767	−1.45
4 Control MD gross	67,174	78,909	17.47
6 Experimental MD net	38.975	37,146	−4.70
4 Control MD net	36,531	39,285	7.54

SOURCE: W.O. Spitzer, B.C. Hackett, W.A.M. Russell, 'Financial consequences of employing a nurse practitioner. II: Changes in income of physicians and nurses' (1973)
41 *Ontario Medical Review* 269

TABLE 2
Changes in actual income of nurses and nurse practitioners
(Southern Ontario trial)

	Average income ($)		
	1970	1972	Change (%)
4 Nurses	6,208	6,618	6.60
4 Nurse practitioners	6,185	8,044	30.06

SOURCE: W.O. Spitzer, B.C. Hackett, W.A.M. Russell, 'Financial consequences of
employing a nurse practitioner. II: Changes in income of physicians
and nurses' (1973) 41 *Ontario Medical Review* 269

A social perspective
Important as profitability of new health professionals is in the assessment of the
applicability of the new approach, the evaluation of the economic effects from
the standpoint of society and of government is paramount. Two categories of
results from the Burlington trial illustrate the evidence that can be obtained to
determine the efficiency of a new health professional from the standpoint of

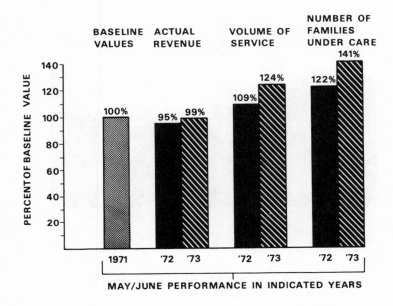

FIGURE 6 Financial performance of the study practice (Burlington trial).
Comparison of baseline period with final two months of trial (1972) and the
follow-up period (1973). SOURCE: W.O. Spitzer, R.S. Roberts, D.L. Sackett,
M. Gent, et al., 'Effects of nurse practitioners on use of health services: Report
of a randomized trial,' paper presented at Medical Care Section, American
Public Health Association Meeting, San Francisco, 5 Nov. 1973

society. Records of over 24,076 encounters of visits to the practitioners were
kept in the study practices during fourteen months. The productivity performance of the study practices is summarized in Figure 6. The first column, designated 100 per cent, is a baseline for the three parameters of performance. The
second set of columns shows that the actual gross revenue to the practice dropped
by 5 per cent after one year and was still slightly under baseline after two years.
The third set of columns shows the changes in volume of services rendered, regardless of permissible reimbursement. The volume grew 9 per cent after one

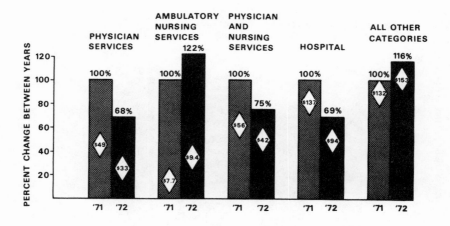

FIGURE 7 Health services utilization in five categories (Burlington trial). Comparisons for combined study practice before and after the trial. SOURCE: W.O. Spitzer, R.S. Roberts, D.L. Sackett, M. Gent, et al., 'Effects of nurse practitioners on use of health services:·Report of a randomized trial,' paper presented at Medical Care Section, American Public Health Association Meeting, San Francisco, 5 Nov. 1973

year and 24 per cent after two years. The fourth set of columns shows the increase in number of families under care in the practice: 22 per cent after the first year and 41 per cent after two years.

Expressed otherwise, the evidence in Figure 6 indicates that nurse practitioner–family physician teams can augment primary care resources where they are needed to a major degree and with remarkable efficiency. Compared to baseline levels, after two years such teams assumed responsibility for 41 per cent more patients while increasing the volume of service delivered only by 24 per cent and holding constant the costs to the government insurance plan.

The second category of data from the Burlington trial was obtained by household interview on a sample of 817 patients who were questioned before and after the experimental period to ascertain whether there were changes in patterns of utilization of health services. The Composite Index of Health Care Costs

TABLE 3
Changes in index of health costs in Burlington sample from 1971 to 1972

	Cost per person per year ($)		
Category of service	1971	1972	Change (%)
Physician	48.69	33.08	−32
Nurse	7.65	9.37	22
Dentist	32.52	35.78	10
Social/welfare worker	1.28	Nil	−100
Optometrist/optician	24.35	24.35	0
Chiropractor	2.06	1.85	−10
Podiatrist	0.27	0.81	200
Hospital and related	136.60	94.49	−31
Laboratory	20.01	27.16	36
Diagnostic X-ray	15.89	25.50	60
Direct cash expenditures	35.55	37.39	5
Composite index of health care costs (total)	324.87	289.78	−11

SOURCE: W.O. Spitzer, R.S. Roberts, T. Delmore, 'Nurse practitioners in primary care. VI. Assessment of their deployment with the Utilization and Financial Index' (1976) 114 *Canadian Medical Association Journal*

was developed as a method to measure various important categories of health service by interview and to report them in identical units. The units are 'dollars per person per year.' The details on methods of developing the Index have been reported elsewhere.[13] For the purpose of this presentation we only state that the Index does not provide the actual average amounts expended by the experimental population on health services. Rather, it conveys the approximate magnitude of health expenditures, and it provides a baseline level against which to compare the differences between groups under assessment or changes within one group over time. We now have good evidence, after validation procedures, that the val-

13 W.O. Spitzer, R.S. Roberts, T. Delmore, 'Nurse practitioners in primary care. V. Development of the Utilization and Financial Index to measure effects of their deployment' (1976) 114 *Canadian Medical Association Journal* 1099

ues indicated by the Index correlate well with actual expenditures both in the total amount and in various categories. Table 3 shows the changes that were observed between 1971 and 1972 for all study practices. There is an 11 per cent reduction of total costs of services used by the patients of the practice. In the category of service corresponding to physician visits there was a reduction of 32 per cent of the cost per person per year; there was a concurrent increase of 22 per cent for nurses. Most significantly, costs for hospital and related services dropped by 31 per cent. As seen in Figure 7, when physicians and nurses' services are combined, a reduction of 25 per cent is still observed. If all categories other than physician, nurse, and hospital are combined, there is an increase of 16 per cent, suggesting that a partial shift from hospital-based service to ambulatory service may have occurred after adoption of the new form of practice.

The reduction in hospitalization of 31 per cent determined by interview in the sample of 817 patients seemed so important that the rates in the total population of 4,300, which had been under surveillance throughout the baseline period and the experimental year, were verified. In doing so, a 21 per cent reduction was found in hospital days used by patients in the practice. The reduction was caused by fewer admissions rather than by a reduction of the length of stay per admission. The pattern suggests that patients who formerly would have been admitted were being managed at home or on an ambulatory basis. These findings have administrative significance in long-term planning because reductions in the number of admissions result in greater savings than reductions in length of stay.

In a setting where the changes in rate of utilization for various categories of service were evaluated using similar techniques to those in Burlington, but where the study had a 'before/after' design, the differences in utilization in the 'after' phase between patients of the interdisciplinary centre using the nurse practitioner and patients in the same township receiving conventional care are remarkable. Particularly noteworthy is the 57 per cent reduced utilization of hospitals demonstrated by patients with whom the nurse practitioner had a key role.[14] Table 4 shows selected cross-sectional comparisons for a cohort of 1,130 patients who were assessed in the study reported.

Our data have provided part of the empirical evidence needed to develop new

14 W.O. Spitzer, R.S. Roberts, T. Delmore, 'Nurse practitioners in primary care. VI. Assessment of their deployment with the Utilization and Financial Index' (1976) 114 *Canadian Medical Association Journal* 1103

227 The introduction of new health professionals

TABLE 4
Selected crossectional comparisons in the Utilization and Financial Index
in the Smithville sample (derived from the 1132 patients in interview cohort)

| Category of service | 'After' determinations as of 1973 ($) | | Difference (%) |
	TWP	FMC	
Physician	25.76	44.20	72
Nurse	3.14	14.05	347
Physician and nurse	(28.90)	(58.25)	(102)
Hospital	165.69	71.83	-57
Other	66.62	80.51	21
Total	261.21	210.59	-19

NOTE: TWP means township; FMC means family medicine centre.
SOURCE: W.O. Spitzer, R.S. Roberts, T. Delmore, 'Nurse practitioners in
primary care. V. Development of the Utilization and Financial Index
to measure effects of their deployment' (1976) 114 *Canadian Medical
Association Journal* 1099

formulas for reimbursement that could make the new method of primary care practice financially attractive to both physicians and nurses while retaining the economic advantages for society.

ACCEPTANCE AND SATISFACTION

Providers
In the Southern Ontario trial we assessed job satisfaction of physicians and nurses in the experimental and control groups by means of a questionnaire with sixty-seven items that explored job content, relationship with colleagues, challenge and achievement, available time and energy for the job itself and for other activities, prestige, and remuneration. The maximum possible scores for all six components of job satisfaction were calculated for the individual respondents, and then the individual scores were averaged. The scores of physicians are shown in Figure 8 and those of nurses in Figure 9. With the exception of remuneration, satisfaction scores were high in all components for doctors and nurses of both the experimental and control groups. For remuneration, satisfaction in the experimental group declined among doctors and rose among nurses. As part of the

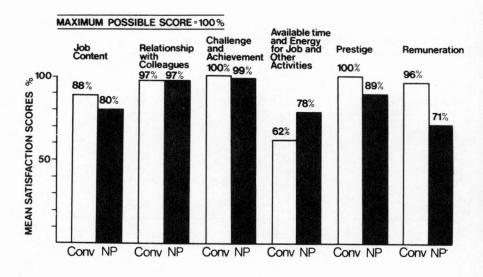

FIGURE 8 Satisfaction of physicians with certain aspects of their work at conclusion of Southern Ontario trial (March 1972). 'Conv' means conventional control practices; NP means nurse practitioner experimental practices. SOURCE: W.O. Spitzer, D.J. Kergin, M.A. Yoshida, W.A.M. Russell, B.C. Hackett, C.H. Goldsmith, 'Nurse practitioners in primary care. III. The Southern Ontario randomized trial' (1973) 108 *Canadian Medical Association Journal* 1005

over-all evaluation that accompanies introduction of a new health professional, satisfaction levels of all health professionals affected directly or indirectly by the change need to be assessed. Without such information, serious errors about the feasibility of widespread implementation of a new concept of health care can be made.[15]

15 Spitzer et al., supra n. 11; W.O. Spitzer, R.S. Roberts, D.L. Sackett, M. Gent, et al., 'Effects of nurse practitioners on use of health services: Report of a randomized trial,' paper presented at Medical Care Section, American Public Health Association Meeting, San Francisco, 5 Nov. 1973

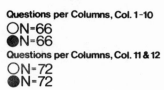

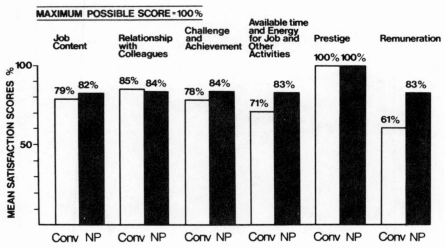

FIGURE 9 Satisfaction of nurses with certain aspects of their work at conclusion of Southern Ontario trial (March 1972). For explanation and source see Figure 8 caption.

Consumers

More important, however, is the acceptance and satisfaction level of those receiving care from a new health professional through the required new arrangements in the organizing of delivery. Surveys of patients' attitudes provide direct information. Table 5 shows the acceptance by a sample population of a nurse in health maintenance and sickness surveillance situations in a study of a rural population in the Niagara peninsula done before nurse practitioners were introduced. Table 6 shows that over 85 per cent of respondents gave a positive assess-

TABLE 5

Acceptance by sample population of a nurse in health maintenance and sickness surveillance situations (Niagara rural survey; before introduction of nurse practitioners)

	Response frequency (%) for total adult respondents ($N = 931$)		
	No	Yes	Don't know
Would you say it is better to get advice about medicines from a nurse rather than use home remedies?	12.7	83.1	4.2
Would you say that it is worth the trouble to see a nurse at a nearby clinic if physicians cannot possibly see everyone promptly?	14.6	82.0	3.4
When you go to see a doctor, do you sometimes depend on the nurse to explain the details of what he is doing to you?	73.4	22.6	4.0
Do you believe that the advice nurses can give you about your health would help you avoid more illness in your lifetime?	29.5	62.8	7.7
Do you think that nurses try to take more responsibility for the health of patients than they are trained to take?	56.6	26.6	16.8
Is it best to get as much advice as you can from nurses in addition to doctors before you decide what you should do if you are sick?	59.7	35.2	5.1
For most kinds of common illnesses, do you think a nurse can be as helpful to you as a doctor?	39.6	56.2	4.2
Would you find it reassuring if you knew that a nurse would be easily available to answer your questions on the telephone whenever you thought you or someone in your family was getting sick?	15.1	82.5	2.4

SOURCE: N.D. Chenoy, W.O. Spitzer, G.D. Anderson, 'Nurse practitioners in primary care. II. Prior attitudes of a rural population' (1973) 108 *Canadian Medical Association Journal* 998

TABLE 6
Perception of respondents regarding formal inclusion of nurses in health team working under supervision of doctors (Niagara rural survey)

Do you think that doctors should make arrangements for specially trained nurses working under their supervision to make home visits, especially for problems of children and elderly people?	Response frequency (%) ($N = 930$)
Yes	85.7
No	9.2
Don't know	5.1
Total	100.0

SOURCE: N.D. Chenoy, W.O. Spitzer, G.D. Anderson, 'Nurse practitioners in primary care. II. Prior attitudes of a rural population' (1973) 108 *Canadian Medical Association Journal* 998

ment of the concept of a specially-trained nurse working under the clinical supervision of doctors in home-visit situations. It has been very interesting to observe, during two years after the survey from which the cited results were completed, that there were very few instances of rejection of nurse practitioner services by patients, even in worry-inducing situations, in spite of the clearly unfavorable attitude about her role before the respondents had had personal experience with such a nurse.

In the Burlington trial, of 1,598 families eligible to enter the project, only seven families refused their assignments, two in the conventional group and five in the nurse practitioner group. It was also determined that during the year of trial, 0.9 per cent of the conventional families and 0.7 per cent of the nurse practitioners' families left the practice because of dissatisfaction. In the followup survey, 97 per cent of the patients in the conventional group and 96 per cent of the patients in the nurse practitioner group were found to be satisfied with health services received during the experimental period. The patients were also asked to rate the acceptability of the nurse practitioner concept, without regard to their satisfaction with total health services. On a five-point scale of unacceptable to highly acceptable, the rank of acceptable or higher was given by 82 per cent of the conventional group and 79 per cent of the nurse practitioner group.[16] The acceptance

16 Spitzer et al., supra n. 8

and satisfaction results of the Burlington trial are especially meaningful because a unique characteristic of the experimental setting was that the patients, if dissatisfied, had complete freedom to seek care from another source. Not only were there several family physicians in the community accepting new families, but health insurance covered costs completely, regardless of the chosen source of care.

ASSESSMENT OF TRANSFER OF FUNCTION

Analysis of daysheet data from the Burlington trial showed that during the baseline period physicians had been involved in 86 per cent of all visits to the practices and the conventional nurses dealt with the remaining 14 per cent of encounters on their own. This is indicated in Figure 10. In the nurse practitioner practices, immediately after the trial began, the doctors were able to reduce their level of involvement to 45 per cent of visits during the first eight weeks. The percentage fell to 28 per cent by the twentieth week. It rose from the twenty-third to the forty-fourth week, when many new families were being seen for the first time, and stabilized at about 33 per cent during the last eight weeks. The physicians in the conventional group continued to be involved in about 86 per cent of all patient visits throughout the trial, as had been the case in the baseline period.[17]

In the Southern Ontario trial, time-motion studies were done to ascertain whether exposure to the educational program was associated with any change in the mix of clinical and non-clinical activities undertaken by the family practice copractitioners in representative work weeks. The observations were done on nurses and physicians and the experimental and control groups. The results for nurses are shown in Figure 11. Activities designated as diagnosis and management with the patient present occupied 33 per cent of the conventional nurses' time, in contrast to 56 per cent for the nurse practitioners. For diagnosis and management by telephone, the corresponding values were 10 per cent and 4 per cent. Case study and professional reading during working hours accounted for 0.3 per cent of time in the control group and 5 per cent in the experimental practices. Clerical and housekeeping tasks took nearly twice as much of the conventional nurses' time (39 per cent) than of nurse practitioners' time (20 per cent). There was a minor difference for other miscellaneous activities. It was also

17 G.P. Sweeney and W.I. Hay, 'The Burlington experience: a study of nurse practitioners in family practice' (1973) 19 *Canadian Family Physicians* 101

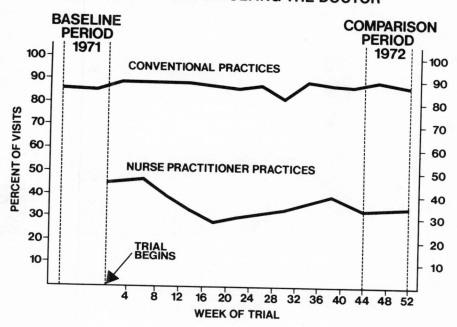

FIGURE 10 Percentage of patient visits involving the doctor (Burlington trial). During the baseline period the percentages indicated correspond to the merged original practices. The nurse practitioner practices began to function when the trial began. SOURCE: G.P. Sweeney and W.I. Hay, 'The Burlington experience: a study of nurse practitioners in family practice' (1973) 19 *Canadian Family Physicians* 101

determined that, although nurse practitioners spent about 50 per cent more time in clinical work and half the time in clerical/housekeeping duties, the shift in time was not at the expense of physicians' time involvement in clinical activities. Nor did the change noted for nurse practitioners result in a higher proportion of non-clinical clerical tasks done by the corresponding physicians.

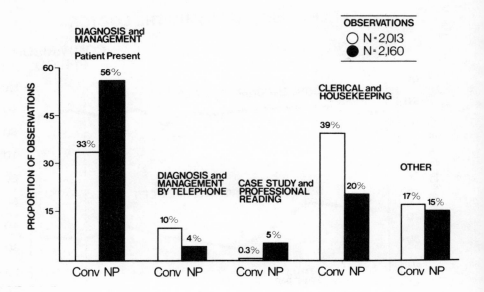

FIGURE 11 Time-motion study of nurses (Southern Ontario trial).
For explanation and source see Figure 8 caption.

The type of analysis described here is also an important aspect of the evaluation of educational programs. It is essential to determine whether the objectives about changes in role and about behavioural characteristics of new health professionals have been met in actual practice. A controlled and randomized design such as that of the Southern Ontario trial, in which the educational program was the independent variable, helps establish whether the observed changes are in fact causally associated with the educational program itself.

LONG-TERM SURVEILLANCE

When the developers of a new drug have given evidence of its safety and efficacy after laborious pilot toxicity studies in animals, after carefully designed and executed randomized controlled trials in humans, and after they have successfully marketed the product following survey evidence of its need, the evaluation process is not over. Long-term surveillance continues to be necessary after a new pharmaceutical is on the market to detect unsuspected or unforeseeable side effects, to identify previously unknown contraindications for its use, and to determine if there is sustained acceptance of the drug by prescribers and patients. The difficulties with chloramphenicol, thalidomide, and potassium-diuretic combinations, to name just three examples, were only identified in long-term surveillance of adverse effects, years after the respective products had been marketed and had successfully passed all the hurdles to which new products are ordinarily subjected.

The introduction of new health professionals, especially in primary care practice, is a relatively new development. Few rigorous evaluative studies analogous to the short-term initial assessments of new modes of therapy or new drugs have been done. The results of almost all these studies conducted to date both in the United States and in Canada have been encouraging. The evidence about safety and efficacy has been favourable. The efficiency of the new method has been satisfactory from the standpoint of society. However, long-term follow-ups are essential if a responsible policy about some of these new methods of practice is to be maintained. The performance of the new health professionals will have to be scrutinized repeatedly to identify any shifts that might cause concern years after graduation from formal educational programs. There may be a change in attitude of the public toward new health professionals, especially in areas where physician/population imbalances can be corrected. The vocational mortality of the new health professionals could reverse the economic advantages of educational programs of short duration. It is conceivable that negative incidents such as preventable deaths, avoidable harm to patients, and lawsuits could occur in such patterns or frequency that they would force second thoughts about the whole concept.

In summary, the data from two studies, a randomized control trial and a before/after study, showed that, in spite of large increases in the use of ambulatory services by practice populations served by family physician–nurse practitioner teams, the net effect has been a substantial reduction in total use of health services. The effect was associated with major reductions in hospital care for the same population. Such economic advantages to society proved feasible in a fee-for-service context and in settings where related evidence demonstrated no concurrent deterioration in the health status of patients or in quality of care. The first survey of one hundred nurse practitioners who graduated in the first year five years of the McMaster University program has been completed. Table 7 summarizes the proportion of nurse-months of employment of those nurse practitioners expressed as a percentage of the maximum total possible nurse-months of employment for all cohorts of nurse graduates taken together. The employment rate has been high up to date, and 82 per cent of the nurses surveyed in

TABLE 7
Average months of employment as nurse practitioner by class of students

Dates of completion of program	Potential months of employment	Average actual months of employment	Percentage of actual months maximum potential = 100%
December 1971 (N = 22)	39	32.3	82.8
Spring 1973 (N = 12)	22	20.4	92.7
Fall 1973 (N = 14)	16	12.4	77.5
Spring 1974 (N = 14)	10	7.1	71.0
Fall 1974 (N = 18)	4	3.8	95.0
Total nurse months	1558	1296.8	
Overall employment rate			83.5

SOURCE: K. Scherer, F. Fortin, W.O. Spitzer, D.J. Kergin, 'Nurse practitioners in primary care. VII. A longitudinal study of 99 nurses and 79 associated physicians' (1977) 116 *Canadian Medical Association Journal* 856-62

1975 were still with the original family physician who had sponsored them under the educational program at Hamilton.[18]

Long-term surveillance has only begun. If, in the exuberance of positive findings, a cautious vigil that will help identify problems and solutions early is not instituted, the ultimate effects of the innovations introduced today might be viewed later as tragic by both critics and proponents of new health professionals.

18 K. Scherer, F. Fortin, W.O. Spitzer, D.J. Kergin, 'Nurse practitioners in primary care. VII. A longitudinal study of 99 nurses and 79 associated physicians' (1977) 116 *Canadian Medical Association Journal* 856-62

LARRY TAMAN

The emerging legal paraprofessionals

The legal profession has become the subject of increasing public scrutiny. A generally more critical posture in the face of established institutions no doubt accounts for some of this activity. In Ontario the ever-mounting public subsidy of legal services through the Ontario Legal Aid Plan has helped to fuel critical inquiry into the structure and work of the legal profession.

The increasing importance of legal aid in the provision of legal services to private individuals focuses concern on access to service, including the pricing behaviour of the profession. The unmet need for legal services, persistently demonstrated by the ready absorption of every new service publicly or privately offered, speaks poorly of the capacity of the existing structure to meet the demands for a just distribution of legal services. This unmet need, substantially a product of high-cost service or simple unavailability of service in many areas, both rural and urban, has invited experimentation with new manpower strategies. Neighbourhood law offices, often university-sponsored, have experimented with the use of non-lawyers in the performance of tasks hitherto exclusively within the preserve of the lawyers. Client interviewing and counselling, representation in the lower courts and before administrative tribunals, legal education in community organizations, all have been undertaken by these newcomers.

Moreover, one suspects that a similar burgeoning of paralegal personnel, perhaps even antedating the neighbourhood law office phenomenon, has taken place inside the private law firm. No solid Canadian data exist to confirm or deny the common perception that so-called law clerks are growing in numbers and in the importance of the work they undertake. Rising cost-consciousness and the possible disappearance of a reliable beast of burden, the articled clerk, form important drives in this movement.

Osgoode Hall Law School, York University

Nor do present data probe the extent of the monopoly of the profession and its adjuncts (like neighbourhood law offices) in the market for legal services. In the private sector, claims adjusters, patent agents, trust officers, and shop stewards all perform tasks requiring at least some of the lawyer's skills. Some, such as tax computation services, sell their wares directly to the public. Others, like claims examiners, are slotted into the internal machinery of the firm. In either case they confine and to some extent erode the lawyer's monopoly.

In this essay, I plan to give some indication of who the paraprofessionals are and to take some measure of the challenge they pose for public policy.

THE EMERGING ACOLYTES

Paraprofessionals are non-professionals who work alongside professionals in positions which require the understanding of some aspects of the profession's allegedly systematic body of knowledge. I choose the word 'alongside' in deliberate recognition that notions of 'superior' and 'subordinate' are often as much self-servicing propaganda as anything else. For example, both lawyers and judges would probably consider the probation officer a subordinate in the sentencing system. Yet, given that some 90 per cent of accused persons plead guilty, the sentence is the only real variable, and in this the pre-sentence report of the probation officer must often, functionally speaking, be the dispositive input. Likewise he, not the judge or the lawyer, will supervise the convicted person for the duration of the probation. One would thus not be surprised to discover that convicted persons see lawyers and judges as assistants to probation officers.

I use 'non-professionals' only as a shorthand way of describing those actors who have not been traditionally included in the established professions. In no way do I seek silently to prejudge any other issue. Because of the complexity of the legal care system there are myriad persons performing work of a paraprofessional nature. Sacrificing comprehensiveness for depth, let me set out some of the paraprofessionals who work alongside the practising lawyer. The titles of the various categories are not presented as being universally accepted.

Legal assistants: Initial interview clerks, process servers, and others are required to understand and carry out limited procedures of a routine nature.

Legal secretaries: Legal secretaries, properly speaking, are not stenographers. Their responsibilities vary widely from office to office and often include the work normally carried out by law clerks.

Law clerks: Law clerks perform tasks which may be considered more standardized than those which lawyers do themselves. Their work is marked by the necessary application of the worker's judgment to his or her knowledge of the ascertained facts and the pertinent rules. There is now a rapidly growing corps of law clerks who are able to perform the bulk of the work done by the legal general practitioner. Incorporations, straightforward estates and real estate deals are their everyday work. On the litigation side, pleadings, motions and even discoveries may be handled by law clerks. Professional conduct rules require that this work be supervised by a lawyer, but it is clear enough that most of it could be and probably is done practically without supervision. My guess is that reliable data on what lawyers in general practice actually do would show that a large part of it could, even given our present legal technology, be done by law clerks.

Lay advocates: Like law clerks, lay advocates are distinguished from legal assistants by reason of the necessity of bringing trained judgment to bear on the meeting of facts and rules. Their work is comparable to that of the law clerks, but is exclusively directed to advocacy. At the moment they have only those rights of audience before judicial and quasi-judicial tribunals enjoyed by all citizens. This restricts their right to represent clients to those tribunals before which the individual is entitled to be represented by a non-lawyer agent – Workmen's Compensation Appeal Board, Social Assistance Review Board, Unemployment Insurance Commission, Small Claims Courts, and others. Very little of this work is presently done by private practitioners. Most of the relatively small number of lay advocates are employed by a few neighbourhood-based law offices throughout the country which specialize in legal work for poor people. There are others, however, in the employ of public and private organizations. A collection agency, for example, may employ individuals to represent it in small claims courts. Of course, the work of the lay advocate is not limited to actual advocacy before tribunals but would normally include all ancillary work – the necessary interviewing, the organization of the paperwork and the application of informal settlement techniques.

Community education and organization: The community law offices to which I just referred have exercised an important role in the development of innovative legal technology in Canada. Some offices have employed paraprofessionals as community educators *cum* organizers. The idea here is more practical than political. It is, in the main, an effort to bring a preventive perspective to legal practice. Of course, lawyers have always acted as problem preventers for wise, paying clients. For the less wise and the less paying, law is a crisis business. The community educators have attempted to teach members of low-income communities about their more important rights (can a landlord change the locks on your door? can your employer lay you off without notice? can the sheriff repossess your furniture because you have signed for someone else's loan?) and to alert them to the more common forms of abuse. In doing this work, community educators have found their most important resource to be other community members. This has led to group action as a most important problem-solving technique, with the legal paraprofessionals leading the way.

Outside the law office: Lawyers and their supervised assistants are commonly said to enjoy monopoly rights over the provision of legal services to the public. However, there are other sellers in the market. Tax consultants, apparently widespread, calculate their customers' income tax liability. In cases of property loss through fire, independent adjusters advise fire victims on their rights and assist in the preparation of claims and in the evaluation of proposals for settlement. Some privately-funded service organizations, such as Injured Workers' Consultants, offer free services direct to the public without the involvement of lawyers.

Business enterprises provide themselves with untold quantities of legal services from internal sources. It appears likely, for example, that the claims department of an accident insurer makes the legal judgments as to liability and quantum of damages in the vast majority of the cases handled. Some of these judgments must necessarily be quite complex. Detailed supervision and elaborate hierarchies of authority attempt to guarantee that adequate sophistication is brought to bear on each case.

THE ACOLYTES AND THE ISSUES

Even on first view, the emergence of the paraprofessionals raises a series of concerns which will need to be addressed in the near future.

The professional monopoly
We are accustomed to speaking of the legal profession's monopoly over legal services. Regrettably, there exists no work with which I am familiar which attempts to measure the market for legal services and to assess the market shares of the various active interests. Clearly, as indicated above, legal services are presently being offered to the public on a fee-paying basis by persons who are neither lawyers nor supervised by lawyers. Moreover, an unknown portion of that service apparently offered by lawyers is actually being carried out by non-lawyers – law clerks, legal secretaries, etc. acting, notionally at least, under the supervision of lawyers. Lastly, corporate interests may be handling relatively sophisticated legal tasks with non-lawyer corporate personnel.

This phenomenon is capable over time of generating substantial pressure on the legal profession. Given the apparently prevailing view that substantial regulation is always better than little or no regulation, calls will no doubt shortly be made for the regulation of the paraprofessionals. A wide range of concerns needs to be canvassed: training requirements, role definition, certification or licensing, quality and availability of service, supervision and continuing education, discipline, working relations with other professionals, public acceptance of paraprofessionals, and others.

I think it most likely that movement on these issues will concentrate on those paraprofessionals who offer service in the market place (rather than, say, inside a corporation). There are already dialogues between the Law Society and the Institute of Law Clerks and the Metropolitan Toronto Association of Legal Secretaries. These groups, working as they do under the direct supervision of lawyers, pose little direct threat to the established order of things.

The tax consultants, the claims adjusters, the title searchers, and others no doubt present a more acute threat to the professional monopoly. Whether they should continue to be allowed to offer their services and, if so, under what regulation, if any, will no doubt raise more pressing questions.

Who regulates?

Self-regulation has long bemused me. It has always struck me as unlikely on the face of it that any important activity in the market place could be self-regulated. My prejudices are, of course, no more self-validating then those of the Law Society, which, as chance would have it, run in the opposite direction. An evaluation of the effectiveness of legal self-regulation and the concomitant monopoly would address itself to the allocative efficiency and distributive adequacy of existing arrangements. The danger signs of high cost of entry and high concentration would need to be examined with some thoroughness.

It seems likely, however, that the paraprofessionals will eventually chafe at regulation by the professionals. Unlike the public at large, they will ultimately represent a group with both the inclination and the capacity overtly to conflict with the established profession. The question of the definition of the role of the paraprofessional, in this context one of the allocation of market shares, will prove particularly vexing.

Legal technique

The de facto emergence of the legal paraprofessionals suggests that lawyers are overtrained for at least some of the services demanded in the legal services market. Individuals with less investment in their professional formation are able, apparently, to perform some law jobs satisfactorily and at less cost. Beginning from this base, role definition, perhaps the key problem, resolves itself into a determination of who is capable of doing which law job under which regulatory regime. We might, for example, suggest that any insured holder of a certain certificate of qualification ought to be allowed to handle residential real estate transactions without supervision. The same individual, it might be suggested, ought not to be permitted to handle the typically more complex commercial real estate transactions except under the direct supervision of a solicitor.

Focusing the enquiry on the complexity of the tasks and the serious consequences of error will no doubt remain a key aspect of the professional response to the demands of the paraprofessionals. It may, in fact, be a sensible approach – as far as it goes.

Legal science, of course, is not a closed book. It represents the existing methods of ordering those human transactions deemed to be of sufficient importance to merit the application of rules, principles, and the binding force of the legal order. Clearly the secrets of some aspects of this science are sufficiently arcane to be accessible only to those with elaborate professional formation. Yet before we leave these areas to the professionals, we might first examine that aspect of the science involved to determine if its simplification would permit its successful operation by less costly human resources.

Consider the following proposition. Real property transactions, largely routine to the trained eye, are nonetheless an intricate business, full of pitfalls for the unwary. Law clerks working in the field probably ought to be qualified as specialists and/or closely supervised. Looking for ways to professionalize law clerks seems a sound policy.

Logical? Yes, of course, but only as long as the major premise holds true. Are transactions involving real estate necessarily as intricate as Ontario lawyers have made them? Probably not. In some jurisdictions a system of title insurance attempts to transfer the whole job into an inexpensive clerical operation. In Ontario, the technology demands (we are told) such skill that the normal legal fee for the simplest transaction may run close to $1,000, giving the legal profession a surtax of between 1 and 2 per cent on all real property transactions. This income is no doubt a mainstay in the fight against increasing overhead. It is also, from a social perspective, an essentially wasteful, unnecessary expenditure.

Other examples abound. Fees averaging $800 may be justified by the amount of work presently involved in an uncontested divorce. In the typical case, however, there is no real dispute over questions of custody of children, division of assets, and maintenance after separation. At least in these cases the work could theoretically be done as easily by someone trained to operate a paper shredder as by a lawyer.

Or again, Canada makes more use of imprisonment for the control and (it is said) rehabilitation of certain kinds of social deviants than almost any other developed country. Given this draconian consequence of deviant behaviour, the participation of lawyers is necessary to ensure that punishment is meted out only after the most scrupulous attention has been paid to the applicable rules. We know perfectly well that this system is very expensive. A day-long criminal trial followed by incarceration for two years in a federal prison will cost in the neighbourhood of $60,000. We also know that the whole procedure is almost completely ineffectual by any known measure. Most tragically, we know that the whole system is heavily biased in favour of the punishment of the poor and the ignorant. Notwithstanding its demonstrated inadequacy, that legal science which deals with the social control of deviant behaviour is firmly grounded in its ancient English roots. Only a smattering of fundamental research and development is taking place. Meanwhile, the law schools annually turn out thousands of graduates trained in the venerable rites of the criminal law.

The argument, then, is simple. By all means, let us perform the existing professional jobs in the most cost-efficient manner we can devise. This is the least onerous of the obligations conferred by our professional monopolies. At the same time, however, we should look beyond that to the prospects of deprofessionalizing legal (and other) professional services.

Ivan Illich has summarized his penetrating critique of health care professionals in this way: 'A professional and physician-based health care system which has grown beyond tolerable bound is sickening for three reasons: it must produce clinical damages which outweigh its potential benefits; it cannot but obscure the political conditions which render society unhealthy; and it tends to expropriate power of the individual to heal himself and to shape his or her environment.'[1] I believe the sense of his critique is perfectly applicable to our 'professional and lawyer-based social problem-solving system.'

CONCLUSION

The emerging legal paraprofessionals give us the opportunity to examine the whole of our work to ensure that each job we do is done in the least expensive, least harmful, most simple, and most effective manner we can devise. When lawyers' work is restricted to jobs that only lawyers can do well, then, and only then, is their professional monopoly arguably necessary in the public interest.

1 Ivan Illich, *Medical Nemesis* (London: Calder and Boyars, 1975) 11

EMPLOYED PROFESSIONALS

MORLEY GUNDERSON

Economic aspects of the unionization of salaried professionals

INTRODUCTION

The growth of professional occupations is a well-documented fact in Canada, as in most developed economies. Census figures indicate that between 1931 and 1961, for example, the professions grew by 166 per cent, compared to the 55 per cent increase for all other occupations. Since 1951 the professions have been the fastest growing occupational group.

Within the growing category of the professions, the number of salaried professionals has been increasing relative to the number of self-employed. Much of this growth comes from the rapidly expanding 'newer professions' such as science, nursing, social work, and economics. In addition, however, many of the traditional professions are becoming increasingly salaried, especially – as is the case with medicine and law – when they become more involved in social security programs like medicare and legal aid.

Census figures indicate the following increases, between 1961 and 1971, in the proportion of the profession that is salaried, as opposed to self-employed: accountants 0.86 to 0.93, dentists 0.10 to 0.24, lawyers 0.31 to 0.43, optometrists 0.13 to 0.25, pharmacists 0.55 to 0.78, physicians 0.34 to 0.46, and veterinarians 0.50 to 0.57. Some professions, such as engineering and science, have not increased their proportion of salaried workers in recent years, because they were already almost exclusively salaried. Unfortunately, estimates of the number of salaried and self-employed professionals are not readily available prior to 1961.

University of Toronto Centre for Industrial Relations, Faculty of Management Studies, and Scarborough College. Without implicating them for the contents of the paper, the author would like to thank Jack Barbash, Dave Beatty, John Crispo, Everett Kassalow, Ernie Lightman, Gerry Starr and Michael Trebilcock for their helpful suggestions and comments.

For lawyers, however, Meltz gives the proportion on salary as being 0.14 in 1931, 0.17 in 1941, 0.27 in 1951, and 0.32 in 1961.[1] Current 1971 census estimates are 0.43.

Unionization - once thought to be the response of manual workers only - has been increasingly discussed and implemented amongst many of the salaried professionals. Unfortunately, comprehensive data on unionization by occupation is not readily available in Canada, so it is not possible to document the exact growth of professional unionism.

Collective action on the part of professionals generally occurs through a professional association, a union, or both. Professional associations sometimes act as mere sounding boards for their members (as is often the case for engineers), and sometimes engage in full-fledged collective bargaining (as is often the case for pilots and for medical associations that bargain with the government over state health insurance fees for doctors).

Trade union affiliation often involves being subsumed in the bargaining unit of existing production or white-collar unions, as is often the case with social workers, health personnel, and librarians. Or it involves separate bargaining units of professional employers, either as independent unions or with national or international affiliation, as is often the case with teachers, university faculty, and musicians. Some professions, such as teachers, university faculty, and engineers, have run the gamut of all of the alternative forms of collective action.

This phenomenon of professional unionism raises many questions. For example, what are the reasons for the growth of professional unionism, and can we expect it to persist in the future? What impact will professional unions have on such factors as professional incomes and working conditions, the price and quality of professional services, and the public interest? Answers to these questions have important policy implications: if the process of professional unionism continues into the future and can be expected to have a substantial impact, then careful scrutiny of the process is in order. Without understanding the underlying process and its effects we would have little basis for legislative policies to govern professional unionism or to alter its impact in a socially desirable fashion.

The purpose of this paper is to outline the *economic* dimensions or professional unionism, with particular emphasis on its causes and consequences. Beyond the direct scope of the paper are various legal aspects of an industrial relations nature, including issues of the appropriate bargaining unit, the appropriate scope of bargaining, and the possible conflict of interest that may occur if a pro-

1 N. Meltz, *Review of Historical Trends and Projections of the Number of Lawyers and Judges in the Ontario Labour Force* (Toronto: University of Toronto Institute for Policy Analysis, 1974)

fessional association both bargains for its salaried members and regulates professional conduct.

REASONS FOR UNIONISM OR COLLECTIVE ACTION

Individuals engage in collective action such as unionization when such activities improve their individual position more than would their own individual action. Professionals will thereby engage in union activity when they have lost individual power and when their activity as a group can be influential. The loss of individual power for the salaried professional is associated with the increased bureaucratization of their work, their declining social and economic status, and increased fluctuations in demand and supply conditions affecting their employment.

Bureaucratization of work
More and more often professionals have found themselves employed as salaried workers in large bureaucratic organizations with their rigid work schedules, formal authority structures, short-term production objectives, and emphasis on seniority. Much of their employment is in the public sector or otherwise dependent upon public funds and public scrutiny. Most important, these large bureaucratic organizations subject the salaried professional to more formal evaluation than do clients or colleagues for the self-employed professional. As Garbarino points out: 'In contrast to the layman, who feels ignorant in dealing with professionals, institutional employers are likely to take the position that they are informed consumers qualified to select their own suppliers of professional services and to judge the quality of their performance.'[2]

This bureaucratization of work has affected most professional groups. Engineers and scientists tend to be employed in large conglomerates; teachers are employed in the larger amalgamated schools with their specialization of labour and administrative specialists and consultants; university professors are employed in the publicly supported 'degree mills'; lawyers are increasingly employed in the large law firms or dependent upon government support through legal aid; and even doctors – the bastion of professionalism – negotiate with the government for their general fee structure under state-supported medicare.

For many, this is the antithesis of professionalism with its emphasis on individuality, autonomy, flexibility, merit, self-determination, and a close relationship with the client. Finding themselves treated as production workers, many of these salaried professionals react as production workers – they organize into unions or they influence their professional associations to behave more like

2 J. Garbarino, 'Professional negotiation in education,' *Industrial Relations* 7 (Feb. 1968) 98

unions. Unionization of industrial workers was essentially a job-security response to the work rationalization associated with industrialization, especially with mass production techniques. The most important objectives were wage and employment stability and protection from the apparently arbitrary whims of management. The same process has occurred with salaried professionals, as they found themselves in a peculiar employment situation, excluded from management decisions, and not afforded the job protection of unionized workers.

The dilemma of the professional working as a salaried employee is compounded by what economists term the 'public-goods' nature of some professional work. With public goods the benefits are equally available to all users, but it is not feasible to extract payment from users. Basic research, especially of a theoretical or academic nature, has public-goods characteristics. Consequently, it is not in the interest of the employing organization to encourage such research, since it is not possible to sell the results, as it could with more practical research through patents, copyrights, or even brand-name affiliation with new products. This may conflict with the objectives of many professionals – especially the better, research-oriented ones – who continue to seek professional recognition through basic research.

Declining social and economic status

The bureaucratization of work has also resulted in a relative decline in social status, especially for the salaried professional. This is reinforced by the sheer increase in numbers of both the traditional and newer professions. No longer a select elite, professionals have lost individual power and influence; hence group power, perhaps through unionization, is a natural response.

This is especially the case as the powers of other interests groups increase and impinge upon professional activity. Consumer groups seek representation on the governing bodies of professions; students and community groups seek representation on the governing bodies of the university; community schools seek to share decision-making responsibility with teachers, administrators, and the public; and white-collar unions are now a prominent force along with blue-collar unions in the corporate and public sector. Recognizing the obvious success of these interest groups, including and perhaps especially those that engage in militant action, professionals also look towards collective action to achieve recognition.

Examples of organizing to achieve recognition and influence abound in the professions. Academics are organizing in part to have sufficient bargaining power to be given an audience with university administrators who are deluged with pressures from other interest groups including students, legislators, alumni, and community groups. In addition, there is the fear that non-unionized universities will lose relative to unionized universities, especially in getting increased budgets

TABLE 1
Earnings of salaried professionals, Canadian males, census years 1931-71

Profession	1931	1941	1951[a]	1961	1971
Average annual earnings					
Architects	2,591	2,246	3,712	6,694	12,496
Dentists	1,925	1,998	4,415	7,304	18,195
Engineers-electrical	2,443	2,363	3,817	7,329	11,139
Engineers-mechanical	2,315	2,232	3,774	7,004	10,864
Lawyers and notaries	3,236	2,833	3,987	7,366	14,597
Librarians	2,046	1,790	2,567	4,691	7,278
Nurses-graduate	n.a.	865	2,205	3,457	5,799
Physicians and surgeons	3,133	2,813	4,268	6,876	19,791
Professors	2,564	2,198	3,608	7,113	13,667
Schoolteachers	1,575	1,416	2,667	5,527	7,042
Veterinarians	2,218	1,971	3,710	6,362	13,068
All professionals	1,978	1,746	3,011	5,507	8,522[b]
All occupations	925	993	2,131	3,660	6,606
Ratio of salaried professionals earnings to earnings in all occupations					
Architects	2.8	2.3	1.1	1.8	1.9
Dentists	2.7	2.0	2.1	2.0	2.2
Engineers-electrical	2.6	2.4	1.8	2.0	1.7
Engineers-mechanical	2.5	2.3	1.8	1.9	1.6
Lawyers and notaries	3.5	2.9	1.9	2.0	2.2
Librarians	2.2	1.8	1.2	1.3	1.1
Nurses-graduate	n.a.	0.9	1.0	0.9	0.9
Physicians and surgeons	3.4	2.8	2.0	1.9	3.0
Professors	2.8	2.2	1.7	1.9	2.1
Schoolteachers	1.7	1.4	1.3	1.5	1.1
Veterinarians	2.4	2.0	1.7	1.7	2.0
All professionals	2.1	1.8	1.4	1.5	1.3

a   Figures for 1951 refer to median earnings.
b   Weighted average of professional incomes for CCDO occupations 21, 23, 25, 27, 31, and 33.
SOURCE: Figures for 1931-61 are from N. Meltz, *Manpower in Canada 1931 to 1961: Historical Statistics of the Canadian Labour Force* (Ottawa: Manpower and Immigration, 1969) 242, 246. Figures for 1971 are from the 1971 Census, *Income of Individuals*, No. 94-765, Vol. 3, Part 6, Bulletin 3, 6-7 (Ottawa: Information Canada, 1975).

from the legislators. Engineers in the United States began organizing in the 1940s and 1950s largely to avoid being engulfed in the bargaining units of production workers' unions that were having marked success. As Kassalow points out, jour-

TABLE 2

Income of salaried vs self-employed male professionals, 1961, 1971

Select profession	Salaried (%)		Salaried income ($)		Self-employed income ($)		Salaried/ self-employed income (ratio)	
	1961	1971	1961	1971	1961	1971	1961	1971
Accountant	0.86	0.93	6,195	9,615	10,593	15,269	0.58	0.63
Architect	0.65	0.61	6,694	12,496	12,545	17,407	0.53	0.72
Dentist	0.10	0.24	7,303	18,195	13,132	22,819	0.56	0.80
Engineer	0.97	0.97	7,228	11,011	11,895	13,826	0.61	0.80
Lawyer	0.31	0.43	7,359	14,597	12,550	23,930	0.59	0.61
Optometrist	0.13	0.25	6,410	15,296	9,430	17,630	0.68	0.87
Pharmacist	0.55	0.78	5,321	11,173	9,168	14,931	0.58	0.75
Physician	0.34	0.46	6,883	19,791	18,006	33,201	0.38	0.60
Scientist	0.98	0.98	6,677	8,022	9,725	8,384	0.69	0.96
Veterinarian	0.50	0.57	6,362	13,068	8,577	17,450	0.74	0.75
All professions	0.87	0.91	5,448	8,522[a]	12,286	19,984[a]	0.44	0.43
All occupations	0.89	0.89	3,679	6,606	5,929	6,413	0.62	1.03

a   Weighted average of professional incomes from CCDO occupations 21, 23, 25, 27, 31, 33.
NOTE Employment income for the self-employed is not available prior to 1961.
SOURCE: Figures for 1961 salaried income are from *1961 Census*, No. 94-539. Vol. 3, Part 3; Figures for 1961 percentage self-employed and self-employed income are from *1961 Census*, No. 98-502, Vol. 4, Part 4. Figures for 1971 are from *1971 Census, Income of Individuals*, No. 94-765, Vol. 3, Part 6, Bulletin 3, 6-7 (Ottawa: Information Canada, 1975).

nalists, musicians, and airline pilots all organized early, in part at least, to achieve recognition as professional groups: without unionizing they had little power because they lacked strong professional associations, formal training requirements, or occupational licensing.[3] This leads Kassalow to speculate that many technical and quasi-professional occupations may seek union status in order to achieve professional recognition.

The declining relative economic position of many salaried professionals is illustrated in Table 1. Males only are included, so that changes in relative incomes do not reflect the changing sex composition of the occupation. However, the age composition of the occupation is not held constant, and consequently a decline in the relative income of salaried professionals may simply reflect an increasing

3 E. Kassalow, 'Prospects for white collar union growth,' *Industrial Relations* 5 (Oct. 1965) 43

proportion of younger, junior-level professionals. As the bottom half of the table shows, earnings of most salaried professionals have consistently declined relative to the average earnings of all occupations. Whereas in 1931 the earnings of all salaried professionals averaged over twice (2.1) that of all occupations, by 1971 they averaged only slightly more (1.3) than all occupations. Based on attitudinal surveys, Seidman and Cain also cite a decline in salaries relative to unionized blue-collar workers as a prime cause of unionization among salaried engineers.[4]

Unfortunately data do not exist to enable a comprehensive comparison of the earnings of salaried professionals with those of self-employed professionals prior to 1961. However, as Table 2 shows, for the years 1961 and 1971 the earnings of salaried professionals were considerably below those of self-employed professionals in the same occupation (although not necessarily of the same age or training). For all professions, salaried persons earned less than half of the self-employed, with this ratio declining slightly between 1961 and 1971 (i.e. from 0.44 to 0.43). This decline in the relative earnings of salaried professionals occurred when the earnings of salaried workers in *all* occupations improved markedly relative to the self-employed in all occupations (i.e. from 0.62 to 1.03). However, when we look at the ratio of salaried to self-employed income for many of the more established and better organized professions (i.e. the select professions of Table 2), we see that compared to their self-employed counterparts these professionals tend to be not as badly off and that their position seems to have improved over the 1960s, in contrast to the position of all other professions, where the income of salaried professionals declined compared to the self-employed. It appears that the declining economic position of the salaried professional, especially in comparison to his self-employed counterparts, was concentrated in the less-well-organized professions. Even for salaried professionals, organization seems to have been a help. Table 2 also illustrates the dramatic increase in the proportion of salaried employees in most of the professions over the decade of the 1960s. Even for the more established professions of law and medicine, by 1971 almost half of the profession was salaried.

In summary, relative to all occupations the economic position of salaried professionals has declined consistently since the 1930s. Relative to their self-employed counterparts, their employment income is considerably lower and has declined slightly during the 1960s. This decline, however, was concentrated in the less-well-organized professions, with the better organized professions having a slight improvement in the earnings of salaried relative to the self-employed in the 1960s. The slight improvement in the earnings of salaried relative to self-

4 J. Seidman and G. Cain, 'Unionized engineers and chemists: a case study of a professional union,' *Journal of Business* 37 (July 1968) 242

employed professionals suggests that economic factors were probably not the prime motive for the unrest amongst salaried professionals that has been occurring in recent years.

Fluctuations in demand and supply conditions
Since most salaried professionals are employed in government or government-supported organizations, fluctuations in government activity have an important bearing on their employment stability. Especially since the 1930s the vicissitudes of government-related employment have been as severe as was the case in the private market for industrial workers at the time of their early organizing drives. Fluctuations in government activity are prevalent in part because Keynesian economics dictates that government activity be used to influence aggregate demand in the economy, and in part because government activity tends to be motivated by rapidly changing political demands ranging from medicare, legal aid, and civil rights to wage-price controls and concern over the environment and cities, all of which have profound effects on the demand for different professional groups.

The interesting thing about such demand fluctuations is that professional discontent seems to rise both in good times and in bad times. Perhaps reflecting an inherent conservatism, professional groups seem content only when there is no change, including change in the demand for their services. Periods of expanding demand and tight labour markets give rise to soaring expectations on the part of professionals (as with all workers), and this often increases rather than decreases their discontent. This phenomenon is discussed by Barbash in the case of academics and by Drucker in the case of engineers.[5] When the expansion is over and labour markets loosen, the threat of job insecurity increases and professionals become further discontented. For some salaried professionals the threat of losing their jobs is real; for most, however, the reduced demand for their services means reduced mobility, smaller salary increases, the inability to work on projects of their own choosing, and the performing of a variety of tasks that otherwise might be performed by subordinates or assistants.

Fluctuations on the supply side of the market have equally important implications for the professional employee. Because of the long formal education required for most professions, the supply side of the market is often characterized by what economists have termed the 'cobweb cycle.' An increase in the demand for the services of a particular profession leads to a rapid increase in the earnings in that profession. This occurs because in the short run it is not possible to in-

5 J. Barbash, 'Academicians as bargainers with the university,' *Issues in Industrial Society* 1 (No. 3, 1970) 25; P. Drucker, 'Management and the professional employee,' *Harvard Business Review* 30 (May-June 1952) 84

crease the supply of professionals nor to utilize other factors of production to do the job of the scarce professional. In the longer run, however, the increase in professional earnings serves as a signal to attract new students to acquire the formal education and training of the profession. It also serves as a signal for the employer to utilize alternative inputs (e.g. paraprofessionals, capital equipment) and to develop alternative production processes that will economize on expensive professional services. By the time the new large pool of professional graduates enters the market (perhaps four years or more for many professions), employers may no longer demand their services. The excess supply of professionals and the reduced demand for their services then decreases professional earnings dramatically. This serves as a new signal for prospective new students not to enter the profession and for employers to utilize professional services in place of alternative inputs. The cycle continues with periods of short supply (and hence high earnings) being succeeded by periods of excess supply (and hence low earnings). When this fluctuating supply is added to the fluctuating demand associated with government-related employment, we see that the employment conditions of many salaried professionals is often characterized by 'boom-and-bust,' and hence the chances for discontent are heightened. Empirical evidence of the cobweb cycle for professionals is discussed by Freeman.[6]

This boom-and-bust scenario is relevant for a variety of professional groups. Associated with the educational boom of the 1960s, the expectations of teachers and academicians soared, only to be dampened in the 1970s by the large supply influx of teachers and academicians, and by budget cutbacks and increased public scrutiny of hours of work, class sizes, paid leaves-of-absence, professional development, and tenure. The high demand for medical personnel – much of it associated with medicare – is only beginning to wane as hospitals close and the organization of the medical care field becomes rationalized. The engineering professions constantly go through fluctuations in demand, especially in the United States, where defence contracts are so important.

IMPACT OF PROFESSIONAL UNIONS

Factors influencing potential impact
The potential impact of professional unions will depend largely on their ability to control labour supply and, on the demand side, from the expected adverse employment effect from any associated wage or cost increase.

6 R. Freeman, 'Legal cobwebs: a recursive model of the market for new lawyers,' *Review of Economics and Statistics* 57 (May 1975) 171-9

On the supply side, professional associations and unions can maintain artificially high earnings by regulating entry into the occupation. Even salaried professionals can do so since they are usually a well-defined homogeneous group with occupational requirements that are capable of being controlled. Academics and doctors can insist upon citizenship requirements, teachers could bargain with school boards for the requirement of a BA and a full year of professional training, and registered nurses could increase their education and training requirements. It is precisely because professionals usually have substantial entrance requirements that they are capable of controlling labour supply, even though the process may be indirect in the case of salaried professional employees.

On the demand side, the ability of professionals to bargain directly for improvements in their wages and working conditions will depend on the extent to which the associated cost increases will result in a reduction in their employment, that is, it will depend on what economists term the 'elasticity of derived demand for labour.' The demand for professional labour will be inelastic, and hence the adverse employment effect of their wage increase small, if 1/ the demand for the output produced by firms employing professionals is inelastic, so that wage-cost increases can be passed on to the consumer in the form of price increases without their being much of a reduction in demand for this output; 2/ there are few good alternative inputs that could be used to substitute for the higher-priced professional services; and 3/ the ratio of the cost of professional labour to total cost is small, so that wage increases for professionals are not a large part of total expenditures. Each of these three factors will be examined in turn.

The demand for the 'output' produced by firms employing professionals would be inelastic if the output were regarded as essential and if it were not possible for consumers to substitute other goods or services or to postpone consumption of the output: they will pay for any cost increases rather than curtail consumption. The extent to which this applies to salaried professionals depends on the particular profession and the nature of the firm employing the professionals. Many professionals are employed in the public sector, which by definition provides output that is often essential and for which alternative sources of output are not readily available. Teaching and health care are examples. For many other professions, however, it is possible to postpone the consumption of their services. Examples include social workers, academics (who do not serve the important babysitting function), economists, statisticians, scientists, engineers, or any other groups engaged in longer-term research or planning. Even with teaching and health care we have seen in recent years that what we once regarded as absolutely essential is now not so essential, or at least it is postponable. In addition, the ability to pass wage-cost increases on to the consumer (taxpayer) in the public sector is not limitless, although there is a belief that the absence of a profit incentive in the public sector is conducive to such wage increases. Salaried employees in the private sector are generally employed by the larger oligopolistic and regulated industries, often dependent upon government contracts: their ability to pass on cost increases to their customers is still the subject of considerable debate. The general impression that emerges, then, is that the demand for the output produced by firms employing most salaried professionals is partially inelastic, so that price increases entailed by salary increases from professionals would not result in drastic cutbacks of the output produced by these firms. Their ability to pass these cost increases to their customers is not limitless, however, and it varies considerably across the professions.

The substitution of alternative inputs to replace higher-priced professional services can occur in a subtle fashion, involving the subcontracting to non-union self-employed professionals, increased use of paraprofessionals, and the use of alternative forms of production, as well as the usual substitution of capital. All of these items are of course negotiable, so that a strong professional union could bargain to prevent these substitutions which would reduce the employability of higher-priced unionized professionals. University faculty could bargain over the use of teaching assistants, librarians could bargain over technological change in automated libraries, accountants could bargain over the use of computers, and pilots could bargain over the use of automated landing and takeoff systems. Even without strong bargaining, such substitution may be limited by the fact that, by definition, a profession often involves personal contact and discretionary judgment – elements for which it may be difficult to find good substitutes.

The proportion of the total cost of the service or output that consists of professional salaries differs dramatically for the various professions. In some cases only a few professionals are involved in a project or in providing a service, and a large increase in their salary will not add much to total cost. This is often the case for airline pilots, lawyers, architects, and some scientists and engineers. In many cases, however, professional services are the main ingredient in producing the output or service. This is usually the case for the large scientific-engineering firms, for social work and the health professions, and for teaching at elementary, secondary, and university levels. For these occupations the overriding importance of the cost of professional labour would serve to reduce professional employment if union wage increases were dramatic.

In summary, for those particular jobs in which the cost of professional labour is high relative to the total cost of providing the service, professional unions could do little to raise professional earnings since increased wages would mean a reduction in potential employment. However, to the extent that this reduction in employment would apply only to new potential recruits, it may not serve as a strong deterrent for existing employed professionals seeking large wage increases.

After all, it is the existing employees, not the potential new ones, who control the union. The incentive for professional unions to go for large wage increases is further strengthened by the fact that the substitution of other factors of production for professional labour is often difficult and could be subject to control by the union. Furthermore, the outputs or services produced by organizations utilizing large numbers of salaried professionals, tend to be regarded as essential in nature or are often produced by oligopolistic or regulated industries that may not be subject to severe price competition.

Actual impact of professional unions on earnings
The previous discussion suggested that in many circumstances professional unions may have the potential to have a substantial impact on the earnings of their members. They could exert control over the supply of professional labour, and in many cases the demand for professional labour would be inelastic, so that they would not have to worry about the threat of unemployment associated with large wage increases.

In contrast to the case of industrial unions, empirical evidence on the impact of professional unions is scant. In summarizing the results of the four major studies of the effect of teachers' unions in the United States, Lipskey and Drotning suggest that teachers' unions have raised their members wages by 3 or 4 per cent.[7] This may not have involved any real cost increase to taxpayers since it was often accompanied by an increase in class size. This impact of teachers' unions is less than the likely effect of industrial unions, which is probably more in the range of 5 to 15 per cent in the long term and higher in the earlier years. Probably the inhibiting factor in raising teachers' salaries is the expected adverse employment effect that would result because teachers salaries are such a high proportion of education expenditures.

Except for teachers, comprehensive studies of the effect of professional unions are rare. In his thorough review of studies of the impact of unionism in the United States, Lewis refers to only one study of a professional union – the Air Line Pilots Association – and he concludes that it raised earnings of its members by a substantial 21 to 34 per cent.[8] This large impact occurs because of the union's strong control over labour supply and because it did not fear any large employment reduction, in large part because pilot salaries are only a small proportion of the total cost of running airline services. The substantial difference

7 D. Lipskey and J. Drotning, 'The influence of collective bargaining on teachers' salaries in New York State,' *Industrial and Labour Relations Review* 27 (Oct. 1973) 34
8 Lewis, *Unionism and Relative Wages in the United States* (Chicago: University of Chicago Press, 1963)

between the impact of teachers' and pilots' unions suggests that further research on the impact of professional unions would indicate substantial variability depending on the ability of the union to control supply, and the different potential adverse employment effects from wage increases.

Impact on non-wage aspects of employment
The previous discussion concentrated on the potential and actual impact of professional unions on the salaries of unionized professionals. For various reasons, however, we may expect professional unions to concentrate on the non-wage aspects of employment. Their salary gains would be subject to high marginal tax rates and, in times of wage and price controls, government scrutiny. The public may be more critical of visible salary increases than other less visible gains. Professionals may be trying to regain some of the influence over policy issues they felt they lost with the increased bureaucratization of their work and dilution of their numbers. Continuing education, retraining, and attendance at professional meetings are important to maintain professional standing, and control over such factors as supply and the substitution of other inputs for professional labour are key to the long-run success of a professional union.

In fact, the limited evidence we have suggests that professional unions will bargain for much more than salary increases. Unionized teachers and social workers have stressed the importance of becoming involved in policy issues that affect students and clients; engineering unions have bargained for employer payment of professional society dues and the cost of attending professional society meetings, as well as tuition expenses and salaries while the engineer advances his professional education; faculty unions bargain for sabbaticals and tenure; and pilots' and musicians' unions bargain for featherbedding clauses that increase their employment.

There is little reason to believe the relationship between the employer and professional employees will dramatically deteriorate or improve as a result of professional unionization. To the extent that a poor relationship was one of the motivating factors causing unionism, then professional unionization may actually improve the working relationship between management and salaried professionals. Informal procedures may give way to more formal processes for hiring, promotion, grievances, and salary determination; the implicit adversary relationship may be made more explicit; seniority may become more important relative to individual merit; the salary structure may be compressed; and working hours may be formalized. Many of these factors could result in the exodus of some top professionals, perhaps to self-employment. Yet professional unionism need not induce such developments to happen any more frequently than they already are as a result of the changing status of the professional employee. To a large extent

these are causes rather than symptoms of professional unions; professional unionism may simply formalize and rationalize what already is occurring in a somewhat haphazard fashion.

The impact of the unionization of professionals will depend on the form of
professional unionization. If professionals became immersed in the bargaining
units of production or white-collar unions, then the typical formalization and
rationalization of the job environment described above will probably result. If
they form their own bargaining units, or exert a strong independent influence
within larger units, then they can be as flexible or rigid as their group interest
dictates.

Impact on prices, quality of service, and public interest
As with all unions, the impact of professional unions will extend beyond salaries
and other aspects of employment. With professional unionism, however, the
repercussions will depend considerably upon the nature of the profession and on
the extent of collective bargaining's effect on the wages and working conditions
of members.

To the extent that the cost increases imposed by the professional unions are
large, then prices (taxes in the public sector) will rise or the quality of professional service will fall. Deterioration in the quality of service may come in such
forms as larger class sizes in schools and universities, larger case loads for social
workers and legal-aid lawyers, shorter visits and longer waiting periods for doctors, fewer nurses per hospital room, or less personal attention from a librarian.
To the extent that unionism improves productivity, perhaps by improving the
work environment, then costs may not increase. However, such a result is probably more wishful thinking than reality: it is just as likely that productivity will
decrease, especially if featherbedding becomes prominent and job security is
guaranteed.

The quality of professional service will also be affected by the way in which
professional unions influence wages. If they control supply, they will probably
do so by using quality-related criterion such as an increased education and training period. If they simply bargain for higher wages, there will be a queue of
applicants competing for the scarce high-wage union jobs. These jobs may be
rationed by selecting only the best qualified candidates. These factors suggest
that professional unionism may result in better qualified professionals doing the
work. However, to the extent that the salary structure is compressed and seniority is substituted for merit, the best professionals may leave their salaried jobs
for self-employment. Clearly, the effect of professional unionism on the quality
of professional service is ambiguous.

The public interest is probably affected more by professional unionism than by unionism in most other occupations. As indicated earlier, professionals tend to be employed largely in the government or government-related sectors and in regulated and oligopolistic industries. Although the employing organization is capable of judging professional quality, it may have little incentive to do so. Public enterprises may be inclined to make political appointments, and regulated industries may want to grant noticeably large wage increases to professional employees, in order to get approval for rate increases. If the consuming public does not approve of the resulting quality of service for the price (tax), it may not be able to take its business elsewhere. The diffuse interest may be sacrificed for the better organized and articulated interest of some professional unions. To a large extent this is what the self-governing regulating bodies do for the self-employed professions.

The public interest would also be affected by the probable redistribution of income that would accompany any large-scale professional unionism. Since individuals engage in union activity in order to improve their own position and since it is difficult to get something for nothing, professional unionism would likely involve a transfer of wealth to professional union members from those who ultimately purchase their services. While this may have been socially acceptable for lower-paid industrial workers, it is probably more difficult to accept for higher-paid professionals. This will be the case especially if the professional mystique of social responsibility and service to the public breaks down as professionals pursue their self-interest through collective action, whether through a union or a professional association.

SUMMARY AND CONCLUDING OBSERVATIONS

The increased numbers of professionals, especially salaried professionals, have been accompanied by growing interest in professional unionism. The impetus for such unionism has come from the increased bureaucratization of work, declining economic and social status, and the severe fluctuations in demand and supply conditions facing many professional employees. Many of these factors are associated with the public sector nature of professional employment. The continued existence of most of these forces suggests that the issue of professional unionism will persist into the future.

Responding to these pressures, salaried professionals have increasingly engaged in collective action, sometimes through their professional association and sometimes through union affiliation either as a distinct bargaining unit or within the bargaining unit of a related union. To the extent that professional associations have co-opted the process of unionism, they have done so by behaving more and more like unions. For this reason, perhaps more attention should be paid to the appropriateness of extending legislation governing union affairs to professional associations.

The potential impact of professional unionism will vary dramatically across the various professions, reflecting differences in their ability to control supply and in the expected adverse employment effect from wage increases. This expected variability is confirmed by the limited empirical evidence we have on the impact of professional unions – raising wages of their members around 30 per cent for the salaries of airline pilots and less than 5 per cent for teachers. Evidence on the impact of professional unions is further complicated by the fact that for various reasons – not the least of which is their high tax rates – professional unions may concentrate on improving the non-wage aspects of their employment. To the extent that professional unions are successful in raising the wages or improving the working conditions of their members, prices will rise, the quality of professional service will be altered in an ambiguous fashion, and the diffuse public interest will probably be sacrificed for the special interests of an already privileged group. For these reasons the process of professional unionism merits careful public scrutiny.

The main policy-related conclusions that can be drawn from this analysis of the economic aspects of professional unionism are as follows:
– The basic causes of professional unionism are continuing: it is not a passing fad.
– The analysis of professional unionism is intricately tied to the analysis of public-sector employment, since most salaried professionals are dependent, directly or indirectly, on public-sector funds.
– Professional unions can have a substantial impact on raising their own earnings, with resulting higher prices for the products and services produced by professional employees.
– The actual impact of a professional union can differ substantially across the various professions: generalizations to all professions are not really possible.
– There is no guarantee that professional unions would represent the public interest.
– Professional associations with licensing and self-governing powers are especially capable of acting as powerful unions; hence, public scrutiny is warranted.

These conclusions highlight the importance of a variety of unanswered public policy questions, most of which involve legal aspects of industrial relations and hence have been beyond the direct scope of this paper. Should professional employees be covered under existing or modified labour relations statutes or under special legislation? Should professional associations be allowed to bargain for their salaried members at the same time as they act as the licensing body for the profession? What is the appropriate bargaining unit for professionals and para-professionals? Is there a basic conflict between management rights and professional standards and ethics? What are the alternative dispute resolution procedures that are applicable to professionals? What is the appropriate role, if any, of self-governing professional bodies in regulating the relationships of employed professionals with their employers? These are only a few of the many public policy questions that will have to be dealt with in this area of growing concern.

G.W. ADAMS

Collective bargaining by salaried professionals

INTRODUCTION

Recent legislative initiatives in many Canadian jurisdictions suggest a growing recognition that the salaried members of many of the prototype[1] or traditional professions are subject to the same social and economic forces confronting other employees. These initiatives have granted salaried members of one or more professions access to collective bargaining and in doing so have generally accorded them special-bargaining-unit treatment. Because the forces that have caused salaried professionals to turn to collective bargaining are accelerating, other jurisdictions will move in the same direction, and many of the current initiatives are likely to be broadened. The number of employed professionals is steadily, in fact dramatically, increasing, and many of the large bureaucracies in which they tend to be employed do not readily and voluntarily adjust to the culture of professionalism. As a general matter professional associations have not been able to respond to the employment problems experienced by their salaried membership, and thus these professionals have had no alternative but to turn to collective bargaining. The first part of this paper surveys the employment problems of salaried professionals that have given rise to these developments.

However these employment problems are not unique to the prototype professions but are common to a growing number of intellectual occupations with whom the prototype professionals often work side by side. This increasing number of intellectual workers and their 'professionalization' therefore raises doubts

Osgoode Hall Law School, York Unversity; formerly assistant deputy minister of labour, Province of Ontario
1 By prototype I mean the architectural, dental, legal, medical, and engineering professions.

about the appropriateness – in fact fairness – of singling out the salaried members of the prototype professions for special treatment in collective bargaining statutes of general application. For example, in a number of jurisdictions recent amendments apply only to salaried members of particular professions and mandate craft bargaining units for them – bargaining units restricted to these individual professions. What is the justification for giving these particular occupations craft status? And is it a desirable policy? How should legislatures and labour boards respond to claims for similar treatment by members of the growing number of intellectual occupations that possess many if not all of the important hallmarks of 'professionalism'? Quite clearly a similar approach with respect to them could lead to an unworkable fragmentation of bargaining units. But does it then follow that no special treatment ought to be accorded to any intellectual occupation whether it is part of a prototype profession or not? In seeking to address this question the paper is critical of most of the approaches adopted in Canada to date and concludes that special treatment along the lines taken in the United States is both necessary and practical.

SALARIED PROFESSIONALS AND
COLLECTIVE BARGAINING: SOME HISTORY

Legislation in Newfoundland, Nova Scotia, Alberta, and Prince Edward Island excludes all of the prototype professions from collective bargaining by providing that the definition of employee does not include 'a member of the medical, dental, architectural, engineering, or legal profession, qualified to practise under the laws of a province and employed in that capacity.' The earliest Canadian labour laws did not make this exclusion. However, after a very short and unsatisfactory experience Parliament decided against their inclusion, and most jurisdictions, save Saskatchewan, followed suit. The principal reasons for exclusion can be briefly summarized. First, because early labour laws made no reference to professionals they were often 'swept' into large heterogeneous bargaining units containing other employees to whom they could not relate. For example, in *British Columbia Distillery Co. Ltd. and Local 203 United Office and Professional Workers of America, Local 203 et al Wartime L.R.B.,*[2] the Board ruled that 'The conditions of employment of the office workers and the professional and technical workers employed by the employer are the same. No good reason has been shown to warrant subdividing this group of employees into separate units.' A similar response to a particular working relationship that continues as a problem today is revealed in *Quebec Federation of Professional Employees in Applied*

2 1947 CLLC para. 10, 513 (Wartime Labour Relations Board)

Science and Research, Unit 4, and Canadian Broadcasting Corporation, Wartime, C.L.R.B.,[3] in which the Wartime Board stated: 'The Board does not consider that for the purpose of collective bargaining there is any important difference in interest between a professionally qualified engineer and an engineer who has no such professional qualifications, provided both are carrying on work of the same or similar nature and under similar conditions. Academic attainment cannot by itself determine the community of interest.' Secondly, collective bargaining by professionals was thought by many to be unethical or at least undignified. The prototype professions are, generally speaking, service-oriented, and all have been granted a statutory monopoly over the provision of their services. Therefore because collective bargaining could result in the concerted withholding of these services, abstract ethical and public policy questions were perceived. Moreover, this reticence was compounded by the fact that the professions had attracted persons into their membership who were very individualistic and in whom this individualism was reinforced by a service-oriented professional training. From their viewpoint, then, collective action centring on monetary matters was not only unseemly but in direct conflict with a profession's chief purpose – serving the public. Thirdly, professional associations were dominated by either non-salaried professionals who lacked identification with the problems of their salaried colleagues or by salaried professionals with either managerial responsibility or ambitions in this regard. Finally, it is likely that governments of the day were affected by a common feeling that professionals were already well served by their status in society. Even today it is difficult for the general public to identify with the employment problems in professional occupations because of the obvious advantages enjoyed by their non-salaried faction.

FORCES OF CHANGE

As fundamental technological and market forces had their impact on labour market structure and business form, these views began to be reconsidered. While the increase in white-collar workers in relation to the total labour force was the most salient aspect of the over-all occupational shift in the first half of this century, the growth of the 'professional' group within this white-collar segment has been the most striking recent change. Between 1951 and 1971 professionals showed the largest percentage increase of any occupational classification, rising in absolute numbers from 385,696 to 848,725, a gain of 120.1 per cent, compared to a

3 1946 CLLC para. 10, 485 (Wartime Labour Relations Board)

114.2 per cent increase in the white-collar work force and only 65.4 per cent in all occupational categories.[4]

Professor Bell believes these changes to be at the heart of what he calls 'post-industrial society.' In describing this same occupational distribution in the United States he writes of 'the pre-eminence of the professional and technical class':

The second way of defining a post-industrial society is through the change in occupational distributions; i.e. not only where people work but the kind of work they do. In large measure occupation is the most important determinant of class and stratification in the society.

The onset of industrialization created a new phenomenon, the semi-skilled worker who could be trained within a few weeks to do the simple routine operations required in machine work. Within industrial societies, the semi-skilled worker has been the single largest category in the labour force. The expansion of the service economy, with its emphasis on office work, education and government, has naturally brought about a shift to white-collar occupations. In the United States, by 1956 the number of white-collar workers for the first time in the history of industrial civilization outnumbered the blue-collar workers in the occupational structure. Since then the ratio has been widening steadily; by 1970 the white-collar workers outnumbered the blue-collar by more than five to four.

But the most startling change has been the growth of professional and technical employment – jobs that usually require some college education – at a rate twice that of the average. In 1940 there were 3.9 million such persons in the society; by 1964 the number had risen to 8.6 million and it is estimated that by 1975 there will be 13.2 million professional and technical persons, making it the second largest of the eight occupational divisions in the country, exceeded only by the semi-skilled workers. One further statistical breakdown will round out the picture – the role of the scientists and engineers who form the key group in the post-industrial society. While the growth rate of the professional and technical class as a whole has been twice that of the average labour force, the growth rate of the scientists and engineers has been triple that of the working population. By 1975 the United States may have about 550,000 scientists (natural and social scientists) as against 275,000 in 1960, and almost a million and a half engineers compared to 800,000 in 1960.[5]

4 Goldenberg, *Professional Workers and Collective Bargaining*, Task Force on Labour Relations (1968) 14, 15; *1971 Census of Canada*, Statistics Canada, Cat. 94-717
5 Bell, *The Coming of Post-Industrial Society* 1973) 15

But is is also important to note another and related feature of 'post-industrial society.' Despite the image of individualism traditionally associated with professional work, almost all teachers and nurses are paid employees, as are 96 per cent of engineers and architects, 97 per cent of economists, and 93 per cent of accountants and auditors.[6] Even in the most traditionally individualistic professions of law and medicine, approximately 43 per cent are not engaged in private practice.[7] Almost all of the 'new professionals,' ranging from social workers to systems analysts, work for an employer. And salaried professionals tend to be concentrated in *large* work organizations that may not easily adapt to the culture of professionalism.[8]

Quite clearly these occupational shifts will continue at an even more rapid rate in the decade ahead. In manpower requirements the growing emphasis will be upon relatively high degrees of skill, knowledge, and specialized training of various kinds. The shift from an agricultural economy to a predominantly urban industrial society has brought with it the need to concentrate large amounts of capital and numbers of people in order to meet the needs of an interdependent urban economy. The result has been an integrated economy comprised of large industrial, scientific, and commercial bureaucracies housing the vast number of specialized white-collar employees needed to co-ordinate complex production and marketing activities. More recently, there has been a distinct trend towards a service-oriented economy which has even accelerated these occupational shifts. As national incomes have risen there has been an increased demand for services and a corresponding occupational shift to trade, finance, transport, health, recreation, research, education, and government activities. These areas represent the greatest expansion of intellectually based occupations. This occupational shift has also been magnified by the dramatic growth of scientific and technical knowledge and the correlative rise of science-based industries (computers, electronics, optics, polymers, health).[9] The end result has been a bureaucratization of the sciences and an increasing specialization of intellectual work. These features of contemporary society challenge the adequacy of our collective bargaining laws as well as any attempt to confine the term 'professional' to the prototype professions.

6 *1971 Census of Canada*, supra, n.4
7 Ibid.
8 By 1962, for example, 54 per cent of all engineers and scientists in the United States worked in establishments employing 1,000 or more employees (see Kleingartner, 'Professional associations: an alternative to unions?' in Woodworth and Peterson, *Collective Bargaining for Public and Professional Employees* (1969) 294).
9 Professor Bell argues that what is distinctive about this stage in our development is the centrality of theoretical knowledge and its exponential growth (Bell, supra, n.5, 20).

Interest of salaried professionals in collective bargaining
These background forces have contributed to the interest of salaried professional employees in the collective bargaining process because they mean that salaried professional employees are exposed to the same economic and social risks as other wage and salary earners.

The bureaucratization of intellectual work and the explosion of knowledge not only in new fields but within existing fields has led to the specialization of intellectual work into minute parts. For example, after the second world war, fifty-four specializations in the sciences were listed in the United States National Register of Scientific and Technical Personnel. Twenty years later there were over nine hundred distinct scientific and technical specializations listed.[10] Skills are inevitably broken down, compartmentalized, and routinized to the point where salaried professionals may be unable to realize the skills for which they were educated. This problem is often aggravated by the immediate profit-making interests of an enterprise which cause it to employ its labour in the most efficient manner.[11] It may be more efficient to have work which a professional considers to be within his profession's exclusive jurisdiction performed by persons with a lesser but related education or at least to intersperse such persons amongst the professional employees. Similarly it may be more economical to require a salaried professional to perform work which a lesser educated but unavailable person, with training, could perform and thereby avoid immediate recruitment and training costs. Salaried professionals may therefore turn to collective bargaining as a method of preserving or recovering what they believe to be an exclusive work jurisdiction.

Another motivating factor may arise out of a desire to play a more significant or active role in the decision-making processes of the enterprise. An interest in direct participation in the decision-making of a firm is but a corollary of professional expertise. In this sense, claims for greater involvement in decision-making are based upon the premise that those persons who have undertaken protracted studies or acquired experience which gives them a special ability to perform a given type of work have the right to participate in decisions relating to that work and to share this decision-making power only with persons of at least equal competence.[12] However, in a bureaucratic setting guided by managerial authority, salaried professionals may have no freedom to choose the direction of work and little or no control over working conditions. Indeed, salaried professionals may

10 See Bell, supra, n.5, 187
11 See Chartier, *The Management of Professional Employees* (1968)
12 See Gross, *When Occupations Meet: Professions in Trouble* (Minneapolis: University of Minnesota Press, 1967) 45

not be considered real workers, or their contribution may be discounted because their efforts seldom result directly in a physical product; such responses only aggravate feelings of alienation.[13] The end result is that salaried professionals, having undergone a training that reinforces a strong sense of competence and autonomy, can find themselves distinctly subordinate, in their perception, to an insensitive managerial authority.

But muffled claims for greater job control may not be the central concern. In many instances salaried professionals turn to collective bargaining simply for economic reasons. For example, employed professionals may be paid in accordance with the internal job hierarchy of a bureaucracy which has little or no relationship to professional status, but then lack personal mobility to react to these 'unacceptable' pay scales because their skills are specific to the enterprise or the similarity in salary scales between firms may make moving pointless.

Financial considerations are very often the primary reason why intellectual workers paid from public funds opt for collective bargaining. In our so-called post-industrial society the government has become the single largest employer of intellectual workers, and indirectly, through public funding, it supports the employment of many more. These workers are caught up in one of today's most perplexing employment dilemmas – the search for an appropriate mechanism to set the terms and conditions of employment of public employees or employees dependent upon public funds. Winning wage increases from the government is a far different matter than from private industry. The multiplication of government functions creates an unremitting need for new revenues and a concommitant public outcry against rising taxes. Increasingly the end result has been a decision to end or limit existing programs and to hold down spending, with an adverse effect on wages and salaries. Indeed, one often gets the impression that the public expect intellectual workers who profess a devotion to work and to public service to be indifferent to economic advantages. Buffeted by these political winds, many salaried professionals have simply been driven to collective action, with public school teachers, university faculty, and hospital employees being good cases in point.

But why turn to collective bargaining? Why did salaried professionals not turn to their professional associations for assistance? The answer is that most did at first, and these professional associations were unable or unwilling to grapple with employment-related problems, leaving no alternative to collective bargaining for the salaried professional. On the whole, professional associations have shied away from direct confrontation with employers. It has been suggested that the

13 See Cuvillier, 'Intellectual workers and their work in social theory and practice' (1974) *Int'l. Lab. Rev.* 291, at 294.

associations have a practitioner orientation and cannot identify with the problems confronting salaried members, or that the associations are dominated by employer-oriented members who are unsympathetic.[14] Whatever the reason, professional associations by themselves were unable to respond to the problems of their salaried members and collective bargaining was opted for by many.

SOME RECENT LEGISLATIVE RESPONSES IN THE PRIVATE SECTOR

In Ontario the Legislature has recently provided professional engineers with access to collective bargaining under *The Ontario Labour Relations Act*.[15] Section 6(3) stipulates that a 'bargaining unit consisting solely of professional engineers shall be deemed by the Board to be a unit of employees appropriate for collective bargaining.' The Board may include engineers in a bargaining unit with other employees only if a majority of the engineers wish to be included – in short, professional engineers have been given craft status in Ontario. New Brunswick has taken this craft concept further by providing that the members of the medical, dental, dietetic, architectural, engineering, and legal professions may engage in collective bargaining, and each profession is entitled to a separate bargaining unit unless the members wish to have other employees included.[16]

Another approach adopted by the federal government[17] and Manitoba[18] concentrates less on the prototype professions by defining a professional employee as 'an employee who (*i*) is engaged in the application of specialized knowledge ordinarily acquired by a course of instruction and study resulting in graduation from a university or similar institution; and (*ii*) is or is eligible to be a member of a professional organization that is authorized by statute to establish qualifications for membership in the organization.'

14 For example, one study observed that a survey of over 3,000 engineers and scientists showed that 38 per cent of them were desirous of a future in administration, rather than in research or engineering (Kleingartner, *Professionalism and Salaried Worker Organization* (1967) 80).

15 R.S.O. 1970, c. 232 as amended by 1975, c. 76

16 *Industrial Relations Act*, R.S.N.B. 1973, c. 1-4, s.1(5)(b). Quebec adopts the same approach essentially, although many more professions are included (lawyers, notaries, physicians and surgeons, inspectors of anatomy, homeopathic physicians, pharmacists and druggists, dental surgeons, engineers, land surveyors, architects, forestry engineers, optometrists and opticians, and dispensing opticians). *Labour Code* R.S.Q. c. 141 as amended s.20

17 *Canada Labour Code* R.S.C. 1970 c. L-1, Part V, S.C. 1972, c. 18, s.107 and s.125(3)

18 *The Labour Relations Act*, C.C.S.M. c. L-10 enacted by S.M. 1972, c. 75, s.1(t) and s.28(3). See also *Organization of Professional Engineers, etc.*, v. *Manitoba Labour Relations Board* (1976) W.W.R. 723 (Man. C.A.).

Partnering this somewhat more expansive definition of a professional employee, the federal government has selected a more flexible approach to professional bargaining unit structures as well. Section 125(3) of the Code reads:

Where a trade union applies under section 124 for certification as the bargaining agent for a unit comprised of or including professional employees, the Board, subject to subsection (2)

(*a*) shall determine that the unit appropriate for collective bargaining is a unit comprised of only professional employees, unless such a unit would not otherwise be appropriate for collective bargaining;

(*b*) may determine that professional employees of more than one profession be included in the unit; and

(*c*) may determine that employees performing the functions but lacking the qualifications of a professional employee be included in the unit.

And subsection 2 of section 125 provides: 'In determining whether a unit constitutes a unit that is appropriate for collective bargaining, the Board may include any employees in or exclude any employees from the unit proposed by the trade union.'

Finally, neither the *Labour Code of British Columbia*[19] nor the *Saskatchewan Trade Union Act*[20] mentions the inclusion or exclusion of professional employees, so that they are subject to those statutes in the same manner as any other employee. This then represents a third approach.

CHALLENGE FOR PUBLIC POLICY

All salaried professionals should be able to engage in collective bargaining, and this principle is gaining widespread acceptance. Facing the same employment problems as others, they ought to have the same rights as others in resolving them. However the challenge for public policy relates to the way in which this result is to be effected. Are the prototype professions to be distinguished from other intellectual workers and provided with craft status, as is the case in New Brunswick, or should the unwarranted exclusions simply be removed, as in British Columbia, and bargaining unit structures determined by reference to the traditional principles underpinning the concept of 'appropriateness'? On the other hand, the *Canada Labour Code* and the *Manitoba Labour Relations Act* adopt positions somewhere between these two extremes.

19 *Labour Code of British Columbia* S.B.C. 1973, c. 122
20 *The Trade Union Act*, 1972, S.S. 1972, c. 137

Who is a professional?
What is the rationale for limiting professional employee definitions to the proto-type professions? While they can be distinguished from other employees because their non-salaried brethren achieved exclusive authority to regulate 'the practis-ing profession,' should the existence of licensing, registration, and certification statutes be relevant to the granting of a special status to these occupations under modern labour laws? Generally these statutes were enacted to protect an inexpert public from the unqualified or unscrupulous practitioner. However where the consumer is a small number of sophisticated employers or where the occupation does not consult or practise with respect to a broadly based lay clientele, licens-ing statutes are less relevant and indeed less likely to exist. For example, Fried-son has observed that 'licensing is much less likely to occur on behalf of the scholar or the scientist, for they are devoted to exploring intellectual systems primarily for the eyes of their colleagues.'[21] Moreover, it is not unusual today to find 'accreditation' privately administered. The occupational qualification of the PHD for a psychologist or university professor and the required eligibility for membership in the vast number of paramedical occupational associations im-posed by hospital hiring illustrate this phenomenon.[22]

This point takes on even greater significance in view of the fact that the ex-plosion of knowledge in modern society has led to the development of a great number of very sophisticated occupations that meet all the characteristics of 'salaried professionalism.' This being so, it appears unfair to grant a special status only to the prototype professions. Many occupations are now based on syste-matic knowledge or doctrine acquired through long-prescribed training, and more often than not those performing such work adhere to a set of ethical norms where such norms are relevant.[23] Obvious examples include scientists, dietitians, occupational and speech therapists, social workers, psychologists, economists, nurses, mathematicians, and professors. Is each group expected to lobby for spe-cial treatment, and would special treatment along craft lines be practical?

The *Canada Labour Code* and the *Manitoba Labour Relations Act* have attempted to meet this problem by using a more comprehensive professional em-ployee definition, but by limiting the term to those occupations having a profes-sional organization authorized by statute to establish the qualifications for its own membership they continue to rely upon an unduly restrictive if not irrele-vant condition. Another problem is their mutual requirement that a professional

21 See Friedson, *Profession of Medicine* (1970) 74.
22 See Hall, *The Paramedical Occupations in Ontario: A Study for the Committee on the Healing Arts* (1970); *Report of the Committee on the Healing Arts* (1970) Vol. 2.
23 These are the two basic criteria of distinction suggested by Wilensky, 'The professionali-zation of everyone' (1964) 60 *Am. J. of Soc.* 137, at 139.

employee must apply specialized knowledge acquired by a course of instruction resulting in graduation from a university or similar institution. In a labour relations context, should a university degree be a crucial factor in separating professional employees from other workers? For example, many technologists in the fields of health, science, and communications are graduates of post-secondary institutions other than universities, such as community colleges and institutes. Would they come within the phrase 'similar institution,' and should they as a matter of policy be so characterized? Many of these occupations possess codes of ethics, and their associations often play vital roles in developing the curricula by which members are educated. Moreover, some of these associations are supported or referred to by private and public statutes.[24]

It is also important to bear in mind that in an area as dynamic as occupational change, many of these occupations are in an evolutionary state. A community college program today may be the basis of a university degree tomorrow. For example, in the United States, laboratory technologists are trained in universities, whereas in Ontario they are educated in community colleges. Indeed it can be asked whether the difference between a community college education and a bachelor of arts program is any more significant than the educational distance between a BA (the dietitian), a MA (the social worker), and a PHD (the psychologist). In fact, some graduates of community colleges, like nurses, have achieved a substantial degree of 'professional' recognition.

Another point to be made is that educational requirements are capable of manipulation by an occupation 'on the make,' and whether or not an occupation is engaged in such deception, educational requirements may not reflect the actual skill exercised in the workplace. While it is easy to identify different levels of education as a general matter, it is much more difficult to determine whether the work performed by one occupation is any more difficult or deserving of special treatment than another. Who is to say that a physiotherapist performs a more complex function than a respiratory technologist, although their levels of educational attainment are clearly distinct? On the other hand a lack of distinction in job duties may be the very reason why the salaried professional wishes to engage in collective bargaining, as in the continued conflict between engineers and engineering technologists and technicians.[25]

24 For example, *The Radiological Technicians Act*, R.S.O. 1970, c. 399, and see generally Elizabeth MacNab, *A Legal History of Health Professions in Ontario*, a study for *The Committee on the Healing Arts* (1970). See also *Ontario Public Service Employees Union and Stratford General Hospital and Association of Allied Health Professionals* (1976) OLRB Rep. 459.
25 See *Association of Engineers of Bell Canada and Bell Canada*, Montreal, Quebec (1976) 1 Canadian L.R.B.R. 345, where a lack of distinction in job duties deprived a group of engineers of professional status under the *Canada Labour Code*.

The most prominent legislative attempt to avoid an overly restrictive definition of professional employee and to accommodate these problems is section
2(12) of *The National Labour Relations Act*[26] in the United States. This section
defines professional employee to mean:

(*a*) any employee engaged in work (*i*) predominantly intellectual and varied in
character as opposed to routine mental, manual, mechanical, or physical work;
(*ii*) involving the consistent exercise of discretion and judgment in its performance; (*iii*) of such a character that the attempt produced or the result accomplished cannot be standardized in relation to a given period of time; (*iv*) requiring knowledge of an advanced type in a field of science or learning customarily
acquired by a prolonged course of specialized intellectual instruction and study
in an institution of higher learning or a hospital, as distinguished from a general
academic education or from an apprenticeship or from training in the performance of routine mental, manual, or physical processes;
(*b*) any employee who (*i*) has completed the courses of specialized intellectual
instruction and study described in clause (*iv*) of paragraph (*a*) and (*ii*) is performing related work under the supervision of a professional person to qualify
himself to become a professional employee as defined in paragraph (*a*).

This definition appears much less restrictive than its Canadian counterparts and
provides the National Labour Relations Board with a greater capacity to respond
to the claims of all intellectual workers. I might also add that the definition
appears most consistent with the dynamics of occupational change.

The appropriateness of craft status
The issue of craft status, as opposed to some form of more broadly based bargaining unit structure, is a very important one. The principle of craft unionism is
maintained when bargaining units are confined to members of a single profession
or to specialized categories within a profession. The alternative, sometimes referred to as industrial unionism, combines two or more professional groups or
professional and non-professional employees. As we have seen, those jurisdictions that have granted salaried professionals access to collective bargaining laws
of general application have not adopted a common formula in this regard.

Ontario and New Brunswick have granted craft status to one or more of the
prototype professions while leaving the evolving or 'new' professions to the discretion of a labour relations board. (An exception is New Brunswick's treatment
of dietitians). As mentioned, the difficulty with this approach is that the proto-

26 49 Stat. 449 as amended by 61 Stat. 136 and 73 Stat. 519, 29 U.S.C.A. s.141 et seq.
   (amended)

type professions are thereby treated differently from other intellectual workers who cannot be significantly distinguished as groups on the basis of skill, training, and responsibility. On the other hand if all these occupations were granted craft status it would mean in many instances an impossible proliferation of bargaining units. For example, consider the effect on hospital labour relations if pharmacists, physiotherapists, occupational therapists, speech therapists, social workers, psychologists, psychometrists, laboratory technologists, x-ray technologists, respiratory technologists, nuclear medicine technologists, dietitians, and medical record librarians were provided with separate bargaining units. Fragmentation on this order would only aggravate counterproductive professional rivalries that already exist (and which tend to cancel each other) and would likely impair meaningful negotiation. In fact, it is more than interesting to note that where this fragmented approach was adopted, as in the construction industry, governments are now gradually moving toward more integrated forms of bargaining and collective agreement administration.[27]

British Columbia, Saskatchewan, and the earlier federal order in council, P.C. 1003, represent a second approach to the problem. This alternative makes no mention of professional exclusions and grants no statutory guarantee of craft status for any intellectual worker. It leaves the treatment of such occupations to the discretion of the labour relations tribunal administering the statute, presumably to be dealt with by reference to general labour law principles that have evolved over the years in defining the 'appropriate bargaining unit.'[28] Unfortunately, however, professionals did not fare very well at the hands of the Canada Wartime Labour Relations Board, and this experience raises questions about the capacity of existing tripartite tribunals to recognize the distinctive interests of intellectual workers. Few, if any, of these tribunals include representation from the occupations with which this essay is concerned, and as we have seen it is all too easy to characterize the claims of professionals for separateness as elitist and snobbish. Without their own representation on labour boards, intellectual workers may therefore find bargaining unit determinations unduly preoccupied by

27 See Province of Ontario, *Report of the Industrial Inquiry Commission into Bargaining Patterns in the Construction Industry*, May 1976; First Report, *Special Commission of Inquiry into British Columbia Construction*, October 1975. However, this is not to deny that the viable protection of craft interests is to a significant extent a function of bargaining unit size. Large numbers of salaried professionals employed within a single bureaucracy, like nurses and teachers, may make it feasible to respect professional distinctions. But unless a special statute is enacted for specific industries or institutions it is difficult to draft statutory language that can guarantee this right and yet provide the flexibility needed to deal with less monolithic work forces.

28 These principles are summarized in *Usarco Ltd* (1967) OLRB Report Sept., 526, and *Essex Health Assoc.* (1967) OLRB Report Nov., 716.

fears of work force fragmentation and concerns for the organizational structure of the employer. Accordingly, without building in sufficient institutional sensitivity to the reasons why salaried professionals wish to engage in collective bargaining, this approach may not be very helpful to them.

The provisions found in the *National Labour Relations Act* (NLRA) and the *Canada Labour Code* represent a mid-point between these two alternatives. Section 9(b)(1) of the NLRA provides that the National Labour Relations Board may not group professional employees and non-professionals in a single bargaining unit unless the majority of the professional employees vote for inclusion. This section has been interpreted to mean that while the Board is required to differentiate professionals from non-professionals for bargaining unit purposes (remember the NLRA's expansive definition of a professional employee) it is not required to differentiate between professionals. However, applying its general principles of appropriateness, the Board has held that professional bargaining units should be confined to professionals having a community of interests.[29] This approach therefore precludes the type of decision made by the Canada Wartime Labour Board and yet provides a tribunal with the flexibility required to tailor bargaining units to the diverse circumstances under which salaried professionals work.

The *Canada Labour Code* contains much more specific language dealing with two prominent work force situations that have caused difficulties in the salaried professional context: first, a large number of persons with different professional backgrounds working side by side and, second, the interdependence often found between salaried professionals and so-called para- or non-professionals (i.e. the engineer and the engineering technician). By conditioning the grant of a craft-like bargaining unit with reference to these two situations, the legislative draftsman has tried to create a presumption in favour of craft bargaining and at the same time provide a more limited flexibility than that possessed by the National Labour Relations Board. Whether he has been successful or not remains to be seen.[30]

CONCLUSION

The earliest debates on this topic centred on whether or not salaried professionals should be permitted to engage in collective bargaining. Many argued that it

29 See for example *Standard Oil* (1954), 107 N.L.R.B. 1524 and *Ryan Aeronautical Company* (1961), 132 N.L.R.B. 1160.
30 In the recent *Bell Canada* decision (supra, n.25) the Board doubted that it could limit the application of section 125(3)(c) to only those situations where the non-professionals would not outnumber the professionals. In the *Professional Engineers* case (supra, n.18) the Manitoba Board refused to include engineers who were not employed in a professional capacity.

was 'unprofessional' to belong to a trade union or that the collective bargaining process, concentrating on money, would undermine the professional status of those who engaged in it. But for the most part these arguments have been overcome. It is now generally understood that salaried professionals have turned to collective bargaining for many of the same reasons as other employees; indeed for the same reasons their non-salaried colleagues established professional associations and sought licensing statutes.[31] There is therefore nothing 'unprofessional' about collective bargaining. In fact it is through collective bargaining that an accommodation of the often conflicting cultures of professionalism and bureaucracy may be achieved. Through the collective bargaining process professionals can achieve greater say in the decision-making processes of the enterprise, working conditions more consistent with professional standards, and salary scales that attract and retain highly qualified members of the profession to salaried positions.

Today, then, the debate centres not so much on whether salaried professionals should be allowed to engage in collective bargaining but rather on how such rights should be accommodated; and here, I suggest, the response has been unduly narrow. The overwhelming reliance on such indicators as the existence of licensing statutes and university degrees ignores the dramatic growth of other intellectual occupations that do not enjoy one or both of these attributes and yet merit the designation 'professional.'

I accept that not all occupations requiring some form of post-secondary training can be considered professional occupations. Lines of demarcation must be drawn even though they may be somewhat arbitrary at the boundary. But in drawing them attention must be paid to the dynamics of occupational change, and, once they are drawn, labour boards ought to be able to group different professionals where a broad community of interest exists or where bargaining unit fragmentation would make labour relations chaotic. However, it must not be forgotten that intellectual workers who can be considered professional employees have, as a group, a community of interest deserving of special treatment, preferably along the lines adopted in the United States. Too often their interests have been resented or misunderstood by both their fellow employees and their employers, and labour relations boards, without direction, have not always been sufficiently sensitive to their central needs.

31 Indeed some might suggest that ethics are merely a form of collective bargaining at the professional level.

D. FRASER

Bicameralism and the professional college

Trade unionism in the earlier part of this century provided a major catalyst for social change in North America which went far beyond the requirements of labour legislation to protect and sanction that unionism. The change embraced the adoption of legislation for safety, injury compensation, and eventually the whole broad spectrum of social welfare. In particular, the unskilled worker became more of a human being in the workplace and less an element of production adding value to the goods on which he worked.

Today, trade unionism is beginning to take on a new character, with the rapid growth of the professional-technical category in the North American labour force. More rapid yet is the growth of the professional group within that category. It is my thesis that insofar as the needs of the professional salaried worker are new, or more pressing, than those which have emerged in traditional unionism, a new catalyst for social change will appear.

How may one explore the nature of that change, when professional unionism is barely past its infancy? First, is it possible at this early date to discover any different or more pressing needs that may be particularly identified with the salaried professional? Second, is it possible to discover a paradigm which will meet such needs, and which will lend itself to development into a process applicable to salaried professionals generally? Finally, what sort of change might we reasonably expect such a process to produce? We shall consider each of these questions in turn.

In the 1940s the psychologist A.H. Maslow formulated a theory of motivation based on the fulfilment of what he described as five basic needs: they are the physiological needs and needs for safety (which includes the need for stability and reliability as well as self-preservation), love, esteem, and self-actualiza-

Department of Law, Carleton University

tion.[1] One modern theorist interested in the question of motivation and productivity, R.H. Sutermeister, has reclassified these needs into three categories which are perhaps more apt for analysis in an industrial relations context: first, physiological needs, as a new grouping for physiological and safety needs; second, social needs, as a redefinition of love needs; and third, egoistic needs, as a new grouping for esteem and self-actualization.[2] Under this new grouping, physiological needs involve such essentials as air, water, food, housing, and clothing, which in our society are fairly well met and not a prime motivation of behaviour[3] Social needs are satisfied by contact with others, and may be satisfied fully both on or off the job.[4] Egoistic needs are defined as 'those that an individual has for a high evaluation of himself, and include such needs as knowledge, achievement, competence, independence, self-respect, respect for others, status, and recognition.'[5]

Sutermeister focuses on egoistic needs as the significant area for professionals:

The area of egoistic needs assumes greater importance when we recognize that the educational level of employees in this nation is rising rapidly and that the number of white-collar and professional people is now greater than the number of blue collar employees. At the higher level of egoistic needs appear those for self-actualisation or self-fulfilment. Such needs are often felt more strongly by professionals such as artists, doctors, and professors.[6]

If the need for self-actualization is felt more strongly by professionals, it is important to consider how that need will become manifest. Some light is cast on that question by the views and findings of Drucker and Gellerman, which I have discussed elsewhere in the following terms:

Peter Drucker, writing in 1952 on the relationship between management and the professional, indicated some clear differences between the basic attitudes of professional employees, and the rest of the business organization. He pointed out the differences between the managerial attitude, which in essence wants to see a job get done, and 'professionality,' which comes from the professional man's 'objectivity, his standards, his refusal to accept uncritically management's defini-

---

1 Maslow, 'A theory of human motivation' (1943) 50 *Psychological Review*, 370
2 Sutermeister, 'Individual's needs,' in Sutermeister, ed., *People and Productivity* (2d edn, 1969)
3 Ibid., 13
4 Ibid., 14
5 Ibid.
6 Ibid., 15

tion of a problem, or management's idea of what the result should be' ... Geller-man has noted the same desire for independence and control among profession-als in discussing what is known as the 'Pittsburgh Studies.' This was a study of work motivation of some 200 engineers and accountants who worked for 11 dif-ferent firms in the Pittsburgh area. The principal reasons for the study were the likelihood of professional workers responding to different motivating forces than clerical or blue-collar workers, and a search generally for 'clues to what kind of motives we can expect to appear among other workers as we move toward a more technologically based economy and a more professionalized labour force.' Gellerman sums up the result of the studies in the following way: 'both the traditional bread-and-butter motivators and the more sophisticated "human rela-tions" motivators didn't motivate ... Control of their own work, rather than the tangible rewards of work, was the motivator.[7]

There is evidence, then, that the principal egoistic need of the professional employee, which may be described as the need for self-actualization, manifests itself in the desire for control over one's own work, the unique aspects of which for the professional are found in his 'professionality.'

A need for control over one's own work undoubtedly exists in various forms for employees at large. For example, it was noted in a recent report of a British committee of inquiry that in the British workforce there is 'an increasing desire among employees to control their working environment and to have a say in decisions which affect their working lives,' and this was considered by the Com-mittee to have been brought about 'especially [by] rising standards of education and higher standards of living.'[8] However, as I will suggest further, the 'profes-sionality' of the professional employee adds a new dimension to his desire for involvement with and control over managerial decisions that goes beyond the aspirations of other employees.

Consider, for example, what 'control over work' involves. Surely, at least for the professional, it will involve not only 'when' and 'where' the work is done, but more importantly the 'how' of doing work, or perhaps more accurately 'how well' the work is done. The latter implies direct concern for, and adherence to, professional standards, and that adherence may require both doing the job well in accordance with the employee's professional education, and doing it within the framework of the appropriate ethical standards and principles subscribed to

---

7 Fraser and Goldenberg, 'Collective bargaining for professional workers: the case of the engineers' (1974) 20 *McGill L.J.,* No. 3, at 461

8 *Report of the Committee on Industrial Democracy* (Bullock Report), Cmnd. No. 6706, at 7 (1977)

by the appropriate professional licensing or governing body. I am thinking here of the engineer who may refuse, for example, to sign and accept responsibility for an engineering report containing a recommended design for an industrial waste discharge system, not only because the system will collapse in a few years from insufficient strength in the piping system but also because the system is in violation of a lawful standard for environmental control. And indeed, with respect to this particular example, it might be noted that in 1970 the Council of the Association of Professional Engineers of Ontario interpreted their Code of Ethics where it related to public welfare as including 'responsibility for meeting all lawful standards for environmental control in all engineering work' and noted that 'failure knowingly or unknowingly to meet such standards is cause for disciplinary procedures to be instituted by the Association against such members.'[9]

There are of course constraints on self-actualization. The professional still has to produce and do the job, and the company still has to be managed efficiently and profitably. However, some control over his professional standards, the 'how' of his work, would fulfil at least partially the professional's needs for self-actualization.

The 'how' of doing work, when it is involved with professionalism, also involves aspects of the 'when' and 'where' of doing work. Control over such things as the pace of work, the hours of work, the freedom sometimes to do the work away from the office environment, the right to time off for study leaves, sabbaticals, professional involvement; all can affect the 'how' of doing work. And so the professional, if he is to have some limited control over his work, needs also some say in the 'when' and 'where.'

In light of the constraints on self-actualization resulting from the freedom management needs to manage and make decisions in accordance with its goals, there are necessarily limits to the extent in which the professional can be involved in managerial decision-making when it affects the 'when' and 'where' of his work, but it may be enough, initially, that he be given a role in the decision-making system by at least being consulted. This need for consultation may be felt more strongly in larger firms, where the professional *en masse* tends to be treated as some sort of faceless anonymity.

For example, again referring to the salaried engineer, J.D. Muir noted, in a speech a few years ago to the Western Congress of Engineers in Canada, that almost 90 per cent of the engineering profession were now in paid employment, and described one result: 'the development of specialization within the engineering profession has led to mass training of engineers on almost a production line basis. As a result, many salaried P. Engs are dissatisfied with being a faceless mass

9 'Report of Conference on Engineers and Environment' (1971) *P. Eng. and Eng. Dig.* II

of engineers with little opportunity of self actualization or reason for incentive. They are thus turning to collective bargaining as a means for asserting themselves.'[10] The same problem has been identified in the United States. Professor Walton has commented that the process of communication in large engineering departments is 'primarily designed to handle the downward flow of authority,'[11] and has proposed that there is a need for 'an independent mechanism for being heard that is influential at the level where decisions are made affecting multifarious terms of engineering employment.'[12] It is not difficult to conclude that such treatment may be viewed as antithetic to a sense of professionality.

Two particular needs of salaried professionals therefore stand out: the need for some direct control over aspects of work directly involved with professional standards; and the need for at least consultation over other aspects of work that have a more indirect effect over aspects of professionality. Needs to control and to be consulted are unquestionably felt generally by other employees in the workplace, but insofar as they become concerned with professional standards they may become a matter of urgency for salaried professionals, because their absence could result in eventual deprofessionalization.

Salaried professionals, of course, have other special problems. Two well-known ones are the problem of managerial exclusions that arise during certification of a bargaining unit of professionals, whereby the size and consequent clout of the unit may be drastically weakened when a broad interpretation is given to the question of who exercises a managerial function, which bars a professional so defined from inclusion in the unit; and the problem of mid-career obsolescence, where a professional with training in a rapidly-evolving specialization finds himself made obsolete in mid-career by advances in knowledge and technique which have passed him by. However, most of such problems may be resolved in a quantitative manner, with mechanisms providing less exclusions, for example, or opportunities provided for more mid-career training.

The two needs of control and consultation are more normative in nature. They would require acceptance in principle by management of a derogation of management rights, and would not likely be achieved normally by quantitative changes over a period of time. What is needed is a new mechanism or process.

A paradigm, or a model, may be found in the bicameral structure of the typical North American university. By that I refer to the dual forums for decision-making and consultation found in most of our universities: the forum of the university board of governors or trustees; and the forum of the university senate.

10 Muir, 'A trade union for P. Engs.?' (Oct. 1970) *Eng. Dig.* 39 at 54
11 Walton, *The Impact of the Professional Engineering Union* (1961), 384
12 Ibid.

Those forums can exist and function co-operatively, in the main, within the context of a formal bargaining relationship between management and a disparate group of salaried professionals such as may be found on a university academic staff.

As a typical example consider Carleton University in Ottawa. The Act establishing the university[13] provides for a Board of Governors in whom is vested the 'government, conduct, management and control of the College,' and it provides for a Senate, composed principally of academics, who not only have control over 'all courses of study, including powers of admission' and such necessary ancillary matters as the conduct of examinations, the publication of calendars, and the granting of degrees, but who also may make recommendations to the Board of Governors.[14] These recommendations may be as particular as ones for 'the establishment of additional faculties, schools and departments,' or they may be quite broad in scope, including 'such recommendations as may be deemed proper for achieving the objects and purposes of the College.'[15] A similar bicameral structure and similar powers granted to a senate may be found in most other university Acts within the Canadian jurisdiction.

Is such a structure truly consultative, in the sense that the management of a university must listen to the university senate before making a decision? Again, one might consider Carleton University as a fairly typical example. A consideration of the problem of denial of tenure shows how the structure works. The president of the university in his capacity as chief executive officer has the final power of decision in such a matter, but by virtue of a set of procedures drafted by the University Senate and amended and approved by the Board of Governors, the faculty must first be consulted by way of a standing committee of the Senate.[16]

The procedures in question establish a standing committee of Senate, known as the Tenure Appeal Committee, comprised of academics other than deans, directors, or departmental chairmen. A candidate denied tenure may make a formal appeal to that Committee, which is required to make recommendations on the matter to the president. After receiving such recommendations, the president is required to provide a written statement of his decision on the matter, with reasons if his decision differs from the recommendations he has received. The entire procedure is incorporated into the collective agreement between the Board of

13 *The Carleton College Act*, 1952, S.O. c. 117, as amended.
14 s. 15; s. 22
15 s. 22(b); s. 22(i)
16 Procedures Concerning Tenure, Dismissal and Related Matters as Approved by the Board of Governors of Carleton University on June 27, 1972, and as Amended by the Board of Governors on October 4, 1972.

Governors and the academic staff, with provisions preventing the alteration, rescinding or suspension of the procedure except by agreement of the parties to the collective agreement.[17]

The particular issue and exact process described might only appear in an academic setting, but the over-all system nonetheless provides an example of a consultative bicameral structure that requires real consultation before a management decision is made, and which protects the decision and makes it enforceable by virtue of its inclusion in a collective agreement.

Similar bicameral structures, providing for consultations before similar types of administrative decisions are made, are incorporated in various forms in all other collective agreements in existence to date between university boards of governors in Canada and the various faculty associations.[18] The question whether such a system has utility, and is transferable, for industry at large will be examined later.

It has been noted earlier in this paper that one university senate had effective control over academic matters; this is true for university senates generally, although there are various ways of describing that control. Academic freedom is both one of the most cherished rights found within the general purview of academic matters and perhaps one of the more difficult rights to define. One typical attempt at definition may be found in Article 4 of the Carleton University collective agreement:

The common good of society depends upon the search for truth and its free exposition. Universities with academic freedom are essential to these purposes both in teaching and scholarship/research. Employees are entitled, therefore, to (*a*) freedom in carrying out research and in publishing the results thereof, (*b*) freedom in carrying out teaching and in discussing his/her subject and (*c*) freedom from institutional censorship. Academic freedom carries with it the duty to use that freedom in a manner consistent with the scholarly obligation to base research and teaching on an honest search for truth.

17 Collective Agreement Between Carleton University and the Carleton University Academic Staff Association, signed 11th December, 1975, s. 6.2, entitled *Existing Policy of the Senate and the Board of Governors.*
18 Collective Agreement Between Board of Governors of Notre Dame University, dated 6 November, 1975, Art. 11; Convention collective entre l'association des professeurs de l'université d'Ottawa and the University of Ottawa dated May, 1976, Art. 33; Collective Agreement between the University of Manitoba Faculty Association, dated 26 September, 1975, Art. XIX, 10; Agreement between Saint Mary's University and the Saint Mary's University Faculty Union, dated 4 December, 1975, Art. 11.40.

Similar clauses are found in most of the other university collective agreements in force in Canada.[19]

The freedom to search for truth in an honest and responsible manner, and to carry out discussion, teaching, and research freely in that search, bears some reasonable comparison to a professional's need for freedom to meet the standards and ethics of his profession. Both are concerned with significant matters of principle which may go to the core or essence of the daily work, and both may occasionally be in conflict with the bureaucratic needs of management. It is significant that university academics have without exception succeeded in protecting the notion of academic freedom in their collective agreements. An analogous process for protecting professional standards in the firm will be suggested below.

In sum, then, the pressing need for self-actualization for salaried professionals may be seen at this point to manifest itself in a need for control over questions involving professional standards, and a need for a consultative form of relationship with the corporate bureaucracy where management of the professional and his work milieu are concerned. A system which largely fulfils both those needs is found in the bicameral structure of university governance, which is protected and made enforceable by its inclusion in a collective agreement.

The most difficult question of all is whether the system is transferable to industry at large. This involves two further considerations. The first concerns its utility and thereby its acceptability; the second is translatability. First, even if the majority of salaried professionals in a firm are clearly in support of such a system, and even if it is advanced in the strongest way during collective bargaining, why should management accept any part of it except under the pressure of the strongest economic threats? It would involve substantial derogations from managerial authority and control, with consequent implications of extra cost, extra time to administer, and the possibility of interference with production.

The answer to that question is necessarily speculative, but there are considerations which indicate that even with the given extra short-term cost in time and money, the corporation may benefit in the long run. The first is that the protection of professional standards by any means, including giving control to the professional, can lead to significant long-term benefits for the firm. If one considers the simple example of design and construction standards in engineering work, examples are legion of cost-cutting by standard-cutting, resulting sometimes in tragedy, with costs in money and human life going far beyond any saving made at the time of construction. For example, in the past year in Ontario, faulty culvert construction caused the crumbling of a cottage roadway in Minden, with a

19 In the collective agreements cited immediately above, see Notre Dame, Art. 4; University of Ottawa, Art. 7; University of Manitoba, Art. XIX, 1; St Mary's, Art. 8.

consequent loss of lives. In the past year in Quebec a fault in the construction of the Olympic Stadium roof had similar tragic results. In both cases construction standards had not been adhered to, and granting not only responsibility but control to the professional engineer in such situations might have saved lives.

Consider the far-reaching question of professional adherence to environmental standards. It was noted earlier that the Association of Professional Engineers of Ontario require their members to adhere to all lawful environmental standards in their work. Numerous examples in the press over recent years show that the long-term costs of cleaning up a polluted environment exceed by a large factor any original cost of adherence to environmental standards during construction. Today those costs are often placed on the polluting company as well as on the community. Thus, long-run economic considerations may frequently provide support for adherence to professional standards where short-term considerations do not.

The second broad consideration is concerned with productivity and can be stated more succinctly. It is that studies of motivation and productivity generally indicate that where an employee is self-actualized by having his egoistic needs met on the job he becomes more concerned with and involved in his work, and his productivity increases as a result.[20]

Both considerations give reason to hope that a corporation involved in long-term planning and reviewing the long-term benefits of the system proposed might thereby find it acceptable.

How, then, might the system be translated into the industrial milieu? First, notwithstanding any possible utility to the firm, it does involve a grant of control from employer to employee when a question of professional standards arises. The achievement of a similar grant for professional engineers has led on occasion not only to difficult collective negotiations but also to a strike threat,[21] so that it is unlikely the system proposed, if it is to go beyond consultation, will be adopted except through a collective bargaining relationship. I therefore suggest that, in a medium-to-large firm or plant with a substantial number of professional employees, they form a group called the 'professional college,' and seek recognition for that body through collective bargaining. The name 'college' is chosen with reference to the Oxford Dictionary definition of college as a 'body of colleagues with common functions and privileges,' which would aptly describe the nature of the group.

20 See, for example, Sutermeister, 'Relationship between needs and motivation,' in Sutermeister, ed., *People and Productivity* (2nd edn, 1969), at 54.
21 Supra, n. 7, 58, 59

Such a college would include the members of all professional groups in the firm, whether engineers, accountants, lawyers, or others, and each professional group would exist as a distinct entity within the college.

If a conflict were to arise between a management policy or instruction and a professional standard, it would seem appropriate that the relevant group within the college would need to have the authority to ensure that the professional standard in question was not breached. The group would accordingly need the right to have a policy or instruction in conflict either modified or withdrawn. In this respect a clear derogation from managerial authority would have to be made, because a professional standard is a norm which does not lend itself to negotiation. In the words of Marc Lapointe, the chairman of the Canada Labour Relations Board, the one professional requirement to be insisted on is the 'inviolability of a professional decision.'[22]

On the other hand when issues arose not over normative standards of a particular profession but over the management of the professional employee and his work milieu, the entire college of professionals within the firm might appropriately form a consultative body which could be approached for advice before a managerial decision is taken. One would not expect the routine business of the firm to go through this bicameral system, but for issues of direct and particular interest to the professional employees as a group, such as the way they are given direction and supervision, it would be quite suitable.

In review, it would seem appropriate that the professional college might act in discrete groups and have some control where issues of professional standards are involved; and it would act in a collegial consultative capacity with respect to other issues affecting professional employment.

The final question is the most difficult and can be answered only in the most speculative way: if such a process is adopted, what sort of long-term change might we expect it to produce? The salaried professional, from being a cog in production, might move perceptibly towards becoming a qualified partner in management. There might be a shift in corporate goals from shorter-term profit motivation towards accommodating work satisfaction and professional standards which may in the long run result in higher quality in production and greater productivity. The most important change in the long run might be that since professionalism involves public duties and public trusts the professional college could be a means through which the professional employee seeks to represent the voice of the public in the corporate bureaucracy, thereby fulfilling the injunction of Francis Bacon:

22 Lapointe, in a speech to the Society of Ontario Hydro Professional Engineers and Associates, in Ryan, 'Engineers must demand share of pie' (1970) *Eng. Dig.* 11.

'I hold every man a debtor to his profession, from the which as men of course do seek to receive countenance and profit, so ought they of duty to endeavour themselves by way of amends to be a help and ornament thereunto.'[23]

23 Bacon, *The elements of the common law*, Preface

ALBERT ROSE

Professional incomes and government restraint programs: the case of the employee professions

THE ANOMALOUS CANADIAN ECONOMY

The performance of the Canadian economy during the decade 1966-75 was, to say the least, curious. On the one hand the GNP at market prices expanded nearly 250 per cent; but in real terms, that is, based upon constant (1961) dollars, the growth was about one-third of the dollar value. Although the rate of unemployment continued to grow and reached a plateau exceeding 7 per cent by the early 1970s, productivity in terms of output per man-hour was, in all analyses, described as 'disappointing.' Wages and salaries expanded at an incredible pace, by comparison with the past, and perhaps closely related to this phenomenon was a drop from 1962 to 1971 of 25 per cent in the purchasing power of the Canadian dollar, measured from 1961. These trends were firmly established by the time the prime minister announced on 13 October 1975 that a program of wage and price controls was essential if Canada were to escape the twin evils of unemployment and price inflation and ultimately a social collapse.

In the second half of the 1970s, the Canadian economy exhibits features that are anomalous from the point of view of most political scientists, economists, social scientists, and public administrators. For more than five years, Canada's national economy has exhibited, not unlike the situation in several other western industrial nations, a combination of an increasing proportion of unemployment within the labour force and an increasingly rapid rate of inflation in the price level. This combination was not conceivable in either classical or Keynesian economics, but it has been a reality with us for so many years that many people have come to accept it as inevitable.

Formerly dean, Faculty of Social Work, University of Toronto

Unemployment has become one of Canada's most serious and chronic problems not simply because the rate, as measured by the monthly labour force survey, has hovered about 7 to 8 per cent for the better part of three years but also because the components of this degree of unemployment bode ill for Canada's future. First of all, there is the matter of age distribution among the unemployed; the most recent figures indicate that the rate of unemployment among Canadians aged 15 to 24 who are in the labour force is double that within the nation as a whole. The second major feature about Canadian unemployment is its regional distribution. We know that unemployment in the Atlantic provinces is two or three times the national average, and that during recent years unemployment in Newfoundland has been as high as 25 per cent. In a time of economic constraint it is difficult to visualize techniques and expenditure sufficient to correct this situation in the most underdeveloped areas. The solution for many persons during the past three decades has been migration to the central provinces or to the West Coast. But the situation – in Ontario at 6 per cent plus, in Quebec at 9 per cent plus, and in British Columbia at 9 per cent to 12 per cent unemployment – does not augur well for speculative internal migration.

Nevertheless, to be very blunt about it, most Canadians 'have never had it so good.' Those who remain employed, and even in families where at least one income recipient of the previous two or three remains employed, there is far more income than was evident during the past two decades. Not only are Canadians earning more but the proportion of gross national income recorded for wages and salaries has consistently risen during the past fifteen years. Mysteriously, Canadians seem to be spending more and saving more simultaneously; retail sales were higher in 1975 than had been anticipated and continued to remain buoyant during 1976.

The past decade has been the most disturbing in Canadian economic history. On the one hand the total population increased by nearly 3 million persons. This fact was substantially due to new immigration, but the nation was beginning to be strongly pressed by the vast numbers of young native-born Canadians who constituted the so-called baby boom of the post-war period. Canada's birthrate began to rise in 1944 and reached rates approaching 30 live births per thousand within the first post-war decade. By the mid-1960s, the birthrate had dropped sharply, but the number of new births each year remained far above that of the period before the second world war. The unprecedented natural increase in the population began to be felt most sharply in those sectors of the Canadian economy which provide essential services, specifically education, health, and social welfare.

THE GOVERNMENT SECTOR OF THE ECONOMY

Canadian governments, in common with those of most western industrial nations, have come to bear an increasing volume and variety of responsibilities, many resulting directly from the growth of population. Post-war population growth was accomplished by a significant upsurge in the concentration of Canadian people in urban centres. Although the balance between urban and rural populations was not reached in Canada until 1931, by 1961 Canada's urban population was more than three-fifths of its total, and by 1971 the urban sector was approaching three-quarters of the national population. Urbanization in itself creates a demand for new services in housing, transportation, health, and social welfare, not to mention educational services, which for many years were a principal source of expansion in government spending across the nation.

The expansion of income is of course the first prerequisite for increasing demands in the service sectors of the economy. Income is very closely associated with demand for health services, and together with the increase in essential educational services the government sector has been carried along on a floodtide of population, expanding income, and demands for services.

In the midst of the second world war, all governmental spending required 50 per cent of the GNP, but by 1950 the proportion had dropped to about 24 per cent. In the midst of the past decade of great monetary expansion and price inflation, governments reached 38 per cent of the GNP (1971), and, more recently, preliminary estimates indicate that total governmental spending has now reached more than 45 per cent of the GNP, including transfer payments. However, there have been noteworthy changes within government spending. Unlike the past, defence spending has been relatively stable in dollars, and as a result its proportion of governmental expenditures has dropped to about one-quarter of its previous share of all governmental outlays. The same comment can be made for general governmental administration and for expenditures on the protection of persons and property.

The largest increases have taken place, both in dollar terms and in proportion, in the fields of education, health, and social welfare, but it is important to emphasize also that these expenditures have been accompanied by a substantial increase in the proportion of outlays for debt charges. Insofar as pressures for increasing services in education, health, and welfare have meant an expansion of social capital in the form of schools, colleges, universities, hospitals, day-care centres, and institutions for the elderly and a variety of handicapped persons, debt charges are an expanding and inflexible component of no mean significance in examining programs of economic constraints.

In the expanding 1960s, the federal government undertook a series of new shared-cost programs for post-secondary education (1967), for social welfare expenditures at the provincial and local levels under the Canada Assistance Plan (1966), and for the development of medicare in 1968. A very important component in the economic restraint program has been the reduction of federal participation, and even the projected elimination of such participation in these and other shared-cost programs. The complaints of the provincial governments and in turn of their creatures, the municipal governments, have been very strongly related to the federal response to their own spending programs.

THE INFLEXIBILITY OF CURRENT GOVERNMENTAL EXPENDITURES

If we examine recent budgets for the government of Canada and the government of Ontario or those of most other provinces, we would find that there was little flexibility in government accounts long before the anti-inflation and restraint program was imposed upon the nation late in 1975. In the federal budget from 1946 to 1970 there had developed a series of commitments to expenditures that could not easily be restricted for political reasons and were universal and open-ended. There were also some federal departments which could not easily be restrained but could perhaps be held to expenditures commensurate with the rate of inflation, departments such as Agriculture, Fisheries, and Transport.

Among the most significant areas of federal governmental expenditure are those in the fields of health, education, and welfare services. These are indeed the very heart of our society, and most of us support them with conviction. Canadians have felt, for example, that every person over the age of 65 should receive a specific old age security allowance, and we indicated strongly in 1972 that we did not wish to introduce a system of selectivity to this process. Most Canadians support the program of family allowances, and, although a good many of us do not need the modest supports which come forward, we indicated very strongly, again in 1972, that we wanted no reversal of the universal nature of this program through the introduction of a system of selectivity, means testing, or the drawing of income lines beyond which the allowance would not be paid.

These programs, together with federal contributions for the health and hospitalization services within our ten provinces and to post-secondary educational institutions throughout the nation, are the very life blood of a decent responsible society. They encourage better provision for our children, assist in creating more adequate standards of living for elderly persons, provide that no individual or family shall be ruined by virtue of catastrophic medical and hospitalization costs; and for the future they provide for increasing numbers and proportions of young Canadians to proceed beyond secondary education towards the development of knowledge and skills in the service of their fellow men.

Governmental expenditure patterns are rigid not only because of the obvious pressures to improve the quantity and quality of services provided to individuals and families but also because of the rising expectations of an increasing population. Most middle-aged Canadians would scarcely have expected some thirty years ago that universal access to medical care through the payment of modest premiums and governmental expenditures from general revenues would be a fact in their lifetime. Moreover, those who completed their secondary education in the 1930s would scarcely have expected that the proportion of young persons completing secondary education and proceeding to college would rise from perhaps 4 per cent of the cohort age group, 16-24 years of age, to nearly 30 per cent of that group by the 1970s.

What would have been considered luxuries or wild dreams at the beginning of the post-war period have become realities and are taken for granted: the benefit programs which all new Canadians, native born or immigrant, find upon growing up or arriving in this country and expect to be provided. It is perfectly understandable that most people assume that life will become better and better, that each generation will be better educated, more healthy, and more secure than the previous one. The ultimate cost in terms of the benefits and manpower required to provide the health and welfare services is rarely calculated, if indeed it is calculable, as much as five or ten years ahead.

'SOFT SERVICES' AND THE EMPLOYEE PROFESSIONALS

The professions in Canada may be crudely divided into two major groups: those whose members are self-employed, either in private general practice or as consultants, and those whose members are the employees of public or voluntary organizations. This difference in simple status has profound effects in several areas of importance: the demand for professional manpower, the utilization of professional or para-professional persons, the remuneration that members of these professions receive in relation to other groups in the community, and the opportunity which the members of these two groups have to maintain or improve their situations in a period of economic restraint.

This attempt at taxonomy does not provide an analyst with a clear-cut dichotomy. The medical, dental, and legal professions are usually considered the characteristic examples of the self-employed, private practice group. Yet an important number of members of each of these professions serve the community as employees of government departments, voluntary organizations supported by so-called charitable dollars, and professional associations. They may also be employees of private enterprise, notably banks, insurance companies, large manufacturers of steel, home appliances, automobiles, and so on. On the other side of the line, teachers, nurses, social workers, physiotherapists and occupational therapists are most often employees, but a small number are already engaged in private practice on their own account. Nor is the problem of classification solved by designating an entire area, such as 'health services,' as 'self-employed' and a field, such as 'social services,' as 'employee.' Most nurses and an increasing number of pharmacists are employees of some organization, public or private. Moreover, a substantial proportion of highly trained social workers (those with MSW degrees) are employed within the health care system, most often in hospitals and related institutions.

Nevertheless, a consideration of the case of the professionals who serve as employees of governmental bodies (including school boards) or voluntary agencies does indicate the relative vulnerability of the employee professional in comparison with the typically self-employed professional. Status and prestige cannot be ignored, nor can the nature and quality of the legislation governing the profession, if any. But the situation is far more complicated than these observations would suggest. In a period of economic restraint, the capacity of each profession to maintain its standards of practice and an appropriate income depends both on society's view of the priority which should be accorded to the service offered by the professional and also upon its view of the clients of the several professions as 'needy' or 'deserving' of the service. Thus the highway accident victim or the person suffering an acute attack of renal colic or asthma must be treated on an emergency basis; but the deserted mother with dependent children may or may not receive the day-care services essential to her entry into the labour market and a state of self-support, depending on the attitudes of the community, or the local elected officials, or the appointed administrators – both to the social situation and the apparent available financial resources. The latter in turn are often dependent upon social attitudes.

On the other hand the major impact of the federal-provincial economic constraint program upon educational services is the clear and obvious decline in the demand for teachers at the elementary and secondary levels. This reduction in demand, however, is largely a consequence of the substantial drop in the birthrate in Canada after 1961. In short, the restraint program insofar as it affects elementary and secondary school teachers has simply confirmed the tendency or the trends which were inevitable, given the demographic facts. But teachers are well organized and to some degree have a 'closed shop,' by virtue of provincial legislation requiring their membership in a teachers' federation. The normal reaction of employees in this situation has been followed, namely, a proposal that the quality of the professional service be improved through a reduction in class size. The total constraint program, however, makes this extremely difficult to attain, and the consequence has been a substantial imbalance between the supply of and the demand for teachers.

At the post-secondary level, a similar situation pertains, but university professors have less of a tradition of unionization. This situation is changing very rapidly, with four universities in Ontario and others elsewhere in Canada now unionized not merely in maintenance and support staff but in the professorial area. The problem here is that the tremendous expansion in post-secondary education has become a severe burden within the budgets of provincial governments, and because their revenues have stabilized and their grants from the federal government have been or may be reduced they concede that the expansion of the 1960s and early 1970s must come to a halt. Moreover, it is clear that the graduates of many university programs now substantially exceed the demand for university-trained personnel. There is in Canada the potential of a terrible tragedy with a highly educated population suffering a serious degree of unemployment or underemployment.

A large proportion of the health and social welfare services is offered by such professionals as nurses and social workers and a host of paraprofessionals trained at the post-secondary but non-university level of education. Many of the services provided by these professionals or subprofessionals are 'soft,' in the sense that the individual or family is apparently not as dependent upon them as it is upon those of the lawyer or the physician for its very survival. A great many obvious social problems may or may not benefit from the 'soft services' offered by professionals in the health and welfare fields. Unfortunately, despite our relative affluence, the economic restraint program has meant that a good many Canadians who do require service and/or might benefit from the work of these professionals will be denied this service. The most obvious examples are the failure to expand day-care services, social and recreational programs for the elderly, and individual counselling for persons whose marital situation and/or mental stability may depend upon an appropriate counsellor.

There is no doubt that on most criteria the professional is in a far better position self-employed than as an employee. The self-employed are protected through a series of laws covering the practice of their professions and malpractice, and by the tax laws which in effect designate them small businessmen. The significance of gross versus net income in a comparative analysis of the two major groups of professional persons in our society has always been evident but is no longer lost on the general public or on employed professionals.

In a period of economic restraint, society's differential treatment of these two major groups becomes more evident by virtue of the community's judgment concerning the 'worth' of varied forms of professional practice. The term 'worth' refers not simply to the way people view the lawyer, physician, or engineer as an important contributor to social development but also to the way they view the clients of these professionals by comparison with those of a professor, social worker, or occupational therapist. The person who visits a doctor is assumed, in most cases, to be ill and in need of medical service. The operative notion in that situation is the fact that the client has voluntarily sought help. On the other hand social work services are less likely to be delivered on a voluntary basis and often are the response of a government or community agency when the client exhibits a disability or disadvantage identified in some form of legislation. This exposition does not neglect the fact that there is a small element of private practice within nursing, social work, and various related therapies but is intended to emphasize that such practice is rare.

There is a further important difference between the self-employed and some employee professionals. Members of professions based upon private practice are almost always regulated by provincial statute. Such regulation implies control over educational preparation for the profession by an elected or appointed regulatory body, a code of ethics disseminated by the governing body, and the exercise of discipline and sanction when this code is violated, including disbarment or removal from the rolls of licensed practitioners. Members of certain employee professions are, in fact, subject to similar provincial statutes; but the governing bodies often cannot deny admission to practice and in other cases cannot revoke the right to practise. Moreover, from the code of ethics the definition of non-ethical behaviour by a social worker, a schoolteacher, or a physiotherapist, for example, is less clear. Unethical behaviour is more likely to be subject to interpretation within the criminal code.

The known process of self-regulation and control of practice implies a responsibility to the public. In addition, most people agree that each year of practice adds a sufficient dimension to the qualifications of a self-employed professional, that he or she may be viewed as proceeding from level to higher level of competence. Thus the notion has emerged of a first-year lawyer (one year beyond admission to the bar), a second-year lawyer, and so on; in the field of medicine the progression from internship to residency to private practice creates a similar impression. The Canadian program of constraining the income of professional persons has accepted these conceptual frameworks, allowing members of many professions income increases well beyond the limit of $2,400 per annum enunciated by the prime minister on 13 October 1975. On the other hand the income of employee professionals is easy to control through regulatory mechanisms binding upon their employers. These constraints are reinforced by the stringent allocation of funds to school boards, hospitals, social service agencies, community organizations, and a variety of health and social service organizations.

It is equally not surprising that human services performed by professionals who are employees fall generally under the rubric 'soft services.' Since the employers (voluntary agencies, hospitals, school systems, universities, and government departments) are maintained through budgets that are not as inflexible as interest on the public debt, the costs of the defence establishment, and the mandatory health and welfare services, the employed professional is in a very exposed position. Most employer groups engaging professional persons – through which the largest amount of employment is afforded – fall under immediate attack when governments find themselves short of resources sufficient to maintain and expand their activities. Thus the first group to find their employment opportunities reduced, their salaries sharply controlled, and their normal responsibilities reassigned, in part to paraprofessionals, are those persons whose services do not command an absolute or top-flight priority in the community and thus have relatively less bargaining power in the total society.

IMPACT ON DISADVANTAGED OR LOW-INCOME FAMILIES

The end product of all these tendencies is a strong pressure upon the disadvantaged in our society and a further humiliation of those who are 'truly poor' through illness, accident, or physical or emotional incapacity. This tendency is justified as an attempt to lessen the burden on ordinary taxpayers caused by those who either are taking advantage of the human service systems or in theory could be induced through training and rehabilitative programs to enter or re-enter the mainstream of economic life.

This argument leads to the ultimate paradox in the anti-inflation program which Canadians have experienced for some two years. When the program was first announced by the prime minister and when the premiers of several provinces indicated their ready acceptance of the program and their willingness to sign an agreement with the government of Canada, major emphasis was placed upon those groups that needed and would be afforded 'protection.' Individuals and families whose capacity to earn income was already restricted by one or more of the major elements of disadvantage – modest education, relatively little skill in the labour market, less than average intelligence, disabling illnesses – were said to be the important beneficiaries of the restraint program. The elderly and other persons whose prime source of income is a pension not adjusted to increases in the Consumer Price Index were frequently cited as suffering most from rapid price inflation.

The paradox is the denial of services to those very groups of disadvantaged persons and families. The poor and the aged were to be protected, but what they have been receiving from social and health programs is a combination of income and social support services. A basic income for simple physical survival has been provided within federal-provincial-municipal programs. The level of income support varies from province to province, although there has been serious question concerning its adequacy. It is in the area of support services, however, that the quality of life for the poor and the disadvantaged is determined. Some elderly persons need meals-on-wheels more than a quarterly adjustment in their universal Old Age Security Allowance; many mothers who are the sole support of dependent children need a day care service so that they can work part-time more than an annual adjustment in their Family Benefits Allowance. These services, and a great variety of others, are the most obvious casualty of the economic constraint program.

The poor and the elderly were promised protection. If a reduction in the rate of inflation from 12 per cent to 7 per cent per annum consitutes protection, then they have received it. But this is not the kind of support a great many people in our society really require. They need more and better educational opportunities, recreation and leisure time services, and opportunities to reduce or remove the isolation which is so obvious in the lives of many elderly persons and many single heads of families. In this context the program of income constraint is nothing new to those unable to keep pace in an affluent society, despite the promises which accompanied the initiation of the program. They have lost rather than gained protection, by virtue of the reduction or insufficiency of protective and preventive services.

CONCLUSIONS

It has become obvious that in a period of economic restraint society as a whole turns sharply 'to the right.' This means that the services provided for those members of society considered to be in need are sharply questioned. Social need is considered optional in comparison with a criminal law charge or even with a tooth in need of extraction. There has thus been mounted a considerable attack on so-called frills. There is a denial of the capacity to expand services previously considered essential, such as protective services for children in danger of abuse. There is the substitution of less well-trained and well-remunerated paraprofessionals for highly qualified professionals, without full attention to the appropriate responsibilities of either group.

The major finding of this analysis is that governmental programs of economic restraint are far more than formal rules and regulations governing the movement of wages and salaries and the incomes of professional persons however the latter may be classified. This is not to deny that the incomes of physicians and other health professionals who offer services to individuals and families 'insured' under mandatory medical and hospital plans are subject to restraint. Professional associations in some provinces have in fact become the formal negotiating bodies to work out annual or biennial contracts with government bureaucrats. Moreover, governmental interference has extended into the modes of professional practice, and the few situations of malpractice or outright fraud uncovered are gleefully publicized by the media with obvious assists by diligent civil servants.

What has not been said sufficiently or emphasized is the continued degradation, by virtue of the restraint programs, of those individuals and families in our society who are already in a position of involuntary restraint. Social units or households who were by no means well served by the health, welfare, and educational systems in Canada before October 1975 have since that time been even less well served. This is not a matter of the postponement of elective surgery through the closing of hospital beds or of dental care through the limitations of local welfare budgets. This is a matter of the further tightening of already stringent budgets, first at the level of governmental and voluntary services and almost immediately at the personal and familial level. Moreover, the extent of this reduction in the quality of life for Canadians whose lives already had little quality extends throughout one-quarter or one-fifth of the entire population, depending upon whose estimate of the poverty line one cares to accept.

Denial of employment to large numbers of potentially employable professionals is an important part of this tapestry of neglect. Individually, they are not expensive – starting salaries for teachers, nurses, social workers, for example, range from $600 to $1,000 per month – but there is no question that the accumulation of physical, emotional and social need in Canada would require vast numbers of such professionals. At this time in our history we are assured that we cannot afford the cost of their services. Ultimately we shall have to pay for our neglect and our prejudices.

REGULATING CONTINUING COMPETENCE

J. ROBERT S. PRICHARD

Professional civil liability and continuing competence

I

There is considerable debate about the relationship between professional civil liability and continuing competence. In Canada, the Committee on the Healing Arts has stated that 'rather than operating as a quality control it may reasonably be argued that the [medical] malpractice action has reduced the quality of medical care [in the United States]'[1] and 'for all intents and purposes, the malpractice action may be ignored in any realistic assessment of the adequacy of existing quality controls.'[2] However, Professor Linden has reached a different conclusion:

All professional groups come under the aegis of tort law. The expertise of doctors, lawyers, engineers and accountants may be impugned in a tort suit. Of course, negligence law normally adopts as its own the standards that the professions require of themselves. But this does not make negligence law redundant, because professional groups are less than zealous in policing themselves. Hardly ever does a doctor, for example, lose his licence to practice medicine because of his incompetence or professional misconduct. It is far more common for a physician to be sued by a patient injured by his malpractice. Consequently, it is the

Faculty of Law, University of Toronto
1 Ontario's *Report of the Committee of the Healing Arts* (1970) Vol. 3, 70
2 Ibid., 71. The Report goes on to rely heavily on programs of compulsory continuing education and limited licences to deal with quality control and continuing competence. See 69-76; 'But the issue today is not whether a practitioner once licenced should be required to submit to continuing education so that his knowledge does not become obsolete but rather what feasible means ought to be employed to this end. The existing formal mechanisms are quite inadequate for this task.'

judges, not the College of Physicians and Surgeons, who by default become the regulators of the quality of medical practice.[3]

A similar divergence of opinion exists in the United States. While introducing a bill creating a federal no-fault compensation system for medical injuries, Senator Daniel Inouye said:

I believe that good doctors practice good medicine in spite of, not because of the threat of malpractice, and that they will continue to do so after the threat is lessened. Conversely, it is questionable whether a deficient or careless doctor can be made to practice good medicine by an external threat. In his case, it is more important that we identify him and take steps to prevent him from endangering the health and lives of his patients.[4]

The opposite view was expressed in the *Waxman Report* issued by the California Assembly Select Committee on Medical Malpractice which stated that: 'It is thus fair to conclude that while there do exist quality control mechanisms, they are not sufficiently effective. At the present time, malpractice litigation is clearly the most significant external pressure prompting physicians to practice quality medicine.'[5]

These contradictory opinions reflect genuine uncertainty about the relationship of civil liability and competence in the medical profession. Recent analytical work in the medical malpractice area in the United States has taken place in an atmosphere of crisis,[6] and analogous Canadian writing has felt at least the

3 Linden, 'Tort law as ombudsman' (1973) 51 *Can. Bar Rev.* 155, at 160
4 121 *Cong, Rec. S.* 414 (1975) quoted in Havighurst, '"Medical adversity insurance" – Has its time come?' (1975) *Duke L.J.* 1233, at 1234. For a similar position, see Carlson, 'A conceptualization of a no-fault compensation system for medical injuries' (1972) 7 *Law and Society Rev.* 329.
5 *Waxman Report* (1974) California Assembly Select Committee on Medical Malpractice, quoted in Cartwright, 'Medical malpractice: a trial lawyer's view,' at 61, which is reproduced in Warren and Merritt, *A Legislator's Guide to the Medical Malpractice Issue* (1976). See also Roemer, 'Controlling and promoting quality in medical care' (1970) 35 *Law and Contemp. Prob.* 284, at 297: 'There is no question that the threat of malpractice suits is an inducement to elevate the diligence of medical performance.'
6 The American 'medical malpractice crisis' has been presented in many forms: 'The most common was the alarm of physicians and hospitals that they could not afford to pay the dramatic new premium increases the insurance companies were demanding for malpractice liability coverage. Even more threatening was the announced intention of many companies to terminate malpractice insurance coverage altogether in some states. This highly charged atmosphere led to reports of physicians closing their doors, hospitals tak-

shadow of the same crisis.[7] Although the medical profession has attracted the greatest attention in this regard, the same issue must be faced in all professions: is civil liability an effective mechanism for ensuring the continuing competence of the members of the profession?[8]

This essay addresses that issue. It considers the possible and proper role of civil liability as a means of gaining continuing competence and, much less extensively, compares this mechanism with those of discipline and continuing education. The thesis of the article is that the relative effectiveness of each of these three mechanisms will vary from profession to profession, and that where there are distinct delivery modes within a profession it will vary within the profession. Certain characteristic variables of a profession enable predictions of effectiveness and thus should be considered in the choice of institutions for maintaining com-

ing only emergency patients, and even doctor strikes' (*Legislator's Guide*, supra n. 5, at v). In 1970, approximately 16,000 malpractice claims files were closed, with some payment in 45 per cent of all claims. Of the successful claimants, more than half received less than $3,000, and only 6.1 per cent received more than $40,000. It is estimated that there were not more than seven payments for $1 million or more. In 1970, a claim was asserted for one out of every 226,000 patient visits to doctors. Based on 1970 data, if the average person lives seventy years, he will have approximately four hundred contacts as a patient with doctors and dentists, and the chances that he will assert a claim are one in 39,500. See *Medical Malpractice*, Report of the Secretary's Commission on Medical Malpractice (1973), 5-12.

7 Commenting on the American situation, Dr Bette Stephenson, past president of the Canadian Medical Association, has warned: 'The Canadian medical profession cannot afford the luxury of smug, chauvinistic, national complacency.' Quoted in Geekie, 'The crisis in medical malpractice: will it spread to Canada?' (1975) 113 *C.M.A.J.* 327. A review of statistics from the Canadian Medical Protective Association indicates that while the frequency of malpractice actions is still slight, it is increasing quite rapidly. In 1965, forty-nine new claims were brought, but in 1974 there were 220, an increase in frequency from one per 325 physicians to one per 132. Membership fees for the *C.M.P.A.* (which acts as a form of insurance company for physicians) have increased from $15 in 1965 to $200 in 1976. See *Annual Reports of the Canadian Medical Protective Association* for the relevant years.

8 See Note, 'Professional negligence' (1972-3) 121 *U. Penn. L. Rev.* 627; Roady and Anderson, *Professional Negligence* (Vanderbilt University Press, 1960); Huszagh and Molloy, 'Legal malpractice: a calculus for reform' (1976) 37 *Montana L. Rev.* 279. Canadian writing in the non-medical professional negligence area is quite limited. For an introduction, see Hoyt, 'Professional negligence,' *LSUC Special Lectures on New Development in the Law of Torts* (1973); Glos, 'Note on the doctrine of professional negligence' (1963) 41 *Can. Bar Rev.* 140; Nelson, 'The source of professional liability – tort or contract?' *LSUC Special Lectures on New Development in the Law of Contracts* (1975); Bastedo, 'A note on lawyer's malpractice' (1969) 7 *Osgoode Hall L. Rev.* 311; Linden, *Canadian Negligence Law* (Butterworths, 1972) 37-51 and Suppl. (1975) 6-8.

petence in that profession. In addition, a number of features of the civil liability mechanism common to all professions affect its viability.

It is important to realize that exclusive reliance on any one of the three mechanisms (or indeed on any other mechanism) is unlikely to lead to an optimal solution to the continuing competence problem. Experience in the United States with medical malpractice teaches that progress will be made by relying on a mix of the mechanisms while refining each of them. Thus the American legislative responses have included procedural and substantive modifications of the civil action, increased reliance on and investment in continuing education, and heightened sensitivity in the disciplinary process to problems of competence.[9]

This article is not concerned with compensation for injuries resulting from professional services. If the sole reason for professional civil liability were to provide compensation, the civil suit would be of limited use; the well-known failures of the tort system as a compensatory vehicle could be overcome (although not without some difficulty) by an insurance scheme unrelated to fault. It is only if one believes that the civil liability action also has a role in ensuring acceptable levels of quality in the delivery of professional services that the tort suit may be justified.

The malpractice action should effectively stimulate continuing competence. The basis of professional civil liability was stated clearly in *Lanphier* v. *Phipos* as early as 1838:

Every person who enters into a learned profession undertakes to bring to the exercise of it a reasonable degree of care and skill. He does not, undertake, if he is an attorney, that at all events you shall gain your case, nor does a surgeon undertake that he will perform a cure; nor does he undertake to use the highest possible degree of skill. There may be persons who have higher education and greater advantages than he has, but he undertakes to bring a fair, reasonable, and competent degree of skill.[10]

Glos explains:

As the standard of care required of a professional man is not simply to exercise reasonable care, but to display such care and skill that is possessed by a man of

---

9 For a summary of these developments, see *Legislator's Guide*, supra n. 5, 3-21. The same mixed approach has been taken for the regulation of accountants and lawyers. See Huszagh and Molloy, supra n. 8.

10 *Lanphier* v. *Phipos* (1838), 8. *C. & P.* 475, at 479. See also *Crits* v. *Sylvester* [1956] O.R. 133, at 143; affirmed [1956] S.C.R. 991: 'He is bound to exercise the degree of care and skill which reasonably could be expected of a normal, prudent practitioner of the same experience and standing.'

average competence exercising a particular calling, the standard may vary from calling to calling depending on the degree of knowledge and perfection attained in the particular calling. The fundamental requirement, however, is common to all professions, trade and callings. Professional men are expected and bound to exercise that degree of care and skill which is displayed by the average practitioner in that particular profession. A fair and reasonable standard of care and competence is thus required. The practitioner possessing the average skill and confidence in the exercise of his profession is looked upon by the law as the standard-giving entity.[11]

There are therefore two possible grounds for success in a professional negligence action: first, that the professional failed to use reasonable care despite being adequately skilled and, second, that the professional lacked the requisite minimum level of skill.[12] The first is concerned with care and diligence, the second with continuing competence and skill.[13] Civil liability should stimulate both care and competence. The stimulus is the threat of an award of damages against the professional and the stigma in both the profession and the community of a judicial determination of fault.

In a sense, civil liability is a negative incentive; by using reasonable care and maintaining his competence the professional avoids adverse consequences. The award of damages acts as a deterrent against carelessness and incompetence. It is thus different, for example, from specialized professional education for which the incentive is the right to hold oneself out as a specialist and presumably reap the benefits therefrom.

Civil liability is also an indirect, flexible mechanism. Initial professional certification is usually achieved by following a specified set of educational requirements as well as displaying competence upon examination. However, the civil liability requirement of continuing competence can be met by any number of individualized routes – attendance at courses, reading, collegial consultation, and the like. Each member of the profession is able to choose the method of main-

11 Glos, supra n. 8, at 142. See also Prosser, *Law of Torts* (West Pub. Co., 1971), at 161; Fleming, *The Law of Torts* (Law Book Co., 1971), at 109. Similarly, a specialist must exercise the degree of skill of an average specialist in his field, *Wilson* v. *Swanson* [1956] S.C.R. 804, at 817.

12 Prosser, *Law of Torts* (West Pub. Co., 1971), at 161: 'Professional men in general, and those who undertake any work calling for special skill, are required not only to exercise reasonable care in what they do, but also to possess a standard minimum of special knowledge and ability.'

13 'Skill is that special competence which is not part of the ordinary equipment of the reasonable man, but the result of aptitude developed by special training and experience' (Fleming, supra n. 11, 109).

taining competence that is most effective for himself. He may rely on institutions to provide the alternative methods – continuing education programs, peer group reviews, professional journals, etc. – and may select that combination of activities which he feels most efficiently allows him to maintain his skills. The emphasis is on the result – competence – rather than the method by which it is achieved. Performance, not compliance, is stressed. In this way it is quite distinct from mandatory continuing education which specifies a form in the hope that it will achieve the desired result. It is coercive only in demanding a certain result, not the method for achieving it.

In addition to being flexible, civil liability is a dynamic mechanism in that it continually adjusts the required level of competence to incorporate any changes in customary professional practice. The standard of care against which the members of the profession are measured is the skill and learning commonly possessed by members of the profession in good standing.[14] As this standard is raised or altered as a result of new methods and learning, the civil liability mechanism requires all members of the profession to maintain their competence as measured by this new standard.

To the extent that the courts adopt the customary practices of the profession as the standard of care, professionals are a privileged group in civil liability actions. Most other types of defendants are unable to set the requisite standard of care. Rather, the court, after hearing evidence about an activity, determines the proper standard of care even if it departs from the customary manner of carrying on that activity. The justification for this delegation in professional negligence situations is 'the healthy respect which the courts have had for the learning of a fellow profession, and their reluctance to overburden it with liability based on an uneducated judgment.'[15] The danger is that in the absence of judicial review of the standard of care, the adoption of the customary practices of the profession may perpetrate, and indeed require, non-optimal professional behaviour.[16] Some of the most noteworthy professional negligence cases have been those in which the court rejected the profession's customary standard and required a different one. For example, in *Anderson* v. *Chasney*,[17] in which a sponge was left behind in an adenoid operation, the court held that a counting precaution should have been used, although it was not proved that it was customary to do this. In these rare cases where following the customary practice is

---

14 Prosser, supra n. 12, 162
15 Ibid., 165. Another explanation which is offered sometimes is that the professional implies that he will follow customary methods and thus has undertaken to do so.
16 It is sometimes said facetiously that professionals are liable for negligent behaviour unless they are customarily negligent.
17 [1949] 4 D.L.R. 71 (Man. C.A.), affirmed [1950] 4 D.L.R. 223 (S.C.C.). See Linden, 'The negligent doctor' (1973) 11 *Osgoode Hall L. Rev.* 31, at 32-5.

not a conclusive defence to a negligence action, the court is taking a much more active role in the promotion of quality professional services. However, in most cases the court is prepared to rely on institutions within and surrounding the profession to dictate the appropriate standard of competence and to limit itself to assessing whether or not the standard is breached.

Before turning to a consideration of the practical limitations on the effectiveness of the civil liability action, it is necessary to clarify one further aspect of a system of civil liability: that not all accidents or risks of accidents should be avoided. An ideal system of accident law (and maloccurrences resulting from incompetent professional services are a form of accident) minimizes the sum of the costs of accidents and the costs of avoiding them.[18] Properly applied, the negligence standard (or at least Judge Learned Hand's conception of it) will find negligence in situations only where the cost of avoiding the accident is less than the expected cost of the accident.[19] That is, negligence law should only encourage the avoidance of accidents which are worth avoiding; accidents too expensive to avoid should not be avoided.

Applications of this principle are common in the medical field where diagnostic tests must constantly be evaluated for their cost-effectiveness. For example, Tay-Sachs disease is a rare form of hereditary brain degeneration found in children. There is a test which can be administered to potential parents which enables the physician to identify carriers of Tay-Sachs disease and therefore to discourage reproduction. Despite this, good medical practice does not require that the test be administered to all potential parents because of the enormous cost of such a testing program. The rare occasions which can be predicted for the general population are not cost-justified, and thus we incur the alternative costs, both medical and human, of children born with Tay-Sachs disease. These are avoidable accidents, but the cost of avoidance is too great. At the same time, there is an identifiable subgroup of the general population – East-European Jews – for whom the incidence of carriers of Tay-Sachs disease is much higher. For this subgroup, the diagnostic test is cost-justified, and the testing procedure should be encouraged.[20] To the extent, then, that the court adopts the profes-

18 Calabresi, *The Costs of Accidents* (Yale Univ. Press, 1970) 24-33
19 *United States* v. *Carroll Towing Co.*, 159 F. 2d. 169 (2d. Cir. 1947); *Conway* v. *O'Brien*, 111 F. 2d. 611, 612 (2d. Cir. 1940) rev'd on other grounds, 312 U.S. 492 (1941): 'The degree of care demanded of a person by an occasion is the resultant of three factors: the likelihood that his conduct will injure others, taken with the seriousness of the injury if it happens, and balanced against the interest which he must sacrifice to avoid the risk.' See Posner, 'A theory of negligence' (1972) 1 *J. Leg. Studies* 29.
20 Indeed, using the Learned Hand definition of negligence, the failure to administer this test to the subgroup should be actionable. For a case making such a finding, see *Howard* v. *Lecher*, 386 N.Y.S. 2d 460 (1976).

sion's practices as defining competent services, we must be confident that other mechanisms are ensuring that the proper tradeoff of accident costs and avoidance costs is achieved, or in other words that the customary professional practices are those that the negligence test would require.[21]

II

Despite the advantages cited above of civil liability as a mechanism for gaining continuing competence – indirectness, flexibility, individuality, and dynamism – many observers of the professions reject the notion that incentives generated by legal liability for negligently caused maloccurrences can adequately promote the quality of professional services. Rather, historically, the professions have displayed a marked preference for internal controls – discipline, licensing, institutional review, etc. – as opposed to liability incentives. Although willing to accept the deterrent and incentive functions of civil liability for many kinds of activity in society, these observers suggest that inherent in the nature of a profession and professional services are factors incompatible with this mechanism. Commenting on the medical profession, Havighurst explains:

The preference for controls and against incentive is traceable ... to an abiding faith in professionalism and ethics as an adequate guarantor of high quality performance by all but a small minority of physicians, which is presumed to be amenable to governmental or professional policing ... [This theory] has a slightly elitist ring, suggesting that physicians as a class are worthy of society's trust and that specific guarantees of their good performance can be dispensed with, except around the fringes.[22]

Havighurst argues further that the incentives created by civil liability can play a useful role in the medical profession:

[It] is not necessary to cast any aspersion on the average doctor's ethics or motives to suggest that financial incentives may be a useful adjunct to his sense

21 See Bovbjerg, 'The medical malpractice standard of care: HMOs and customary practice' (1975) *Duke L.J.* 1375, at 1376: 'Not all avoidable risks should be avoided, however, since many are unlikely either to occur or to cause significant harm, and the resources that would be consumed to avoid them always have valuable applications elsewhere. Individuals and society must somehow decide how much medical risk reduction is appropriate given the alternatives, their costs, and the relative values of the expected outcomes. The law of medical malpractice exerts a large and apparently growing influence on the risk reduction actually undertaken by medical care providers.'
22 Havighurst, supra n. 4, 1244-5

of professional responsibility. One can concede that a highly developed sense of ethics is a hallmark of the profession – I personally believe that it is – yet recognize that this ethical sense is not distributed in precisely equal proportions. For the physician who feels no overwhelming ethical responsibility to limit his practice so as to honor the principle that he should 'first, do no harm,' it is highly likely that ... financial incentives will be quite meaningful.[23]

Although I am somewhat less sanguine than Havighurst about the effectiveness of civil liability in the medical profession because of certain characteristics of the market for medical services which are discussed below. I believe that in most professions the civil liability mechanism should play an important part in the calculus of institutions for the maintenance of minimum standards of competence. However, before discussing some of these characteristics, a brief survey of some prominent features of the negligence action and the adversarial system will clarify the basis of this assertion.

III

The requirement of victim initiative
The civil liability mechanism is a system of private enforcement of continuing competence and therefore rests upon victim initiative. However, there are significant barriers in the system which will discourage action by someone who suffers a loss as a result of incompetent professional services. The victim must recognize first that he has been injured and, second, that the injury is the result of negligence, not just a negative outcome of competent services. Given the arcane nature of professional services – particularly medicine, dentistry, and law – this identification and evaluation generally requires the services of another member of the same profession. At this point the victim is likely to find something less than enthusiastic assistance, given the understandable reluctance of members of a profession to report on or testify against their colleagues.[24] This

---

23 Ibid., 1245-6
24 On the 'conspiracy of silence' see Grange, *'The Silent Doctor* v. *The Duty to Speak'* (1973) 11 *Osgoode Hall L.J.* 81; Haines, 'The medical profession and the adversary process' (1973) 11 *Osgoode Hall L.J.* 41; Wright & Linden, *Canadian Tort Law* (Butterworths, 1975) 187; *Report of the Attorney-General's Committee on Medical Evidence in Civil Cases* (1965); Sharpe, 'The conspiracy of silence dilemma' (1973) 40 *Ont. Med. Rev.* 25. In the United States, see Markus, 'Conspiracy of silence' (1965) 14 *Clev. Mar L. Rev.* 520. As a partial response to this problem, the Ontario Medical Association appoints a specialist to advise plaintiff's counsel. However, to the extent that this appointment depends on some prejudging of the merits of the plaintiff's case, there is still a significant limitation on the civil action.

absence of enthusiasm is surely heightened when most members of the profession – as in the case of Canadian physicians – are members of the same insurance organization and can thus foresee a direct financial impact on their own insurance rates.[25]

Once the victim has identified and evaluated the cause of his injury, he must then approach the legal system, present his claim and depend on the tort system to resolve it. At this point, the cost disincentives of Anglo-Canadian civil procedure face him squarely.

Costs rules

In Canadian civil cases, the general rule is that costs follow the disposition of the case; that is, the losing party bears not only his own legal fees but also a substantial proportion of the successful party's. In contrast, the American rule is that each party bears his own legal costs regardless of the outcome on the merits. The effect of the Canadian rule is to increase the variance in the expected return to the litigation, which should discourage nuisance suits and encourage meritorious ones.[26] However, in fact, because of the generally risk-averse nature of victims, it probably has the effect of discouraging both meritorious and nuisance suits, particularly when the potential damages award is not large. The defendant, if represented by an insurance company which is able to aggregate numerous claims and thus eliminate the unsystematic risk in the outcomes, will not be similarly discouraged by the Canadian costs rule.

Contingent fees

Contingent fees are often included in the litany of complaints about the civil liability mechanism in the United States. The *American Medical Malpractice Report* stated: 'No subject in the entire field of medical malpractice has evoked more bitter feelings between physicians and lawyers than the contingent legal fee system.'[27] In Canada, Ontario, Newfoundland, Prince Edward Island, and Saskatchewan do not allow contingent fees, while they are allowed in some form in the other provinces.[28] Despite this availability, the Canadian Medical Protective Asso-

---

25 The Canadian Medical Protective Association represents almost all Canadian physicians – more than 30,000. All members pay the same annual fees regardless of previous involvement in a successful civil claim. See Geekie, supra n. 7.
26 Posner, *Economic Analysis of Law* (1972) 351. See also Phillips & Hawkins, 'Some economic aspects of the settlement process: a study of personal injury claims,' 39 *Mod. L. Rev.* 497 (1976).
27 *Medical Malpractice*, supra n. 6, 32
28 See Williston, 'The contingent fee in Canada' (1976) 6 *Alta. L. Rev.* 184; Arlidge, 'Contingent fees' (1974) 6 *Ottawa L. Rev.* 374; Bulbulia, 'Contingent fee contracts: policy

ciation 'believes that to date contingency billing has not been a major factor in the increase in legal actions or the size of awards in Canada.'[29] At the same time, the Association warns, 'if contingency billing were to become a widespread practice and if lawyers were to alter their normal system of practice and to begin active promotion of medical malpractice law suits on the basis of contingency billing, both could contribute to a major problem in the not-too-distant future.'[30] Presumably other professional organizations have similar fears.

The contingent fee arrangement does *not* encourage non-meritorious suits. Rather, it discourages them and encourages only meritorious actions because the plaintiff's counsel will refuse to take cases in which he is unlikely to recover. Further, the arrangement does *not* encourage meritorious low-recovery cases for the same economic reason that the plaintiff himself is discouraged in such cases if required to pay counsel on an hourly basis: the expected gain from the suit is too low. The American *Medical Malpractice Report* confirmed this conclusion: 'The Commission finds that the contingent fee arrangement discourages the acceptance of meritorious low-recovery cases. The Commission further finds that on a fee-for-service basis potential clients would be similarly discouraged from pursuing these same meritorious low-recovery cases, since the average citizen cannot financially support the required lawyer's services.'[31] The Commission viewed this discouragement of legally meritorious but potentially low-recovery suits 'as a wholly undesirable and unfair result of the system.'[32] Also, the contingent fee does not lead to a bonanza for lawyers; the *Medical Malpractice Report* found that if reduced to an hourly basis 'there does not appear to be any gross discrepancy between the resultant rates charged by the plaintiff bar and those charged by the defence bar in medical malpractice.'[33]

What the contingent fee does facilitate is the shift of some of the risk of failure in the suit from the plaintiff to his counsel. For two reasons, this is likely to encourage some meritorious actions that otherwise would not be brought. First, counsel are able to diversify away the unsystematic risk of failure by taking numerous similar cases (in a way analogous to the insurance company defendant).[34] By way of contrast, a plaintiff normally has only a single claim and, in

and law in New Brunswick' (1971) 49 *Can. Bar Rev.* 603. For a comprehensive discussion of contingent fees in the United States, see MacKinnon, *Contingent Fees for Legal Services* (Aldine Pub. Co., 1964).

29 Geekie, supra n. 7, 333
30 Ibid.
31 *Medical Malpractice*, supra n. 6, 33
32 Ibid.
33 Ibid.
34 Lawyers may further diversify the risk in suits by forming firms of lawyers handling similar cases or by taking on a co-counsel.

the absence of a market for legal claims, is unable to sell the claim for a certain payment or reduce the risk by diversification. As a result, at the margin, even if the plaintiff and his counsel are equally risk-averse,[35] counsel acting on a contingent fee arrangement will proceed with some suits which the plaintiff would not pursue if required to reimburse his counsel on a fee-for-service basis. Second, counsel is in a better position than the plaintiff to evaluate the merits and consequent worth of potential suit. By sharing the outcome of the suit with his counsel the plaintiff is able to rely on his counsel's self-interest to ensure that a proper decision about whether to proceed is taken and need not spend resources monitoring the quality of his counsel's advice.

If one concludes that civil liability is an efficient and important mechanism for maintaining professional competence, then a fee arrangement which facilitates its operation should be encouraged, not attacked.[36] On the other hand if one concludes that the malpractice action's dysfunctions outweigh its strengths as a competence-inducing mechanism, reform should be directed at the substantive cause of action and not at a procedural device which merely facilitates meritorious claims.

The damages requirement

A negligence claim must include proof of damages to succeed.[37] Therefore, incompetence which does not give rise to actionable damages to the client will not be remedied by the civil liability action. In situations where the client does not pay directly for the professional services – for example, under universal health insurance – and where the lack of professional skills results not in physical harm but merely in inefficient services – for example, unnecessary diagnostic tests – no civil liability action by the client is possible. Unless an alternative mechanism is developed, the professional will not face incentives to overcome this form of incompetence. Indeed, as is suggested below, in the absence of constraints he may substitute this form of incompetence to avoid the threat of malpractice liability for incompetence which might be actionable.

35 This assumption is probably unrealistic. Since risk aversity usually decreases with wealth and lawyers as a class are wealthier on average than victims, the victim will normally be more risk-averse than his counsel. This increases the extent to which the contingent fee facilitates meritorious litigation.

36 The desirable feature of the contingent fee – that it discourages non-meritorious suits – can be favourably compared with legal aid schemes where, if the counsel receives hourly compensation regardless of results, the primary incentive on the counsel may be to continue the suit regardless of its merits. There are, of course, potential abuses of the contingent fee arrangement, many of which are canvassed in Mackinnon, supra n. 28. However, adequate means can be found to control these abuses: see *Legislator's Guide*, supra n. 5, 10, and *Medical Malpractice*, supra, n. 6, 34-5.

37 *Long* v. *Western Propellor Co. Ltd* (1968) 67 D.L.R. (2d) 345 (Man. C.A.).

The effect of insurance on deterrence
The intensity of the incentive for continuing competence is reduced if the professional is able to insure against the award of damages. To the extent that insurance premiums do not vary following adverse assessment and to the extent that there is only a small or non-existent deductible requirement, the financial incentive is eliminated. However, by the same token a significant incentive can be created by mandating either risk categorization in the calculation of premiums or, perhaps more importantly, a substantial, uninsurable, deductible requirement.[38]

Also, as was pointed out earlier, the financial incentive is usually accompanied by a fear of a finding of blameworthiness and the consequent adverse publicity for the professional. This incentive is uninsurable and can be strengthened by means of widespread publication of the outcome of the civil action.[39]

The determination of fault in the adversarial system is expensive
In addition to minimizing the cost of accidents and the costs of avoidance, a model accident control system must include the costs of administration.[40] The fault standard as applied in the adversarial system is notoriously expensive. Mr Justice Haines has written: 'Under the adversary system a medical malpractice case is one of the most difficult, expensive and unsatisfactory, to all involved.'[41] Although the fault system is undoubtedly expensive and cumbersome, it is important to recognize the potential costs of any other proposed mechanism which requires an assessment of either the quality of the professional's services or the cause of the maloccurrence. For example, if disciplinary proceedings for incompetence are adopted as the best mechanism, it must be understood that they are also likely to involve an adversarial format and essentially the same issues of fact

38 Although mandatory deductibles can create financial incentives, if the deductible is the same for all maloccurrences from an incentive point of view professionals will not distinguish among injuries resulting in damages greater than the deductible limit. As a result, the most serious injuries and many lesser ones would presumably be avoided with the same frequency. This could be corrected by correlating the deductible level with the amount of damages, or, less precisely, with the type of injury.
39 However, see Schwartz and Skolnik, 'Two studies of legal stigma,' 10 *Social Problems* 133 (1962), which found that a malpractice judgment had no adverse effect on a doctors' practices and that in some cases the practices improved.
40 *The Seventy-Fifth Annual Report of the Canadian Medical Protective Association*, 32, indicates that 57 per cent of the Association's expenses in 1975 were incurred for administrative and legal costs in defence of members and 43 per cent were paid in damages to successful plaintiffs.
41 Haines, supra n. 24, 44. Mr Justice Burger, chief justice of the United States Supreme Court, is reported to have said in response to a question as to how to improve the Constitution: 'Put an end to the adversary trial': see Morris, 'Medical report: malpractice crisis – view of malpractice in the 1970s' (1971) 38 *Insurance Counsel J.* 521.

will be at stake. Similarly, even a no-fault compensation system for maloccurrences requires, in the absence of universal and uniform social welfare, a factual determination of the cause of the maloccurrence and a consideration of whether this causative factor qualifies the claimant for compensation. It is not clear that such mechanisms will be substantially less expensive administratively than the malpractice action (although the expense may be borne by the general taxpayer instead of the individual claimants) and may incur other costs if they are less effective in the minimization of accident and avoidance costs.

IV

It is argued below that the single most important factor influencing the effectiveness of the civil liability mechanisms for a given profession is the extent to which the practice of the profession is subject to competitive market pressures. In professions constrained by competitive market forces, the civil liability mechanism should be relatively more effective. Conversely, where market forces are weakened or essentially non-existent, considerable inefficiencies of the mechanism can be predicted.

A number of characteristics of a profession influence the presence of market pressures.[42] First, the method of payment for services is probably the dominant factor. To be contrasted are the medical profession in Ontario, where payment is made through universal state insurance, and the design and building professions – architects and engineers – whose services are usually purchased in market transactions. The second factor is the extent to which substitute services are available. While competition in the market for legal services is restricted by the virtual monopoly granted to lawyers,[43] a considerable degree of competition exists in the market for design services as a result of the relative substitutability of the services of architects, engineers, and builders. The third factor is the amount of information available to consumers about the profession's services and its members. For example, whether or not price advertising by pharmacists or optometrists is allowed will directly effect the degree of competition in the respective professions. Similarly, the ability of consumers to select their professional rather than depend on a referral by another will strengthen competition. The fourth factor is the complexity of the services. Only if consumers are able to evaluate the price/quality combinations offered in the marketplace is competition effec-

---

42 See generally, Arrow, 'Uncertainty and the welfare economics of medical care' (1963) 53 *Am. Econ. Rev.* 941; Note, 'Comparative approaches to liability for medical maloccurrences' (1975) 84 *Yale L.J.* 1141.
43 See Ontario's *Solicitors Act*, R.S.O. 1970, S.1.

tive, because competition depends on the presence of discriminating consumers. To the extent that the services are complex and the price/quality combinations are subtle, consumer sovereignty is diminished.[44]

The relationship between a competitive services market and an effective civil liability mechanism is illustrated by two problems: non-actionable incompetence and the 'defensive medicine' syndrome. The problem of non-actionable incompetence was outlined above; certain forms of incompetence will not lead to damages in the traditional sense but rather will lead primarily to inefficient professional services. For example, despite achieving the desired result, the services may be slow or employ wasteful methods of analysis because of the professional's failure to learn new skills and adopt new methods of practice. If the services are delivered in a competitive setting, we need not worry about this form of incompetence; the market will cure it. Just as the competitive market constantly forces firms to adopt new efficiencies in order to survive economically, the professional in a competitive market is forced to maintain efficient and contemporary skills or face the financial discipline of the marketplace. An inability to offer services in competitive price/quality packages will lead to a loss of clients. As a result, in a competitive market we need only be concerned with incompetence leading to damages – actionable incompetence – and this is congruent with the effective range of the civil liability mechanism.

In contrast to the competitive situation, if, as in the medical profession, the practitioner does not face all the costs of his inefficiency resulting from his lack of competence, then the situation will *not* be self-correcting. For example, if neither consumer nor physician directly bears the cost of a diagnostic test, which rather is paid for by a universal insurance scheme, market forces cannot be relied on to ensure that such tests are utilized efficiently. Similarly, assuming the test is harmless although unnecessary, the inefficiency is not actionable. As a result, in the absence of market forces, civil liability is not a sufficient control over competence, and other mechanisms must be sought.

The 'defensive medicine' syndrome is a variant of the same problem. The concern was expressed by Dr Bette Stephenson, past president of the Canadian Medical Association:

Perhaps the most hazardous result of malpractice litigation phobia is defensive medicine. In order to protect themselves in the possible event of suit, physicians may submit each and every patient to the full range of laboratory testing proce-

44 Arrow, supra n. 42, argues that an additional factor is the uncertainty of demand for the services. He concludes that this uncertainty in the medical area is a major determinant of market failure.

dures and radiographic examinations. Already some evidence of this phenomenon has been exhibited in physicians' practice profiles. Widespread application of such superdefensive practice is fraught with real dangers for both individual patients and society as a whole. The individual may be subjected to bad medical care and the hazards of excessive investigation and at the same time be denied access to the benefits of relatively new treatments. Society as a whole suffers the impedence of advances in medical science and the intolerable burden of explosively expanding costs of medical care.[45]

There are two major reasons why the defensive medicine problem arises: the absence of a competitive market in the delivery of medical services and, consequently, the use of custom as the standard of competence in professional negligence actions. The absence of market forces allows the physician to adopt defensive practices without financial penalty or consumer disapproval, and the customary practice standard incorporates suboptimal practices and indeed, over time, may require them.

A competitive market can be viewed as a self-contained system; any cost or saving in the provision of a product or service is reflected in the final price/quality package offered in the market. When the market discipline is removed, certain kinds of costs can be externalized. The practitioner will therefore overinvest in procedures the cost of which can be externalized to him if he believes that the procedure will reduce his exposure to actionable damages, the cost of which cannot be externalized. Defensive practices are therefore a rational and predictable response to professional civil liability exposure in the absence of the containing influence of a competitive market.[46] The decision on the degree of competition

45 Geekie, supra n. 7, 333. Defensive procedures are of two types: additional precautionary steps and failure to use new or high (but justified) risk procedures. Although always cited as a symptom of medical malpractice (see *Medical Malpractice*, 14-15), there has been suprisingly little empirical work measuring the magnitude of the problem. One of the major studies found that there is virtually no serious effect on practice: see Note, 'The medical malpractice threat: a study of defensive medicine' (1971) *Duke L.J.* 939. On the other hand it has been estimated that in the United States the cost of defensive medicine is between 3 and 7 billion dollars annually: see Weinberger, 'Malpractice – a national view' (1975) 32 *Ariz. Med.* 117, cited in Brook, Brutoco, and Williams, 'The relationship between medical malpractice and quality of care' (1975) *Duke L.J.* 1197.
46 The difficulties involved in developing a complete system of market incentives for medical services are enormous. For an attempt to do it on a limited basis see Havighurst, 'Health maintenance organizations and the market for health services' (1970) 35 *Law and Contemp. Prob.* 716. For a further consideration of the problem and the likelihood of its solution, see Calabresi, 'The problem of malpractice – trying to round out the circle' (1977) 27 *U.T.L.J.* 131.

appropriate for the regulation of a particular profession will be based primarily on factors other than the impact of competition on civil liability and continuing competence. However, once the decision is taken, it becomes the dominant variable in determining the relative effectiveness of civil liability.

If the absence of market forces leads to deficient cost-justifications and risk evaluations, the standard of care will perpetuate and even exacerbate those deficiencies because it is based on custom and not on independent judicial assessment.[47] As a suboptimal procedure becomes customary in the profession, it will be adopted as part of the required minimum skill for the profession and all practitioners will be forced to adopt it in order to avoid potential liability. In the absence of effective cost constraints or market forces, this process will progress (or perhaps more accurately regress) continually.

A second major variable influencing the relative effectiveness of the civil liability mechanism is the ability of victims to identify an injury and determine its cause to be the failure of the professional to exercise reasonable care or skill.[48] As stated earlier, civil liability is a private enforcement mechanism which relies exclusively on victim initiative. To the extent that the victim is unable to identify and evaluate his injury, the mechanism fails both because only a portion of the potential meritorious suits will be brought and because those that are brought will arise in a haphazard manner.

It seems likely that the incidence of such inability is higher in those professions which are most esoteric and/or most highly professionalized. By definition, the most esoteric professions create the greatest difficulty for independent client identification. This phenomenon is magnified to the extent that a high degree of professionalism promotes group loyalty and common interests which then create disincentives for assisting individuals with potentially actionable injuries. Also, the inability to recognize injury is inversely related to the sophistication of the client and the client's frequency of use of the service. For example, a homeowner who engages the services of an architect for a one-time renovation of his home is less likely to be able to recognize substandard care or skill than a construction company which frequently uses the services of architects.

47 Bovbjerg, supra n. 21, at 1377: 'The apparent result has been a contemporary standard of care that exposes to substantial legal risks any provider who fails to imitate existing patterns of care, thus aggravating an already serious tendency of medical care providers to adopt even more procedures without careful consideration of the expense and results involved. Many providers, indeed, are said to practice "defensive medicine" in response to this perceived legal threat, performing extra tests and taking additional precautions prompted more by legal fears than by medical expectations.'
48 It is important to realize that this problem of injury recognition is not unique to the civil liability mechanism. It is equally endemic to a disciplinary mechanism if that process also depends on victim initiative in the form of a complaint.

v

In summary, the extent of the absence of competitive market pressures on the delivery of professional services and the barriers of knowledge and expert assistance in the identification and evaluation of injuries both detract from the effectiveness of the civil liability mechanism. When designing the mechanisms for continuing competence in a profession, these factors should be influential.

Numerous similar secondary factors should be investigated. These include the type and role of delivery institutions in the profession,[49] the information mechanisms within the profession, the importance of blameworthiness, and the use of paraprofessionals. These and other factors will have varying degrees of influence on the effectiveness of the civil liability mechanism. In aggregate, when combined with the two primary factors, they may be persuasive in the choice of mechanism.

The other difficulties of the civil liability system – cost barriers, suit-financing barriers, and diminution of deterrence by insurance – must also be considered. However, these are much more amenable than competition and victim initiative to modification to refine the civil liability system. Contingent fees can be encouraged, costs rules altered, and deductibles and risk categories mandated to facilitate suits and the beneficial results thereof. These steps should be taken once a decision is reached that civil liability is, on balance, a desirable mechanism for maintaining competence in the professions or at least a major subgroup of them. Once the civil liability mechanism is selected it should be facilitated, not burdened by unnecessary procedural or substantive barriers.

In conclusion, in the apparent absence of a superior alternative mechanism, civil liability, with its advantage of flexibility, dynamism, indirectness, and individuality, is a relatively attractive and effective tool for gaining minimum levels of continuing competence. An enlightened policy should in most cases include civil liability as one element in the calculus of institutional arrangements in the search for competence.

---

49 For a preliminary discussion of the importance of the delivery institutions to the maintenance of competence in the medical profession, see Huszagh and Mulloy, supra n. 8, at 293-5.

CLAUDE-ARMAND SHEPPARD

Enforcing continuing competence

CONTINUING COMPETENCE:
A PREREQUISITE TO THE RIGHT TO PRACTISE

Members of professional corporations enjoy the exclusive right to practise their profession, or at least the exclusive use of the corresponding title. This monopoly is handed to them by law. In theory at least, the privilege has been granted not to advance the economic and social interests of professional minorities but because it appeared in the public interest to restrict to individuals of certified competence the right to practise certain professions or to hold themselves out as so qualified.

Experience has shown that in many cases the most suitable instrument for the screening of applicants to the professions, and for ensuring and controlling their competence, is the self-regulating professional corporation set up under the law. In this situation, the general criteria for admission are determined by the legislator, with the precise determination of what constitutes competence and admissibility left to the individual corporations. As a variation, for some professions, in some jurisdictions, particularly in the United States, the task of defining and checking competence is entrusted to various types of official boards and commissions rather than to self-governing corporations.

In addition to controlling competence as a prerequisite to admission – and hence as a condition of the right to practise and to use the title – professional corporations (or boards and commissions) have also often been given the task of setting standards of professional conduct and ethics and of enforcing compliance with these standards. This is done through inspection, investigation, and eventually through the initiation of disciplinary proceedings which can result in penalties varying from mere reprimand to suspension or expulsion.

Member of the Bar of Quebec

In recent years there has been a growing insistence by the general public and by the authorities on the obligation of professional corporations to protect the public first and foremost, rather than the material interests of their members. For example, section 23 of the 1973 Quebec *Professional Code* enunciates: 'The principal function of each (professional) corporation shall be to ensure the protection of the public ... For this purpose it must in particular supervise the practice of the profession by its members.'[1] As well, there has been a rapidly increasing awareness that competence is not permanent – a status acquired once and for all – but is to be assessed in the light of the rapidly evolving state of the art, of ever-widening scientific knowledge, and of changing and more stringent professional standards. In other words, knowledge adequate to gain admission to a profession in one year might no longer be sufficient to practise it in another. While the public may not be entitled to demand of all practitioners that they keep abreast of the most avant garde developments in their fields, it certainly has the right to expect that they will meet improved standards with reasonable speed and provide the best care and services possible. Patients have the right to good contemporary medical care, and litigants can demand that their counsel keep up with legislation and jurisprudence. In other words, competence, from a mere condition for admission, has now become a continuing concept. The underlying principle is now the duty of a professional to provide services which conform to improved and current criteria, experience, and knowledge.

Furthermore, competence is no longer judged only in terms of intellectual knowledge, practical experience and use of modern methods. It can also be a matter of physical or mental suitability. This relatively new dimension has only recently become the subject of public discussion and legislative interest. It has become obvious that someone who is physically unable to practise a profession, or who suffers from mental or psychological impediments which interfere with his ability to render professional services, should neither be admitted to practise nor permitted to continue unchecked. It is easy to imagine the harm that might be done by an alcoholic lawyer, an epileptic surgeon, or a deranged engineer.

The widening concept of professional competence and the requirement that the public be protected against all forms of incompetence have confronted lawmakers and the corporations, boards and commissions controlling the professions with complex and disquieting problems. Not only do they have to verify continuing professional, physical, and mental competence, but they must also assist professionals in keeping up to date with developments in their field, as well as deal with the very real difficulties of practitioners who face obsolescence due

---

1 1973, S.Q., c. 43, as amended by 1974, S.Q., c. 22 and c. 65, and 1975, S.Q., c. 32 and c. 62

to one form or another of incompetence. Indeed, while the protection of the public must be of paramount concern, it would be unfair and unwise to subject to insecurity, arbitrary rejection, and unemployment professionals who have trained for long and arduous years and acquired considerable experience.

Furthermore, inadequate knowledge, poor physical condition, or mental problems do not necessarily wholly incapacitate a professional or render him completely unfit. The consequences of such disabilities will depend on the nature of the profession, the character of an individual's practice, and all the circumstances of the case. Incompetence, like competence, is a subjective and variable concept. Perhaps to the concept of continuing competence might be added the notions of partial competence, limited rights to practise, or practice under supervision. These notions would enable society to reconcile the public interest with the continued use of available professional skills and knowledge often acquired at great cost. It would also be a more flexible and charitable approach to the problem.

Since we are dealing with a relatively new area of legislative concern, it would be appropriate to examine how one jurisdiction which recently completely revised its professional laws has dealt with these problems. How have the Quebec *Professional Code* and the laws and regulations governing a number of professional corporations coped with these difficulties and sought to achieve a balance between these apparently conflicting objectives? The Quebec provisions were adopted after a long inquiry, massive research, and prolonged public debate. While experience with these rules has necessarily been limited, they at least have the merit of constituting a systematically thought out and integrated program of legislation.

VERIFICATION AND ENFORCEMENT OF
CONTINUING COMPETENCE UNDER QUEBEC LAW

There are currently thirty-eight professional corporations recognized under Quebec law. In varying degrees, they are governed by individual statutes. However, the *Professional Code* adopted in 1973 establishes basic principles applying to nearly all of them. Thus, continuing competence for all of these professions is regulated by the *Code*, subject to occasional minor supplemental rules in the regulations of some professions, and with the notable exception of the Bar, which is governed by the very detailed provisions of its own Bar Act.[2]

2 1966-67 S.Q., c. 77, as amended by 1968 S.Q., c. 69, and c. 48; 1972 S.Q., c. 10; 1973 S.Q., c. 44, c. 64, and c. 65; and 1975 S.Q., c. 32 and c. 62

Professional competence

The *Professional Code* deals only indirectly with the question of continuing professional competence and does not even attempt to define what must be understood by this principle.

Section 92 (*j*) empowers the Bureau which administers each corporation, by regulation, to 'determine the cases in which professionals may be obliged to serve a period of refresher training and fix the terms and conditions concerning the imposition of such refresher training and limiting their right to practise their professional activities during such period.' A complementary provision is to be found in section 54, which enables the Bureau to 'limit the right to engage in professional activities of any member ... whom it obliges to serve a period of refresher training in accordance with the regulations made under paragraph *j* of section 92.' Legislators aware of the substantial nature of this power have entrusted it to the highest governing body – the Bureau – of each corporation. A professional inspection committee consisting of at least three members appointed by the Bureau is established for each professional corporation.[3] In this connection, Section 110 of the *Code* provides:

The committee shall supervise the practice of the profession by the members of the corporation and it shall in particular inspect their records, books and registers to such practice.

At the request of the Bureau, the committee or one of its members shall inquire into the professional competence of any member of the corporation indicated by the Bureau; the committee or one of its members may also act of his own initiative in this regard. The committee or one of its members may, with the authorization of the Bureau, retain the services of experts for the purposes of such inquiry. The Bureau may also appoint investigators to assist the committee in the exercise of its duties.

The committee shall make a report to the Bureau on its activities with the recommendations it considers appropriate.

Section 111 adds: 'Upon the recommendation of the professional inspection committee, the Bureau of a corporation may oblige a member of such corporation to serve a period of refresher training and limit the right of such member to engage in professional activities during such period, in accordance with the regulations made by the Bureau.' It appears that the Bureau may accept the professional inspection committee's recommendation in whole or in part, or reject it. Without a recommendation, the Bureau is not entitled to act; with a recommendation, there is no obligation for the Bureau to act.

3 Section 107 of the *Professional Code*

Committees on discipline – which are not to be confused with professional inspection committees and which hear complaints of misconduct against professionals and may impose various sanctions – are permitted by section 156 to include in their decision a recommendation to the Bureau that 'it require the professional to serve a period of refresher training and that it limit his right to practice certain professional activities during such period in accordance with the regulations.' Again, the Bureau is not obliged to follow such recommendation but could not *proprio motu* impose such sanctions without the recommendation to that effect of the committee on discipline.

Hence, with refresher training and professional restrictions the Bureau can act only on the recommendation of either the professional inspection committee or the disciplinary committee of the corporation. But it cannot order refresher training or limitations on professional activities without such recommendations. Interestingly enough, contrary to what we shall see in the case of an order of suspension or expulsion on the grounds of health, the decision of the Bureau to impose refresher training or limitations on the right to practise is final. It cannot be appealed to the Professions Tribunal, which is a special Court of last resort in professional matters and consists of five judges of the Provincial Court.

There do not appear to be related provisions in any of the individual statutes governing the various professional corporations except for somewhat cryptic sections of the Bar Act. Section 13(2)(b) allows the General Council of the Bar to adopt a bylaw to 'ensure professional training, define its modalities, give the appropriate instructions and, for such purposes, establish and administer a professional training school.' There is no reference to refresher training. However, section 114c, which was added in 1973, states that the Committee on Discipline which hears disciplinary complaints and can impose various sanctions 'may include a recommendation to the General Council that it require the respondent advocate to take a course or to serve a period of refresher training and that it limit his right to practice for the duration of such course or training period.' This provision is vague and unsatisfactory since it leaves complete latitude to the Committee on Discipline and to the General Council as to the required courses, the refresher training and its duration, and the limitations on the right to practise. Obviously the exercise of such drastic power should be predicated upon the adoption of the appropriate regulations, if only to avoid arbitrary sanctions.

The duty to maintain continuing professional competence is also provided for in the Regulations governing a few professions. For instance, physicians are required to practise their profession 'according to the highest current medical standards [and] must, therefore, keep up-to-date and improve [their] knowledge.'[4] Failure to do so constitutes 'an act derogatory to the honour and dignity

4 Section 52 (4) of the Regulations of the Order of Physicians of the Province of Quebec

of the profession' which can result in disciplinary sanction. The Deontology Code of Pharmacists[5] is even more specific. Sections 16 and 17 state:

16. The pharmacist is obligated to maintain high professional standards by keeping his professional knowledge up to current norms and inform himself of the latest developments, scientific and otherwise, in his profession.
17. The pharmacist must take continuing education and refresher courses given by the College of Pharmacists and he must reply to the questionnaires or any other requests relative to these courses.

The principle of continuing competence is thus recognized in Quebec law, but its implementation has barely begun. The law allows the imposition of refresher training in blatant cases of incompetence, but it does not deal, either by statute or generally in regulations – except in the two cases noted above – with the duty of professionals to keep their knowledge current. Furthermore, there is very little positive action by the professional corporations to ensure and enforce the continuing education of their members or to make it available to them. The matter is really left to the initiative and conscience of individual professionals. Without doubt there must be many incompetent or unfit professionals who are not being retrained but whose right to practise remains unrestricted.

Continuing physical and mental competence
Section 52 of the *Professional Code* imposes on every professional the duty of refraining 'from practising his profession or performing certain professional acts to the extent that his state of health is an obstacle thereto.'[6] If a professional does not voluntarily so refrain, section 53 allows the Bureau, which must give the reasons for its decision, to 'order the medical examination of such professional and he must submit to such examination, which shall be made by three physicians.' One of these physicians shall be named by the Bureau, another one shall be designated by the professional concerned, and the third by the first two. Section 51 decrees that the Bureau of each corporation may order the corporation's secretary 'to refuse to enter on, or strike off, the roll any person who: (*a*)

5 Quebec Statutory Regulations, Quebec Official Publisher, Vol. 9, 9-259 to 9-263
6 The Regulations of the Quebec Order of Physicians provide in section 52 for a list of acts considered 'derogatory to the honour and dignity of the profession' and subsection 35 thereof states: 'The physician must refrain from ... (*m*) practising medicine while his own mental or psychic condition is impaired.' An examination of the Regulations of other leading professional corporations – such as The Professional Corporations of Pharmacists, of Engineers, of Chartered Accountants, and of Advocates of Quebec – failed to produce any analogous provisions

according to the report of three physicians, is in a physical or mental condition incompatible with the practice of the profession governed by such corporation, or (*b*) refuses to undergo a medical examination by three physicians to determine whether he comes under subparagraph *a*.' The section adds that every decision of the Bureau shall be subject to appeal to the Professions Tribunal.

It should be noted that section 52 of the Code does not define what constitutes a 'state of health' detrimental to continued practice. Any decision under section 51 would obviously be a subjective judgment, which must depend on the specific requirements of the particular profession concerned.[7]

An obvious deficiency of these provisions is that in case of defective health there seem to be only two alternatives: inaction or removal from the rolls. The intermediate solution envisaged in the case of professional incompetence – restrictions on the right to practise or medical treatment (by analogy to refresher training) – is not available. This is regrettable, and the law ought to be amended. In fact, as stated, section 52 of the Code seems to imply that there are cases where it would be sufficient to refrain from 'performing certain professional acts to the extent that [a professional's] state of health is an obstacle thereto.'

CONTINUING COMPETENCE
AND THE DISCIPLINARY PROCESS

We have seen that, generally speaking, continuing professional competence, as well as physical and mental suitability, are dealt with in Quebec law outside the scope of the traditional disciplinary process. It is true that disciplinary committees, in addition to imposing normal disciplinary sanctions, are allowed to make recommendations about refresher training, and that in at least two professions the rules of ethics require practitioners to keep abreast of progress in their fields on pain of disciplinary sanctions. But continuing competence is essentially enforced through a non-disciplinary approach.

This is as it should be. Indeed, historically the purpose of disciplinary proceedings inside a professional corporation has been to investigate and punish unprofessional conduct, negligence, and dishonesty. A punitive approach to problems of health or continuing education is not very constructive and is not likely, in the overwhelming majority of cases, to produce very satisfactory results.

To my surprise I found in a survey of reported disciplinary decisions in Quebec between the middle of 1974 and the autumn of 1976 that there were several cases in which the punitive or penal process had been used to deal with questions of health and competence, perhaps largely because in these specific instances bad

7 Similar provisions are found in the *Bar Act*, s.-s. 90 *l-u*

health or inadequate professional knowledge were inextricably bound up with issues of professional misconduct. For instance, in one early case a doctor was suspended for life because his alcoholism and unbalanced mind constituted a danger to the public.[8] In two other cases, nurses were reprimanded for having taken drugs while on duty.[9]

Problems of professional competence in the traditional sense occur more frequently. For instance, an engineer was reprimanded and fined for failing to prepare plans in accordance with the standards of the profession and failing to take into account possible risks to the life and property of the construction workers concerned and the public in general.[10] In another case, a dentist was found guilty and suspended for thirty days for conduct contrary to the precepts of dental science.[11] Several doctors have been punished for neglecting to treat their patients according to current recognized medical standards.[12]

ELEMENTS OF A SUITABLE PUBLIC POLICY

In the light of the foregoing considerations and the limited but valuable Quebec experience, what should be the basic elements of a suitable public policy with respect to continuing competence? I propose the following outline:

1 For most professions, whether they enjoy exclusivity of practice or only of title, and particularly where the body of special knowledge is evolving, continuing intellectual, professional and practical competence should be required in order to protect the public.

2 The level of necessary continuing competence, the scope of continuing education and refresher training, and the specific needs of each profession in these

8 Comité-Médecins-4 (1974) D.D.C.P., 51-2, Disciplinary decisions of Quebec Professional Corporations and relevant Court decisions are published periodically since 1974 by the Quebec Official Publisher in '*Decisions Disciplinaires concernant les Corporations Professionnelles*' (D.D.C.P.)

9 *Comité-Infirmières-1* (1975) D.D.C.P., 167-8, and *Comité-Infirmières-2* (1975) D.D.C.P., 168-9

10 *Comité-Ingénieurs-2* (1975) D.D.C.P., 24-33; see also *Comité-Ingénieurs-3* (1975) D.D.C.P., 173-4

11 *Comité-Dentistes-7* (1975) D.D.C.P., 160-2

12 *Comité-Médecins-1* (1975) D.D.C.P., 35-7; *Comité-Médecins-4* (1975) D.D.C.P., 47-52; *Tribunal-Médecins-2* (1975) D.D.C.P., 77-87; *Comité-Médecins-9* (1975) D.D.C.P., 181-4 (reference was made to current medical standards); *Comité-Médecins-10* (1975) D.D.C.P., 184-6; *Comité-Médecins-12* (1975) D.D.C.P., 189-91; *Comité-Médecins-14* (1975) D.D.C.P., 193-9; *Comité-Médecins-15* (1975) D.D.C.P., 199-204; *Comité-Médecins-20* (1975) D.D.C.P., 213-15; *Comité-Médecins-21* (1975) D.D.C.P., 204-18; et *Comité-Médecins-22* (1975) D.D.C.P., 219-20

respects are best dealt with inside the respective professional corporations, bodies, or commissions. Some official supervision, such as is provided in Quebec by the Office des Professions set up under the *Professional Code*, might be desirable.

3 Continuing physical and mental competence is also necessary for the protection of the public. However, here again, the degree of physical or mental impairment which will interfere with competence will vary from profession to profession, and control is best exercised by the professional corporation, board, or commission governing the profession.

4 To the extent possible, the regulation, control, and enforcement of professional, physical, and mental competence should be distinct from the disciplinary process within the profession and be handled in a flexible and non-punitive manner. Non-compliance, however, should be punished. Appropriate safeguards ought to be available against arbitrary or discriminatory enforcement, and some judicial supervision ought to be provided.

5 To avoid unfairness and unnecessary waste of human resources, a flexible approach to the problem of individual incompetence should allow in applicable cases for limitation on professional activities rather than outright suspension, for practice under supervision and control, or for probation or voluntary compliance with refresher or rehabilitation programs, as long as these are consonant with the protection of the public.

6 The Government and the professional corporations have a responsibility to provide positive programs of continuing education, updating, and professional information to enable practitioners to maintain satisfactory levels of continuing competence. Depending on circumstances, professionals might even be required to attend periodic refresher courses or seminars and submit to inspections or examinations.

7 Greater specialization might be an additional solution, with the possibility of requiring in some cases that practice be limited to a specialty.

8 The jurisdictions of professional corporations, boards, and commissions on the one hand and of civil courts on the other hand ought to be kept separate. The courts should continue to deal with matters of liability to third parties and the professional bodies ought to be concerned with competence and misconduct.

9 Professional corporations, boards, and commissions ought to be required to report to the public authorities, such as the Office des Professions, on their efforts to ensure continuing competence and on their enforcement policies.

10 The experience of each professional corporation, board, or commission in this respect should be closely monitored and the appropriate legislative incentives provided in default of adequate self-regulation.

ALAN M. THOMAS

Learning, compulsion, and professional behaviour

The time is not long past when a professionally trained and identified person was obliged to exercise considerable skill in subterfuge in order to disguise the fact that he or she was taking part in a program of professional instruction. To do so openly would have been to admit that there was something of which he was ignorant, a fact that might incline patients or clients to select professional assistance from an individual who felt obliged to make no such admission. This attitude applied unless the person was clearly engaged in acquiring additional knowledge that would lead to an equally clearly defined change in status, such as the obtaining of a specialized credential in medicine, which permitted a new role and undoubtedly a higher fee. The association in the public mind of large fees and competence seems difficult to challenge. However, such a change in status was almost always associated with relatively young men and women engaged in the early stages of their professional practice, and with full-time study perhaps mixed with a brand of closely supervised apprenticeship.

Yet times have changed. While the notion of combining study of a professional nature with continuing practice, involving professionals of all ages and experience, is a relatively new concept, individual professionals and their associations now draw attention to their commitment to continuing professional education. The public may well be choosing on grounds of information they have about who is participating and who is not. In addition, the state, representing the public, has served notice in most jurisdictions in North America that it will take a very definite interest in such activities and will move to enforce them if they do not see clear indications of professional associations and professionals themselves engaging systematically and voluntarily in their own professional growth.

Chairman, Department of Adult Education, Ontario Institute for Studies in Education

Among the profusion of diplomas and certificates that increasingly decorate the walls of professional offices, most of them extremely impressive in form and mostly unintelligible in content since they are usually in Latin or in very small print, or both, there are not many to be found which provide the appearance of continuing participation in study, or of continuing certification. But perhaps such types will begin to appear. Presumably they will present the impression, if not of total and complete competence, at least of appropriate effort in a professional world in which to 'complete' one's 'formal' training once and for all is no longer possible. The forms for conveying such information are already available, for instance in the certificates of continuing competence issued annually by the College of Nursing in Ontario and other bodies. The problem remains, however, of determining with any clarity what such certificates will mean. The circumstances of this argument, related as it is to the general issues of the professions and public policy, allows us further room to speculate on what they should mean.

Any educator, other than those with some experience with the unavoidable untidiness and often luxurious disorder common to adult education, must be both astounded and appalled at the apparent chaos of practice and thought attendant on continuing education in the professions. However, experience with adult education of all kinds over a period of time does allow one to make at least one distinction even in the face of such tumult. A lack of order or tidiness in practice is, and will remain, an inescapable feature of this type of education. Indeed it should be encouraged and welcomed. Professions differ in their nature. Practice of them differs, not only from period to period but also from region to region. To accommodate these realities, both professional groups and the overseeing governments must be persuaded that uniformity in application, a principle so dear to the bureaucratic heart, if not its mind, is not an ideal to be aimed at.

However, we need not endure or welcome the same or similar lack of order in thinking about the issues involved. We should all be aware that it is the nature of making policy about the education of adults, of which continuing education in the professions is a component, that the decisions involved are made amid the ordinary demands of everyday application of human skills. In contrast to such decisions involving the education of the young, where the beneficiaries are sequestered from daily life and a generation may pass before their consequences are manifest, decisions about what adults should or should not learn have immediate human consequences. Especially in a complex society, adult ignorance is frequently the stuff of tragedy, even more so when it apparently could have been avoided by the provision of instruction. An awareness of this condition, however, does help to explain the presence of considerable confusion surrounding such decisions, as well as the passion and argument frequently involved.

We are dealing with a number of factors. First, a concept of knowledge as related to practical application in human affairs. Second, a concept of what it means to be competent in the present world, and whose agreement to its criteria must be sought and won. Third, the problem of how such competence is both achieved and maintained, as distinct from being enhanced. And, finally, the matter of how and by whom indication is given that such a state of public and individual proficiency is being, if not achieved, at least attempted.

These are all familiar issues to anyone interested or involved in education, professional or otherwise; in fact they are so familiar that we have only recently begun to stop taking traditional solutions to them for granted. Much of the concern over them has focused on limited environments of full-time study or on the early stages of life. When we examine them afresh in the new context of an ongoing everyday society we find that we have to think them out anew.

We are immediately faced with two facts. The first, which extends beyond the world of professional activity, is that the present world, with its demand for the application of both skill and intelligence on a broader scope than would have been dreamed of half a century ago, insists that mere practice of a set of skills, founded on a complementary group of attitudes, is not sufficient to maintain competence in the tasks one is expected to perform. Experience derived solely from the day-to-day performance of the role is not sufficient to allow one to retain the right to fulfil that role indefinitely. In other words, practice no longer necessarily makes perfect. This view is now so widespread in all our major activities as to be virtually taken for granted. The result is that we believe that we are forced to intervene in the day-to-day practice in a conscious formal way so as to maintain, if not to enhance, competence. We make that distinction deliberately because it is quite plain that all of us will much more willingly endure the intervention if it is seen in our eyes and in the eyes of others to result in the enhancement of our skills and knowledge. We are much less willing to undertake such activities if they are seen to result in merely retaining what we already have.

The intervention may be individually initiated and pursued, as we know from the work of my colleague, Allen Tough, on learning undertaken by individual adults.[1] A very great deal of that learning goes on, and one would have expected it to have been relatively greater among individuals with professional training. However, while it appears to be more common among the middle class, that is, among those people with more initial schooling, there is not much evidence that those with specific professional training engage in it more than others.

1 Allen Tough, *The Adult's Learning Projects* (Toronto: Ontario Institute for Studies in Education, 1971)

Such an intervention may be initiated by a group, a professional association, a teaching institution, public or private, or finally by the state acting in the name of the protection of the public. In this case, problems of persuasion, program, and evaluation, the last being the most difficult of all, become of more public consequence.

Obviously such an undertaking must be a combination of both collective and individual initiative. The individual must wish to undertake the learning program, since it is clear that no one can be forced to learn anything specific. We can be compelled to take part in things; we cannot be compelled to learn something which requires a willing participation. On the other hand the individual needs the collective resources of the society to accomplish his or her learning. In the case of the specialized knowledge and skill characteristic of the professions, the information and cultural resources provided for everyone in libraries, museums, broadcasting networks, and the like, taken by themselves, are not likely to be sufficient. Therefore some combination of individual and collective initiative and performance is necessary, and it is at the conjunction of these two things that the confusion and debate occurs and the spectre of 'compulsion' is both potential and actual. A second factor puts the matter more specifically in the immediate context: should the fact that it is 'professions' we are examining make a substantial difference to the choices we make in these matters, publicly and privately?

The debate about what actually constitutes a 'profession' is too long and varied to deal with exhaustively here. However, if one wishes a 'feel' for a mass of complicated and evolving meanings a dictionary is sometimes useful. In this case the complete Oxford Dictionary is helpful in providing a sense of the emerging meaning of the word over seven hundred years and some of the expectations that surround its current use.[2] From the earliest usages of the word 'professional,' in this case the twelfth century, until the most recent, the following consistent characteristics emerge: involvement in some way with public policy; the notion that it is more than the practice of explicit skills but involves beliefs and indeed a way of life; continuing competence; and the notion that professionals deal with those things of the greatest human concern. One might note with reference to the last characteristic that learning is, itself, a central human characteristic, and that in this sense too the practice of a profession and engagement in learning are inseparable.

Talcott Parsons sums up the contemporary characteristics as follows: 'All professions share the following: a requirement of formal technical training accom-

2 *Oxford English Dictionary* (London: Oxford University Press, 1961)

panied by some institutional mode of validating the adequacy of the training and the competence of the individual ... Training must lead to some order of mastery of a generalized cultural tradition in a manner giving prominence to an intellectual component ... The cultural tradition must be mastered, in the sense of being understood, but skills in some form of its use must also be developed ... There must be some indication of means of making sure that such competence is put to socially responsible uses.'[3]

The distinction between culture and skill is interesting if one asks which is the most likely to need refreshment in the contemporary life of professionals and which is attended to most. Where we have unashamedly and relentlessly used compulsion to achieve educational ends, that is with the young, it would appear that we have been much more successful in the order of skill than in the order of culture. A reference to the early arguments for compulsory education, that it would ensure devoutness, piety, and knowledge of the moral code of the society, that it would fill the churches and temples of cultures and empty the jails, is sufficient to convey the argument.

At the heart of this definition lies surely a sense of individual responsibility for those characteristics which are supposed to inhere in any professional. While such responsibility, in the face of the obvious technical ability provided to professionals to accomplish either good or evil, obviously keeps the vast majority from accusations of malpractice, can it apply to the maintenance of competence? We seem to be moving away from the notion that competence is assumed unless malpractice is proven, but to what enlarged notion of competence in the contemporary world are we moving? Until recently the professions themselves were generally left within their legislative privileges and responsibilities to decide this matter, but considerable evidence suggests that this is no longer the case.

The idea of competence is obviously derived from some theory of knowledge that often remains obscure. The French professional who commented in the face of the endless outpouring of medical journals that he rises in the morning a little more ignorant than he was when he went to bed the night before, and the IBM witticism of some years ago when computers were the glamour knowledge and development industry, to the effect that if product engineers were allowed more than half an hour for lunch they would have to be retrained when they returned, contain, perhaps, some uncomfortable truths. Or are they founded on an outdated concept of knowledge and competence, that is, that one should know everything that can be said to be known by anyone about the practice and theory of his profession? It is argued that such was a possibility a mere hundred

3 'Professions,' *International Encyclopedia of the Social Sciences* (Macmillan – The Free Press, 1968)

years ago. Even Hugh MacLennan,[4] writing in *Each Man's Son* of Osler and the great physicians, has his medical hero observe that they had fulfilled their careers happily, exuberantly, and nobly in a period before the world had discovered its nerves.

Perhaps most practising professionals who have been through all of this are tired of its intellectual conceits and intricacies. Nevertheless, the next task is to make these definitions of competence apparent and intelligible to the rest of us, and probably more intelligible within their own professions. Until standards of that kind are developed, however provisional, temporary, and inadequate they may seem, and however difficult in acceptance, there will be little improvement in the situation.

Where we have excelled in innovation and imagination is in the second order of problem and solution, the provision of forms of intervention, that is, of learning programs. In this area various professions have been very imaginative indeed, experimenting with new devices and techniques in instruction. Perhaps more progress has occurred and more imagination been involved here than in any other educational sector of the society recently, with the possible exception of the military, which probably should be included among the professions anyway. Here also one encounters the factor already mentioned, the inescapable differences among the professions to which educational programs must be free to adapt. One problem lies with the density or lack of it, of members of a particular profession in any one location in Canada. A second lies with the existing or emerging nature of conditions of employment; are they self-employed for the most part, or employees of professional or other sorts of organizations? The educational or instructional problems differ. What are their career patterns? A study by Dormer Ellis indicates how few engineers are actually practising engineering twenty years after graduation, and yet even those who have turned to other pursuits wish to remain accredited as engineers.[5] One measure of success in pharmacy is to operate a large, diverse retail establishment instead of manipulating drugs and chemicals; similar observations can be made for many others. Yet all wish, and in fact need, to retain their professional licences. What sorts of programs should be available to them? More important, what should be a measure of competence for them if the licence is to mean anything at all?

As a society we seem to prefer technical to moral, political, or intellectual problems, and the professions are no exception. Because we are good at solving

4 Hugh MacLennan, *Each Man's Son* (Toronto: Macmillan, 1971)
5 Dormer Ellis, *Engineering Careers Over a Twenty-One Year Period*, XIV UPADI Convention, Rio de Janeiro, Brazil (Toronto: Ontario Institute for Studies in Education, 1976)

technical problems related to instruction or teaching, we are allowing the other issues associated with competence and its maintenance to be resolved in those terms. In other words, rather than deal with the difficult problems of standards of competence, with the moral and political problem of evaluation (the most notable absence from discussions in the current literature), we are allowing a form of education to become institutionalized, that is, the ritual form of attendance at prescribed events where instruction is provided with nothing more than the hope that learning will occur and competence be maintained.

There are now in existence required programs of participation in continuing education for several professions, notably dentistry and pharmacy. Some are prescribed by law, as in Quebec and several American states, some prescribed by professional associations, as in Ontario. In Alberta, dentists must complete five hundred points of continuing education credit over a period of five years; in Manitoba, thirty hours a year are required. In Manitoba there are rumours of litigation over the act of revoking of a dentist's licence for failure to participate. A similar challenge to the legislation requiring such participation in the state of Ohio was denied by the courts, and the legislation was declared to be within the bounds of the constitution.

It will be interesting to see the results of such litigation if it appears in Canada, though from the scholar's point of view Canadians have a depressing habit of settling out of court. But one cannot imagine that it will be struck down substantially. Essentially, the law is being used, either directly by the securing of special legislation on behalf of the professional association or indirectly by means of a threat, to support an educational system which extends compulsory activity into adult life in an unprecedented manner. While the reason for such extension can be argued in terms of public protection, and even of the protection of the profession against the more slothful of its members, the real question is whether such compulsion will achieve the stated ends. Will it in fact accomplish even those goals or will it visit on the professions all the casuistry of mechanical credit accumulation that is said to be the curse of existing formal education even where compulsion is of an indirect nature.

Certainly the provision of imaginative and stimulating events and materials for promoting professional learning by the professional associations is to be welcomed and encouraged. The mere act of making them available probably provides much stimulation and excitement throughout the professions as a whole. This would be particularly true if members of the professions themselves are consistently engaged in their creation. Such materials and events would occur naturally as a result of the number of alive, energetic, and self-motivating members that one finds in any important profession. However, no profession or occupation of any size can depend entirely on the critical mass of gifted, energetic, and self-motivated individuals. There is probably a period in the life of any profession when that can be true, but it may only be brief, and most of us know better than to depend upon it for very long. The same observation can be made of any individual who is more energetic and creative at some periods of his or her life than at others, though the profession is practised during all periods.

If one accepts the notion that at the heart of all the definitions of a profession we have examined lies a commitment to competence, and thereby in the contemporary world to continuous improvement of that competence, then the place to begin is with the process by which individuals become professionals in the first place. What do they learn in their entry requirements about the need to maintain their competence in a deliberate manner and about the demands and practice of continuing learning? To what degree is that responsibility imbedded in both the cultural and technical aspects of their initial education? In other words do they learn that they must continue to learn their whole professional lives, and do they learn something of how to do that in other than a full-time setting? Any profession in which the voluntary participation in some form of continuing education over a period of time involves fewer than two-thirds of its members had better examine with some care the impact of the initial education in this respect.

The problem in continuing education with the simple use of compulsion with no evaluation component is that it conceals from the leadership the real state of commitment to the kind of continuing education that will in fact contribute to competence.

A second question is how imaginative and well adapted to the realities of professional practice are the programs being offered. In adult education in recent years we have been trying to translate our teaching and educational problems into learning problems. How do they look from the learner's perspective? Does the learner need help in learning how to learn, as well as assistance with the substance of the task? Many programs show considerable imagination in these areas, based on very limited resources. The impact of compulsion can have the effect of reducing rather than increasing such imagination, since the programmer no longer has to win the attention of the learners: they have to come.

Finally, little may happen of real substance, and much of a ritualistic nature, if the problems of standards and evaluation are not addressed directly. Here one can make a distinction in forms of, or sources of, compulsion. If it results from the legislation of an impersonal state, then not only is it hard to change, but its very distance provokes token conformity, especially in so intimate and personal a matter as learning. If the compulsion emerges from the collective decision of the practitioners, who are supposed at least to share a common culture and some common practices and thus to understand one another better than the public as a whole, and if the nature of the practice is clearly communicated beyond the bounds of the professional group, then it seems a different sort of self-imposed compulsion, to be distinguished from any other. However this cannot happen until these two questions are addressed: first, that 'this is the minimum and maximum of what can reasonably be expected of me by myself and others'; and second, 'I am in fact performing above the minimum and in this relation to the maximum.' There are many ways to provide such an evaluation even in so politically charged an atmosphere of real incomes and real careers. If the professions cannot do so without resorting to the law, which tends then to become residual instead of normative, then we shall have to look to some nobler ideal of mankind than that embodied in the professions. Frankly, I would not know where to look.

I have tried to illustrate the new relations occurring between the professions and public policy in the context of the maintenance of competence. I have tried to indicate the present developments, or what they seem to me to be, and where development is lacking. We have obviously used the term public policy in the broadest sense and have done so deliberately. To have spoken of law only would have been a betrayal of the potential of the situation. We assume that law is the proper way to deal with malpractice, but what we are dealing with seems far more sensitive and fragile than that, and we need a more flexible and sensitive set of mechanisms for dealing with it. One can, by law, prevent an individual from doing evil and punish him if he persists. One cannot, by law, compel an individual to use all of his or her wit, intelligence, humanity, and expertise in the excellent practice of a profession. Such excellence must be won, it must be willed, and it must be deserved. All this of course applies even more to the matter of learning about how to perform that profession.

A society gets the professional practice it deserves. This statement is meant to reflect the delicate balance in which we both demand and reward, expect and are grateful for, professional competence. In this society the professionals more than anyone else, represent the zenith of what we hope for from the application of intelligence, head, and heart in applied activity. The politician can always blame chance, to a degree correctly; the worker, deprivation; the citizen, ignorance or lack of opportunity. None of these are open to the professional or to our thinking about professional practice. It can be no wonder that an educator takes this view, since in many respects the state of professional practice is the measure of the success of an educational system.

In individual terms the question is the difference between what one expects of oneself and is willing to do to achieve it, and what one perceives others expect and is willing to do to achieve that. In combination, at their worst they are a downward spiral of deception, contempt, and perversion; at their best they are vitality, imagination, and creation. The issue at hand can be the key to which of these two we can, as a society, expect and command.

A CONCLUDING PERSPECTIVE

IVAN ILLICH

The need-makers

One way to close an age is to give it a name that sticks. I propose that we name the mid-twentieth century The Age of Disabling Professions, an age when people had problems, experts had solutions, and scientists measured both abilities and needs. This age is now over, just as the age of energy splurges is over. The fallacies that made both ages possible are increasingly visible. Either social awareness will now turn these fallacies into compulsory political creeds, or they will soon be remembered as ephemeral follies. To choose requires us first to confront who, during this age – and thanks to professional dominance – got what, at what cost, and why.

The Age of Disabling Professions will be remembered as the time when politics withered, when voters, guided by professors, entrusted to technocrats the power to legislate needs, the authority to decide who needs what, and a monopoly over the means by which those needs shall be met. It will be remembered as the Age of Schooling, when people for one-third of their lives were trained how to accumulate needs on prescription and for the other two-thirds were clients of prestigious pushers who managed their habits.

It would be pretentious to predict whether our age will be remembered with a smile or with a curse. I do, of course, hope that it will be remembered like the night when father went on a binge, dissipated the family fortune, and obliged his children to start anew. Much more likely it will be remembered as the time when our pursuit of impoverishing wealth rendered all freedoms alienable and politics became organized griping.

I do not believe that this descent into technofascism is unavoidable. But a return to participatory politics is possible only on condition that we clearly

Cuernavaca, Mexico; author of *The Limits to Medicine: Medical Nemesis* (McClelland and Stewart and Marion Boyars, 1976). This paper has been published in expanded form in I. Illich, I.K. Zola, J. McKnight, J. Caplan, and H. Shaiken, *The Disabling Professions* (Marion Boyars and Burns and MacEachern, 1977). It is published here in this form with kind permission of the author and the publishers.

understand the nature of professional dominance, the effects of professional establishment, and the characteristics of imputed needs. I shall outline these points and then describe five myths that enslave us to professional management.

Let us first face the fact that the bodies of specialists that now dominate the creation, adjudication, and satisfaction of needs are a new kind of cartel. They are more deeply entrenched than any guild, more international than any labour union, more stable than any party, endowed with wider competences than any clergy, and equipped with a tighter hold over those they protect than any mafia. In common with guilds and unions they give specialists power over the work they do. By the monopoly which enables them to preclude you from shopping elsewhere or from making your own booze, they at first fit the dictionary definition of gangsters. But gangsters for their own profit hold a monopoly over basic necessities by controlling supplies. The new professionals gain legal endorsement for creating the need that, by law, they alone will be allowed to serve. Their control over human needs, *tout court*, distinguishes them from yesterday's liberal professions, which did not go further than imputing a need to individuals who sought help.

Professionalism is just one of many forms that the control over work has taken. Unions and guilds control who shall work what hours for what pay: these are trade associations that control *how* work shall be done and by whom. Professions go further; they determine *what* shall be done and *for whom*. Thus professionals implicitly exercise tutelage over clients who are ward-like.

Professionals tell you what you need. They claim the power to prescribe. They not only advertise what is good, but ordain what is right. Not every competent healer is a 'doctor.' The physician became a 'doctor' when he left commerce in drugs to the pharmacist and kept for himself the authority to prescribe what clients shall need.

But let us further beware: not every doctor or professional fits into the new class that now dominates the commonweal. To acquire the power it now holds, medicine during the last twenty-five years had to mutate again. It had to turn from a liberal into a dominant profession by obtaining the power to indicate what constitutes a health need for people in general. Only when health specialists as a corporation have acquired the authority to determine what health care must be provided to society at large has the liberal profession turned into an established, almost clerical, mafia. Its members, the new disabling professionals, are experts in public need. They claim a monopoly over the definition of deviance and the remedies for which it calls. The public acceptance of such dominant professions is essentially a political event equivalent to the establishment of a church. Inevitably each such establishment encroaches on lawmaking, judging, and public executing. Power passes from the layman's elected peers into the hands of a self-accrediting elite.

Again, health care provides the example; when medicine recently outgrew its liberal restraints, it invaded legislation by establishing public norms. Physicians always determined what constitutes disease; dominant medicine now determines what diseases society shall not tolerate. Medicine invaded the courts: physicians had always diagnosed who is sick; dominant medicine, however, brands those who must be treated. Liberal practitioners prescribed a cure: dominant medicine has public power of correction; it decides what shall be done with or to the sick. In a democracy, these three powers, legislation, judgment, and enforcement, are not only assiduously kept under citizen control, but are also carefully separated.

Professions could not have become dominant unless people had learned to experience as a lack that which the expert imputes to them as a need. A surreptitious abuse of language moulds this loss of autonomy into a form of respectable greed. When I learned to speak, 'problems' existed only in math or chess, 'solutions' were saline or legal, and 'need' was mainly used as a verb. The expressions 'I have a problem' or 'I have a need' both sounded silly. As I grew into my teens, and Hitler worked at solutions, the 'social problem' also spread. 'Problem' children of ever newer shades were discovered among the poor as social workers learned to brand their prey and to standardize their 'needs.' Need, used as a noun, became the fodder on which professions were fattened into dominance. Poverty was modernized. The poor became the 'needy.'

During the second half of my life, to be 'needy' became respectable. Computable and imputable needs moved up the social ladder. It ceased to be a sign of poverty to *have* needs. Income opened new registers of need. The greedy pursuit of new needs became a sign of status. Spock, Comfort, and vulgarizers of Nader trained laymen to shop for solutions to problems they learned to cook up according to professional recipes. Needs became almost completely coextensive with commodities offered. The citizen was transmogrified into the consumer of professional services. To be ignorant or unconvinced of one's own needs became the unforgivable antisocial act.

The expert dominance over laws, decisions, and routines is reflected in the skyline of the city. Professional buildings look down on the crowds that shuttle between them to tap the silos of health, education, and welfare. Healthy homes become hygienic apartments where one cannot be born, cannot be sick, and cannot die decently. Not only are helpful neighbours a vanishing species, but so are liberal doctors who make house calls. Work places fit for apprenticeship turn into opaque mazes of corridors that permit access only to functionaries equipped with 'identities.' The transformation of society into a service-delivery system constitutes the most profound – and generally overlooked – form of environmental degradation.

The prevailing addiction to imputable needs would indeed be irreversible if people actually fit the calculus of needs. But this is not so. Beyond a certain degree of dominance, medicine engenders helplessness and disease; education turns into the major generator of a disabling division of labour; fast transportation systems in Canada turn urban people for 17 per cent of their waking hours into passengers and for an equal amount of time into members of the road gang that works to pay Ford and the highway department. In the process our major institutions have acquired the uncanny power to remove society consistently from those same purposes for which they originally had been engineered and financed. Under the government of our major professions, paradoxical counter-productivity has been built into our major tools.

Our major institutions spend a growing part of their energies on the maintenance of five myths which are all delusions that enslave the client to salvation by experts.

1 The first enslaving myth is the doctrine that people are born to be consumers and can attain any of their goals by purchasing goods and services. In fact, though, the usefulness of staples is intrinsically limited. Congestion, which is a measure of the degree to which staples get in their own way, explains why cars in Manhattan are useless, but not why people remain prisoners to immobile cars. People become prisoners to time-consuming acceleration, stupefying education, and sick-making medicine because staples destroy human potential, and do so each in their own specific way. Only up to a point can staples replace what people do without thought of exchange. Valued experiences, free movement, dwelling arrangements, the sense of security and participation in community affairs, each springs from two distinct sources: personal aliveness and engineered provisions. Staples inevitably frustrate the consumer when their delivery paralyses him.

The measure of well-being in a society is thus never like an equation by which these two modes of production are added; it is always like a balance that shows how fruitfully use-values and commodities mesh in synergy. Only up to a point can heteronomous production of a staple enhance and complement the autonomous production of the corresponding personal purpose. Beyond this point the synergy between the two modes of production paradoxically turns against the purpose for which both use-value and staple were intended.

The fundamental reason for counterproductivity must be sought in the specific environmental impact that results from every form of mass production. Medicine makes culture unhealthy; education tends to obscure the environment; vehicles wedge highways between the points they ought to bridge. At some point in every domain the amount of services or goods delivered so degrade the environment for action that specific, marginal disutilities grow.

2 The second enslaving myth makes out of each engineering advance a licence for more professional domination. This delusion says that tools, as they become

more efficient in the pursuit of a specific purpose, inevitably become more complex and inscrutable and therefore require operators who are more highly trained and who can be more securely trusted. Counterproductivity due to the paralysis of use-value production is fostered by this technocratic imperative.

Just the opposite is true and ought to happen. As techniques multiply and become more specific, their use often requires less complex judgments. They no longer require that trust on the part of the client on which the autonomy of the liberal professional, and even that of the craftsman, was built. From a social point of view we ought to reserve the designation 'technical progress' to instances in which new tools expand the capacity and the effectiveness of a wider range of people, specially so when new tools permit more autonomous production of use-values.

3 The third disabling myth expects that effective tools for lay use will first be certified by professional tests. Many proponents of soft technology stay hooked on professional service because they assume that appropriate technology in the hands of the layman will compete with industry only when present tools have been redesigned for the man in the street. They wait for the ultimate bicycle, the supreme windmill, the safe pill, the perfect solar panel.

Such people remain entranced by the professional dream that the tools with which everyman will beat the multinationals must of necessity come out of research and design rituals as solemn as those that synthesize the miracles at Dupont and LaRoche.

4 The fourth disabling myth looks to experts for limits to growth. Entire populations trained to need what they are told are ready to be told what they do not need. Growing scarcity pushes controls over needs upwards. The same multinational agents that for a generation imposed an international standard of schooling, deodorant, and speed on rich and poor alike, now sponsor the Club of Rome. Obediently, UNESCO got into the act and trained experts in the regionalization of imputed needs. For their own imputed good the rich are thus destined to pay for more costly professional dominance at home, and provide the poor with imputed needs of a cheaper and tighter brand. The central planning of output-optimal decentralization has become the most prestigious contemporary job.

In each of seven UN-defined world regions a new clergy is trained to preach the appropriate style of austerity drafted by the new need-designers. Consciousness-raisers roam through local communities inciting people to 'need' the decentralized production goals that have been assigned to them. Milking the family goat was a liberty until more ruthless planning made it a dutiful contribution toward an economic indicator.

5 The fifth enslaving myth is this year's radical chic. As the prophets of the sixties drooled about development on the doorsteps of affluence these myth-

makers mouth about the self-help of professionalized clients. I have seen adver-tised bathroom cabinets that open their locks only to a duly certified self-medi-cator. In the United States alone, about 2,700 books have appeared since 1965 that teach you how to be your own patient, so you only need see the doctor when it is worthwhile for him. Some books recommend that after due training and examination graduates in self-medication should be empowered to buy aspi-rin and dispense it to their children. Others suggest that professionalized patients should receive preferential rates in hospitals and benefit from lower insurance premiums. Only women with a licence to practise home birth should have their children outside hospitals since such professional mothers can, if needed, be sued for malpractice on themselves. I have seen a 'radical' proposal that such a licence to birth could be obtained under feminist rather than medical auspices.

Many voters are now willing to look beyond the Age of Disabling Professions and its shopping centres for goods and for services. Thousands of small groups are at present challenging professional dominance over themselves and over the sociotechnical conditions in which they live, and they do so without regard to the cost to themselves. In the social wasteland that sprawls between the union-ized dullness of Middle America with its slums and the spiritual comfort of the islands of orthodox protest, I constantly run into these tribes. They are still a disparate lot, each group seeing through the smog, darkly, what they have to abandon, but each group also amazed at its own tolerance for the quite different style in which the tribe squatting on the next plot choose to live.

What would turn these non-ideological minorities into a political force is a sober philosophical and legal clarification of what in common *they do not want*. The advantages of self-chosen joyful austerity that are demonstrated by these new minorities will acquire political weight only when combined with a general theory that places freedom within voted limits above claims for ever more costly 'packages of rights.' What free men can do, when they are equipped with mod-ern tools that are respectfully constrained, cannot be summed up. It is more colourful and diverse than all the cultures of present and past taken together.